THE PHILOSOPHY OF NATURAL THEOLOGY

WORLD PHILOSOPHY

Additional books in this series can be found on Nova's website
under the Series tab.

Additional e-books in this series can be found on Nova's website
under the e-books tab.

WORLD PHILOSOPHY

THE PHILOSOPHY OF NATURAL THEOLOGY

WILLIAM JACKSON

snova
New York

Library of Congress Cataloging-in-Publication Data

ISBN: 978-1-53613-829-0

Published by Nova Science Publishers, Inc. † New York

CONTENTS

To the Most Noble
THE MARQUIS OF SALISBURY,
Chancellor of the University of Oxford,
&c., &c., &c.,
The following pages are, with his lordship's permission, respectfully inscribed by their Author.

From the "Oxford University Gazette" of June 14th, 1870.
Prize Essay.

Circumstances have induced an Individual, who wishes to remain unknown, to offer a Prize of £100, to be competed for by Members of the University of Oxford of not less standing than Master of Arts, and by any above that standing, for the best Essay in confutation of the Materialism of the present day by arguments derived from Evidences of Intelligence, Design, Contrivance, and Adaptation of Means to Ends, in the Universe, and especially in Man considered in his Moral Nature, his Religious Aptitudes, and his Intellectual Powers; and in all Organic Nature. The observation also to be made and supported in the course of the Essay that the Will and Wisdom of the Creator may be a sufficient cause for deviations from the established course of nature, and that the Free-will of man, in things within his power and influence, may be a cause of similar deviations.

It is desired that all arguments used against Materialism should be independent of those of Hegel, and of what is called the Spiritual Philosophy, which had its rise in Germany.

A period of two years will be allowed after the Public Announcement of the subject before the competing Essays will be required to be sent in to the Judges: and it is a condition of the competition that the Copyright of the successful Essay shall be the property of the Donor of the Prize; but that if published, the profits (if any) shall belong to the Writer.

The Very Reverend the Dean of St. Paul's, the Regius Professor of Divinity, and the Rev. C. Pritchard, Savilian Professor of Astronomy, have consented to act as Judges.

Essays must be sent to the Registrar of the University on or before the 12th of June, 1872. The Essays are to be distinguished by mottoes, the writer's name being sent at the same time in a sealed envelope, in the manner prescribed for the Chancellor's Prizes.

F. K. LEIGHTON, Vice-Chancellor.
All Souls College,
June 13, 1870.

After the decease of Dean Mansel the last clause but one of the above notice was thus modified in the Gazette for Dec. 5th, 1871:—

The Very Reverend the Dean of Canterbury, the Regius Professor of Divinity, and the Rev. C. Pritchard, Savilian Professor of Astronomy, have consented to act as Judges.

The following announcement appeared in the Gazette for Nov. 26th, 1872:—

Prize Essay.

The Judges appointed to award a Prize of £100 offered for the best Essay in confutation of Materialism have adjudged the Prize to the Rev. W. Jackson, M.A., F.S.A., late Fellow of Worcester College.

H. G. LIDDELL,
Vice-Chancellor.

November 25, 1872.

In a letter dated Dec. 26th, 1872, the Donor of the Prize surrendered any claim that he might have upon the Copyright of the Essay, and requested the Author to proceed with its publication.

LIST OF ADDITIONAL NOTES AND ILLUSTRATIONS

PREFACE[*]

The Essay now published is the expansion of a thin volume by the present writer, which was printed more than four years ago [1]. Natural Theology, considered as a science, had been at that time pronounced extinct and impossible by very eminent authorities. From this decision I felt myself constrained to differ; and thought it worthwhile to put on record a plea for what appeared to me an unduly neglected branch of Philosophy.

Such contempt of a pursuit possessing so many claims on the favourable attention of educated minds, seemed a fact to be accounted for in some way. After considerable thought, I ventured on asserting that the method latterly employed in treatises on this once popular science, furnished the true reason of its decline and fall. That method I could not avoid condemning as both inadequate and suicidal.

The publication of my Sermon in 1870, was followed by a number of letters and critiques from scientific and literary men. Not one amongst them alleged any worse fault than novelty against the matter of my book, and undue compression against its manner. Many of their remarks were of the most encouraging description, and affected me deeply by reason of the celebrity of their writers, whom I had previously known only by their works and their reputation. One most generous letter from the Author who, above all others, had called my own intellectual life into active energy, excited, in my mind, a warmth of feeling absolutely indescribable.

When, therefore, a Prize on this subject was offered for adjudication subject to the appointment of my own University, I felt glad to embrace an occasion which might be called in the truest sense an "Opportunity." What I have produced is to be found in the following pages. When engaged in writing them, it was my most anxious wish and endeavour to be honest: to advocate what I thought and still think true, without disguising the difficulties of my own conclusion, or assailing its antagonists by gratuitous insinuations or unfairnesses of any sort. Should such a meanness appear, I would earnestly desire the leaf on which it is printed to be torn from my book.

The delays which have befallen these pages since they were first sent to press in the former half of 1873, have caused much regret to both author and publishers. Our troubles began with a singular misadventure to a quantity of MS.; which, together with other circumstances, delayed printing till after the time originally fixed for publication. The next

---

[*] This is an edited, reformatted and augmented version of "The Philosophy of Natural Theology: An Essay in Confutation of the Scepticism of the Present Day" by William Jackson, published by A. D. F. Randolph & CO., Broadway MDCCCLXXV

season was lost in consequence of severe domestic affliction. Those of my readers who have ever gone into print, will most readily commiserate the anxiety caused by such unlooked for disappointments.

The ensuing line of argument was suggested to my mind when a young Oxonian, in consequence of circumstances with which it is needless to trouble my readers. What I then thought its special strength, lay in the point of its combining two totally different kinds of proof:—one, drawn from a survey of the world we live in,—the other, from what is nearer to ourselves—the moral truth given us by our personal consciousness. I also thought that any particular weakness alleged against one proof, could not be incident to the other; and, therefore, that since both lines of evidence, (kept apart while under examination), met at last in one and the same result, my inquiry had arrived at a demonstrably certain conclusion. At the same time, I could not but feel a wholesome distrust of my reasonings on a subject, which, though often discussed, had never, as I then believed, been looked at exactly from my own point of view.

Somewhat later in life, I learned from Paley's commentators and continuators, that the attack and defence of Natural Theology had for years been conformed to the position taken up by the Archdeacon, so far at least as the popular science of this country was concerned. But the sceptical tactics of Hume shewed me a much wider plan of assault; and in studying his great German antagonist I saw that a double line of defence had been contemplated by him. I have since observed that no part of Kant's philosophy is less commonly known to English readers than his method and results in those most priceless of his critical investigations, the treatises forming a ground-work of Moral Science. As may at once be supposed, the discovery that I really had a sort of sympathiser in Kant, was the greatest possible encouragement to my mind.

Yet there remained a very heavy discouragement. Evidently, any one who should try to pursue two very separate but convergent lines of reasoning, must undergo a most toilsome task, and one little likely to be performed without long and continued effort. And, harder yet to answer was the question next following: Who will read your patiently obtained results, to say nothing of the collateral topics which must in logical fairness be argued by the way? After all, the inevitable drawback to Natural Theology lies in the fact that, in order to be held a valid science, it must necessarily become a complex one.

This last difficulty remains my chiefest apprehension still. Neither in the Essay itself, nor yet in the additions made to it, have I introduced any one point which it seemed permissible to omit with justice to the real issue. Yet I dare not hope that many eyes, except those of the practised student, will easily perceive how germane to that issue are several among the subjects discussed. One class of thinkers will, however, welcome the whole of these inquiries; and this class contains the earnest men for whom above all others I have written.

The amount of MS. sent to the Registrar was much less in compass than the present volume. But Notes and Illustrations were intended from the first, and, had there existed a doubt as to their propriety, it would have been at once removed by the counsel of competent advisers. The risks attaching to the Essay in its smaller shape were said to be two: (1) An evident appearance of unwilling brevity, and (2) a possible charge of novel thought, bordering on paradox. In attempting to overcome these obstacles to favourable attention, I have pursued the following course:—

The text of the Essay is printed as originally written, with only a very few verbal changes for the sake of improved clearness. A number of foot-notes belonging to its first draft, remain distinguished by the ordinary marks of reference [2].

In reperusing the text, I set myself to consider how many sympathisers I could find. The best answer to any possible charge of Paradox, seemed to be a roll-call of thinkers who, for their own purposes, have asserted positions more or less approaching those I had attempted to maintain. The number of auxiliaries I have thus succeeded in assembling, is, I confess, a matter of considerable self-gratulation. Yet, I do not appeal to such opinions as authorities, in any other sense than so far forth as they are the decisions of experts in different provinces of knowledge. In whatever concerns his own department, each scientific worker has assuredly a right to be heard. The weight of confirmation thus given to my own previous results, is enhanced by the fact that most of the authors cited, pursued different objects from mine, and wrote without any bias favourable to Natural Theology. Respecting more than one of them, I feel inclined to repeat the ancient adage, "My antagonist has become my helper."

The Quotations themselves have been divided into separate classes. The greatest number illustrate particular expressions, sentences, and paragraphs. These are arranged as foot-notes on the several pages of Text, and are referred to by the small letters of the alphabet. Others, explaining or confirming principles, of general importance to the argument, have been distinguished by capital letters, and placed at the end of the chapters to which they appertain. With this latter division are classed a third set of extracts, which aim at expounding certain special thoughts, and opening out to the real student useful paths of prolonged investigation.

One circumstance connected with the Additional Notes, is alluded to at the bottom of page 27. Originally, I had made only a few citations from thoroughly sceptical writers. But, against this plan were urged the following objections. (1.) In arguing questions of all kinds, definite points are present to the mind of every disputant, and against them he directs his argument. His expressions are always antithetic to these points, and should they be left in the shadow, all antithesis is lost, and the real force of the argument obscured. Sometimes it is even mistaken;—a truth which may be illustrated by comparing the positions of great leaders in politics or theology with the positions occupied by their disciples. The former always speak by way of antithesis,—the latter seldom construe their leaders' words antithetically. Hence, the disciples never fail to outrun their teachers. Antithesis is in truth a verbal counterpoise; and where it disappears, balance is not seldom overthrown. Thus, said my advisers, your reasoning must necessarily suffer by a general loss of clear definition. Again, (2) they continued;—Since the time when you began your Essay, Scepticism in general, Materialism and Mechanism in particular, or, to speak briefly, the various denials of Theism, have ceased to be subjects on which reticence is feasible. An Address of Mr. Gladstone's delivered in a room, and spoken to a company of youths, soon became world-wide; it has been, and will be read, quoted, and commented on, wheresoever the English language is understood. One daily newspaper attractively written, devotes many of its clever pages to making known in a forensic manner the many different phases of sceptical opinion. And some religious journals explain, with complete freedom, what the disbeliefs are which they consider most reprehensible. Reticence, therefore, is simply thrown away. Some may desire to see it practised towards young people, but such "economizers" are, in effect, theoretical. They forget that the Battle of Thought comes to educated young minds along with the Battle of Life; and woe to the unprepared either way! They become, one and all, bewildered.

These reasons have satisfied my own judgment up to a certain point. I have consequently added such quotations from sceptical authors, as seemed desirable for the purpose of limiting my several positions with antithetic distinctness; a kind of definition which I admit to be the most distinct of all. And to these extracts I have appended some others, plainly expressing the conclusions which the opponents of Theism ought to reach, provided their views are carried out with fairness and consistency. Conclusions of this kind can only be obtained from Sceptics themselves. In what are called "logical consequences" put by an author into the mouth of his adversaries, I, for one, have no confidence whatever. To draw such inferences and glory in their wrong-headedness, is like inventing both sides of a controversial dialogue, defeating the party destined to defeat, and then laying claim to a philosophic victory. Or, we may take the reverse supposition. A writer is too honest for such ill-gotten triumph. This same quality of candour will, most probably, induce him to put the case he opposes in a light so advantageous, as to throw fresh doubt upon his own.

If, then, I have erred in over-quoting upon these accounts, I cannot plead that the error is committed unadvisedly.

It seems right to say, that, in mustering auxiliaries, I found the best friends to my argument were the most truly philosophic Biologists. It would indeed be strange and sad, should the genuine leaders of thought in any among the Natural Sciences be reckoned real adversaries of Natural Theology. But, in order to convey an exact impression to the reader's mind, I must beg him to peruse, in connection with this statement, the note on Materialism appended to Chapter 3; and, more particularly, its concluding pages. Towards the hybrid class mentioned p. 246, I cannot help entertaining a sentiment the reverse of complimentary.

To several distinguished persons who have bestowed upon this undertaking the aids of advice or sympathy, I offer a tribute of respectful gratitude. In one particular they will, I hope, think their kindness not utterly thrown away; since, unlike many recipients of good counsel, I have followed the opinions given me. It is with a deep solemnity of emotion, I thus venture on recording my heartfelt indebtedness. One, who was glad that words of his had helped me, now adorns no longer the noblest of assemblies by his eloquence. To my personal sorrow, he will not cast a glance on the pages over which his favour threw a ray of encouragement.

That same last change, O half-sceptical yet whole-earnest Reader, awaits both thee and myself. To thee, I am no more than the unseen utterer of certain thoughts, nourished through a period of blended hope and anxiety. It is now thine, to take unto thyself such reasonings as may fairly lay claim to some serious consideration. It is mine to accept the mixed consequences of their utterance;—the kindness and contempt which follow believing advocacy always. Through all, and above all, there will remain with me—and perchance with thee also—the sense of a new Responsibility.

These two shares in this slight book on the largest of subjects, belong in a fashion to earnest reader and anxious author for the time present. Soon they will be ours, and not ours. As days pass by, thought and utterance will bring less to both of us. We shall both have tinctured our lives more deeply with the Divine, or the Not-Divine; we shall both have sealed the secret fountains of our hearts, in readiness for the Grave and its inevitable Futurities.

"Natural Theology attempts to demonstrate the existence of a personal First Cause, supreme Reason, and Will. The relations of mankind towards such a Being, are called natural religion.

We look upon the starry heavens and say, as man creates within his own soul, and gives to airy nothing a thought, a name, a purpose, and a reality, so Almighty God created the Divine poem of this universal frame; His will is its substance, His majestic thought and purpose shine out in its adornment, and we—we are hidden in the hollow of His hand. Every marvel of the visible raises our sense of the infinite variety and beauty of the invisible, until, attracted by Him Who is the first mover of the outward and the inward alike, we make of this wonderful orb we tread upon a solid ground of support from which to mount, to fly to God and be at rest."

These paragraphs are taken from the Appendix to my little volume on Natural Theology alluded to in the beginning of this Preface. They were intended as comments on the words with which the Sermon itself concluded:—

"I have only to add that time could not permit my carrying this fruitful subject beyond its obscure and dry first principles. There is a brighter district of thought, an upland territory, as it were, rising towards our highest inheritance; a border country where Natural Theology melts into Spiritual Religion, and where the true offspring of God learn the lineaments of their Father's divine love. I turn with regret from this land of living light."

Such, then, were the feelings with which I could not help regarding the scientific limits of Natural Theology. I felt it nothing less than a disappointment to traverse the paths of positive fact and argument, and to close just at the very point where the human head gains a response from the human heart. It seemed like the task of a landscape painter, who, after depicting successive plains made shadowy by tangled brushwood and dark forest-growth, should be compelled to lay down his pencil, and forbear transferring to his canvas the beautiful downs and sun-lighted hills overlooking those more obscure regions. Compared with the painter's regrets, were mine, I asked, less natural? The attributes of Deity already dwelt upon through the chain of my argument, were not only fitted to bring His existence home to Reason, but also to move earnest spirits by a strong sense of elevated hopes and duties, devotion and aspiration. These religious sentiments might have yielded the purest lights of my landscape. All that had gone before seemed more negative than affirmative;—rather to have been sketched in neutral tints than in radiant and glowing colours.

A similar feeling of deep concern attended the conclusion of the present Essay; increased by an inevitable thought that the reiterated disappointment seemed likely to be a disappointment always. It was, therefore, a very great gratification to find in the honour of an election to the Bampton Lectureship for 1875, the possibility of adding a crown and completion to all my foregone work. The scheme of these Lectures enables me to treat of Natural Religion; to penetrate the upland territory, the border country where Man may view, as he walks heavenwards, the lineaments of his Father's Divine love.

Before this time next year, I may, therefore, hope to have realized my purpose. The volume of Bampton Lectures for 1875, may then have become the appropriate conclusion of this present book.

Oxford,
Nov., 1874.

"Finis vitae in primis noscendus est, ut ad eum actiones omnes dirigere valeamus; non minus quàm naviganti portus ad quem deveniat ante omnia statuendus."

Ficinus in Platonis Philebum, Cap. I.

Chapter 1

INTRODUCTORY: MOTIVES OF ESSAY— DIVISION INTO CHAPTERS— METHOD OF STUDY— CONSILIENT PROOFS

"Flower in the crannied wall,
I pluck you out of the crannies;—
Hold you here, root and all, in my hand,
Little flower—but if I could understand
What you are, root and all, and all in all,
I should know what God and man is."
—Tennyson.

"I have written under the conviction that no Philosophy of the Universe can satisfy the minds of thoughtful men which does not deal with such questions as inevitably force themselves on our notice, respecting the Author and the Object of the Universe; and also under the conviction that every Philosophy of the Universe which has any consistency, must suggest answers, at least conjectural, to such questions. No Cosmos is complete from which the question of Deity is excluded; and all Cosmology has a side turned towards Theology."
—Whewell, *Philosophy of Discovery*, Preface, p. vi.

"All science is but the intercalation, each more comprehensive than that which it endeavours to explain, between the great Primal Cause and the ultimate effect."
—Professor Allman's Address to the British Association at Bradford, 1873.

"Glory about thee, without thee; and thou fulfillest thy doom,
Making Him broken gleams, and a stifled splendour and gloom.
Speak to Him, thou, for He hears, and Spirit with Spirit can meet,—
Closer is He than breathing, and nearer than hands and feet."
—Tennyson.

SYNOPSIS OF CHAPTER 1

This Introductory Chapter consists of three parts. The first lays down the questions proposed, and shows the necessity of asking them. The second illustrates what may be termed in Art-phrase the motives of the Essay. The third briefly describes its method, and explains the readiest mode of studying Natural Theology.

Analysis — Inquiries underlying Natural Theology—Way in which they are answered by our Instinctive Persuasions—How far this answer is sufficing; how far influential.

Phases of Doubt; undeclared Scepticism and Indifferentism—Origin and leaders of the modern Sceptical and Materialistic Schools—Doubts of Intellect distinguished from Scepticism of Immorality—Social dangers and alarms exemplified.

Method of this Essay, and requests as to the mode of reading it—Divisions of Argument; their separate and consilient effect.

Additional Notes and Illustrations

    A. The Right Honourable W. E. Gladstone and others on Modern Scepticism.
    B. On Corruption of the Judgment by misdirected Moral Sentiments.
    C. On Special Pleading in History and Morals.
    D. On the Method employed throughout this Essay.
    E. On the Effect of Consilient Proofs.

INTRODUCTORY

No subjects of thought have ever been proposed more essential to the culture and happiness of mankind than the two following inquiries.

Upon the first, human minds dwell unweariedly through every change of circumstance from childhood to advanced age. It is this:—What reason have we to look for a future life after that hour of dissolution which inevitably awaits us all?

The second question unites itself closely, as by indissoluble links, to the first. We always proceed to ask, Is there sufficient ground for believing in the existence of a Supreme Moral Being, to whose righteous care and kindness we can calmly commit ourselves when we come to die?

Suppose any man to maintain that the universe we inhabit,—and we who are a portion of its occupants—came into existence by chance, he renounces at once every right and title to expect a life succeeding his bodily death. Chance—if the word means anything—means absolute uncertainty; and from that which is in its own nature uncertain, what continuing effects, what conclusive expectation, can be drawn?

Neither is the prospect improved by Materialists [a], in whose opinion the being of man comprehends no element differing essentially, and in kind, from the natural world he rules over. We see actually consequent upon every death-bed the decay of our material frame; if, therefore, that frame be not the casket of a brighter jewel, we can assuredly affirm no hope higher or happier than corruption.

The feelings of most human beings revolt from a destiny so ignoble. And many persons are satisfied that this revolt of feeling is in itself a sufficient ground for some belief in Immortality. Why, they ask, should so powerful an instinct dwell in the breast of our race with only a misleading issue? The higher instincts of creatures below us do not mislead them regarding that which is to come. Insects innumerable make provision for the certain sustenance of a progeny they never can live to behold. They also anticipate for themselves a futurity of life and development. The caterpillar invests himself with the web he has spun, and sinks into a chrysalid-sepulchre, to emerge from it in sun-lighted beauty. Can any valid reason be assigned why the intuitive aspirations of man should be more fallacious than such practical foresights of the merely animal world below him?

So far as the writer of these pages is aware, no one has ever alleged a reason why mankind should be thus deluded. And without going further than our own country, it seems probable that this instinctive persuasion is seldom wanting amongst the greater part of our people. Although the moral consequences of such a persuasion, sometimes merely passive, may be far less than good men could desire, yet they are frequently strong enough to assist the weak and wavering when exposed to sudden temptations. In the "short and simple annals of the poor," may be read countless instances of the fact. Neglected men and women, the scorned outcasts of society, have been often held back by it from greater criminality. They have found themselves unable to acquiesce in the belief of their world's opinion—the opinion of their evil friends and companions—that death must be to all creatures the certain end of all things.

If, on the other hand, absolute knowledge of a future state were the natural gift of each person's understanding, there are thousands amongst our educated classes to whom the trial and terror of their own hearts would be incalculably mitigated. Numbers feel that speculative doubts concerning the Being of a God, and life after death, are sources of a continual perplexity and distress, under which they find little or no sympathy. In every fresh affliction or anxiety, such a mind has to sustain a double burden of sorrow, and concerning such it seems emphatically true, that "the heart knoweth his own bitterness." There may, however, be suggested one alleviation for every similar instance of despondency. The same rule holds in this respect as in all human pursuits,—labour is, and will always continue, the appointed path by which we must attain. The more noble the object sought, the more arduous the task and toil,—and what can be nobler than a well-grounded belief in God and Immortality?

Another very large class of educated persons bear their doubts with stoical composure, account them an inevitable burden, and consider it lost time to ask questions concerning "the Unknowable." This class is sustained in its attitude by the prevalence [b] of really sceptical writings;—writings (that is) which deny the possibility of knowledge beyond the circle of positive phenomena. Maxims to this effect are not uncommonly disseminated through the periodical press, books of fiction, and other kinds of light literature. The rapidity of modern life leads men to take opinions upon trust, and keeps them back from serious investigation. An ephemeral satirist becomes in their eyes as valuable an authority as the most deeply-thinking reasoner. Much work is saved by this valuation, to say nothing of the great gain in self-complacency. And, no doubt, many persons feel particularly complacent in taking their tone from minds which are evidently no better informed, and no more finely strung than their own [c].

The class of sceptics just described, cannot be reckoned in figures. They make up multitudes never enumerated apart in any religious census. They live and die and make no sign,—and how can quiet unavowed disbelief obtain a separate place in the columns of the Registrar-General? Among the audible tones of respectable people it finds no utterance, and therefore occupies no position. Every one experienced in the world knows that this species of Indifferentism is usually regular at public worship, and reticent where sceptical phrases pass current. The only sure test is a moral one—of very slow application, since it takes time for a decent sceptic to balance the pleasures against the risks of immorality. Meantime, there remains some possible hope for a happier choice during the period of indecision.

Far fewer, because far more strongly declared, are the literary lodestars of that harbourless sea, where all beyond the horizon of cloud and billow seems veiled and uncertain. Some amongst them may, after all, be but wandering lights themselves [d], floating and drifting like meteors which glimmer at nightfall across shadowy waters. Others appear really fixed in a dim and joyless firmament where the Present only is true, the remote Past a conjecture, and the Future altogether inscrutable. According to them this bounded prospect is the true goal and real aim of our transitory life,—within it the trials and griefs of humanity assume their proper dimensions and pale their ineffectual terrors, while peace, like a river of Eden, flows out over the once martyred but now ransomed race of man. Even in our own imperfect struggling day, the human creature may be happy who certainly knows that this mixed existence is his All—that outside it he can live no life except in the memory of his fellow-men—that there is no God, no futurity of individual progress or perfection; but that one thing happens equally to the good and the bad—the wise and the unwise. This knowledge brings happiness, because it chases from the breast self-centred hope and fear: the man who accepts this blank beholds himself, as he really is, an atom of the Universal Whole—borne now by the irresistible tide of force into sunlight—borne soon by the same irresistible tide into a darkness of the shadow of death.

Compared with this creed, the martyrs of Monotheism were self-loving—for did not they hope? Compared with this simple creed, all who have stopped short on the threshold of frightful crimes, and hesitated to stain their souls, were also self-loving—for did they not fear?

A great variety of remonstrances have been addressed to writers of this latter type [e]. Social consequences have been eloquently urged against hypotheses which, if realised, would weaken, or perhaps destroy, self-control, foresight, and self-improvement. In reply we are told that these objects of pursuit still appear good and useful to benevolent eyes. But it should be remembered that our age is one of transition—half-developed as it were in Doubt. Our benevolent men have not yet been fully disciplined in the coming school. Who, therefore, shall safely predict for us the effects of its proposed discipline? Add that, looking at the civilised world in general, certain ideas (illusions, as they are sometimes called) respecting a Futurity influenced by our present right and wrong-doing, are ingrained in cultured man, and may perhaps be described as connate with his nineteenth-century existence [f]. Is it possible, then, for any one to say beforehand what may or may not be the consequence of uprooting cherished principles fitted in their own nature to exercise so practical an influence?

Remonstrances of this kind, however truthful and valuable in themselves, would be out of place in the ensuing pages. A contribution to the constructive science of Natural Theology must rest its arguments upon the reason of the case, to the exclusion of many interesting and persuasive considerations. All questions of Sociology, have, however, a special fascination for numerous thinkers who are unlikely to overlook negative conclusions lying close upon the confines of their own science, and to them the treatment of such questions must be remitted.

That these phases of thought have not, in fact, escaped the consideration of benevolent observers, may be inferred from the special circumstances under which this Essay is composed. Into every condition (each being required by the exigencies of the subject) the present writer enters with honest cordiality. His wish and aim is to place before those who, while they doubt, still debate, certain reasonable considerations which have appeared convincing to other speculative minds. And he may defend himself from any possible charge of causeless intermeddling with other men's concerns, in the words of one amongst our most genuinely English poets:—

> "'Twere well, says one sage, erudite, profound,
> Terribly arch'd and aquiline his nose,
> And overbuilt with most impending brows,
> 'Twere well could you permit the World to live
> As the World pleases: what's the World to you?
> Much. I was born of woman, and drew milk
> As sweet as charity from human breasts.
> I think, articulate, I laugh and weep,
> And exercise all functions of a man.
> How then should I and any man that lives
> Be strangers to each other?" [3]

There are, however, doubters whom the writer can scarcely desire to address—human beings in whose hearts to deny God kindles a vivid delight, because belief in Him would compel the renunciation of some darling wickedness. The true spring of their Materialism, Pantheism,—or whatever else happens to be the adopted form of Negation—lies within the will [g] itself. And, therefore, the wish to be better must precede the wish to hear any one who reasons of righteousness, temperance, or judgment to come.

To those who doubt, yet desire that Truth—whichever way Truth may incline—shall distinctly prevail, the ensuing pages are dedicated. And one main endeavour to be kept in view by both writer and reader is, that, laying aside passion and prejudice, these questions may be discussed under the *siccum lumen* —the purified ray—of Right Reason. To argue for victory may be allowed an advocate who pleads subject to the intervention of a judge. But here we have no arbiter to say what is or is not allowable; here, too, the matter is in itself something graver than corporeal life, or death, or all else beneath the sky; here, finally, the case is personal, since each reasoner first settles an account with his own heart; next, tries and decides a conclusive issue, and by his own sentence, accepts more than any human foresight can declare. Here, then, special pleading [4] is altogether out of place on either side, and we must, if we aim at what is best, argue for nothing more or less than the plain and simple truth.

There must, of course, be difficulties in keeping this straight and honest road. Few men like making admissions apparently at variance with their own conclusions; fewer still like to forego pleas which, though in their own judgment unsound, are certainly specious, and to many minds persuasive. Such, however, is the wish and aim of the present essayist. And, that he may bind himself the more firmly to his own resolution, he requests his readers to believe that any over- statement or other error of which he may fairly be found guilty, is occasioned by the unpleasantly common cause of ignorance,—a cause which Dr. Johnson confessed was his reason for defining "pastern" as a "horse's knee." "Ignorance, madam, pure ignorance," he replied, to the surprise of his fair critic, who expected an elaborate defence. Per contra, the essayist may equitably claim that he shall not be convicted by a too summary and inconsiderate process. At the first blush, there will certainly appear in the eyes of many readers numerous seeming mistakes, which, if carefully scrutinized, may afterwards be held the reverse. At all events, plain dealing and honest purpose demand that, when Truth is the issue truly sought, those who approach it from opposite sides must (if they desire to do right) sift their objections and difficulties as well as their favourite arguments.

Reasoning on Natural Theology falls necessarily into two divisions. The first is made up of arguments drawn from the world without us. The second, of arguments drawn from the world within [h]. Each path of reasoning is subject to a cross division. We may argue affirmatively to a definite conclusion. We may also argue negatively with the same end in view;—we may show how much more difficult and less tenable is the contradictory hypothesis.

It would be an awkward and almost impracticable task to keep these kinds of reasoning far apart. The natural procedure of thought, is to combine, rather than to dissever, when we marshal facts for the purpose of a full and wide generalization. Yet it does seem practicable to mark every transition of thought distinctly; and, if clearly marked, the distinction may easily be kept in mind. With this precaution, it may appear allowable to treat Natural Theology in a more discursive manner than could otherwise be permitted. The object of so doing will be to divest discussion as much as possible of a dry, logical stiffness; and, by ranging round each topic [i] to look at it in various lights; a process which generally discovers both the weakness and the strength of reasoning. Any one who has read Plato will understand the advantage of Dialogue in this respect. A more familiar book, Coleridge's "Friend," is another apt illustration. Each of its series of essays takes a sweep of the kind; and each "landing-place" affords a rest to the reader, and a fresh beginning to the intellectual tour. Without venturing to copy the quaint invention of landing-places, the present writer intends making every Chapter the occasion of a fresh start. The separate trains of thought will thus proceed from distinct points, and travel by separate routes, so as to admit of full inspection in their progress. Each argument allowed by the reader to be valid, will finally link itself to its neighbours; and all thoughtful persons know how to estimate the strength of convergent conclusions.

The writer trusts, also, that he may be allowed to escape the two alternatives,—either circumlocution, or the use of an objectionable pronoun singular, by employing the plural "we." This word may perhaps have a further good effect; it may remind both reader and writer that they are engaged as pilgrim-companions on a journey of joint exploration.

At the head of all their reasonings, Natural Theologians usually place the celebrated argument from Design. It would be impossible, in discussing it, to reproduce here the many illustrative examples of Design which have been collected. It would likewise be useless; partly, because they are all easily accessible and mostly well known; partly, because their appositeness as illustrations is now fully admitted; and the controversy turns upon questions of another and more abstract kind. It is asked whether the analogy founded on these instances is relevant?—whether it proves too little, or too much?—and, how far the inferences drawn from such examples really go? Our plan will, therefore, be to devote our second Chapter to the examination of such objections; to the review and elucidation of the argument from Design. But if the reader wishes really to study the various questions closely connected with this celebrated line of thought, and to view the reasoning in a shape so complete as to be at once relevant and satisfactory, he may be pleased to bestow a leisure hour on the consecutive perusal of Chapters 2, 5, and 6, with their appended notes and illustrations.

The third Chapter is intended as a critical propaedeutic or foundation for the constructive science of Natural Theology. So far as our experience of men in great cities teaches anything with respect to the speculative difficulties which keep them from God, it seems to teach one undoubted fact. There is grounded in their minds a persuasion (underlying all further objections), that, whatever else we can know, little or nothing is to be learned concerning God. The idea of Theism is thus isolated from every other idea; and there is a presumption against all reasoning which in any way leads up to a determinate thought of the Divine Being or the Divine attributes.

Some such doubters allege the necessary limitation of human knowledge in general:—

"Know then thyself, presume not God to scan;
The proper study of mankind is man."

But, is not one chief object in knowing man, to acquaint ourselves with God? In this spirit Quarles says:—

"Man is man's A B C; there's none that can
Read God aright, unless he first spell man."

We may be perfectly sure that every human being, who (as Pope continues) hangs between the sceptic and the stoic,—

"In doubt to deem himself a god or beast,"

will never arrive at any knowledge of God whatsoever.

Others, again, who suppose mankind to know a great deal, conceive all special thought which transcends the every-day human circle, to be encompassed by a number of difficulties exceptionally its own. If, it is said, there are angelic natures, they must needs pity our poor attempts to survey super -human or extra -human spheres of existence:—

"Superior beings, when of late they saw
A mortal man unfold all nature's law,
Admir'd such wisdom in an earthly shape,
And show'd a Newton as we show an ape." [5]

Pope's cynicism has been lately re-echoed in various comparisons. A death-watch has been supposed to speculate on the final end of a clock; a timepiece on the nature of its makers. Writers who use similitudes may be asked to remember that if Man really possesses reason (to say nothing of an immortal spirit), he cannot be ranged in analogy with apes, death-watches, and timepieces. The moment brute organisms, or inorganic constructions, are represented as reasoning, they cease to be what they are—a Thing suddenly becomes a Person. If this were all, the speech and faculties of Man would be represented as intact, though veiled beneath some shape worthy of the invention of a Babrias or an AEsop. But this is not all. The monstrous shape is at once both Thing and Person, and its thinkings in this double character are supposed to show by their grotesque failures the absurdity of our human endeavour to reason concerning God or Immortality.

To this whole kind of preoccupation the third Chapter is addressed. There are really no special difficulties in the way of Theism. It argues from the known to the unknown; so do all the inductive sciences. It accepts more than it can explain; so do we, each and all, in accepting the truth of our own individuality and personal identity, of the world outside us, and the mind within, which scrutinizes that changing world. The more thoroughly questions relating to our first sources of knowledge are debated, the more surely shall we perceive how safe is the starting-point of Natural Theology.

Against Materialism, on the other hand, there may be urged a series of difficulties properly its own, and this may be most easily seen by placing it in contrast with pure Idealism. The Materialistic starting-point is from an unauthorized postulate—in common parlance, an unfounded assumption; each step it takes is attended with a fresh need of postulation, amounting at last to the gravest burden of improbability. And when the materializing goal is reached we gain nothing—no treasure is discovered—no vista opened into new realms of intellectual or moral empire. We are only told that our supposed insight was but a dream. We are only warned to dream no more. Materialism has murdered insight.

With the argument of this Chapter there arises a very important question, which the reader is entreated to put to himself more than once, and bestow upon it from time to time a pause of serious thought. In a negative form the question runs thus: Since the difficulties supposed to bar the first march of Natural Theology are in no wise peculiar to it, but attach themselves equally to a multitude of our daily grounds of thinking and acting, must we not, if, on account of such difficulties, we deny Natural Theism, also deny those persuasions of ordinary life? How else can we maintain our critical consistency? Let no man henceforward be confident that there exists an outward world of either men or things—let him not carelessly suppose that he has even an individual mind to speak of as his own—let all that concerns other ness—all that concerns self ness be relegated along with the Divine Being to the region of the Unknown and the Unknowable. But we may imagine that, instead of denying these truths of common life, many men will be hardy enough to affirm them. If so, in accepting these they clearly accept a great deal more. To be consistent they must accept also the reasonable beliefs and first principles upon which reposes Theism.

The question thus put is therefore a dilemma or choice between two alternatives. And there may seem to remain no great doubt as to which alternative most practical reasoners will accept. This kind of dilemma will recur at many several steps of our inquiry, but having been illustrated in one instance at considerable length, its examination on other occasions may be safely left to the intelligence of the thoughtful reader.

The four following chapters argue for the truth of Theism on four several and independent grounds. These arguments are purely constructive; and each is so far apart from the other three as to stand or fall upon its own merits. But, when each of these four arguments has been separately examined, if admitted either wholly or in a modified shape, their consilient and conjoint effect must be taken into consideration [j].

To minimize impediments in the way of true knowledge; and to rise into clearness;—these should be the hopes and aims of us all. Life is full of foiled endeavours; but let us onward now with the hopeful!

ADDITIONAL NOTES AND ILLUSTRATIONS TO CHAPTER 1

A. The Right Hon. W. E. Gladstone and Others on Modern Scepticism

Extract from Mr. Gladstone's Address Delivered at the Liverpool Collegiate Institution, December 21st, 1872.

"It is not now only the Christian Church, or only the Holy Scripture, or only Christianity, which is attacked. The disposition is boldly proclaimed to deal alike with root and branch, and to snap utterly the ties which, under the still venerable name of Religion, unite man with the unseen world, and lighten the struggles and the woes of life by the hope of a better land.

"These things are done as the professed results and the newest triumphs of Modern Thought and Modern Science; but I believe that neither Science nor Thought is responsible, any more than Liberty is responsible, for the misdeeds committed in their names. Upon the ground of what is termed evolution, God is relieved of the labour of creation; in the name of unchangeable laws, He is discharged from governing the world; and His function of judgment is also dispensed with, as justice and benevolence are held to forbid that men should hereafter be called to strict account for actions, which under these unchangeable laws they may have committed. But these are only the initial stages of the process. Next we are introduced to the doctrine of the Absolute and the Unconditioned; and under the authority of these phrases (to which, and many other phrases, in their proper places, I have no objection) we are instructed that we can know nothing about God, and therefore can have no practical relations with Him. One writer— or, as it is now termed, thinker—announces with pleasure that he has found the means of reconciling Religion and Science. The mode is in principle most equitable. He divides the field of thought between them. To Science he awards all that of which we know, or may know, something; to Religion he leaves a far wider domain,—that of which we know, and can know, nothing. This sounds like jest, but it is melancholy earnest; and I doubt whether any such noxious crop has been gathered in such rank abundance from the press of England in any former year of our literary history as in this present year of our redemption, eighteen hundred and seventy-two." (pp. 22-3.)

The writer, or thinker, mentioned by Mr. Gladstone is thus described at the end of the address, p. 33:—

"My reference is to Mr. Herbert Spencer. See his 'First Principles,' and especially the chapter on the 'Reconciliation of Science and Religion.' It is needless to cite particular passages. It would be difficult to mistake its meaning, for it is written with great ability and clearness, as well as with every indication of sincerity. Still it vividly recalls to mind an old story of the man who, wishing to be rid of one who was in his house, said, 'Sir, there are two sides to my house, and we will divide them; you shall take the outside.'

"I believe Mr. Spencer has been described in one of our daily journals as the first thinker of the age."

To some people the Premier will appear more than reasonably disturbed by the journal's description. There is (as we have remarked) a very advanced type of the genus journalist in

England, and its anonymous zealots are liberal in distributing titles of honour—that is, among their friends. Per contra, upon authors of Mr. Gladstone's calibre and lofty mode of thought they bestow epithets very much the reverse of complimentary. They seem, in fact, somewhat to resemble those critics of whom Nathaniel Hawthorne wrote, that "though excellent fellows in their way, there are no gentlemen in the world less sensible of any sanctity in a book, or less likely to recognize an author's heart in it." So far, however, as Mr. Herbert Spencer is concerned, the journal censured might observe in justification of its approval that his system seems a good deal read by the students of more than one school in our Premier's own University—a proud distinction shared by Mr. Spencer with several other eminent thinkers of the same speculative tendencies as himself.

The eloquent speaker next passes under brief review two other typical books,—one by a German, the second by an Englishman. Respecting the opinions of the former author (Strauss [6]) Mr. Gladstone writes thus (*Authentic Report*, p. 24):—

"In his first chapter he puts the question, 'Are we still Christians?' and, after a detailed examination, he concludes, always speaking on behalf of Modern Thought, that if we wish our yea to be yea, and our nay nay, if we are to think and speak our thoughts as honourable, upright men, we must reply that we are Christians no longer. This question and answer, however, he observes, are insufficient. The essential and fundamental inquiry is, whether we are or are not still to have a Religion?

"To this inquiry he devotes his second chapter. In this second chapter he finds that there is no personal God; there is no future state; the dead live in the recollection of survivors—this is enough for them. After this he has little difficulty in answering the question he has put. All religious worship ought to be abolished. The very name of 'Divine Service' is an indignity to man. Therefore, in the sense in which religion has been heretofore understood, his answer is that we ought to have no religion any more. But proceeding, as he always does, with commendable frankness, he admits that he ought to fill with something the void which he has made. This he accordingly proceeds to do. Instead of God, he offers to us the All, or Universum. This All, or Universum, possesses, he tells us, neither consciousness nor reason. But it presents to us order and law. He thinks it fitted, therefore, to be the object of a new and true piety, which he claims for his Universum, as the devout of the old style did for their God. If any one repudiates this doctrine, to Dr. Strauss's reason the repudiation is absurdity, and to his feelings blasphemy" [7].

Many readers will agree with the Premier in calling these "astonishing assertions." Many will also speak of Strauss's positions as something worse than astonishing when they read in the Illustrative Passages (Address, p. 34) a declaration which he holds it his duty as well as his right to make without any kind of reserve [8].

Most persons will likewise agree with the Premier's further observation (p. 38):—

"I have made a statement that these ideas are not a mere German brood, though I fear that we owe much of their seed to Germany, as France owed to England the seed of her great Voltairian movement, so far as it was a movement grounded in the region of thought."

In illustration of the statement that "there are many writers of kindred sympathies in England, and some of as outspoken courage" (Address, p. 26), Mr. Gladstone quotes four passages from Mr. Winwood Reade's "Martyrdom of Man." The three first cited possess a painful interest for the Natural Theologian. They are as follows:—(1.) "When the faith in a personal God is extinguished; when prayer and praise are no longer to be heard; when the belief is universal that with the body dies the soul; then the false morals of theology will no longer lead the human mind astray." (2.) "We teach that the soul is immortal; we teach that there is a future life; we teach that there is a Heaven in the ages far away: but not for us single corpuscles, not for us dots of animated jelly, but for the One of whom we are the elements, and who, though we perish, never dies." (3.) "God is so great that He does not deign to have personal relations with us human atoms that are called men. Those who desire to worship their Creator must worship Him through mankind. Such, it is plain, is the scheme of Nature." (pp. 38-9.)

On account of his Address and pièces justificatives, Mr. Gladstone has been already (like a prophet of old) "wounded in the house of his friends." It may therefore be well to support his judgment by some additional testimony. Now the Pall Mall Gazette, whatever faults may be imputed to it by its adversaries, cannot be justly charged with harshness or discourtesy towards materializing writers. And it so happens that both Dr. Strauss and Mr. Reade have lately been criticised in its columns. From these notices, therefore, I shall venture on making some extracts. Strauss's "Der Alte und der Neue Glaube" was reviewed at considerable length in the number for November 27, 1872. I quote two passages only.

After an interesting introduction the reviewer proceeds thus:—

"As the title of the book indicates, the work to be effected divides itself into two main parts. First, it is necessary to settle the relations to be adopted towards the old Church faith, or Christianity. That accomplished, the outlines at least of the new views that take its place must be sketched out. Of course, before that can be done it must be settled whether or not there is anything to put in place of Christianity. It is logically correct to ask, first, whether 'we'—meaning 'the thinking minority,' who have grown dissatisfied with 'the old faith'—'are still Christians' in any sense. Having answered that question in the negative, it is in order to ask next 'whether we have any religion,'—which cannot be answered by a simple negative or affirmative, or without further explanations as to the nature of religion. We must see 'how we regard the world,' or the system of existing things; what results we are led to by modern researches as to its origin, purpose, and destiny. Although in the light that flows from these, Strauss maintains that the old idea of a personal God must disappear, he finds a Divinity in the All or totality of nature, whose forces and course exhibit purpose or design—subjectively speaking—and order, and to which we are bound, recognizing the wisdom that regulates them, piously to resign ourselves, seeking to fulfil that order of which we ourselves are a part."

The following extract concludes the notice:—

"We have seen that Strauss refuses to acknowledge Christianity because on examination its assertions appear to him incredible, and its claims therefore inadmissible. That is the result of an examination of the nature of Christianity, in which we have nothing new, as it is substantially a synopsis of the fuller process of reasoning contained in 'The Life of Jesus.' But it is not Christianity alone that must be dispensed with. In accordance with the old declaration that miracles are impossible, the supernatural also disappears. It is not merely relegated, as by Herbert Spencer and Comte, to the sphere of the Unknowable; it is not recognized in any manner whatsoever. In place of creation, we have in these pages a process of continuous development through immense periods of time; instead of God, as the source of law and authority and order, nature proceeding harmoniously in an unending process; instead of individual immortality, the conclusion that every individual fulfils his destiny in this world. The divinities and the after life of man are, as with Feuerbach, declared to be simply his own desires. 'What man might be but is not, he makes his god; what he might possess but cannot win for himself, that shall his god bestow upon him.' In reference to the argument that man must somewhere realize all the possibilities that are in him, and as he does not do so in this life there must be a future one, Strauss asks whether all seeds in nature come to maturity. Having dispensed, then, with the supernatural, are we necessarily without any religion? We have seen that Strauss answers in the negative, though not very confidently. The fundamental views on human life, the existence of the world, and so forth, are without doubt a religion, or the theoretical side of one. If in order to a religion it be necessary to believe that the universe fulfils a rational purpose through a rational order, we have that presented to us. There is constant process and continuous development. There is an ascent, as it were, of the forces of nature which perform their mighty cycles through the ages, and a consequent descent and vanishing away. The All remains ever the same, is at no moment more complete than in the preceding, nor vice versâ, but there is a process of becoming and disappearing which goes on, or may go on ad infinitum. The design or purpose of every part is being fulfilled at every moment, for at every moment there is the richest possible unfolding of life in the total system of things. The highest idea to which we can attain is that of the universe.

"Many people were scandalized when a few years ago Mr. Mill maintained that the idea of a God was not indispensable to a religion. Comte's 'Religion of Humanity' was then in view. Strauss's religion, though equally without a God, is deformed by no such crudities of thought and feeling as Comte's. Rather is his book a representation in brief compass of the views to which, whether we regret it or not, the majority of educated and thinking men are in our day more and more attracted."

One remarkable circumstance dwelt upon in this notice, as well as in Mr. Gladstone's Address, is that Strauss, like Comte, finds a substitute for the worship of a Deity—a something which both are pleased to call a Religion. Strauss takes the theoretical, Comte the sentimental view. According to the Frenchman, men are to worship "Humanity" with a leaning to the female side. The un- deformed religion of the German centres upon an Optimistic theory of the All or Universum [9]. Both would seem practically to confess the real necessity of some Religion to mankind, and the question naturally occurs whether these succedanea are more wholesome and elevating than Theism, or whether (it may be added) they are as likely to be true after all.

Mr. Winwood Reade's "Martyrdom of Man" had been criticised four days earlier (Pall Mall Gazette, Nov. 23). As he is an English writer, I take the liberty of making more copious extracts, but would recommend such of my readers as have not perused the article to bestow half an hour's steady thought upon it.

"Mr. Reade," writes the critic, "puts forth his book as a sort of review, or survey, or abridgement of the general history of the human race, and he has given to it the strange title it bears because he is of opinion that 'the supreme and mysterious Power by whom the universe has been created, and by whom it has been appointed to run its course under fixed and invariable law; that awful One to whom it is profanity to pray, of whom it is idle and irreverent to argue and debate, of whom we should never presume to think save with humility and awe; that Unknown God has ordained that mankind should be elevated by misfortune, and that happiness should grow out of misery and pain.' But, although the work is in the main historical, it is also partly cosmological, partly physiological, and partly polemical. It deals with the past, the present, and the future of the world as well as of humanity....

"In what he has to say on the present occasion Mr. Reade lays no claim to originality. On the contrary, he warns us that he has borrowed, 'not only facts and ideas, but phrases and even paragraphs from other writers.' The purpose he has in view is to illustrate the investigations and enforce the conclusions within a moderate compass of higher and more voluminous authorities. But still there is quite enough of his own handiwork in the volume to entitle him to be regarded as far more than a mere compiler; and we venture to think that many readers will find those portions of it which are the fruits of Mr. Reade's personal experience as an African explorer, and his reflections upon that which he has himself seen, among the most interesting and instructive of all.

"In the writings of Mr. Darwin, Mr. Mill, Dr. Draper, and Mr. Herbert Spencer, the authors to whom Mr. Reade seems to be chiefly indebted, the assumed antagonism between the conclusions of modern science and the premises of popular theology is latent rather than manifest. With them it is left as a matter of inference, and is nowhere forced upon the attention as a matter of fact. Mr. Reade endeavours to supply this deficiency, and he does so distinctly and abruptly enough.... In order to build we must destroy. Not only the Syrian superstition must be attacked, but the belief in a 'personal God,' which engenders a slavish and oriental condition of the mind, and the belief in a posthumous reward which engenders a selfish and solitary condition of the heart.... What Mr. Reade is pleased to designate 'the Syrian superstition' is still the direct or indirect source of all the really practical sympathy existing both between the higher and lower classes of society and the higher and lower races of mankind. As to the belief in a personal God, the passage we have quoted above from Mr. Reade seems to show that he shares it, or the language he uses is mere nonsense. It would be absurd to talk about anything except a personal God creating the universe, appointing fixed and invariable laws, and ordaining the destiny of mankind. And if Mr. Reade is referring merely to force collectively or in the abstract, we cannot perceive why it 'should be idle and irreverent to argue and debate about' it, or why 'we should never presume to think, save with humility and awe' about it, more than about its particular and concrete manifestations; for instance, light, heat, or electricity. Moreover, if we admit that the universe is in any sense the work of a supreme and mysterious Power who has in any sense predestined an unalterable course for it to run, we cannot understand how such a belief is fitted to remove the 'slavish and oriental condition of mind' of which Mr. Reade complains. We should have thought rather that the unmitigated fatalism it implies would be far likelier to generate such an intellectual state than reliance on providential superintendence and interposition carried to no matter what extravagant lengths. Mr. Reade's proposition that the belief in a posthumous reward engenders a selfish and solitary condition of the heart appears to us likewise wide of the mark. As long as we continue to be individual beings, our conduct will continue to be the result of our individual feelings, present or anticipated. Practically, at all events, the Stoic, the Sadducee, and the Christian equally will fulfil instead of neglecting their duty—first, because they are conscious that it is their duty, and secondly, because they know that fulfilling it will bring them satisfaction, and that to neglect it will bring them remorse. The only difference is that the Christian trusts that his satisfaction in the one case, and fears that his remorse in the other case, will be infinitely prolonged."

Mr. Reade's reviewer concludes his critique with a piece of wit from Voltaire, which he views as enunciating a pretty fair summary of the moral contained in the "Martyrdom of Man." Voltaire compares the Creator of the world to the builder of a great house, and men to the mice who inhabit its chinks and crannies. The Divine builder has not enlightened us mice. This comparison has often since been repeated in new and improved shapes by sceptical moderns, who treat a considerate Death-watch as a typical thinker on problems of reason, such as Design and Final Causation.

As author of a Lecture on Positivism in 1871, I cannot but be gratified to perceive that Mr. Gladstone's views of Comte's character and system are coincident with my own. (Authentic Report, pp. 25 and 36.)

This note began with extracts furnished by one Premier—it may not inaptly close with quotations from the writings of another.

Mr. Disraeli, in his preface to the new edition of "Lothair," expresses himself as follows (p. xv., seq.):—

"It cannot be denied that the aspect of the world and this country, to those who have faith in the spiritual nature of man, is at this time dark and distressful. They listen to doubts, and even denials, of an active Providence; what is styled Materialism is in the ascendant. To those who believe that an atheistical society, though it may be polished and amiable, involves the seeds of anarchy, the prospect is full of gloom.

"This disturbance in the mind of nations has been occasioned by two causes: firstly, by the powerful assault on the divinity of the Semitic literature by the Germans; and, secondly, by recent discoveries of science, which are hastily supposed to be inconsistent with our long-received convictions as to the relations between the Creator and the created."

On the first cause of disturbance, Mr. Disraeli continues:—

"Man brings to the study of the oracles more learning and more criticism than of yore: and it is well that it should be so. The documents will yet bear a greater amount both of erudition and examination than they have received; but the word of God is eternal, and will survive the spheres."

On the second, he observes:—"Scientific, like spiritual truth, has ever from the beginning been descending from Heaven to man. He is a being who organically demands direct relations with his Creator, and he would not have been so organised if his requirements could not be satisfied. We may analyse the sun and penetrate the stars, but man is conscious that he is made in God's own image, and in his perplexity he will ever appeal to 'our Father which art in Heaven.'"

Both these sources of doubt and denial have been exemplified in the preceding note. I might indeed have hesitated to exemplify them so fully were it not for the considerations mentioned in my preface to this essay.

B. On Corruption of the Judgment by Misdirected Moral Sentiments

Talfourd—then Mr. Serjeant Talfourd—thus describes what passed in his own mind when viewing the site of Gibbon's abode at Lausanne:—

"That garden in which the Historian took his evening walk, after writing the last lines of the work to which many years had been devoted;—a walk which alone would have hallowed the spot, if, alas! there had not been those intimations in the work itself of a purpose which, tending to desecrate the world, must deprive all associations attendant on its accomplishment of a claim to be dwelt on as holy! How melancholy is it to feel that intellectual congratulation which attends the serene triumph of a life of studious toil chilled by the consciousness that the labour, the research, the Asiatic splendour of illustration, have been devoted, in part at least, to obtain a wicked end—not in the headlong wantonness of youth, or the wild sportiveness of animal spirits, but urged by the deliberate, hearted purpose of crushing the light of human hope—all that is worth living for, and all that is worth dying for—and substituting for them nothing but a rayless scepticism. That evening walk is an awful thing to meditate on; the walk of a man of rare capacities, tending to his own physical decline, among the serenities of loveliest nature, enjoying the thought that, in the chief work of his life, just accomplished, he had embodied a hatred to the doctrines which teach men to love one another, to forgive injuries, and to hope for a diviner life beyond the grave; and exulting in the conviction that this work would survive to teach its deadly lesson to young ingenuous students, when he should be dust. One may derive consolation from reflecting that the style is too meretricious, and the attempt too elaborate and too subtle, to achieve the proposed evil; and in hoping that there were some passages in the secret history of the author's heart, which may extenuate its melancholy error; but our personal veneration for successful toil is destroyed in the sense of the strange malignity which blended with its impulses, and we feel no desire to linger over the spot where so painful a contradiction is presented as a charm."— *Vacation Rambles*. Ed. 2, p. 238.

We may gladly give Gibbon the benefit of the doubt with which the great judge closes. But surely most attempts to address the mental state depicted must needs be found impotent. There is great force in a dictum of Schelling's ("Idealismus der Wissenschaftslehre") to the following effect—

"The medium by which spirits understand each other is not the ambient air, but the deep-stirred sympathetic vibrations propagated by a community of spiritual freedom. When a soul is not pervaded by this atmosphere of conscious freedom, all inward communion with self or with another is broken,—what wonder, then, if such a one remain unintelligible to himself and to others, and in his fearful wilderness of spirit wearies himself by idle words, to which no friendly echo responds, either from his own or from another's breast?

"To remain unintelligible to such an one is glory and honour before God and man. Barbarus huic ego sim, nec tali intelligar ulli. This," concludes Schelling, "is a wish and prayer from which no man can keep himself."— Sämmtliche Werke, I. 443.

C. On Special Pleading in History and Morals

A few emphatic sentences from Lord Macaulay's strictures on historical special pleading will repay perusal:—

"This species of misrepresentation abounds in the most valuable works of modern historians. Herodotus tells his story like a slovenly witness, who, heated by partialities and prejudices, unacquainted with the established rules of evidence, and uninstructed as to the obligations of his oath, confounds what he imagines with what he has seen and heard, and brings out facts, reports, conjectures, and fancies in one mass. Hume is an accomplished advocate. Without positively asserting much more than he can prove, he gives prominence to all the circumstances which support his case; he glides lightly over those which are unfavourable to it; his own witnesses are applauded and encouraged; the statements which seem to throw discredit on them are controverted; the contradictions into which they fall are explained away; a clear and connected abstract of their evidence is given. Everything that is offered on the other side is scrutinised with the utmost severity; every suspicious circumstance is a ground for comment and invective; what cannot be denied is extenuated, or passed by without notice; concessions even are sometimes made; but this insidious candour only increases the effect of the vast mass of sophistry.

"We have mentioned Hume as the ablest and most popular writer of his class; but the charge which we have brought against him is one to which all our most distinguished historians are in some degree obnoxious. Gibbon, in particular, deserves very severe censure."— *Macaulay's Miscellaneous Writings*—History.

The reader may very advantageously carry along with him the above quoted just remarks, if he has occasion to travel into Hume's sceptical writings. Respecting these, where every feature of the author's character appears with intensified distinctness of expression, it is not too much to say that their influence, which had suffered suspended animation [10], is now felt in almost every cultivated circle in Europe. Checked for a time under the empire of Kant and his successors, it has been revived by the German Darwinists (so-called), who are bent on evolving all that can be got from the theory of Evolution. Comte speaks of Hume as his own master—an intellectual debt all the more readily acknowledged, because Hume's treatment of most subjects leans towards the French, rather than the Teutonic, side of English speculation. The master's influence over numbers who, without being Comte's disciples, are addicted to thinking Positively upon questions connected with Mind and Morality, was never greater than at present.

Here, therefore, the disciplined inquirer will obtain a prolific field of discovery, if he wishes to convince himself how little originality pervades the set of opinions just now in fashion.

But the student of Hume ought surely to be a disciplined inquirer. Many senior residents at our Universities will, therefore, join me in regretting that his sceptical treatises should be so commonly found in the hands of very young men. So far as such readers are concerned, it does not much signify whether Hume's fallacies are due to one siddedness of intellect or (as has been said by a critic, once himself a doubter) whether he was influenced "by vanity, appetite, and the ambition of forming a sect of arguescents." An opinion scarcely libellous, considering what Hume has said respecting the validity of his own paradoxes. However this may appear, the fallacies remain fallacies, and are less easy of detection than they would have been were their author a systematic thinker, instead of a philosophical dilettante. Under any circumstances, it is not every aspirant to the "Round Table" for whom the quest after secret spells is fitted. The youthful knight has his own ward to keep, and needs help—not hindrance, much less betrayal—inasmuch as:—

> "Tis his to struggle with that perilous age
> Which claims for manhood's vice the privilege
> Of boyhood;—when young Dionysus seems
> All glorious as he burst upon the east,
> A jocund and a welcome conqueror;
> And Aphrodite, sweet as from the sea
> She rose and floated in her pearly shell,
> A laughing girl;—when lawless will erects
> Honour's gay temple on the mount of God,
> And meek obedience bears the coward's brand;
> While Satan, in celestial panoply,
> With Sin, his lady, smiling by his side,
> Defies all heaven to arms!"
> *Hartley Coleridge's Poems*, Vol. II., p. 202.

D. On the Method Employed in This Essay

The advantages which ensue from this mode of "ranging round each topic" are well described by the late Sir B. Brodie (*Psychological Inquiries*, 1st series, p. 18).

> "Our minds are so constructed that we can keep the attention fixed on a particular object until we have, as it were, looked all around it; and the mind that possesses this faculty in the greatest degree of perfection will take cognisance of relations of which another mind has no perception. It is this, much more than any difference in the abstract power of reasoning, which constitutes the vast difference which exists between the minds of different individuals; which distinguishes the far-sighted statesman from the shallow politician; the sagacious and accomplished general from the mere disciplinarian. Such also is the history, not only of the poetic genius, but also of the genius of discovery in science. 'I keep the subject,' said Sir Isaac Newton, 'constantly before me, and wait until the first dawnings open by little and little into a full light.' It was thus that, after long meditation, he was led to the invention of fluxions, and to the anticipation of the modern discovery of the combustibility of the diamond. It was thus that Harvey discovered the circulation of the blood; and that those views were suggested to Davy, which are propounded in the Bakerian lecture of 1806, and which laid the foundation of that grand

series of experimental researches which terminated in the decomposition of the earths and alkalies."

Dr. Tyndall also considers the case of Newton ("Fragments of Science," p. 60).

"Newton pondered all these things. He had a great power of pondering. He could look into the darkest subject until it became entirely luminous. How this light arises we cannot explain; but, as a matter of fact, it does arise." Dr. Tyndall had before remarked on the question thus suggested, that "There is much in this process of pondering and its results which it is impossible to analyse. It is by a kind of inspiration that we rise from the wise and sedulous contemplation of facts to the principles on which they depend. The mind is, as it were, a photographic plate, which is gradually cleansed by the effort to think rightly, and which when so cleansed, and not before, receives impressions from the light of truth. This passage from facts to principles is called induction, which in its highest form is inspiration; but, to make it sure, the inward sight must be shown to be in accordance with outward fact. To prove or disprove the induction, we must resort to deduction and experiment."—Ibid, p. 57-8.

This last remark concerns the process of verification which the accomplished writer discusses through several subsequent pages.

Notwithstanding a passing observation of Dr. Tyndall's that "this power of pondering facts is one with which the ancients could be but imperfectly acquainted," some readers will be struck by the thought that it forms the nearest approach which can be made by any inductive discoverer to the old philosophical method of Dialectic. Janet says, in a volume to which those who have not encountered it will thank me for introducing them,

"La dialectique logique dans Platon est parfaitement conforme aux lois de la raison. Elle ne sert qu'à réfuter les idées fausses, ou à éclaircir les idées données antérieurement par une sorte de synthèse, qui, suivant les uns, n'est que le progrès de la généralisation, et, selon nous, est le progrès de l'intuition." (Études sur la Dialectique dans Platon et dans Hegel, p. 393.)

For a more complete appreciation of what is here stated in few words, the student should peruse pp. 244, seq. The account given by Janet appears in some measure to coincide with Dr. Tyndall's idea, though perhaps the word "Intuition" might be more entirely approved by Schelling or Coleridge than by any Physicist.

Be this as it may, Dr. Tyndall's outline of the Inductive process in its highest form is evidently one which describes the prerogative of Genius—the exercise of Imagination as distinguished from Fancy—the child, that is, of Reason, rather than a stray bantling of sportive wit.

To bring his general conception within the grasp of every-day workers, and describe a procedure which may be adopted as a kind of practical rule or maxim, let us look at this subject in the following manner.

Suppose we take the example of a great idea; that, for instance, of the constitution of Great Britain, or any other nation which subsists in tolerable freedom from revolutionary change. There are clearly two elements involved—one, Permanence; the other, Progress. These, in the actual working constitution, form its factors, or moments (as they may be better termed); and in the idea or mental representation of the same, we may liken them to complementary colours in the spectrum, which appear separately contrasted in tint, but blend together in a wave of white light. Now, our analysing faculty of mind is, in point of fact, our intellectual prism. It separates each bright and strong idea into elements so antagonistic as to be apparently incompatible. Like clear yellow and shadowy violet, one component seems excellent in beauty, another its foil or opposite. To one class of minds truth consists in Permanence, and Progress is a note of evil omen. Of another class the contradictory is true. The real statesman alone knows that their blending is a question of measure and degree, of human affairs,—time, circumstance, and opportunity.

We may ask with reason what gain accrues to the statesman by looking at his country's constitution from this point of sight? Evidently a good deal. He will soon discern that practically it cannot exist in vigour if either factor be eliminated. Each is given in the analysis of his prolific idea, and, however great may seem the apparent incompatibility, both must be capable of co-existence and correlation. Now, there could be no synthesis if, on the one hand, Progress did not imply a something which remains identical and in unity with itself, while it flourishes and grows;—or, on the other hand, if Permanence were not safest, when its strength is manifested by its vital increase. Consequently, to grow is to continue essentially the same;—to be permanent is to live and bear fresh fruit every passing year.

A precisely similar advantage accrues to the Ethical Philosopher from a process of the like description. He considers (it may be) the concrete idea of moral activity. Obviously, there must be found in it an unfettered power of choice, and a conformity to the rule of moral law. Submitted to the analytic prism, the two elements come out at opposite poles in very decided contrast. At the pole of necessary conformity we find what looks like Determinism;—at the pole of choice appears its irreconcilable antagonist, a sense of Responsibility, logically unexplained, but inalienable from our moral nature. And our Ethical inquirer finds the only possible synthesis of his two contrasted moments of morality in the deep truth that each righteous man is a Law unto himself. And hence it is, that the righteous shines out over the lower world of mechanical arrangement—a faint, it may be, but still a visible image of the God who made him what he is [11].

By the same process of analysis and reconstruction the Natural Theologian arrives (as may be shown) at a synthesis of Faith and Reason. Yet these two are antagonistic in the eyes both of the sceptic and the superstitious. Les extrêmes se touchent, and by both extremes faith is relegated to the region of sentimental aesthetics.

Reason, say both, is Faith's natural enemy; and must fail to yield any expectation of future happiness in the presence of a righteous God, together with its long train of present hopes and fears. Our plain answer is that the true synthesis of Natural Theism lies in the chief primary fact of our human nature—the undeniable existence of its Reasonable Beliefs. They originate deep down, and we may affirm respecting the birth of each and all, as Dr. Tyndall affirms of the inward vision which dawns upon the philosophic mind when photographically cleansed by its own efforts to think rightly,—"how this light arises we cannot explain, but as a matter of fact it does arise." In its degree it may be (to use Dr. Tyndall's word) "a kind of inspiration." And what endowment has a higher claim to such a representative kinship?—what nobler gift can be conceived from God to man than a Belief of Reason? Dr. Tyndall's further requirement that "the inward sight must be shown to be in accordance with the outward fact," a Natural Theologian may hope to meet by a sufficient verification. He may meet it in the case of this particular Belief by showing, as we shall try to show, our actual human experience of its working and its worth.

We might pursue similar examples through the regions of Discovery and Production, but the three instances already adduced may fairly suffice. It is, perhaps, more interesting to observe the real gains which accrue from pondering over an idea in the manner exemplified. How much political charlatanerie is at once disposed of when men distinctly acknowledge that two reputed incompatibilities, however useful as war-cries, are essentially conjoint elements in all truly statesmanlike action: what countless angry controversies die in the moral principle that each righteous man is a Law unto himself! And not only to Natural Theology, but to other parts of knowledge, it is of the greatest utility to perceive with equal distinctness that Reason has its beliefs as well as Unreason; and that when we accept reasonable beliefs as the basis of scientific investigation, we affirm their value for the conduct and government of life. The true amount of that value as a mainspring of our hopeful activities is estimated on another page. Meantime, we may remark from the three examples above discussed, how regularly an idea of Reason, analysed into its complementary factors, resumes a concrete form when we employ it as a maxim of practical life. The politician who separates progress from stability is really preparing his country for revolution. The man on whose heart the law is not written (like the necessity laid upon St. Paul [12] is as yet imperfectly righteous. And so too, if in our Beliefs we lose sight of the gift that makes us human, we are likely to ring the changes between superstition, atheism, and effeminate sentimentality.

When, from results, we pass to the easiest method for attaining them, there seems but little to add to the extracts with which this note commenced. And if the object be clearly defined, the labour of the mental workshop need not be a severe discouragement. It is true that no man can take his Thought—the offspring of his inward Light—pull it to pieces, and reconstruct it, as he would deal with a thing of brass or iron. But every earnest ponderer may keep his prolific idea steadily in view, and hold conversations with himself respecting it. This is the well-known method by which Aristotle virtually obtains his conclusions before he finally proceeds to deduce them. From the same conception of Method, real thinking appears to Plato as a Dialogue without speech. And, doubtless, actual discussion between two or more living men would be the surest way of arriving at the goal of insight, provided those most uncommon of all endowments, common sense and common honesty, could be assured to the dialecticians [13].

Thus much, then, may serve as an illustration of the task we are attempting, and of the means by which we hope to accomplish it. If achieved, it will form a contribution to the great work thus characterised by the Rector of Lincoln College from the University pulpit, as reported in the *Oxford Undergraduates' Journal* for October 26, 1871:

"The Natural Theology of the last century is no longer found to be satisfactory in presence of the geological and biological sciences as they now stand. The answer that the sciences are wrong and the theologians are right does not admit of being discussed or refuted, for it is the answer of ignorance. The answer of the Catholic Church, which is to take refuge in its own authority, can only be practically tendered where there is an infallible living authority, as in the chair of S. Peter. It seems to be the business of the English Church especially—a Church which has never yet broken with reason or proscribed education—to fairly face these questions, to resume the Natural Theology of the past age, and to re-establish the synthesis of Science and Faith."

E. On the Effect of Consilient Proofs

The expressive word "Consilience" has been adopted on the authority of Dr. Whewell and Professor Pritchard, both of whom employ it in preference to the commoner expression convergence. Upon the force of consilient proofs, Dr. Whewell writes thus:—

"The cases in which inductions from classes of facts altogether different have jumped together, belong only to the best established theories which the history of science contains. And as I shall have occasion to refer to this peculiar feature in their evidence, I will take the liberty of describing it by a particular phrase, and will term it the Consilience of Inductions.

"It is exemplified principally in some of the greatest discoveries. Thus it was found by Newton that the doctrine of the attraction of the sun varying according to the inverse square of the distance, which explained Kepler's Third Law of the proportionality of the cubes of the distances to the squares of the periodic times of the planets, explained also his First and Second Laws of the elliptical motion of each planet; although no connexion of these laws had been visible before. Again, it appeared that the force of universal gravitation, which had been inferred from the perturbations of the moon and planets by the sun and by each other, also accounted for the fact, apparently altogether dissimilar and remote, of the precession of the equinoxes. Here was a most striking and surprising coincidence, which gave to the theory a stamp of truth beyond the power of ingenuity to counterfeit....

... The theory of universal gravitation, and of the undulatory theory of light, are indeed full of examples of this consilience of inductions. With regard to the latter, it has been justly asserted by Herschel, that the history of the undulatory theory was a succession of felicities. And it is precisely the unexpected coincidences of results drawn from distant parts of the subject which are properly thus described." ("Philosophy of the Inductive Sciences," B. XI., chap. v., s. 3.)

And again,

"It is true, the explanation of one set of facts may be of the same nature as the explanation of the other class; but then, that the cause explains both classes, gives it a very different claim upon our attention and assent from that which it would have if it explained one class only. The very circumstance that the two explanations coincide, is a most weighty presumption in their favour. It is the testimony of two witnesses in behalf of the hypothesis; and in proportion as these two witnesses are separate and independent, the conviction produced by their agreement is more and more complete. When the explanation of two kinds of phenomena, distinct, and not apparently connected, leads us to the same cause, such a coincidence does give a reality to the cause, which it has not while it merely accounts for those appearances which suggested the supposition. This coincidence of propositions inferred from separate classes of facts, is exactly what we noticed in the last book, as one of the most decisive characteristics of a true theory, under the name of Consilience of Inductions.

"That Newton's first rule of philosophizing, so understood, authorizes the inferences which he himself made, is really the ground on which they are so firmly believed by philosophers. Thus, when the doctrine of a gravity varying inversely as the square of the distance from the body, accounted at the same time for the relations of times and distances in the planetary orbits and for the amount of the moon's deflection from the tangent of her orbit, such a doctrine became most convincing: or, again, when the doctrine of the universal gravitation of all parts of matter, which explained so admirably the inequalities of the moon's motions, also gave a satisfactory account of a phenomenon utterly different—the precession of the equinoxes. And of the same kind is the evidence in favour of the undulatory theory of light, when the assumption of the length of an undulation, to which we are led by the colours of thin plates, is found to be identical with that length which explains the phenomena of diffraction; or when the hypothesis of transverse vibrations, suggested by the facts of polarization, explains also the laws of double refraction. When such a convergence of two trains of induction points to the same spot, we can no longer suspect that we are wrong. Such an accumulation of proof really persuades us that we have to do with a vera causa. And if this kind of proof be multiplied,—if we again find other facts of a sort uncontemplated in framing our hypothesis, but yet clearly accounted for when we have adopted the supposition,—we are still further confirmed in our belief, and by such accumulation of proof we may be so far satisfied as to believe without conceiving it possible to doubt. In this case, when the validity of the opinion adopted by us has been repeatedly confirmed by its sufficiency in unforeseen cases, so that all doubt is removed and forgotten, the theoretical cause takes its place among the realities of the world, and becomes a true cause." (Ibid. B. XII., chap. xiii., art. 10.)

The reader of this Essay will be pleased to remark as he proceeds that its argument is made up of a diversity of proofs (very many among them being inductive), and that they all lend each other mutual support and become consilient at last.

Chapter 2

PHILOSOPHY OF DESIGN: HOSTILE CRITICISMS EXAMINED—EXPLANATIONS AND RESTATEMENTS

"It is an assured truth, and a conclusion of experience, that a little or superficial knowledge of Philosophy may incline the mind of Man to Atheism, but a farther proceeding therein doth bring the mind back again to Religion: for in the entrance of Philosophy, when the second causes, which are next unto the senses, do offer themselves to the mind of man, if it dwell and stay there it may induce some oblivion of the highest Cause; but when a man passeth on farther, and seeth the dependence of causes and the works of Providence; then, according to the allegory of the poets, he will easily believe that the highest link of Nature's chain must needs be tied to the foot of Jupiter's chair."
—Lord Bacon's *Advancement of Learning*, Book I.

"Deus sine dominio, providentiâ, et causis finalibus nihil aliud est quam fatum et natura. A caecâ necessitate metaphysicâ, quae eadem est et semper et ubique, nulla oritur variatio. Tota rerum conditarum pro locis ac temporibus diversitas, ab ideis et voluntate entis necessario existentis solummodo oriri potuit."
—Sir Isaac Newton, Scholium at close of Principia.

"Tax not my sloth that I
Fold my arms beside the brook;
Each cloud that floated in the sky
Writes a letter in my book.

"There was never mystery But 'tis figured in the flowers; Was never secret history
But birds tell it in the bowers."
—*Emerson's Poems*—The Apology.

SYNOPSIS OF CHAPTER 2

This Chapter enters upon an examination of the kind of reasoning involved in the Argument from Design, and an inquiry into its special force. These investigations are accompanied by illustrative examples of Analogy in different shapes. The most powerful objections against this argument, and the various modes of stating it, are then described and criticised.

A re-statement of the whole line of thought is followed by the outline of a proposed method for the constructive science of Natural Theology.

The Chapter closes with a corollary on Efficient and Final Causes.

Analysis —Argument from Design—Its Popular Form, and the Popular Objections raised against it—Art and Nature dissimilar—Organic and Inorganic Worlds, their Unlikeness and their Likenesses—Difference between Similitude and Analogy, whether the latter be Illustrative or Illative, and easiest ways of stating both Analogies.

Scientific Difficulties—Charge of proving too much—Anthropomorphism and Dualism—Physical and Moral Antithesis—Was Paley to blame for introducing these Questions?—Answer to the charge of proving too much—On how many points need Analogy rest?—Examples.

Charge of proving too little—Design assumes Designer as a Foregone Conclusion—Process observed is test of Designer in Art, but fails in Nature—Criticism on these Objections.

Baden Powell compared with Paley—Wide Views and Inductions—Argument analysed into Gradations of Proof, Order, and Intelligence—Means, Ends, and Foresight—Physical and Moral Causation—Argument analysed into various Lines of Proof—Their Separate and Consilient Force. Value of Powell's views on Causation—Objections against some peculiarities of his language—Natural Theology and Natural Religion distinguished—Professor Newman—Use of Words on subject of Design.

Statement of the Constructive Method now to be employed—Corollary on Efficient and Final Causes.

Additional Notes and Illustrations

A. On the abstract reasonings involved in Natural Theology.
B. On the phrase "Design implies a Designer."
C. Hume on the analogies of Art and Nature.
D. The Pantheistic consequences charged upon Physical Speculation.
E. The extent and divisions of the Science of Natural Theology.
F. On Teleology.

PHILOSOPHY OF DESIGN

The argument from Design in Nature has been made familiar to most readers in Natural Theology by Paley's well-known book. It is probable that no argument has ever been more praised, and at the same time more strongly controverted. Our business lies, of course, with the controversy; and we must say a few words on our present mode of dealing with it.

Nothing could be more useless than to repeat illustrative examples of Design already thrice told by an endless variety of treatises. Of so wide a subject everything may be quoted as an illustration, from a pebble to a world, if only the principle illustrated—the pivot on which the argument turns—be understood and admitted. In modern times, this turning-point is precisely the centre of the dispute. Untrained minds misapprehend the meaning of the word Design, and are further still from apprehending the real force of argument from analogy. And when these subjects come to be discussed by skilled writers, various questions are always raised which generally issue in irreconcilable differences of opinion.

Our plan here will be to take the argument in its best-known shape, and examine it from the points of view occupied by several classes of objectors, beginning, as is reasonable, with the most popular difficulties and misapprehensions. It does not seem necessary to load the page with references to controversialists of the ordinary sort, particularly as we endeavour to look at the whole question through their eyes.

Respecting the more philosophic questions it is necessary to observe, that the Evolution-theory will not form a topic of the present chapter. It is excluded for two reasons. One, that we are now trying to put a value on the argument from Design per se, and not to compare it with rival theories. The other reason springs from the subject of Evolution itself—it is too extensive to be thus briefly treated—and the sum of this Essay must be taken together as furnishing a counter statement to the manner in which it has been employed by certain of its ardent advocates [14].

We hope for a further advantage from the method proposed. The cause of truth ought to gain from being looked at on more than one side; and, whatever be the worth and true effect of reasoning from Design, we may expect by this method to display it adequately.

The word itself, like all figurative terms—or words used in a secondary sense—is by no means free from ambiguity. It has, in common parlance, several shades of signification. Design being the centre of Paley's argument, and containing the one idea which gives force to all the rest: his first object was to fix the sense in which he employed it. He did so by using an illustration.

To explain by comparison is always a popular resource, some serious drawbacks notwithstanding. Almost every one prefers that an author should use a sparkling similitude which tells a great deal, rather than write what looks like a grammar and dictionary of his science. Analysis and induction require thought on the part of him who employs them—thought also on the part of a reader determined to understand what he reads. Paley saw all this thoroughly, and at the beginning of his book employed the now celebrated comparison taken from a watchmaker and a watch. His judgment received support from the popularity he enjoyed, and from the way in which everybody borrowed his illustration [15].

Yet Paley's deference to the popular understanding gave rise to the first general misapprehension of his treatise. He sets out from a kind of surprise—the surprise his readers would feel at finding a watch upon a heath. Now this feeling was immediately alleged as a conclusive objection against Paley's comparison, and as a ground for distrusting the whole argument founded upon it. The world, it was said, cannot be likened to a watch, nor yet to any other sort of mechanism. Between things natural, and the things which men make, the difference is not a mere contrast of perfection with imperfection. The real reason why we are surprised to see Paley's watch lying on a moor—and not at all surprised to see Paley's stone lying beside it—springs from this very difference. And though the history of a stone, common, coarse, and worthless, is really more wonderful than the history of any watch, and though the stone has an infinitely longer pedigree, we should never speak or think of it in the same way. We feel that the objects are dissimilar, and our surprise testifies the fact. A heath is given up to nature, a watchmaker's shop to art. The watch is out of place among stones, the stone among watches. The idea raised at the outset, therefore, is that Art and Nature would seem to be thoroughly unlike.

At a first view of the subject, these remarks appear open to one obvious rejoinder. The sort of surprised feeling which Paley describes, is not in itself a proof of real unlikeness. A weed is a plant out of place; we do not expect thriving crops of cabbage or teazle in a carefully kept rose-garden, nor gooseberry bushes amongst azaleas. The proudest flower that blossoms is a weed in a vineyard, in a plot of opium-poppies, or mixed with other herbs medicinal. So, too, a rough diamond would not be out of place in a watchmaker's shop; but if we saw a stone of no selling value inside a case of watches we should certainly experience some surprise. And the feeling would remain even though we were quite unable to explain how the poor pebble differed chemically from the priceless gem. We know that the latter would appear to a jeweller's customers like a rose among flowers, but the former worthless as a weed. The jeweller would consider it a trespasser fit only to be turned out of doors.

But does this rejoinder satisfactorily dispose of the difficulty? Is not the true reason why we might observe with some wonder a watch lying upon a moor resolvable into the fact of our knowing its use and being quite sure that some one had dropped it there? [k] A savage might not feel in the least surprised, unless, indeed, he happened to suppose that the watch was a kind of animal he had never seen before, and took notice of the singular sound it made. In this event he would probably break it to pieces without discovering the purpose or mode of its contrivance.

Throughout all disputatious matter, a thought on one side leads to a thought upon the other—at least, amongst tolerably fair people. The idea which we have just imagined our savage to entertain respecting a watch suggests a further question. What effect ought in reason to be produced upon cultured minds by the contemplation of some unknown or half-comprehended phenomenon?—a question this, closely bearing upon the whole subject under discussion. Now surely it is from intelligent wonder—a contrast of the unknown with what we already know—a feeling of mystery to be solved by us, that inquiry and science perpetually spring. A fossil-shell, the former habitation of a marine animal, found upon some mountain top, presents a contrast and a mystery of this kind. Moreover, the highest triumph of inquiring science is the discovery, not of difference anywhere, but rather of resemblances in objects apparently diverse. An uninquiring mind will never perceive any common attribute, either ideal or structural, between a stone and a watch.

But did Paley himself perceive any such community of attribute? So far does he appear from the perception that he speaks of the stone as an "unorganised, unmechanised substance, without mark or indication of contrivance," and adds, "It might be difficult to show that such substance could not have existed from eternity." Paley's day was meagre in natural science, and Paley was as meagerly acquainted with its results as he was with metaphysical philosophy. Few people, however, even now-a-days, know enough of the laws which govern inorganic products to find their investigation a slight or easy task. For a purpose of comparison with any human work or mechanism, most inquirers will prefer having recourse with Paley to the world of organisation. The flower and fructification of a plant or shrub growing on the heath beside Paley's watch, though carelessly passed over a thousand times, and exciting no surprise from anything unusual in its habitat, will, when observed, raise the most sincere admiration. And the same may be said of the bony skeleton of the lizard [16] racing round plant and shrub, the forehand of the mole which burrows beneath them, and the wing of the bat circling nightly in upper air.

Take, then, replies the objector, an organism, vegetable or animal, whichever you or Paley may prefer. The difficulty formerly urged at once recurs, slightly altered in shape, but with augmented point and force. Your organisms are not put together like the parts of a watch (undique collatis membris)—brass from this place, steel from that, and so on, with china dial-plate, covering-glass, and gold case. All these things were apart in nature, they were severally chosen, manipulated, and brought together. What we see is a successful union of materials possessing inherent adaptation to definite purposes—such as the freedom of brass from rust, or the superior elasticity of steel, qualities indicating the skill and workmanlike knowledge of some human artificer, and showing by their utilization the truth of what was before asserted. Watches and worlds, the products of Art and of Nature, are obviously and thoroughly unlike.

By way of answer, it might be observed that in organization we do really see very distinct constituents combined. In a plant, for instance, there is the combination of a growing point, a humus or pabulum that feeds it, and the stimuli, air, water, light, and all the "skiey influences" by which its passive vitality is excited and sustained. We see plant life, by reason of these concurrent adaptations, swelling into leaf, stem, bud, corolla, and fruit, throughout all the brighter tribes of vegetable beauty that bloom apparent to the unassisted eye. And the like holds true respecting animals, but with increased variety and complication of conditions, made necessary by their higher mode of existence. The marvels of their many powers, habits, and perfections of form and movement are great, but greater still the vast multitude of ministering aids put in requisition to ensure their earliest appearance and after continuance in life and enjoyment. When we contemplate microscopic Nature, a like sweep of combination is again evident to the skilful naturalist, and excites his constant wonder, especially when observed in connection with the exquisite finish of minute creatures and their infinitesimal parts, both alike unperceived by our ordinary human senses. And a similar idea of invisible, and perhaps almost incomprehensible, harmony might be raised by a consideration of the elements, metallic and non-metallic, brought together in numberless inorganic productions, as well as of the forces which bind them in hard cohesion, and give them such properties as we may discover in the commonest block of granite. And what if we could extend our field of view to a world—to the universe?

The answer suggested by this last paragraph has its value, and the principle involved in it will occur for our scrutiny further on. But at present this train of thought, if pursued, might be likened to the weed we spoke of,—it would not be altogether in place here. The truth is that the whole objection thus parried appears more out of place still, and is therefore itself not a flower, but a weed of popular rhetoric. And the reason of its irrelevancy is plain. Paley's argument does not really turn upon the similitude of any two objects of simple apprehension, but upon an analogical comparison; the discovery, that is, of the likeness between two ratios, a process known in common life under the name of Proportion. Hence it is from the illative force of analogy that this topic of Design derives its value. The analogy does, in fact, serve a double purpose,—- first to explain, and secondly to prove. We had better look at it from both points of view.

The easiest method for making an illustrative analogy intelligible is to state it in old-fashioned style as a rule of three sum; the fourth term being the conclusion which completes it. "As a watch is to the watchmaker, so is creation, (exemplified by such and such a specimen,) to its Creator." That is to say, there exists some ratio or relation connecting the watch and the watchmaker, which exists also between the world and its Creator.

To see its illative force used as an argument, we need only alter the position of the four terms, and state our proportion as is more usual in modern day. "As the watch is to such and such specimens of creation, so is the watchmaker to the Author of any and all of these things."

In the first statement Paley's similitude is displayed in full as an asserted illustration of Design. The watch is a thing contrived—that is, a design realized, and the maker is its contriver. Just so, is the world a Design realized by its Creator. And it appears plainly implied in the assertion, that even as the little watch shows the limited power and intelligence of its maker, so the vast and unfathomable universe illustrates the infinite power and wisdom of its incomprehensible Author.

The second mode of statement displays the force of Paley's analogy viewed as a chain of reasoning. The watch is not like the world, but there is something in common between them, and this something it is Paley's purpose, and the purpose of his various continuators, to show at the greatest convenient length. Now such community of character must be sufficient to establish a further community still. When we see a watch we are sure it had a designer,—the watchmaker; and here, again, Paley means to argue that from every example of contrivance which we can adduce and examine, the same inference ensues, and always must ensue. Therefore (he concludes) from the immeasurable designed world we infer the world's omnipotent Designer.

The chief Divine attributes (as, for example, omnipotence) are dwelt upon by Paley towards the close of his treatise. But it seems well to insert the adjective at once. Most thinking persons admit that whoever believes in a Creator may find from the physical Cosmos and its

"Mysterious worlds untravelled by the sun,"

Ample reason for justifying the noblest of such adjectives. They generally go further, and allow that any Theist finds in these endless marvels a full confirmation of his faith—there is, as Coleridge says, a whole universe at hand to ratify the decision. But what many educated people who concede thus much disallow, is the sufficient witness of Design standing by itself to prove what it may fairly corroborate or even extend. To illustrate, confirm, or widen what is already held a truth is one thing; to serve as its sole sufficient witness is another. This conclusiveness some deny, and more scruple to affirm. And one of the drawbacks in arguing from analogy seems to be, that all except the most philosophically trained minds experience a sort of hesitation in estimating its force—a hesitation which they are at a loss to define in words. Consequently, the attack upon its adequacy is always difficult to answer; so many various shades of negation must be classed together for brevity's sake, and met by one or two general lines of defence. The safest way, probably, is to make the negative classes as wide as possible, and to put the scientific doubts in their most fatal form of expression. And it appears hard to imagine anything really destructive of evidence which may not be brought under one of the two following heads. There may be, first, a failure of evidence when it is not strong enough in its facts and circumstances to justify the conclusion drawn—when, in short, it proves too little. Secondly, it is worthless, if its acceptance so damages the position occupied by those who employ it, that their purpose is thereby destroyed, their locus standi demolished—in other words, they have proved too much.

May we not, then, presume it impossible to bring worse charges against any argument than whatever can be urged in support of these two accusations? And we will first put the well-known analogy on its trial for proving too much, because it is from anxiety to avoid this charge that most analogical reasoners are apt to risk proving too little.

Admit, say Paley's most decided antagonists, the relevancy of an argument from human art. It must be taken to show the Creator of the Universe as Theists conceive and acknowledge Him. Let us at once ask in what light He is thereby represented? Is it not, so to speak, as a supreme Anthropomorphic [1] Craftsman sketching a vast plan or design, and moulding the materials necessary for its realization? We begin with the remark that His work—the world—must show some traces of that plastic process and the hand of its Moulder. The requirement seems just and reasonable, and is commonly answered by an appeal to what have been termed the records of creation, the structure of the heavens, and the structure of the earth. Thus, for example, we are referred to Geology and Palaeontology, and are led from age to age, and type to type. In passing from one formation to another we seem (as Goethe said) to catch Nature in the fact. At all events the plastic process is everywhere traceable, and to its evidences the Theist points with triumph.

But no intelligent objector can stop here. He will next inquire what on theistic principles was the origin of this material substance so constantly undergoing transformation. Most sceptical thinkers put the inquiry in a trenchant manner; they not only demand to be answered, but they prescribe beforehand the sort of answer to be returned. It is useless, they tell us, to speak of archetypes existing in the Divine mind, and to illustrate them by the creative thought of musician or sculptor, of painter or of poet. The hard, coarse world must be looked at as it is: an actual material habitation for sorrowing and sinful human creatures; its physical conditions, imperfect in that respect, unhappily corresponding too well with the low moralities of its tenants.

Now, they say, if we examine Paley's common-sense analogy no one can at all doubt what answer is suggested there. The steel of the watch-spring, the brass of the wheel-work, and other materials for all the curious mechanical contrivances required, were taken into account by the watch-designer when he formed his design. Had it been otherwise he could not have calculated on finding the necessary strength, elasticity, resistance to rust, and other properties on which Paley dwells so distinctly. In like manner, it has been said by some physical science Christians since Paley's time: "Let matter and its primary properties be presupposed, and the argument from Design is easy." True, but it seems quite as easy to suppose the world itself eternal. And we know that this supposition was adopted by pagan philosophers, to whom it appeared the easiest of all beliefs.

But other philosophic pagans, holding clearly that the world had a beginning, conceived its First Cause to be like Paley's Designer—analogous to an earthly workman. They carried out the analogy thoroughly—more thoroughly than modern writers, and believed both Artificer and the matter from which He shaped the visible universe, self-subsistent, indestructible, and co-eternal.

In this eternity of matter and its native inflexibilities, these great heathen thinkers found an apology for what they considered the failure of creative power—misshapen things, monstrosities, and imperfections. The Creator never desired them, but His will was thwarted by the material He worked in. Against this dualism the early Fathers protested. Will the modern Theist (his assailants ask) deny himself, and affirm two independent and self-existent principles; or will he deny the parallelism asserted in Paley's analogy? Can he conscientiously believe that its issue is a worthy representation of the Divine and omnipotent Creator? If not, it has failed by proving too much [m] raised. Who can help seeing that several of them lie equally against all rational theories which have ever been suggested to account for the origin of that sorrow and evil which we see and acknowledge everywhere? And does not the same remark apply to every attempt at solving the antithesis of mind and matter? Some thoughtful men have believed that they could see their way to a solution; others believe it altogether above human reason, and point with a kind of triumph to the failures of philosophy. However this may be, the mournful moral enigma [17], and the unexplained antithesis underlying our knowledge of nature, attach themselves equally to every possible conception of the universe, religious or irreligious, common-sense or metaphysical. They have no special connection with our argument from Design, and ought not in fairness to be brought as objections against it.

The more real question just now is, whether Paley's mechanical analogy was to blame for introducing the problem of cosmical matter into the discussion.

On this question the opinions of competent and unprejudiced judges disagree. By an eminent and accomplished writer the case is summed up as follows, in the Harveian Oration for 1865. Having previously included the material factor under mechanical adaptation as distinguished from art in the highest sense, Dr. Acland goes on to say (page 13):

> "The illustration of the watch so quaintly employed by Nieuwentyt, and so entirely appropriated by Paley, only in a coarse way suggests the parallel between infinite art and common mechanical skill. It has done some mischief to the cause it advocates, by making familiar a rude illustration, which minds without imagination, or void of constructive power, have accepted as a recognised explanation of the method of operation by an Infinite Creative Will."

Paley's critics should however observe, that he did not himself intend the objectionable inference. Probably he never even perceived that it might be drawn from his comparison. Abstract inquiries connected with Theism, he banished to the end of his book, where they are discussed in a manner little calculated to satisfy any readers who have ever felt them as substantial difficulties [18]. But then, he would most likely have referred these persons to the writings of professed metaphysicians. It may be wise for us to take warning both by what Paley did and by what he left undone. Some deeper questions are indispensable to the argument from Design, but we shall follow his example so far as to avoid such disquisitions as were current in his day under the name of metaphysics. On the other hand we shall draw the required data from that critical Fact- philosophy of Mind and Human Nature, which forms to so many thinkers the birth-star of a new science, one amongst the rising hopes of our nineteenth century.

Meantime, our business on hand is to rebut the present accusation of proving too much, brought against Paley's analogy. We shall try to complete our answer by setting his argument in the point of view under which he evidently meant it to be looked at.

Either as an illustration or as a means of proof, Analogy need not hold in more than a single point; provided only that this single point is clear and well-established—resting, for example, on a moral law or a causal nexus. Any one who desires to make an analytical investigation into this law of inference will receive valuable aid from Ueberweg's Logic, §§ 131 and 2, particularly if compared with § 129.

To a common-sense mind we may give sufficient satisfaction by adducing one or two good analogies. Thus, for instance, the duties of a religious minister are often explained by saying that he ought to be the shepherd of his flock; that is, his relation to his people ought to resemble that of the shepherd to his sheep. We all understand how truly is here expressed a world of watchful care. But are all points of the relation to be implied? May the spiritual pastor ever become the slayer or the salesman of his flock?

Again,—writers upon political subjects some years ago used very commonly to quote from the days of Alfred the Great supposed precedents for our most modern constitutional dicta. In many cases the thing defended was a legitimate outgrowth of the precedent cited; but to pronounce the two identical seemed sufficiently absurd. In confutation of some such absurdities, clever men argued that the body corporate has, like the individual body, its childhood, growth, and maturity. The argument became generally accepted, and got extended to the distinctions between healthy increase and sickly degeneration, with other like inferences. The further conclusion was next drawn, that every national body resembles the human frame in a necessary decay, and inevitable mortality. Now, whatever opinion may be entertained as to the fact of a death-rate of nationalities, nothing seems more certain than that those who first employed the comparison never contemplated this particular corollary. Whether their first use of it was wise or unwise, has been, like Paley's Watch-analogy, a matter of some considerable dispute.

The general subject of Analogy, rightly or wrongly extended, admits of wider illustration.

Simile and metaphor are often compressed analogies, and many of them gain in beauty from expansion. Pope's celebrated comparison of the traveller ascending the Alps with the student who scales the heights of literature; and how

"Hills peep o'er hills, and Alps on Alps arise;"

is a good example of a poet's successfully expanding his own thought. Still more exquisitely true to nature is the final parallel drawn in Coleridge's description of the divided friends who stood apart,—

"Like cliffs which had been rent asunder,"

while the marks of a former union lingered indestructible. Perhaps few readers of "Christabel" ever looked at Lodore, and "its scars remaining," without feeling how aptly they represent traces of thought and affection engraved upon the soul of man, deeper and more imperishable than the primaeval rocks between which the "dreary sea" now flows.

The wonderful force of many among Shakespeare's metaphors is derived from compressed analogy. But by expanding

"The slings and arrows of outrageous Fortune,"

we should form no better conception of the goddess; and the next line,

"Or to take arms against a sea of troubles,"

might easily be turned into nonsense! Like Paley's "watch," the "sea" holds true only in one point. Shakespeare had before his eye the image of multitudinous vastness. But what arms could we take up to stem the billows of a swelling tide?

No one can read many commentators on the Scripture without feeling how groundless are numberless conclusions arrived at by extending Scriptural analogies beyond their just limits. Preachers and platform speakers are still more guilty. Not content with straining Holy Writ, they add to the mischief by pressing into their service comparisons of double meaning. The above quoted word "sea," has long been a much-enduring similitude in its relation to the countries and islands of the earth. What is it really to us, the earth's inhabitants? Our highway and bond of union? or a waste of waters given to divide rivals, as Horace phrases it, "Oceano dissociabili"? The last is the oldest metaphor [19].

Enough has been said upon various analogies to show how frequently even in their widest use (that of illustration), the effect of extending them beyond their one salient point, is utter confusion. And with respect to illative analogy, this rule becomes obviously more stringent still. Paley meant it to be observed strictly as regards his own analogous reasoning.

But the caution itself must be cautiously applied, where the salient point on which the inference turns is too superficial, or too weak to stand alone. And this is the very thing we have to discuss next,—because a second accusation brought against the argument from Design is, that by reason of weakness in its pivot, it proves far too little.

This second charge is less usual amongst popular than scientific writers, and most of us may learn something by sifting it. Their position may be described in few words as standing thus:—

All examples which men can, of their own knowledge, connect with Design, fall under one sole class, and from this class alone they can argue. It contains the products of human workmanship and manufacture—and nothing else. By its characteristic processes (which together with their result make the sum of what we know about this class) it is so essentially dissociated from the products of Nature, that any appearance of design common between them must be pronounced superficial in the absence of stronger nexus. But since proof of such nexus remains wanting, Paley's analogy is worthless. It will be observed that the effect of this position is to sever between human works and natural things quite as completely as did the popular objection which we put first in our list of assaults upon Paley. Yet, though these conclusions may seem suspiciously coincident, the grounds of argument are really distinct. Scientific persons do not compare two objects natural and artificial, nor yet their two sets of constituents, and say, "These are unlike." They argue rather that the relative or proportionate likeness asserted is insufficiently made out, and that when it is said "Design implies a designer," people are speaking of design worked out in the known way of workmen. We (they observe) need not deny a designer of the world, but we desiderate evidence of his actual workmanship. By this we shall know that he first conceived and then realized the alleged design. We do not feel convinced by being shown certain organic somethings in their perfect state, and being told to observe how very like contrivances they are. They may be very like, certainly, but we want assurances that they can be nothing else. We want to have shown us some work being done, and to ascertain that it is carried on in a workmanlike manner. Then we shall say with confidence, Here is the active hand of a designer. To compress our requisition into a single sentence,—We want not only to catch Nature in the fact, but also to ascertain that Nature's way of performing the fact has something essentially humanlike about it.

To see our meaning clearly (add these objectors) take the instance of some marvellous work of man's art previously unknown to us. We could, if we perceived the marks of human fabrication, reason from a watch, or some other well known machine, to the conclusion that some person had designed it. In other words, we should feel sure that we were looking at a new product of skill, which differed from what we had seen before in the degree of excellence attained. The difference we feel in our transition from Art to Nature appears, on the contrary, to be a difference not only between more or less perfect products or processes, but a thorough difference of kind in the whole manner of bringing about the results placed before our eyes. Or put the case (they continue) as a piece of circumstantial evidence. We say positively of this or that machine, They are contrivances, things designed, because we know the history of their manufacture. We feel positive, because we are arguing from a plain patent fact to a hidden but absolutely essential condition, without which the fact could not exist. As regards natural products we have not got the fact—we do not know the history of their production. We cannot say, Here is the process, because the processes of Nature are mostly unknown to us. Paley therefore would have us assume the fact and argue from it; first to design, next, to something more hidden still,—a Designer. Yet what we do know of natural processes is not encouraging; there is visible about them more unlikeness than likeness to the processes employed by man. The truth may be surmised, that Paley was always seeing in his own examples the footprints, as he thought, of a Designer. Hence he affirmed Design, and then argued back again in a never-ending circle. There is really no reason why he should have travelled round such a circuit. If his argument shows anything, it shows a Designer at once [n].

With some risk of tediousness, this last attack on Paley has been detailed at great length, and placed (as the present writer believes) in several of its most formidable shapes [o]. But for additional security of fair dealing with the strongest of all objections—one which, if established, would be a death-blow to all argument on the subject (since its ultimatum is unconditional surrender)—for these reasons, then, and in order to satisfy the most rigorous understanding, let it be finally rehearsed in the words of a most eminent physicist whom no one will accuse of haste, oversight, or credulity. To this rehearsal the Professor adds what is to us more important still,—his judgment on the point at issue.

But before quoting Professor Baden Powell, it may be worth while to make two short notes on the few preceding paragraphs. Let us take the last paragraph first.

It really does appear that marks of Design and the footprints of a Designer are in common sense very nearly one and the same thing. If we concentrate our attention on the former, we are looking at an object on the side of certain properties,—that is, of certain subjectively perceived relations. For instance, we may think of the eye only as an optical instrument wonderfully constituted, and enumerate the parts of its visual apparatus. But the moment we speak of this apparatus as a provision intentionally made for sight, we have introduced the idea of a Designer in the strongest sense of the word. Now, it is difficult to think of anything as an example of intelligent arrangement, and at the same time give no hint even to our own thoughts of arranging Intelligence. We can hardly look through a pane of glass and admire the perfect transparency of one surface to the exclusion of the other! We are not now speaking of what might be done, if attempted by a man so profoundly skilled in analytics that

"He could distinguish, and divide
A hair 'twixt south and south-west side."

We are rather speaking of what it is natural to do. And it may be doubted whether anybody thinks of a design as design very long without thinking also of the Designer.

One other remark is suggested by the reference to process as contradistinguished from product. Here, again, the real question is, How far is such a distinction maintainable in fact? Does it rest upon any definite separation in Nature? The exact contradictory is the truth; taking the world as it is, the distinction, though clear in thought, becomes essentially fluent when objectively regarded. What we call a production one moment, we say is a process the next. You have, for example, a galvanic current, produced by certain chemical combinations, and often a product per se of some importance. Yet the current itself is a part of the electrotyping process. Suppose this done, you have your electrotype—your coin,—a hard fact,—a solid production, bright, beautiful, admirable! But we will suppose you, while devising all this, to have a further view;—the coin is to be employed in the process of imposture. Here again comes a result—a great fraud committed; but this is not all. The fraudulent procedure turns out a very useful police-trap, and your chemical combination sends the last actor on the scene to Portland, for at least ten years. Consider in this brief history the scientific arrangements, material conditions, and workmanlike execution, discernible in its earlier parts; then, see how mind becomes gradually predominant, and how Law, based on ideas of corrective justice, enters the series. Add the judge and jury, and you admit the force of intellect,—deliberating, deciding, putting further activities in motion; till, perhaps, if the reformatory process succeeds, Portland may have the honour of giving to society the welcome product of (as times go) a passably honest man. We might really frame a curious inquiry as respects this flowing tide of process and production, production and process, with its commingling currents and waves which seem to interrupt each other like circles of diffracted light. We might ask which of all these parts of the moving diorama is most distinctly human. I believe most people would say, those scenes in which mind, not mere workmanship, is most evidently discernible.

Professor Powell seems to have thought so too. The difficulty we have been discussing he states as an objection requiring solution [20].

"In those cases most nearly approaching the nature of human works, such as the varied and endless changes in matter going on in the laboratory of nature, the results, even when most analogous to those obtained in human laboratories, yet present no marks of the process or of the means employed, by which to recognise the analogous workman; and in all the grander productions, the incessant evolutions of vegetable and animal life, which no human laboratory can produce,—in the structure of earth and ocean, or the infinite expanse of the heavens and their transcendent mechanism, still further must we be from finding any analogy to the works of man, or, by consequence, any analogy to a personal individual artificer."

The next paragraph contains his own judgment.

"But the more just view of the case is that which arises from the consideration that the real evidence is that of mind and intelligence; for here we have a proper and strict analogy. Mind directing the operations of the laboratory or the workshop, is no part of the visible apparatus, nor are its operations seen in themselves —they are visible only in their effects;—and from effects, however dissimilar in magnitude or in kind, yet agreeing in the one grand condition of order, adjustment, profound and recondite connexion and dependence, there is the same evidence and outward manifestation of Invisible Intelligence, as vast and illimitable as the universe throughout which those manifestations are seen."

This second extract may be analysed into distinct propositions somewhat as follows:— In a manufactory,—

Mind is no part of the visible apparatus—nor are its operations visible,— But the effects make the operations manifest.—

In the universe,—

Effects may be seen differing from Human productions in many ways,—but agreeing in one common characteristic,—order—adjustment—hidden interdependence.

Such effects make manifest the operation of an Invisible Intelligence as vast as the Universe itself.

The majority of people might suppose this a conclusive inference from Nature to the Being of a Personal God. But Professor Powell does not so intend it; and therefore some readers may feel disposed to blame his use of words. It is, however, only fair that before so doing, they should carefully consider his whole mode of apprehending the subject in its completeness. And the easiest way of understanding Powell is, most probably, to compare him with Paley.

The latter is confident that when he has derived the design and arrangement of the world from a mind analogous to the mind of man, but immeasurably vast as the Universe which man inhabits,—little more need be said. He thinks the infinite intelligence thus demonstrated, is clearly no other than the Great First Cause, and Creator of all things. "Contrivance, if established, appears to me to prove everything which we wish to prove." This sentence begins Chap. xxiii., and the rest of Paley's Natural Theology is intended to demonstrate and verify its correctness.

Powell thinks that the step from a mind or intelligence, even if conceived illimitable as the Universe, to a First Cause, Supreme Mind, or Moral Cause, is a very much longer ascent [p] than Paley thought it. By these latter terms he meant—as Paley did—the Divine Personality believed in by Theists, and evidenced, first, as mind by a reign of law, order, and arrangement, so far as the world can evidence Him;—but manifest, secondly, in His higher nature as the fountain and originator of law—that is, a true Cause, a manifestation due to the causal structure of our own human minds. The point of difference is the length of the step to be taken from Law to Causation; but Powell agrees with his predecessor in asserting it, though arduous, to be absolutely safe. The point he insists on is that we cannot take it by a contemplation of the world without us only. "Ever- present mind" he says [21], "is a direct inference from the universal order of nature, or rather only another mode of expressing it. But of the mode of existence of that mind we can infer nothing." From this view he draws conclusions in opposite directions. Pantheism [22], the co-existence or identification of mind with matter, "is at best a mere gratuitous hypothesis, and as such wholly unphilosophical in itself, and leading to many preposterous consequences." There are also grounds on which Theism appears certain and Pantheism extravagant, absurd, and contradictory [23]. To see these grounds we are to carry out the analogy given us by the common characteristics of order, adjustment, and interdependence visible through their effects as in the human workshop or laboratory, so, too, in the vast illimitable Universe, and described in our second extract as manifestations of Mind or invisible Intelligence. In the paragraph immediately following that extract [24] he continues:—

> "It is by analogy with the exercise of intellect, and the volition, or power of moral causation, of which we are conscious within ourselves, that we speak of the Supreme Mind and Moral Cause of the Universe, of whose operation, order, arrangement and adaptation, are the external manifestations. Order implies what by analogy we call intelligence; subserviency to an observed end implies intelligence foreseeing which by analogy, we call Design."

The last sentence of the paragraph now quoted is very remarkable. The eminent writer directs attention to a distinction between two several inferences which can be drawn from the observed manifestations of Order, and of Foresight. From the first, he says, we infer Intelligence, from the latter we infer Design. It seems singular that Powell should have defined this distinction so clearly, and made no further use of it.

He might naturally have insisted upon the separate and diverse evidences thus afforded by the physical world. Amid the variety of human minds, some may feel impressed by the contemplation of Nature in one of these ways, some in the other. To many persons the magnificent spectacle of a law-governed Universe, infinitely manifold yet everywhere harmonious, appears to justify the belief in one supreme Reason and sovereign Will. Separate parts of this same Universe—or the whole in its entirety of vastness—when considered as manifesting purpose—that is, intentional adaptation to separate ends or to one end—are to other minds a more convincing line of thought.

With many writers on Natural Theology the different shades of meaning implied in the word Design [25] may prevent clearness of conception in this respect. But our author (like Paley) appears to use this word in its strongest signification.

And this usage of Powell's brings into view another point in his reasoning even more singular than the one to which we have just adverted. Surely, if in the natural world we observe the manifestations of an Intelligence foreseeing an End, and employing means in subserviency to that end, it seems strange to conclude that respecting the mode of existence of such Intelligence we can infer nothing, yet the words occur on the very next page. It would seem almost an impossibility to suppose such a mind existing as anything less than a Personality under the twofold aspect of a Reason and a Will. Paley's common sense drew this conclusion at once, and very profound thinkers have agreed with Paley on the topic.

> "That," says F. H. Jacobi, "which, in opposition to Fate, makes God into a true God, is called Foresight. Where it is, there alone is Reason; and where Reason is, there also is Foresight. Foresight in itself is Spirit, and to that only which is of Spirit do those feelings of admiration, awe, and love, which announce its existence, correspond. We can indeed declare of any object that it is beautiful or perfect, without previously knowing how it became so, whether with or without the operation of Foresight;—but the power which caused it so to be, that we cannot admire, if it produced the object, without aim or purpose, according to laws of mere Necessity of Nature" [26].

In point of fact Professor Powell was himself of the same opinion, for in another place he writes thus:—

"Now, the bare fact of order and arrangement is on all hands undisputed, though commonly most inadequately understood and appreciated.

"The inference of design, intention, forethought, is something beyond the last mentioned truth, and not to be confounded with it. This implies intelligent agency, or moral causation. Hence again, we advance to the notion of distinct existence, or what is sometimes called personality; and thence proceed to ascribe the other Divine attributes and perfections as centring in that independent Being" [27].

It appears only just to the Archdeacon that we should notice this variation of language on the part of his censor [28]. Of this variation itself the true account seems undoubtedly to be as follows. The writer was engaged in tracing the progress of conviction in his own mind. He first observes order, adjustment, interdependence, throughout the Universe. Hence he is penetrated by the impression of pervading Intelligence. Next, he perceives that these results could never have taken place unless foreseen and provided for by a designed subserviency of means to ends, and this convinces him of the Personality of that universal Mind. Finally, he draws, from the analysis of Causation, a full definition of the great Originator of all things.

The fact, however, remains that each of these gradations of reasoning may be stated just as easily and more logically as separate and convergent lines of thought, because each can be rested on a separate combination of proofs. But the elucidation of this subject cannot be compressed into few words, and must be deferred to our fifth and sixth chapters.

Still there is a very peculiar and special satisfaction in following the path of argument which persuaded an acute and practised reasoner, accomplished in several departments of knowledge, and himself of a turn of mind which would appear naturally adapted to the utmost refinements of sceptical investigation. We shall, therefore, now return to our comparison of Powell with his predecessor.

These two distinguished writers do, in fact, come at last to the same conclusion. But they reach it through a difference in the paths travelled over by such logic of evidence as may after all seem natural enough to a theological pleader on one side, and on the other to a scientific physicist. Professor Powell, of course, leads us more deeply than his predecessor into the thorny thickets surrounding Natural Theology. No one can read his essays without remarking the subtlety of his thought, which to many readers appears over refined, and to some as employed on points in themselves unimportant. Mr. Baden Powell's own deliberate judgment was the other way, as we find from the last [29] of his considerable performances on our subject.

"Points," he writes, "which may be seen to involve the greatest difficulty to more profound inquirers, are often such as do not occasion the least perplexity to ordinary minds, but are allowed to pass without hesitation.... On the other hand, exceptions held forth as fatal by the shallow caviller are seen by the more deeply reflecting in all their actual littleness and fallacy."

We may add that a subtle argument is often like a sharp thin blade, cutting clean into the very heart of a question. If it indeed prove a home thrust, few things ought to be more fearlessly and cheerfully welcomed by those who desire to dissect out the naked, intrinsic truth. We will, therefore, dissect a little deeper, following the Professor's track of demonstration.

We find him, then, reaching down to a septum, or, as botanists prefer to speak, a strong dissepiment between a law of Nature or physical causation, and a true Cause in the highest and most emphatic sense [q].

Such a separation is not to be sought from a writer of Paley's date, when the modern notion of law was unformed, or rather was in process of formation. Thus Newton's discoveries were thought by many persons irreligious, because the stability of the heavens appeared like something necessarily determined. Respecting this opinion, Powell observes (and from his point of view with truth), that "such necessity of reason is the highest proof of design." Paley, on the contrary, felt inclined to despair of discovering much evidence of Design in Astronomy, but he looked upon the starry heavens as affording the most ample and glorious confirmation of the agency of an intelligent Creator, when proved from some other source. In his next chapter (the 23rd) he proceeds to reprehend the mistaken sense of law, growing up amongst physicists in his own day. "It will," he says, "be made to take the place of power, and still more, of intelligent power," and will "be assigned for the cause of anything or of any property of anything that exists." In this remark he shows his accustomed penetration. Law, antecedent and consequent, with their series of physical evolutions, have been talked of by men who confuse physics and metaphysics, as if they could thereby account for a whole universe [30]. Now, from this cloudy confusion [r], Professor Powell is exempt. He accepts (as obviously he must accept) the natural-science idea of law, which looks at it as an orderly expression of force, and tells us that "law and order, physical causation and uniformity of action are the elevated manifestations of Divinity, creation and providence" [31]. But from the conception of Mind or Intelligence thus given us, which, though invisible to the eye, is yet, in its effects, plainly visible, he distinguishes, over and over again, the idea of a true originating first Cause [32]. We see the necessity of a moral Cause as distinguished from a physical antecedent, when we survey Nature. But Nature does not contain the idea in an explicit shape. She only necessitates its acceptance. This idea, we find, he tells us, manifest in our own moral nature,—by analogy we discern it in the Divine. He likewise severely blames those who commingle in words the two contrasted thoughts and lines of inference, and mentions Coleridge and Sterling [33] by way of example. As concerns his own mode of establishing the idea of causation in its proper and peculiar force, Professor Powell agrees with a large number of metaphysicians, ancient and modern. It might seem superfluous to name as an instance the late Dean Mansel, were not a passage in his "Prolegomena" so full of good matter on the topic [34].

In this view of causation, then, Powell advanced nothing new. But what he did advance was really valuable. The man who can rise no higher than law or succession as he sees it impressed on outward nature, stands in a totally different position from the man whose insight into Reason and Will has shown him the idea of true Causation. For, he has seen that whoever is the author of his own act, does something which puts in movement a new series of antecedence and consequence,—a new train of events, the issue of which no man can foresee;—though of what has come, and is coming, he, the individual man, is the truly responsible cause [s]. But if he can introduce into the order of the outward world a new antecedent carrying after it a chain of new consequents, what shall he think respecting the absolute Cause of all worlds, things and beings, the thinker himself included? Who shall persuade him to deny the reasonableness of a Providence following creation? Who can reprove the man when he feels and asserts his own moral power, for a belief in Miracles? Above all, who will demonstrate that prayer is inefficacious, if we can rise (as Baden Powell says we can rise) "by analogy with the exercise of intellect, and the volition, or power of moral causation, of which we are conscious within ourselves, to the Supreme Mind and Moral Cause of the universe?"

It is no slight praise to say that Professor Powell clearly saw, and no less clearly expressed, a truth not always apprehended among physicists. By giving it expression, he rendered a substantial service to Natural Theology. It is, indeed, a serious drawback and impediment to Natural Theologians that their argument requires some acquaintance with more than one wide field of knowledge. They have to reason from the material world,—they have also to reason from the world of mind; and in countries like England, France, and Germany, where division of labour penetrates every calling, literary as well as manufacturing, a combination of this sort is a matter of infrequent occurrence. To this retarding circumstance may be ascribed the want of progress in several mixed sciences [35], which, like the subject we are treating, occupy two distinct tracts of border-land territory.

The separating wall between Law and Cause built up by Professor Powell, was founded on fact, and will probably remain unshaken. But he added to it a theoretical limitation of the term, Natural Theology, which, like many changes in verbal usage, does not appear defensible,—particularly as its bad effects are plainly shown in Professor Powell's own book.

Within two pages of the passage on Causation last quoted, he startles the unwary reader by saying (p. 173) that "Natural Theology confessedly 'proves too little,' because it cannot rise to the metaphysical idea or scriptural representation of God." It is generally vain to inquire what may be meant by "Metaphysical." Few people are aware that everybody, learned or unlearned, talks metaphysics either well or ill; and usually (as M. Jourdain talked prose) without knowing it. The epithet "metaphysical" figures often enough as another name for what is unintelligible;—and most Englishmen apply it to all "ideas" not strictly commercial or practical. Here it seems to stand along with Scripture, in opposition to Natural Theology; while the latter term is in turn opposed to the science of the human mind. Yet does not Powell distinctly trace a Mind and Intelligence analogous to the mind and intelligence of Man, throughout the world of outward Nature; and does he not further determine that this same analogy, fairly carried out, leads to what he now calls "the metaphysical idea, or scriptural representation of God?" In other words, when discussing the question of Evidence, he finds Mind pervading outward Nature,—he treats Mind as the ordering and sovereign part of the Natural world, which visibly shows the effect of its invisible direction, and bids us follow up this higher nature in its analogies to God, of Whose operation the order and arrangement of the Universe are external manifestations. But, when he speaks of Natural Theology, that higher nature seems to disappear; intellect, volition, and the power of moral causation, slip out of sight, and are blotted from his catalogue of natural facts. Human nature must thus be treated as no part of universal Nature, in order that a needlessly narrow and purely theoretical fence may be drawn round the science of Natural Theology! Natural Theology and Natural Religion are, in truth, terms originally adopted as mere antitheses to Revelation. The first signifies what mankind might have known, or may know, of the Divine Being, prior to, or apart from, any direct message sent by Himself. The second is intended to comprehend those relations between that Divine Being and ourselves, which must ensue immediately upon the acceptance of Theism [36]. The ideas expressed by these two terms are as old as Revelation itself,—a strong reason why their meaning should not be lightly altered [37]. But this antithetic usage was never intended to prejudge the question whether the results of Natural Theology and Religion do not coincide to a very great extent with the teaching of revelation.

Much less was there any idea of answering this question in the negative, as a hasty reader of certain isolated passages in Professor Powell's book might easily be led to answer it [38].

Our strictures may be aptly concluded by a quotation taken from another recent writer. Professor Newman understands the evidence of Design in the same breadth of meaning which we have attached to it. Under it he comprehends the evidence of Mind naturally known to us, as may be seen by the following extracts:—

> "A lung," says Mr. Newman [39], "bears a certain relation to the air, a gill to the water, the eye to light, the mind to truth, human hearts to one another: is it gratuitous and puerile to say that these relations imply design? There is no undue specification here, no antagonist argument, no intrusion of human artifice: we take the things fresh from nature. In saying that lungs were intended to breathe, and eyes to see, we imply an argument from Fitness to Design, which carries conviction to the overwhelming majority of cultivated as well as uncultivated minds.... If such a fact stood alone in the universe, and no other existences spoke of Design, it would probably remain a mere enigma to us; but when the whole human world is pervaded by similar instances, not to see a Universal Mind in nature appears almost a brutal insensibility.... Of the physical structure of mind, no one pretends to know anything; but this does not weaken our conviction that the mind was meant to discern truth. Why should any philosopher resist this judgment? One thing might justify him; namely, if there were strong à priori reasons for disbelieving that Mind exists anywhere except in man. But the case is just the reverse. That puny beings who are but of yesterday, and presently disappear, should alone possess that which of all things is highest and most wonderful, is à priori exceedingly unplausible. As Socrates and Cicero have pointedly asked: 'Whence have we picked it up?' Its source is not in ourselves: there must surely be a source beyond us. Thus the tables are turned: we must primâ facie expect to find Mind in the Universe, acting on some stupendous scale, and of course imperfectly understood by us. Consequently, such Fitnesses as meet our view on all sides bring a reasonable conviction that Design lies beneath them. To confess this, is to confess the doctrine of an intelligent Creator, although we pretend not to understand anything concerning the mode, stages, or time of Creation. Adding now the conclusions drawn from the Order of the universe, we have testimony, adapted to the cultivated judgment, that there is a Boundless, Eternal, Unchangeable, Designing Mind, not without whom this system of things coheres: and this Mind we call God."

To take stumbling-blocks out of the reader's way has been the main object of this Chapter. It has discussed the meaning and force of several words. The discussion may have seemed somewhat intricate,—but if honest, and, so far as it goes, thorough, no one will deny its utility. For facts are known to us as words, and words are facts to our intellect, since they express our apprehension of objects. They are, in brief, the interpreters of a world-wide human consciousness. And in the strength of consciousness our knowledge stands, if it does stand;—unfaithful to consciousness, it must fall, and ought to die the death of a traitor [40].

The word most discussed has been that one upon which turns the best known argument by Natural Theology—"Design." We trust also, that it may hereafter gain additional clearness under sidelights from other trains of thought [41]. And what next follows will be essentially a discussion of thoughts and things—in which words are to be treated less as their representatives, and more as our servants and implements. For this Chapter will have been written to very little purpose if the reader has failed to perceive that Natural Theology [42] includes at the very least two distinct elements—two separate sets of premises drawn from different sources. One of these factors rests upon our human knowledge of the natural world we live in—the other requires a deeper kind of knowledge, and one far less cultivated upon inductive principles—the know ledge, that is to say, of our own nature—our essential humanity and self-ness.

The investigation of this last element is of paramount importance for the purpose we have in hand, since, without some ascertained principles and conditions of truth, men may fold their hands and view all behind and above the moving diorama of present impressions as ideas sublime but hopeless [43] —too high for us, who surely can never attain to them. The plan, therefore, of this essay is to take from the point now reached a fresh start—to set out, not from a consideration of what we may desire to know, but of how much or how little can be known, and the conditions of our knowing it.

An honest wish to be sure of one single thing soon shows us the impediments we meet in making quite sure of anything. Soon, also, we painfully learn that these impediments arise from two persistent sets of causes. Difficulties on the one hand occasioned by the obscurity, complication, or many-sidedness of objects actually existing in rerum naturâ. Difficulties on the other hand, which, like barnacles and remora attached to a good ship's wooden bottom, act as drags and retardations on our own apprehending faculties. Barnacle-like, they can only be kept at a distance or detached by carefully-devised contrivances. And these again give rise to troubles of other kinds,—just as copper-sheathed keels or iron vessels are not without their drawbacks.

The inquiry we propose will have a great collateral advantage, both to him who doubts and to him who accepts Theism. For we shall at least get rid of what may fairly be termed a stupid prejudice. Persons who read and think little, are apt to base upon their own ignorance a vague presumption that the path of knowledge is plain and easy, until men try to know God. Then all is hard; the pleasant path becomes a rough and toilsome road. Others who read, but think less than they read, are aware that very real obstacles beset all deep inquiry, yet form hazy and imperfect notions as to the true extent of those obstacles. They little think how often we are all obliged to accept and maintain first truths;—difficulties objective, and difficulties subjective, notwithstanding.

Of one practical conclusion resulting from these difficulties, we may feel assured beforehand. Many objects of the greatest interest and importance to truth can never be truly known as they are in themselves;—our utmost hope is to know, not them, but as much as we can discover respecting them. And sometimes this limited knowledge is invaluable. If it does not gratify our natural desire for speculation, it may often guide and govern our lives. Unspeakably important, for example, in itself and in its consequences, must be an affirmative answer to our anxious question concerning the existence of a God.

Corollary. —It plainly appears from what has been said, that the knowledge of an "efficient cause" (in physics) does not, and cannot, at all preclude the inquiry after a purpose or "final cause"; but, on the contrary, leads to its investigation. In a watch's action, the former is represented by the moving power—that is, the spring; the latter, by the watch's function—that of indicating hours, minutes, and seconds. Would any uninformed person, examining a watch for the first time, and knowing no more than what he sees,—be able to give to himself any real account of the watch, if spring, train of wheel-work, and pointers, were shown him; but no hint given of the purpose and object of the whole construction? Now, to tell him this, would be to convey the idea,—a principle which resides in Mind, and in Mind alone;—and, so residing, leads to intelligent adaptation;—that is, a law or laws apprehended by the active exercise of certain mental faculties.

Let the intelligent reader ask himself whether any functional structure can be comprehended on any lower terms?—As however this latter question will be fully discussed further on, it is unnecessary to say more respecting it at present.

ADDITIONAL NOTES AND ILLUSTRATIONS TO CHAPTER 2

A. On the Abstract Reasonings Involved in Natural Theology

In his discourse on Natural Theology, Lord Brougham writes thus (p. 78):—

"The whole reasoning proceeds necessarily upon the assumption that there exists a being or thing separate from, and independent of, matter, and conscious of its own existence, which we call mind. For the argument is, 'Had I to accomplish this purpose, I should have used some such means'; or, 'Had I used these means, I should have thought I was accomplishing some such purpose.' Perceiving the adaptation of the means to the end, the inference is, that some being has acted as we should ourselves act, and with the same views. But when we so speak, and so reason, we are all the while referring to an intelligent principle or existence; we are referring to our mind, and not to our bodily frame."

... "The belief that mind exists is essential to the whole argument by which we infer that the Deity exists. This belief ... is the foundation of Natural Theology in all its branches; and upon the scheme of materialism no rational, indeed no intelligible, account can be given of a first cause, or of the creation or government of the universe."

In a foot-note, Lord Brougham adds:—

"It is worthy of observation that not the least allusion is made in Dr. Paley's work to the argument here stated, although it is the foundation of the whole of Natural Theology. Not only does this author leave entirely untouched the argument à priori (as it is called), and also all the inductive arguments derived from the phenomena of mind, but he does not even advert to the argument upon which the inference of design must of necessity rest—that design which is the whole subject of his book. Nothing can more evince his distaste or incapacity for metaphysical researches. He assumes the very position which alone sceptics dispute. In combating him they would assert that he begged the whole question; for certainly they do not deny, at least in modern times, the fact of adaptation. As to the fundamental doctrine of causation, not the least allusion is ever made to it in any of his writings,—even in his *Moral Philosophy*."

It is when reviewing this last-named treatise that Dr. Whewell remarks (*History of Moral Philosophy*, p. 169):—

"The fact is that Paley had no taste, and therefore we may be allowed to say that he had little aptitude, for metaphysical disquisitions. In this there would have been no blame, if he had not entered into speculations which, if they were not metaphysically right, must be altogether wrong. We often hear persons declare that they have no esteem for metaphysics, and intend to shun all metaphysical reasonings; and this is usually the prelude to some specimen of very bad metaphysics: for I know no better term by which to designate the process of misunderstanding and confounding those elements of truth which are supplied by the relations of our own ideas. That Paley had no turn or talent for the reasoning which depends on such relations, is plain enough."

The reader may with little trouble collect for himself what is meant by bad metaphysics from the following extracts. The first is Lord Macaulay's criticism on the metaphysics of the Schools, which he introduces into his essay on Francis Bacon, as follows:—

"By stimulating men to the discovery of useful truth, he" (Bacon) "furnished them with a motive to perform the inductive process well and carefully. His predecessors had been, in his phrase, not interpreters, but anticipators of nature. They had been content with the first principles at which they had arrived by the most scanty and slovenly induction. And why was this? It was, we conceive, because their philosophy proposed to itself no practical end—because it was merely an exercise of the mind. A man who wants to contrive a new machine or a new medicine has a strong motive to observe accurately and patiently, and to try experiment after experiment. But a man who merely wants a theme for disputation or declamation has no such motive. He is therefore content with premises grounded on assumption, or on the most scanty and hasty induction. Thus, we conceive, the schoolmen acted. On their foolish premises they often argued with great ability; and as their object was "assensum subjugare, non res" (Nov. Org. I. Aph. 29), to be victorious in controversy, not to be victorious over nature, they were consistent. For just as much logical skill could be shown in reasoning on false as on true premises" [44].

Of course, if any genuine metaphysical philosophy exists at all, its right and real object must be to try and discover true premises of the more abstract sort—premises, the truth of which affects the procedure of all the ancillary series [45].

Our next quotation contains Hume's sentence of execution rather than critique upon metaphysics as he saw them in connection with dogmatic theology. First, for his fiery anathema:—

"When we run over libraries, persuaded of these principles, what havoc must we make? If we take in our hand any volume of divinity or School metaphysics, for instance, let us ask, Does it contain any abstract reasoning concerning quantity or number? No. Does it contain any experimental reasoning concerning matters of fact and existence? No. Commit it then to the flames: For it can contain nothing but sophistry and illusion."

(Inquiry concerning Human Understanding, § XII.) Alas for certain of Hume's own speculations!

The student of Positivism knows how this fierce invective was echoed and re-echoed by Comte and his followers. They, however, omitted the qualifying word "School," which Hume prefixed to metaphysics. With Comte, metaphysic of every kind was "anathema maranatha"; and even psychology got excommunicated, by way of making "a clean sweep."

Hume, on the contrary, had an idea of what philosophy ought to be, and thus outlined his preparation for a Metaphysic of the Future:—

"The only method of freeing learning, at once, from these abstruse questions, is to inquire seriously into the nature of human understanding, and show, from an exact analysis of its powers and capacity, that it is by no means fitted for such remote and abstruse subjects. We must submit to this fatigue in order to live at ease ever after: and must cultivate true metaphysics with some care, in order to destroy the false and adulterate. Indolence, which, to some persons, affords a safeguard against this deceitful philosophy, is, with others, overbalanced by curiosity; and despair, which at some moments prevails, may give place afterwards to sanguine hopes and expectations. Accurate and just reasoning is the only catholic remedy, fitted for all persons and all dispositions; and is alone able to subvert that abstruse philosophy and metaphysical jargon, which, being mixed up with popular superstition, renders it in a manner impenetrable to careless reasoners, and gives it the air of science and wisdom.

"Besides this advantage of rejecting, after deliberate inquiry, the most uncertain and disagreeable part of learning, there are many positive advantages, which result from an accurate scrutiny into the powers and faculties of human nature. It is remarkable concerning the operations of the mind, that though most intimately present to us, yet, whenever they become the object of reflection, they seem involved in obscurity; nor can the eye readily find those lines and boundaries which discriminate and distinguish them. The objects are too fine to remain long in the same aspect or situation, and must be apprehended, in an instant, by a superior penetration, derived from nature, and improved by habit and reflection. It becomes, therefore, no inconsiderable part of science barely to know the different operations of the mind, to separate them from each other, to class them under their proper heads, and to correct all that seeming disorder in which they lie involved, when made the object of reflection and inquiry. This task of ordering and distinguishing, which has no merit when performed with regard to external bodies, the objects of our senses, rises in its value when directed towards the operations of the mind, in proportion to the difficulty and labour which we meet with in performing it. And if we can go no farther than this mental geography, or delineation of the distinct parts and powers of the mind, it is at least a satisfaction to go so far; and the more obvious this science may appear (and it is by no means obvious), the more contemptible still must the ignorance of it be esteemed, in all pretenders to learning and philosophy." Ibid. Section I.

It seems worth while to consider what the effects might have been, had Hume been faithful to his own idea [46]. In the first place he would have remedied the weakness pointed out by Macaulay in the premises of the schoolmen, which were in fact little better than sententious maxims often derived from mistranslated passages of Scripture, one-sided opinions of the Fathers, and other sources of doubtful value. These, Hume would have abscided altogether, and rested his "true metaphysics" upon such principles as survived a searching inquiry into the conditions of Human knowledge. Hence, secondly, he would have rendered a great service to Divinity itself, which can never be benefited by such arguments as have been described, but must look for a safe alliance to a synthesis of Faith and Reason. And in the third place he might have probably given to his country a critical Philosophy adapted to English modes of Thought. Kant's mind was fired by a spark of Hume's kindling, but when we think what might have been the shape and acceptance of Kant in this country had Hume heralded him by a critique of Reason, it is impossible to read the great Scotchman's writings without a feeling of disappointment [47].

It would however be unjust to omit the fact that Hume did really entertain a serious intention of dealing with these difficult questions. Thus much is expressed in his earliest work, and we may conjecture that literary disappointment was at least one cause of that later preference for "easy philosophy" which contrasts so strongly with the programme of his treatise on Human Nature. Few programmes were ever more vigorously outlined, than the ensuing.

"From hence," he says, "in my opinion, arises that common prejudice against metaphysical reasonings of all kinds, even amongst those who profess themselves scholars, and have a just value for every other part of literature. By metaphysical reasonings, they do not understand those on any particular branch of science, but every kind of argument, which is any way abstruse, and requires some attention to be comprehended. We have so often lost our labour in such researches, that we commonly reject them without hesitation, and resolve, if we must for ever be a prey to errors and delusions, that they shall at least be natural and entertaining. And, indeed, nothing but the most determined scepticism, along with a great degree of indolence, can justify this aversion to metaphysics. For, if truth be at all within the reach of human capacity, 'tis certain it must lie very deep and abstruse; and to hope we shall arrive at it without pains, while the greatest geniuses have failed with the utmost pains, must certainly be esteemed sufficiently vain and presumptuous. I pretend to no such advantage in the philosophy I am going to unfold, and would esteem it a strong presumption against it, were it so very easy and obvious."—*Treatise on Human Nature*, Introduction, p. 12.

In these sentences Hume has sufficiently condemned the vulgar objections brought against abstract reasoning. Deep and difficult questions can be discussed in no other manner; and what is often called a popular treatise on some subject of philosophic inquiry can never be more than a statement of its writer's opinions, or possibly of his sentimental prejudices.

The next paragraph contains Hume's earliest [48] sketch of that critical inquiry into Human Nature on which he proposed to base all future philosophy. It is of course deeply interesting.

"'Tis evident that all the sciences have a relation, greater or less, to human nature; and that however wide any of them may seem to run from it, they still return back by one passage or another. Even Mathematics, Natural Philosophy, and Natural Religion, are in some measure dependent on the science of Man; since they lie under the cognizance of men, and are judged of by their powers and faculties.

"'Tis impossible to tell what changes and improvements we might make in these sciences were we thoroughly acquainted with the extent and force of human understanding, and could explain the nature of the ideas we employ, and of the operations we perform in our reasonings. And these improvements are the more to be hoped for in natural religion, as it is not content with instructing us in the nature of superior powers, but carries its views further, to their disposition towards us, and our duties towards them; and consequently we our selves are not only the beings that reason, but also one of the objects concerning which we reason."

"If, therefore, the sciences of mathematics, natural philosophy, and natural religion, have such a dependence on the knowledge of man, what may be expected in the other sciences, whose connection with human nature is more close and intimate?... In these four sciences of Logic, Morals, Criticism, and Politics, is comprehended almost everything which it can any way import us to be acquainted with, or which can tend either to the improvement or ornament of the human mind.

"Here then is the only expedient, from which we can hope for success in our philosophical researches, to leave the tedious lingering method, which we have hitherto followed, and instead of taking now and then a castle or village on the frontier, to march up directly to the capital or centre of these sciences, to human nature itself; which being once masters of, we may everywhere else hope for an easy victory. From this station we may extend our conquests over all those sciences which more intimately concern human life, and may afterwards proceed at leisure to discover more fully those which are the objects of pure curiosity. There is no question of importance, whose decision is not comprised in the science of man; and there is none, which can be decided with any certainty, before we become acquainted with that science. In pretending, therefore, to explain the principles of human nature, we in effect propose a complete system of the sciences, built on a foundation almost entirely new, and the only one upon which they can stand with any security" [49]. Ibid. pp. 13-14.

The present writer has a special interest in citing these passages, because they do in fact defend as well as describe the procedure of his very next chapter.

Such then at an early age was Hume's keen-edged critical appreciation of those intellectual conditions required for a Philosophy of the Sciences, or as he calls it, the "true Metaphysics." In order to supplement his clever and clear idea by a very practical delineation of the metaphysical territory, we turn to another great thinker, the founder of our modern natural science, the great Lord Verulam [50].

Bacon divides Philosophy according to its objects, which are three,—God, Nature, Man. Take, then, Natural Philosophy; it is well said that the truth of nature lies deeply hidden, and it is also well said that the Producer imitates Nature. Natural Philosophy divides itself accordingly into the inquisition of causes and the production of effects; it is both speculative and operative. There is indeed an intercourse between causes and effects, and both these kinds of knowledge. All true and fruitful Natural Philosophy has a double scale or ladder,—ascendent and descendent; ascending from experiment to first causes; descending thence to fresh experiment and always fresh productiveness [51].

The ascending half is divided into two moieties, of which one is the science of Physics, the other of Metaphysics. In distinguishing these two, Bacon so far agrees with antiquity as to say,—

"That Physic supposes in nature only a being and moving and natural necessity; whereas Metaphysic supposes also a Mind and Idea. For that which I shall say comes perhaps to this" [52].

Or, to put it in another light, he writes elsewhere:—

"Physique, taking it according to the derivation, and not according to our idiom for medicine, is situate in a middle term or distance between natural history and Metaphysique. For natural history describeth the variety of things; Physique, the causes, but variable or respective causes; and Metaphysique, the fixed and constant causes" [53].

In order to clear the way for his Metaphysic of the future, Bacon subjects what had been called by that name to a critical process. He separates from it a kind of theoretical philosophy, the attainment of which he considered doubtful, though he desired that it should be attempted, as the ultimate goal of human wisdom. The object of the separation is, therefore, to leave his metaphysical science within the limits of what is certainly attainable,—a fact not to be lost sight of in its relation to the abstract subjects in which we are now specially interested. The separated realm of knowledge Bacon calls "First and Summary Philosophy"; it is a "common ancestor to all knowledge" [54], whereas Metaphysic belongs to the philosophy of Nature. It is at the apex of his pyramid of knowledges [55], —the basis being a collection of natural facts—the "stage next the basis," (an investigation of causes variable and immersed in material existence,) is called "Physique—the stage next the vertical point is Metaphysique" [56]. To enter clearly into Bacon's meaning, two questions should be answered: one, what was the wisdom that older Metaphysicians pursued, respecting which he did not himself feel sanguine? and the other, what remained in his thought the province of practical Metaphysique?

It is obvious that a wisdom which shall gather up all that every other realm of wisdom produces, cast it into Thought's winepress, and extract the rarest vintage of Truth, has been the vision of every age since men began to inquire and to reason. If this wisdom were possible, it would become to us an alphabet of the Universe; we should obtain a clear insight into the world as it is, and the foregone work of its Creator. Each of us might truthfully say:—

"Der du die Welt umschweifst,
Geschäftiger Geist, wie nah' fühl ich mich dir!"

It needs but a glance at Bacon's indefinite outline of a First and Summary Philosophy [57], to see that it must always be greeted by two opposite sentences of condemnation. A large section of its censors will pronounce the meagreness of its contents "a gentle riddance," or perhaps describe the contents themselves still more harshly as "rubbish shot here." Another section may compare all that it leaves for Metaphysics to the year without its spring, or Shakespeare's masterpiece of philosophy with the part of Hamlet left out.

Let us see then how the reserved province was parcelled out.—Bacon himself remarks:—

"It may fairly therefore now be asked, what is left remaining for Metaphysic? Certainly nothing beyond nature; but of nature itself much the most excellent part."

Most excellent because

"Physic handles that which is most inherent in matter and therefore transitory, and Metaphysic that which is more abstracted and fixed. And again, that Physic supposes in nature only a being and moving and natural necessity: whereas Metaphysic supposes also a mind and idea" [58].

This search into the Mind of Nature is divided into the investigation of two kinds of causes, still called the Formal and the Final. Bacon's doctrine of Forms—the Philosophy in which is embraced "Natura naturans"—nature engendering nature—the Queen of Art—and the Regent of Production, constitutes one of the most difficult parts of the Novum Organum, the Advancement, and the De Augmentis; and may have been one chief provocative to King James' irreverent similitude. It might, according to some writers, even now prove a veritable "peace of God" could we only grasp its full meaning. "From the discovery of Forms," says Bacon, "results truth in speculation and freedom in operation" [59]. And his latest commentator believes that this field of discovery has not been truly explored, because its very idea has been only imperfectly apprehended. The whole question, however, belongs to a future Chapter of this Essay, where we propose examining the Law of Production in its most refined and abstract shape. Yet one further remark may be allowed here. According to Francis Bacon, one

> "respect which ennobles this part of Metaphysic, is that it enfranchises the power of men to the greatest liberty, and leads it to the widest and most extensive field of operation.... For physical causes give light and direction to new inventions in similar matter. But whosoever knows any Form, knows also the utmost possibility of superinducing that nature upon every variety of matter, and so is less restrained and tied in operation, either to the basis of the matter or to the condition of the efficient" [60].

We are more concerned, at the present stage of this Essay, with the second portion of Bacon's Metaphysique—the Inquiry into Final Causes. They are described in the Advancement as not having been neglected before its great Author's time, but as having been "misplaced."

> "For they are," he writes in the De Augm. (E. & S. iv. p. 363) "generally sought for in Physic, and not in Metaphysic. And yet if it were but a fault in order I should not think so much of it; for order is matter of illustration, but pertains not to the substance of sciences. But this misplacing has caused a notable deficience, and been a great misfortune to Philosophy. For the handling of final causes in Physics has driven away and overthrown the diligent inquiry of physical causes." ...
> "And I say this, not because those final causes are not true and worthy to be inquired in metaphysical speculations; but because their excursions and irruptions into the limits of physical causes has bred a waste and solitude in that track. For otherwise, if they be but kept within their proper bounds, men are extremely deceived if they think there is any enmity or repugnancy at all between the two." (Ibid. p. 364.)

Bacon's meaning is indeed clear enough to those who consider his examples. We do not learn how clouds are produced by being told they serve for watering the earth. It is no history of our earth itself, to say that its "solidness is for the station and mansion of living creatures." "To know the actual nature of a thing," observes an Oxford commentator on the Organum, "we must investigate it in and for itself, not for its results" [61].

Perhaps one of the most curious facts relating to the "misplacement" of Final Causes is that few more flagrant instances of that abuse can be found than some which occur in the field, not of physical but of moral science. The following remarkable example is from an argument framed by Mr. James Mill against Sir J. Macintosh, which appears all the more worthy of quotation, because it is reproduced and approved by Mr. J. Stuart Mill. The whole argument deserves perusal as showing how easily an acquired and customary kind of association will sometimes predominate over free thought; but for our present object a few passages will suffice. The italics are not Mr. Mill's, but are here marked for the purpose of guiding the reader's eye to those steps which lead from final cause (or motive) to interest, from interest to Utility in its grossest form, the artificial creation, namely, of our spur to interested action, dignified by this author with the sacred name of Morality, both in essence, i.e., what makes an act to be moral—and in respect of our moral sense, i.e., what are the sentiments with which we regard our own actions and those of other persons.

"Men make classifications, as they do everything else, for some end. Now, for what end was it that men, out of their innumerable acts, selected a class, to which they gave the name of moral, and another class, to which they gave the name of immoral? What was the motive of this act? What its final cause?

"Assuredly the answer to this question is the first step, though Sir James saw it not, towards the solution of his two questions, comprehending the whole of ethical science; first, what makes an act to be moral? and, secondly, what are the sentiments with which we regard it?

"We may also be assured, that it was some very obvious interest which recommended this classification; for it was performed, in a certain rough way, in the very rudest states of society.

"Farther, we may easily see how, even in very rude states, men were led to it, by little less than necessity.... They had no stronger interest than to obtain the repetition of the one sort, and to prevent the repetition of the other.... And here we clearly perceive the origin of that important case of classification, the classification of acts as moral and immoral. The acts, which it was important to other men that each individual should perform, but in which the individual had not a sufficient interest to secure the performance of them, were constituted one class. The acts, which it was important to other men that each individual should abstain from, but in regard to which he had not a personal interest sufficiently strong to secure his abstaining from them, were constituted another class. The first class were distinguished by the name moral acts; the second by the name immoral.

"The interest which men had in securing the performance of the one set of acts, the non- performance of the other, led them by a sort of necessity to think of the means. They had to create an interest, which the actor would not otherwise have, in the performance of the one sort, the non-performance of the other. And in proceeding to this end, they could not easily miss their way. They had two powers applicable to the purpose. They had a certain quantity of good at their disposal, and they had a certain quantity of evil.... And this is the scheme which they adopted; and which, in every situation, they have invariably pursued. The whole business of the moral sentiments, moral approbation, and disapprobation, has this for its object,—the distribution of the good and evil we have at command, for the production of acts of the useful sort, the prevention of acts of the contrary sort. Can there be a nobler object?" [62].

Some people may think that all nobleness is here taken away from moral distinctions. Others may wonder how such refined calculation could take place "in the very rudest states of Society." Many more will feel that this factitious interest is not the moral sentiment of which they are themselves conscious. We defer these points, however, to a future chapter, and are satisfied now with calling attention to the "misplacement" of final causes. To any modern versed (as Bacon was) in the wisdom of the mediaeval schools, the following parallel might appear complete. Ask two questions—what are clouds?—what are moral distinctions?—let a "why" be substituted for the "what." Both are classified by men, both may be defined by their subserviency to human interests,—it is sufficient to discover some use in each. Moral distinctions exist for the benefit of society, clouds are for watering the earth. An earth-watering contrivance describes not only one use but the whole nature of a cloud; and for morality can a nobler definition be found than that of a notion invented and named on Utilitarian principles and promoting a public interest? [63] Doubt less morality does benefit mankind—doubtless clouds do water the earth. But in either case is the good effect its full and comprehensive "why?"—to say nothing of the desiderated "what?"

Francis Bacon (as we have seen) strongly affirmed that between Physical Causes and Final Causes "kept within their proper bounds, men are extremely deceived if they think there is any enmity or repugnancy at all." The manner in which, according to the Baconian doctrine, these two sets of causes harmonize and supplement each other, so as conjointly to subserve the highest purpose of Natural Theology, cannot be better explained than in the words of Bacon's late lamented Editor, Mr. R. Leslie Ellis:—

> "It is not sufficiently remarked that final causes have often been spoken of without any reference to a benevolent intention. When it is said that the final cause of a stone's falling is 'locus deorsum,' the remark is at least but remotely connected with the doctrine of an intelligent providence. We are to remember that Bacon has expressly censured Aristotle for having made use of final causes without refer ring to the fountain from which they flow, namely the providence of the Creator. And in this censure he has found many to concur.
>
> "Again, in any case in which the benevolent intention can be perceived, we are at liberty to ask by what means and according to what laws this benevolent intention is manifested and made efficient. If this question is not to be asked, there is in the first place an end of physical science, so far as relates to every case in which a benevolent intention has been or can be recognised; and in the second, the argument à posteriori founded on the contrivance displayed in the works of creation is entirely taken away.
>
> "This is, in effect, what Bacon says in the passage of the De Augmentis, in which he complains of the abuse of final causes. If, he affirms, the physical cause of any phenomenon can be assigned as well as the final, so far is this from derogating from our idea of the divine wisdom, that on the contrary it does but confirm and exalt it" [64].

Before passing from this subject the reader's attention may be drawn to two notes by the same eminent commentator. Bacon remarks (Nov. Org. I. 48) that Final Causes are "ex natûra hominis" i.e., have relation to the nature of Man.

> "It is difficult," writes Mr. Ellis, "to assent to the assertion that the notion of the final cause, considered generally, is more ex natûra hominis than that of the efficient. The subject is one of which it is difficult to speak accurately; but it may be said that wherever we think that we recognise a tendency towards a fulfilment or realisation of an idea, there the notion of the final cause comes in. It can only be from inadvertence that Professor Owen has set the doctrine of the final cause as it were in antithesis to that of the unity of type: by the former he means the doctrine that the suitability of an animal to its mode of life is the one thing aimed at or intended in its structure. It cannot be doubted that Aristotle would have recognised the preservation of the type as not less truly a final cause

than the preservation of the species or than the well-being of the individual. The final cause connects itself with what in the language of modern German philosophy is expressed by the phrase 'the Idea in Nature." [65].

The epigrammatic comparison of a Final Cause to a consecrated Virgin [66] has been reviewed by numberless disciples as well as critics of our author. Mr. Ellis annotates the Latin text thus:—

"Nihil parit, means simply, non parit opera, which though it would have been a more precise mode of expression would have destroyed the appo siteness of the illustration. No one who fairly considers the context can, I think, have any doubts as to the limitation with which the sentence in question is to be taken. But it is often the misfortune of a pointed saying to be quoted apart from any context, and consequently to be misunderstood."

And this seems to be a scholarly explanation [67].

To complete the sketch of Baconian Metaphysic it appears only needful to add that his respect for the science of Quantity is sufficient to make him class under this higher philosophy—this near approach to the apex of his Pyramid—the whole circle of Mathematics.

Our long note will not have been written in vain if the reader bears its contents in mind when considering the abstract arguments advanced throughout this Essay. It is well to see what very great authorities have thought concerning the true use of Metaphysics;—it is well also to see how they ought to be applied in questions of physical science, and for the purpose of grounding a science of Natural Theology.

B. On the Phrase "Design Implies a Designer"

"It has been contended," says Professor Baden Powell, "that in one sense it is mere tautology to say that Design implies a Designer." (*Connexion of Natural and Divine Truth*, p. 183.)

As a matter of fact there can be no doubt that verbal-sounding phrases, however useful in a system of Mnemonics, and much in favour as political war-cries, always tend to discredit the sober course of a philosophic argument. But Paley, though writing popularly, did not intend a mere ad captandum effect, as may be seen by a reference to his second chapter. He meant by Design and Contrivance to express in brief the conditions he had laid down as characteristic of the intentional adaptation of means to definitely purposed ends,—with which conditions he appears to have been fully satisfied.

In his 23rd and 24th chapters, where some hasty writer might have said "law implies a lawgiver," the Archdeacon prefers to state that "a law pre-supposes an agent," and proceeds to argue the statement on its merits. "Law," he says, "is only the mode according to which an agent proceeds: it implies a power, for it is the order according to which that power acts. Without this agent, without this power, which are both distinct from itself, the 'law' does nothing; is nothing." (Chapter 23.) He is well satisfied with this argument also, and repeats it (slightly varied in form) during the course of his next chapter.

In our comparison of Powell with Paley we were led to remark on the diverse meanings of the word Design, and the facility with which some authors have glided from one to another among its significations. If any thinker believes that the examples he adduces are distinctly instances of Foresight, Intention, and Will, he has the Designer full in mind before he employs the term Design. But if his instances fall short of thus much implicit force, the argument founded on them is a worthless verbality [68].

Those who protest against the popular phrase, "Design proves a Designer," say it is a temptation to assume this point—(the one point at issue)—over which it skims with such secure ease. But to any person in earnest, few things are more irritating than a piece of cool, thorough-going assumption. It is like catching a cat and persistently calling it a hare. Many visitors at certain Roman Hotels are aware that when deprived of ears and tail more Italico and well roasted, the resemblance between these two animals may give rise to questions of disputed identity. Imagine, now, a party of cat-catchers, who not only assume the Identity, but persevere in calling their mongrel curs harehounds, and themselves huntsmen. No truer claim in reality do a multitude of Design-hunters possess to any higher title than the leguleii of Natural Theology. And the blame of their discredit must in a great degree be laid upon their words. It is easy to say, "A thrown-stone implies a thrower." But suppose the stone about which you and I are talking was thrown by the fiery force of a volcano? Must we hence infer the existence of a Cyclops or a Titan?

This mode of popular speech reached the climax of absurdity when it was gravely argued that "Evolution implies an Evolver." So it might appear to the peculiar mind of the speaker; but how about the mind of him who promulgated the evolution-hypothesis? Stones (as we may observe) fly from more than one cause, and there is more than one account to be given of the theory of Evolution.

Enough has been said to show that the phrase commented on in this note, prejudices the argument it is intended to assist. It wears the appearance of embodying a foregone conclusion; and gives trouble to the honest inquirer, who, in order to estimate reasonings at their true value, must translate them into accurate forms of speech.

We may aptly finish these remarks by a quotation from Whewell's Aphorisms on the Language of Science. (Aphorism I., *Philosophy of the Inductive Sciences*, II. 483.)

"Words borrowed from common language, and converted by scientific writers into technical terms, have some advantages and some disadvantages. They possess this great convenience, that they are understood after a very short explanation, and retained in the memory without effort. On the other hand they lead to some inconvenience; for since they have a meaning in common language, a careless reader is prone to disregard the technical limitation of this meaning, and to attempt to collect their import in scientific books, in the same vague and conjectural manner in which he collects the purpose of words in common cases. Hence the language of science, when thus resembling common language, is liable to be employed with an absence of that scientific precision which alone gives it value. Popular writers and talkers, when they speak of force, momentum, action, and reaction, and the like, often afford examples of the inaccuracy thus arising from the scientific appropriation of common terms."

A similar line of reflection led Coleridge to remark (Biog. Lit., Chap. x.) that "the language of the market would be in the schools as pedantic, though it might not be reprobated by that name, as the language of the schools in the market. The mere man of the world, who insists that no other terms but such as occur in common conversation should be employed in a scientific disquisition, and with no greater precision, is as truly a pedant as the man of letters, who, either over-rating the acquirements of his auditors, or misled by his own familiarity with technical or scholastic terms, converses at the wine-table with his mind fixed on his museum or laboratory."

And such pedantry is, we may add, not uncommonly just as perspicuous as the definition which, says old Glanvill, "was lately given of a Thought in a University Sermon —viz. A Repentine Prosiliency jumping into Being." (Defence of the Vanity of Dogmatizing, *Actio Decima*, p. 61, ed. 1.)

C. Hume on the Analogies of Art and Nature. [Referred to in Footnote (E) in the Preceding Chapter.]

The statement in the text is shaped as a not unfairly urged scientific objection of the kind which might be raised by some actual craftsman or producer. An objection identical in essence is thrown by Hume into a refined semi-metaphysical shape, and made to turn upon our general acquaintance with Human nature contrasted with our general ignorance of the Divine. It runs as follows:—

"The infinite difference of the subjects, replied he," (Hume's dramatic Epicurus,) "is a sufficient foundation for this difference in my conclusions. In works of human art and contrivance, it is allowable to advance from the effect to the cause, and returning back from the cause, to form new inferences concerning the effect, and examine the alterations which it has probably undergone, or may still undergo. But what is the foundation of this method of reasoning? Plainly this; that man is a being, whom we know by experience, whose motives and designs we are acquainted with, and whose projects and inclinations have a certain connection and coherence, according to the laws which nature has established for the government of such a creature. When, therefore, we find that any work has proceeded from the skill and industry of man; as we are otherwise acquainted with the nature of the animal, we can draw a hundred inferences concerning what may be expected from him; and these inferences will all be founded in experience and observation. But did we know man only from the single work or production which we examine, it were impossible for us to argue in this manner; because our knowledge of all the qualities, which we ascribe to him, being in that case derived from the production, it is impossible they could point to anything farther, or be the foundation of any new inference....

"The case is not the same with our reasonings from the works of nature. The Deity is known to us only by his productions, and is a single being in the universe, not comprehended under any species or genus, from whose experienced attributes or qualities, we can, by analogy, infer any attribute or quality in him." (*Enquiry Concerning Human Understanding*. Section xi.)

Hume himself gives in his own character a reply partially veiled by the same half-metaphysical style which characterises the objection:—

"There occurs to me (continued I), with regard to your main topic, a difficulty which I shall just propose to you without insisting on it, lest it lead into reasonings of too nice and delicate a nature. In a word, I much doubt whether it be possible for a cause to be known only by its effect (as you have all along supposed), or to be of so singular and particular a nature, as to have no parallel and no similarity with any other cause or object that has ever fallen under our observation. It is only when two species of objects are found to be constantly conjoined, that we can infer the one from the other: and were an effect presented which was entirely singular, and could not be comprehended under any known species, I do not see, that we could form any conjecture or inference at all concerning its cause. If experience and observation and analogy be, indeed, the only guides which we can reasonably follow in inferences of this nature; both the effect and cause must bear a similarity and resemblance to other effects and causes which we know, and which we have found, in many instances, to be conjoined with each other. I leave it to your own reflection to pursue the consequences of this principle." (Ibid.)

The consequences which ought in fairness to be deduced may be stated thus. The effect we contemplate, (i.e., Nature,) is not singular but can be compared with other effects—those of Art. The comparison is made in respect of certain specific attributes or properties upon which the Design analogy turns, so that we may reason upwards to certain specific analogies of Causation.

Art manifests the foreseeing attributes of the human artist, and from comparison of these we infer in the Creator like attributes,—what Hume elsewhere calls the natural attributes of the Deity. But this likeness is properly termed analogical, because of the vast difference in the magnitude of the effects from which we thus reason, and of the causes to which we reason. As our wisdom and power are proportionable to our earthly works, so are the Divine wisdom and power proportionable to the whole majestic Universe. There is, then, a comparison in species, but not in grandeur—the attributes are not similar, but analogical. As the Heavens are high above the Earth, so are His thoughts higher than our thoughts.

D. The Pantheistic Consequences Charged Upon Physical Speculations

The following is the passage from Professor Baden Powell referred to in note (h) of the preceding chapter. Some short extracts were also made from it on a previous page.

"Nothing but the common confused and mistaken notions as to laws and causes, could give any colour to the assertion that ... physical speculations tend to substitute general physical laws in the place of the Deity; and that scientific statements of the conclusions of Natural Theology are nothing but ill-disguised Pantheism.

"The utter futility of such inferences is at once seen, when the smallest attention is given to the plain distinctions above laid down between 'moral' and 'physical' causation; and to the proper force of the conclusions from natural science establishing the former by means of the latter.

"This distinction obviously points to the very reverse of the assertion that physical action is identical with its moral cause; the essential difference and contrast between them is the very point which the whole argument upholds and enforces.

"Of all forms of philosophical mysticism, the idea of Pantheism seems to me one of the most extravagant. Ever-present mind is a direct inference from the universal order of nature, or rather only another mode of expressing it. But of the mode of existence of that mind we can infer nothing.

"To assert, then, that this universally manifested mind is co-existent, or even to be identified, with matter, is at best a mere gratuitous hypothesis, and as such wholly unphilosophical in itself, and leading to many preposterous consequences. But if further supposed to apply in any higher sense as to an object of worship, trust, love, obedience, or the like (as is implied in the term Pan theism), it appears to involve moral contradictions of the most startling kind.

"There are, however, many who, though rejecting Pantheism as untrue, do not conceive it absurd or contradictory. Much, however, will, in all such cases, depend on the precise sense in which it is maintained. With some it seems to have been upheld on a fanciful analogy with the conception of the human frame animated by an indwelling spirit; as if in a somewhat similar manner the supreme mind might animate nature. Without disputing this in a certain sense, the cases surely cannot be considered at all parallel: we do not infer the existence of the human mind, from the arrangement and adaptation of the bodily organs, nor is it the moral cause of their organisation.

"If Pantheism were asserted merely in the sense of a kind of vital or animating principle pervading the material world, I would admit that such an idea involves no absurdity, or contradiction, but still I should regard it as visionary and unphilosophical. I could but class it with the 'vital forces' which Kepler fancied necessary for keeping up the motions of the planets, with the 'plastic powers of nature,' 'her abhorrence of a vacuum,' and the like chimaeras. But it is when men elevate such a supposed animating principle into a Deity, a being of supreme wisdom, power, beneficence, and goodness, yet residing in every atom of matter, and participating directly in every form and case of material action, that the contradiction arises." *Spirit of the Inductive Philosophy*, pp. 176-9.

E. The Extent and Divisions of the Science of Natural Theology

The following passages from Professor Powell's Essay "on the Spirit of the Inductive Philosophy" will go far to justify the praise and blame bestowed upon his mode of procedure in the text of the foregoing chapter. But we would recommend his own pages to the student's discriminative perusal.

In extract No. 1, Baden Powell shows with equal truth and force that universal Law must be contemplated as a manifestation of one supreme Intelligence presiding over the whole Universe. A philosopher who looks on Nature with this majestic breadth of view does not need for his own deepest convictions to follow Design through a multitude of smaller evidences.

If extract No. 2 could be admitted as a full account of the conditions and limitations of Natural Theology, our science would seem to result in an obscuration of the magnificently Supreme Power already accepted. So far as its letter goes, the Creator of the Universe might appear to be shut out from the world which He has made. We cannot (as has been said) consent to this narrow consideration of Natural Theology, nor yet of Powell's meaning.

Extract No. 3 acknowledges what all physical investigators ought to acknowledge,—that although their sciences contribute very much towards solving the problem of the Universe, and although their results readily harmonize with the solution maintained by the Theist—yet there rests over that vast problem a cloud which the physical sciences cannot completely dispel. This (as we shall see in Chapter 5.) is indeed the confession of the greatest minds at present engaged upon the philosophy of Natural Science.

Extract No. 1.—

"From the inductive philosophy we derive our belief in the harmony, order, and uniformity of natural causes, perpetually maintained in a universally connected chain of dependence. And hence it is, that we arrive at those sublime ideas of a presiding Intelligence of which law and uniformity, universal mechanism once for all adjusted, are the proper external manifestations.

"To the truly inductive philosopher, fate and chance, necessity and accident, are words without meaning. To him, the world is made up of recondite combinations of physical laws, and the existence and maintenance of those laws are the very indication of a Supreme Mind. But chance is irreconcilable with laws, fate with mind, regulated and fixed order with blind destiny, fortuitous accident, or arbitrary interruption.

"All rational natural theology advances by tracing the immediate mechanical steps and particular processes in detail, and the physical causes in which the influences of the Great Moral Cause or Supreme Mind are manifested. The greater the number and extent of such secondary steps and intermediate processes through which we can trace it, the greater the complexity and wider the ramifications of the chain of causes, the more powerful and convincing the instruction they convey as to the existence and operation of the Divine wisdom and power.

"Yet it is a common mode of illustration to speak of the chain of secondary causes reaching up to the First Cause. Or, again, fears are entertained of tracing secondary causes too far, so as to intrench on the supremacy of the First Cause. But this is an erroneous analogy: the maker or designer of a chain is no more at one end of it than at the other. The length of the chain in no way alters our conviction of its skilful structure, except to enhance it. If the number of links were truly infinite, so much the more infinite the skill of its framer.

"Mr. F. Newman observes [69], I think most truly, that the common arguments from what are called 'secondary causes' to the 'First Cause' are unsatisfactory: and I would trace this to the confused sense in which those terms are commonly used, as already explained; and which, I think, might be entirely removed by attention to the distinctions above laid down. While, on the other hand, I fully acknowledge that those arguments, when correctly understood, lead only to a very limited conclusion; and one which falls infinitely short of those high moral and spiritual intuitions on which Mr. F. Newman grounds his religious system, yet in no way discredits or supersedes them." Essay, pp. 151-4.

Extract No. 2.—

"In the present state of knowledge, law and order, physical causation and uniformity of action, are the elevated manifestations of Divinity, creation and providence. Interruptions of such order (if for a moment they could be admitted as such) could only produce a sort of temporary concealment of such manifestations, and involve the beautiful light shed over the natural world in a passing cloud. We do not indeed doubt that the sun exists behind the cloud, but we certainly do not see it; still less can we call the obscuration a special proof of its presence. The main point in the system of order and law is its absolute universality. Exceptions, if real, must pro tanto imply a deficiency in the chain of connexion, and might, to a sceptical disposition, offer a ground of doubt.

"But so overwhelming is the mass and body of proof, that no philosophic mind would allow such exceptions for a moment to weigh against it; they would be as dust in the balance. A supreme moral cause manifested through law, order, and physical causes, is the confession of science: conflicting operations, arbitrary interruptions, abrupt discontinuities, are the idols of ignorance, and, if they really prevailed, would so far be to the philosopher only the exponents of chaos and atheism; the obscuration (as far as they extend) of the sensible manifestation of the Supreme Intelligence." Ibid. 165, 6.

Extract No. 3.—

"The whole tenor of the preceding argument is directed to show that the inference and assertion of a Supreme Moral Cause, distinct from and above nature, results immediately from the recognition of the eternal and universal maintenance of the order of physical causes, which are its essential external manifestations.

"Of the mode of action or operation by which the Supreme Moral Cause influences the universal order of physical causes, we confess our utter ignorance. But the evidence of such operation, where nature exists, can never be lost or interrupted. And in proportion as our more extended researches exhibit these indications more fully and more gloriously displayed, we cannot but believe that our contemplations are more nearly and truly approaching their Source." Ibid. 179.

The reader will not grudge the time he may have bestowed upon this note if it leads him to a distinct apprehension of the true breadth and compass of our science.

"Natural Theology," says Kant, "infers the attributes and the existence of an author of the world, from the constitution of, the order and unity observable in this world, in which two modes of Causality, together with their laws, must be accepted—that is to say, Nature and Freedom. Thus Natural Theology rises from this world to a supreme Intelligence, whether as to the principle of all natural or of all moral order and perfection. In the former case it is termed Physico-Theology, in the latter Ethical or Moral Theology."

This last term he explains by adding,

"Not theological ethics; for this latter science contains ethical laws, which presuppose the existence of a Supreme Governor of the world; while Moral Theology, on the contrary, is an evidence of the existence of a Supreme Being, an evidence founded upon ethical laws." Kant's *Kritik der reinen Vernunft Transscendental Elementarlehre*, s. 7.

It was from the fulness and depth of a personal conviction on this topic that the present writer ventured to assert in 1870 that "The conditions under which Natural Theology becomes scientifically possible, are found when it supplements Natural Science by a science of Right and Wrong," and also that "for the future Natural Theology ought to follow this path and no other—unless it wishes to commit suicide." These assertions were made in a University Sermon [70] on the question, "Under what Conditions is a Science of Natural Theology possible?" and they were censured as novel and unprecedented by critics who ought to have known better.

F. On Teleology

One consequence of the principle on which this Essay has been framed is an endeavour to place before the reader's eye different modes of reasoning in the language of their several authors. The method of looking at any subject-matter in a diversity of lights naturally leads to copiousness of quotation. There can, it is evident, be no varieties of thought so undeniably distinct as those which are the actual products of diverse minds.

The maxim which has governed the following selection is what Bacon would call a marshalling Idea. They posit one central thought and throw light upon it from a circle of separate reflectors.

Let it be observed that such a collection of opinions implies no appeal to authority in the narrow sense of the word. There is indeed a manifest distinction between authority and authorities—and our present appeal is to the latter. No man's ipse dixit can dogmatically settle questions which belong to an inquirer's responsible self; but it is surely the wisdom of every one who acknowledges the awful sense of accountability attendant on the determination of questions affecting his central beliefs, to weigh the reasonings of others who have felt the same deep impression of their paramount importance. If any one is reluctant so to do from an idea that by doing thus much he pays a wrongful deference to prejudices, he has in truth assumed the whole issue which he is bound to examine. How otherwise can he certainly allege that the prejudice is not inherent within himself?

Reluctance of this kind would on the present occasion be thoroughly misplaced. Authorities as here quoted are neither more nor less than the opinions of experts who have a title to be heard each in his own proper department. Throughout the practical conduct of life we all experience the benefit of laying aside our private spectacles from time to time and of looking through the glasses of other men. And in questions such as the one now before us, is it possible to do better than try whether we can see for ourselves what has been pronounced discernible by men who contemplated this world of ours with more than ordinary powers of vision?

The present writer has a personal interest in bringing together the reflections of many who have reached the same resting-place along various lines of approach, and who have expressed their conclusions with some diversity of language. He has ventured himself on viewing the evidences of Natural Theology from a position by no means identical with that most commonly occupied by Natural Theologians. The student, therefore, who takes a wide survey of the field will be the critic best prepared to examine the latter part of this Essay.

The first authority quoted among our ample citations is Hume, whose appearance as a witness for Natural Theology may surprise some readers. As, however, is remarked by an eminent writer in the Quarterly, Hume's hard common sense "enabled him when he liked, to control the excesses of a speculative imagination and subject it to practical reason, as he understood reason's verdict." He even went so far as to say that "The whole frame of Nature bespeaks an Intelligent Author; and no rational inquirer can, after serious reflection, suspend his belief a moment with regard to the primary principles of genuine Theism and Religion." (Natural History of Religion, Intro duction.) Indeed, according to Cucheval Clarigny [71], Hume was an "almost Christian" at certain periods of his life. The repellant forces that kept him back, are "not far to seek."

The following passages refer to the illative analogy which forms the proper shape of the argument from Design.

"That the works of Nature bear a great analogy to the productions of art, is evident; and according to all the rules of good reasoning, we ought to infer, if we argue at all concerning them, that their causes have a proportional analogy. But as there are also considerable differences, we have reason to suppose a proportional difference in the causes; and in particular ought to attribute a much higher degree of power and energy to the supreme cause than any we have ever observed in mankind. Here then the existence of a DEITY is plainly ascertained by reason: and if we make it a question whether, on account of these analogies, we can properly call him a mind or intelligence, notwithstanding the vast difference which may reasonably be supposed between him and human minds; what is this but a mere verbal controversy? No man can deny the analogies between the effects: To restrain ourselves from inquiring concerning the causes, is scarcely possible: From this inquiry, the legitimate conclusion is, that the causes have also an analogy: And if we are not contented with calling the first and supreme cause a GOD or DEITY, but desire to vary the expression; what can we call him but MIND or THOUGHT, to which he is justly supposed to bear a considerable resemblance?" *Dialogues Concerning Natural Religion*, Part xii. in Essays, Vol. II. p. 526 [72].

"If the whole of Natural Theology, as some people seem to maintain, resolves itself into one simple, though somewhat ambiguous, at least undefined proposition, That the cause or causes of order in the universe probably bear some remote analogy to human intelligence. If this proposition be not capable of extension, variation, or more particular explication; if it affords no inference that affects human life, or can be the source of any action or forbearance; and if the analogy, imperfect as it is, can be carried no farther than to the human intelligence, and cannot be transferred, with any appearance of probability, to the other qualities of the mind: If this really be the case, what can the most inquisitive, contemplative, and religious man do more than give a plain, philosophical assent to the proposition, as often as it occurs; and believe that the arguments on which it is established, exceed the objections which lie against it?" Ibid. p. 538.

The following is the opinion of Cleanthes, upon whom Hume confers the palm in the dialogue;—

"Take care, Philo, replied Cleanthes; take care; push not matters too far: allow not your zeal against false religion to undermine your veneration for the true. Forfeit not this principle, the chief, the only great comfort in life; and our principal support amidst all the attacks of adverse fortune. The most agreeable reflection, which it is possible for human imagination to suggest, is that of genuine Theism, which represents us as the workmanship of a Being perfectly good, wise, and powerful; who created us for happiness; and who, having implanted in us immeasurable desires of good, will prolong our existence to all eternity, and will transfer us into an infinite variety of scenes, in order to satisfy those desires, and render our felicity complete and durable. Next to such a Being himself (if the comparison be allowed), the happiest lot which we can imagine, is that of being under his guardianship and protection." Ibid. p.535 [73].

The next three extracts give Hume's opinion on the prevailing principle disclosed by the analogy—design, purpose, and the recognition of final causes:—

"Though the stupidity of men, barbarous and uninstructed, be so great, that they may not see a sovereign author in the more obvious works of nature, to which they are so much familiarized; yet it scarce seems possible, that any one of good understanding should reject that idea, when once it is suggested to him. A purpose, an intention, a design is evident in everything; and when our comprehension is so far enlarged as to contemplate the first rise of this visible system, we must adopt, with the strongest conviction, the idea of some intelligent cause or author. The uniform maxims, too, which prevail throughout the whole frame of the universe, naturally, if not necessarily, lead us to conceive this intelligence as single and undivided, where the prejudices of education oppose not so reasonable a theory. Even the contrarieties of nature, by discovering themselves everywhere, become proofs of some consistent plan, and establish one single purpose or intention, however inexplicable and incomprehensible." *Natural History of Religion XV.*—General Corollary, in Essays II. pp. 422, 3.

"In many views of the universe, and of its parts, particularly the latter, the beauty and fitness of final causes strike us with such irresistible force that all objections appear (what I believe they really are) mere cavils and sophisms; nor can we then imagine how it was ever possible for us to repose any weight on them." *Dialogues Concerning Natural Religion*, Part X. in Essays, II. 509.

"The order and arrangement of nature, the curious adjustment of final causes, the plain use and intention of every part and organ; all these bespeak in the clearest language an intelligent cause or author. The heavens and the earth join in the same testimony. The whole chorus of nature raises one hymn to the praises of its Creator.... I have found a Deity; and here I stop my enquiry. Let those go farther who are wiser or more enterprising." Ibid. Part IV. p. 467.

Hume is conspicuous amongst reasoners on Natural Theology for having distinctly comprehended Human Nature along with Nature in the cycle of its evidences.

"This sentence at least," he writes, "Reason will venture to pronounce, That a mental world, or universe of ideas, requires a cause as much as does a material world, or universe of objects; and, if similar in its arrangement, must require a similar cause. For what is there in this subject which should occasion a different conclusion or inference? In an abstract view, they are entirely alike; and no difficulty attends the one supposition which is not common to both of them." Ibid. Part IV. p. 464.

This statement brings us to the impediments which withheld Hume from forming a sublime idea of the Divine Being, such an idea as kindles the enthusiasm of devout men, and inspires even timidly sensitive souls with deathless confidence in the final triumph of a self-sacrificing virtue destined to survive the grave. These causes were the opinions he maintained respecting human nature. We may lay it down as a universal rule that every one who sees the animal, but not the heaven- aspiring moral element in his own nature, and in our common nature, will fail to represent to himself the lineaments or reflection of the Divine attributes. An acknowledged kinship with brutal passions, the lowering of society and wedlock to animal gregariousness, of moral principle and the rule of Right and Wrong to a perception of Utility, are fatal hindrances in the search after God;—a search arduous to the best of us, since deep as the far translucent heavens, are the majestic thoughts of Him after Whom we strive to feel. Now Hume failed to discern the Godlike in Man.

> "Human life," he remarks in his Sceptic, "is more governed by fortune than by reason; is to be regarded more as a dull pastime than as a serious occupation; and is more influenced by particular humour than by general principles."

Morality is no fixed star in Hume's firmament. To omit the laxity of many moral maxims he lays down, the very nature and foundations of morality were imperilled by his analytics [74].

> "He has," writes Mackintosh, "altogether omitted the circumstance on which depends the difference of our sentiments regarding moral and intellectual qualities. We admire intellectual excellence, but we bestow no moral approbation on it."

And again—

> "He entirely overlooks that consciousness of the rightful supremacy of the moral faculty over every other principle of human action, without an explanation of which, ethical theory is wanting in one of its vital organs." *Ethical Philosophy*, pp. 182, 4.

> "If," says Hume in the Sceptic, "we can depend upon any principle which we learn from philosophy, this, I think, may be considered as certain and undoubted, that there is nothing in itself valuable or despicable, desirable or hateful, beautiful or deformed; but that these attributes arise from the particular constitution and fabric of human sentiment and affection."

And half a dozen pages afterwards—

> "Good and ill, both natural and moral, are entirely relative to human sentiment and affection." So too, "The necessity of justice to the support of society is," he tells us, "the Sole foundation of that virtue;" usefulness, he explains, "is the Sole source of the moral approbation paid to fidelity, justice, veracity, integrity, and those other estimable and useful qualities and principles." It is also "the source of a considerable part of the merit ascribed to humanity, benevolence, friendship, public spirit, and other social virtues of that stamp." *Principles of Morals*, Sect. III. sub fin.

With these sentiments it is not surprising that while he insists on the analogy between human workmanship and the natural universe he cannot argue analogically from moral Truth to the Divine attributes—and even goes so far as to decide that the first causes of the Universe "have neither goodness nor malice."

The student of Natural Theology cannot direct his attention too soon or too steadily to the vast share possessed by our moral sentiments in our apprehension of the Divine nature. It is from our sense of Responsibility attached to each act of Will and Choice that we deduce the idea of causation. It is from our intuitions of immutable moral truth and the irreconcilable antithesis between Right and Wrong that we behold the Martyr as one who has not lived in vain, but lives truly and for ever; and are sure that there exists a God who has regard to the righteous, the oppressed, the fatherless, and the widow. Clear moral insight appears in Socrates, who chose to die rather than offend against the eternal laws. But ought the man to be styled moral or immoral who should balance together two comparative utilities,—that of preserving his father's life and that of acquiring by a judicious neglect, without risk to himself, a property which he resolved to expend usefully? Of one thing we may be sure, God could not be in all his thoughts whilst making such a calculation.

It is thus that a pure Morality and an elevated conception of the Divine Being act and react upon each other. And in this way our speculative and practical Reason become interlaced—the former giving to the logical understanding an account of those ideas which form the essential sublimity and moving influence of our practical beliefs—the springs of our daily and hourly behaviour. There is no more certain characteristic of a mind so ordered than its ability to deal with a moral doubt which casuists might long debate, to solve the enigma within the compass of a moment's thought, and to defend the solution by fair and honest argument. As regards our present question it makes no difference by what means such a condition of mind may have been brought about, but it is plain that a sense of accountability has much to do with this condition. And the connexion between Responsibility and our belief in a life immortal, and in a just and veracious God, will form a subject for future consideration.

Meantime, the reader must take Hume's acceptance of the doctrine of final causes and the Design-analogy, for what it is worth. No candid person ought to condemn Hume as he has often been condemned without remembering the allowance to be made for his excessive vanity [75], his extreme love of paradoxical speculation, and the dramatic irony which runs throughout his writings. These are in fact some of the qualities which make him an unfit schoolmaster for the young, and a shrewd exercise for elder men. One useful lesson we gather just now is learned from the fact that he places a wide gulf between the natural and moral attributes of the Deity, and draws a veil over the latter, because the alleged poverty of our moral ideas precludes any analogy to reason upon, however remote that analogy may appear. Hence Hume's God of Nature becomes a shadow like Wordsworth's Laodamia, scarce fit for the Elysian bowers; He is no longer felt by us to be the God of Human Nature.

We cannot here omit to observe that Hume had no thought of worshipping the Order of the World, or of erecting a temple to immutable Laws, blind Force, or any other blank impersonal Necessity. The limit of his inquiry was what to human reason might appear the easiest and most probable interpretation of nature [76]. This question he asked and answered. Whether modern science has added important data on which to found a more conclusive reply is a further inquiry which we shall have to consider, but meantime it appears certain that if the most sceptical theory of the most sceptical scientist were held true, there would still remain the same necessity for asking Hume's question. For neither our life, nor the world we live in, nor the wide universe, have any real cause or aim scientifically assigned them. We should still have to inquire by what agency and to what purpose we and the All exist? That we really are is a fact for you, O reader, and for me; and we cannot but want to discover whether we shall yet be, when this brief yet tedious life is done; and if so, whether our present acts and choosings must influence our Hereafter? Science has said nothing to annihilate our interest concerning these topics, nor yet to finally decide them.

For the truth of what is contained in this last paragraph, we may cite as witness amongst scientific men, the distinguished President of the British Association for 1872. Dr. Carpenter spoke at Brighton in these words:—

"There is a great deal of what I cannot but regard as fallacious and misleading Philosophy—'oppositions of Science falsely so called'—abroad in the world at the present time. And I hope to satisfy you, that those who set up their own conceptions of the Orderly Sequence which they discern in the Phenomena of Nature, as fixed and determinate Laws, by which those phenomena not only are within all Human experience, but always have been, and always must be, invariably governed, are really guilty of the Intellectual arrogance they condemn in the Systems of the Ancients, and place themselves in diametrical antagonism to those real Philosophers, by whose comprehensive grasp and penetrating insight that Order has been so far disclosed."

And again towards the close of his Address:—

"With the growth of the Scientific Study of Nature, the conception of its Harmony and Unity gained ever-increasing strength. And so among the most enlightened of the Greek and Roman Philosophers, we find a distinct recognition of the idea of the Unity of the Directing Mind from which the Order of Nature proceeds; for they obviously believed that, as our modern Poet has expressed it—
"All are but parts of one stupendous whole,
Whose body Nature is, and God the Soul."

The Science of Modern times, however, has taken a more special direction. Fixing its attention exclusively on the Order of Nature, it has separated itself wholly from Theology, whose function it is to seek after its Cause. In this, Science is fully justified, alike by the entire independence of its objects, and by the historical fact that it has been continually hampered and impeded in its search for the Truth as it is in Nature, by the restraints which Theologians have attempted to impose upon its inquiries. But when Science, passing beyond its own limits, assumes to take the place of Theology, and sets up its own conception of the Order of Nature as a sufficient account of its Cause, it is invading a province of Thought to which it has no claim, and not unreasonably provokes the hostility of those who ought to be its best friends."

Our next extract is from Sir Benjamin Brodie, and it, too, considers the absolute permanence of the laws of Nature in relation to Design:—

Crites. "There have been sceptics who have believed that the laws of nature were, if I may use the expression, self-existent; and that what we now see around us is but a continuation of a system that has been going on from all eternity—thus dispensing with the notion of a great creative Intelligence altogether."

Eubulus. "Under any view of the subject, it seems to me that it would be very difficult, if not impossible, for any of us practically to separate the marks of design, and of the adaptation of means to ends, which the universe affords, but which are more especially conspicuous in the animal and vegetable kingdoms, from the notion of an intelligent Cause. There is not one of the sceptics to whom you have alluded, who would not, if he were asked the question, "What is the use of the eye?" answer, "that it is intended to be the organ of vision, as the ear is intended to be that of hearing, and as the nostrils are constructed for the purpose of smell." But what I said just now requires some further explanation. When I stated that at the present time there is no evidence of any deviation from certain established laws of nature—that if we could thoroughly know and thoroughly appreciate what those laws really are, we should be able to account for all the phenomena around us—I was far from intending to say that there has never been a period when other laws than those which are now in force were in operation, or that the time may not arrive when the present order of things will be in a similar manner superseded. Looking at the structure of the globe, and the changes in its surface which have been disclosed to the observation of geologists, we recognize the probability that there was a time when this planet of ours was no better than a huge aërolite, and in a state quite incompatible with animal or even vegetable life. The existence of living beings, then, must have had a beginning; yet we have no evidence of any law now in force which will account for this marvellous creation" [77]. *Psychological Inquiries*, Part II., pp. 193-4-5.

The great surgeon next discusses the question of "Equivocal Generation" now known by the terms Archebiosis and Abiogenesis. His opinion, together with some later information on the topic, will be found in our additional notes to Chapter 3.

When writing his first series of "Inquiries" Sir Benjamin recorded his judgment regarding our knowledge and conception of the Divine Existence and in terms which show how closely he connected the general subject of Mind and its Essence with his idea of the Creator.

Eubulus. "When I contemplate the evidence of intention and design which present themselves everywhere around us, but which, to our limited comprehensions, is more especially manifested in the vegetable and animal creations, I cannot avoid attributing the construction and order of the universe to an intelligent being, whose power and knowledge are such that it is impossible for me to form any adequate conception of them, any more than I can avoid referring the motions of the planets and stars to the same law of gravitation as that which directs the motions of our own globe. But no one, I apprehend, will maintain that the mind of the Deity depends on a certain construction of brain and nerves; and Dr. Priestley, the most philosophical of the advocates of the system of materialism, ventures no further than to say that we have no knowledge on the subject. But, to use the words of Sir Isaac Newton, 'This powerful ever-living agent being in all places, is more able to move the bodies within his boundless uniform sensorium, and thereby to form and reform the parts of the universe, than we are, by our will, to move the parts of our own bodies.' The remainder of the passage from which I have made this quotation, is not without interest, as indicating the view which Newton took of the matter in question:—'And yet we are not to consider the world as the body of God, or the several parts thereof as the parts of God. He is an uniform being, void of organs, members, or parts, and they are his creatures, subordinate to him, and subservient to him, and he is no more the soul of them than the soul of man is the soul of the species carried through the organs of sense into the place of its sensation, where it perceives them by its immediate presence, without the intervention of any third thing. The organs of sense are not for enabling the soul to perceive the species of things in its sensorium, but only for conveying them thither; and God has no need of any such organs, he being everywhere present to the things themselves.'"

Ergates. "I entirely agree with you in the opinion that we must admit the existence of the Deity as a fact as well established as that of the law of gravitation, and that in doing so we must further admit that mind may and does exist, independently of bodily organization. Be it also remembered that mind, in its humblest form, is still mind, and that, immeasurable as the distance between them may be, it must nevertheless be regarded as being of the same essence with that of the Deity himself. For my own part I find no difficulty in conceiving the existence of mind independently of corporeal organs." (p. 39, seq.)

Those who have read Professor Huxley's article on the Metaphysics of Sensation [78], will feel much interested in the passages selected from Newton by Sir Benjamin. It seems almost a pity that the accomplished Professor did not cite any of Dr. Clarke's explanatory remarks addressed to Leibniz respecting Sir Isaac Newton's expressions. The similitude above quoted, Clarke explains thus:—

"Mr. Newton considère le cerveau et les organes des sens, comme le moyen par lequel ces images sont Formées et non comme le moyen par lequel l'âme voit ou aperçoit ces images, lorsqu'elles sont ainsi formées. Et dans l'Univers, il ne considère pas les choses, comme si elles étaient des images formées par un certain moyen ou par des organes; mais comme des choses réelles, que Dieu lui-même a formées, et qu'il voit dans tous les lieux où elles sont, sans l'intervention d'aucun moyen. C'est tout ce que Mr. Newton a voulu dire par la comparaison, dont il s'est servi, lorsqu'il suppose que l'Espace infini est, pour ainsi dire, le Sensorium de l'Etre qui est présent partout."

A simpler way of putting the case may be to point out that the comparison of a Sensorium is intended, like other similitudes we have reviewed, to hold in only one point. Newton uses it apparently to localize the idea of immediate intuition. In this way all Space, the whole Universe, with its moving contents, which transcend the farthest flight of human imagination are,—not distantly,—but immediately present to the mind of God.

Passing from these thoughts which may illustrate, but cannot explain, a subject dark with excess of splendour, we now enter on a series of extracts so chosen as to furnish an ample examination of the several ideas involved in the philosophy of Design, and an estimate of their several values. It is evidently important that the reader should possess some means of forming clear conceptions respecting the nature of these ideas, and the collection now appended, aims at saving him the trouble of a tedious search. Any points which may have appeared perplexing or obscure in the preceding Chapter will, it is hoped, be made sufficiently plain by a perusal of the following pages.

The first in this class of passages is taken from Whewell's Philosophy of the Inductive Sciences. No one probably was ever much better fitted by training and attainment than that eminent writer for the investigation he here undertakes. We must, however, caution the reader against supposing that Dr. Whewell means to introduce him into a world of Platonism. The ideas he speaks of may be illustrated in this way. Suppose a person constructs a right line according to Euclid's definition and draws it evenly between its extreme points, his mind has immediately an impression of rightness or straightness, which he attaches to all lines actually so constructed or conceived of as theoretically possible. This idea of straightness is absolute and universal. So, again, looking at two such lines, he knows that they, cannot, in the nature of things inclose a space, and this idea likewise is universal and absolutely true.

With the nature of these ideas as a psychological question, the reader need not concern himself for our present purpose. It is sufficient to observe they are brought into activity by a practical occasion. Whether they were wholly or partially pre-existent—or whether they represent a state of our Reason evoked by the occasion—are points which make no difference to their exact strength of validity. We find as a matter of fact in going through life that this particular class of ideas is so very true that it enables us to gauge the material universe. Yet notably enough, *Hume in his Treatise* (I. 247, seq.) reduces applied mathematics to a species of probability.

Other ideas having various degrees of validity and practical necessity are involved in the diverse processes which pertain to the inductive sciences. Dr. Whewell's work was written for the purpose of elucidating them, which he does at great length. To some such ideas, principles, and beliefs we shall advert by and bye.

All that seems now necessary is to remark that the distinguished author's general division (Book IX.) where our extract will be found, is concerned with the Philosophy of Biology, and that the paragraphs quoted are sections of its chapter 6, "On the Idea of Final Causes."

"1. By an examination of those notions which enter into all our reasonings and judgments on living things, it appears that we conceive animal life as a vortex or cycle of moving matter in which the form of the vortex determines the motions, and these motions again support the form of the vortex: the stationary parts circulate the fluids, and the fluids nourish the permanent parts. Each portion ministers to the others, each depends upon the other. The parts make up the whole, but the existence of the whole is essential to the preservation of the parts. But parts existing under such conditions are organs, and the whole is organized. This is the fundamental conception of organization. 'Organized beings,' says the physiologist [79], 'are composed of a number of essential and mutually dependent parts.'—'An organized product of nature,' says the great metaphysician [80], 'is that in which all the parts are mutually ends and means.'

"2. It will be observed that we do not content ourselves with saying that in such a whole, all the parts are mutually dependent. This might be true even of a mechanical structure; it would be easy to imagine a framework in which each part should be necessary to the support of each of the others; for example, an arch of several stones. But in such a structure the parts have no properties which they derive from the whole. They are beams or stones when separate; they are no more when joined. But the same is not the case in an organized whole. The limb of an animal separated from the body, loses the properties of a limb and soon ceases to retain even its form.

"3. Nor do we content ourselves with saying that the parts are mutually causes and effects. This is the case in machinery. In a clock, the pendulum by means of the escapement causes the descent of the weight, the weight by the same escapement keeps up the motion of the pendulum. But things of this kind may happen by accident. Stones slide from a rock down the side of a hill and cause it to be smooth; the smoothness of the slope causes stones still to slide. Yet no one would call such a slide an organized system. The system is organized, when the effects which take place among the parts are essential to our conception of the whole; when the whole would not be a whole, nor the parts, parts, except these effects were produced; when the effects not only happen in fact, but are included in the idea of the object; when they are not only seen, but foreseen; not only expected, but intended: in short when, instead of being causes and effects, they are ends and means, as they are termed in the above definition.

"Thus we necessarily include, in our idea of Organization, the notion of an End, a Purpose, a Design; or, to use another phrase which has been peculiarly appropriated in this case, a Final Cause. This idea of a Final Cause is an essential condition in order to the pursuing our researches respecting organized bodies....

"5. This has already been confirmed by reference to fact; in the History of Physiology, I have shown that those who studied the structure of animals were irresistibly led to the conviction that the parts of this structure have each its end or purpose;—that each member and organ not merely produces a certain effect or answers a certain use, but is so framed as to impress us with the persuasion that it was constructed for that use;— that it was intended to produce the effect. It was there seen that this persuasion was repeatedly expressed in the most emphatic manner by Galen;—that it directed the researches and led to the discoveries of Harvey;—that it has always been dwelt upon as a favourite contemplation, and followed as a certain guide, by the best anatomists;—and that it is inculcated by the physiologists of the profoundest views and most extensive knowledge of our own time. All these persons have deemed it a most certain and important principle of physiology, that in every organized structure, plant or animal, each intelligible part has its allotted office:—each organ is designed for its appropriate function:—that nature, in these cases, produces nothing in vain: that, in short, each portion of the whole arrangement has its final cause; an end to which it is adapted, and in this end, the reason that it is where and what it is.

"6. This Notion of Design in organized bodies must, I say, be supplied by the student of organization out of his own mind: a truth which will become clearer if we attend to the most conspicuous and acknowledged instances of design. The structure of the eye, in which the parts are curiously adjusted so as to produce a distinct image on the retina, as in an optical instrument;—the trochlear muscle of the eye, in which the tendon passes round a support and turns back, like a rope round a pulley;—the prospective contrivances for the preservation of animals, provided long before they are wanted, as the milk of the mother, the teeth of the child, the eyes and the lungs of the foetus:—these arrangements, and innumerable others, call up in us a persuasion that Design has entered into the plan of animal form and progress. And if we bring in our minds this conception of Design, nothing can more fully square with and fit it, than such instances as these. But if we did not already possess the Idea of Design;—if we had not had our notion of mechanical contrivance awakened by inspection of optical instruments, or pulleys, or in some other way;—if we had never been conscious ourselves of providing for the future;—if this were the case, we could not recognize contrivance and prospectiveness in such instances as we have referred to. The facts are, indeed, admirably in accordance with these conceptions, when the two are brought together: but the facts and the conceptions come together from different quarters—from without and from within.

"7. We may further illustrate this point by referring to the relations of travellers who tell us that when consummate examples of human mechanical contrivance have been set before savages, they have appeared incapable of apprehending them as proofs of design. This shows that in such cases the Idea of Design had not been developed in the minds of the people who were thus unintelligent: but it no more proves that such an idea does not naturally and necessarily arise, in the progress of men's minds, than the confused manner in which the same savages apprehend the relations of space, or number, or cause, proves that these ideas do not naturally belong to their intellects. All men have these ideas; and it is because they cannot help referring their sensations to such ideas, that they apprehend the world as existing in time and space, and as a series of causes and effects. It would be very erroneous to say that the belief of such truths is obtained by logical reasoning from facts. And in like manner we cannot logically deduce design from the contemplation of organic structures; although it is impossible for us, when the facts are clearly before us, not to find a reference to design operating in our minds."

It seems well to add here the practical comments made by Müller and Kant on the passages quoted from them by Dr. Whewell in his first Paragraph. Professor Müller writes thus (Baly's translation, Vol. I., p. 19):—

"The manner in which their elements are combined, is not the only difference between organic and inorganic bodies; there is in living organic matter a principle constantly in action, the operations of which are in accordance with a rational plan, so that the individual parts which it creates in the body, are adapted to the design of the whole; and this it is which distinguishes organism. Kant says, 'The cause of the particular mode of existence of each part of a living body resides in the whole, while in dead masses each part contains this cause within itself.' This explains why a mere part separated from an organized whole generally does not continue to live; why, in fact, an organized body appears to be one and indivisible."

Before proceeding to the great Metaphysician, it may be interesting to place in connection with this extract from Müller, certain views of other distinguished physiologists. Sir C. Bell states his own opinions on the connection of Life and Organization in this manner (Appendix to *Paley's Natural Theology* by Sir Charles Bell, commencing with pp. 211-13):—

"Archdeacon Paley has, in these two introductory chapters, given us the advantage of simple, but forcible language, with extreme ingenuity, in illustration. But for his example, we should have felt some hesitation in making so close a comparison between design, as exhibited by the Creator in the animal structure, and the mere mechanism, the operose and imperfect contrivances of human art.

"Certainly, there may be a comparison; for a superficial and rapid survey of the animal body may convey the notion of an apparatus of levers, pulleys, and ropes—which maybe compared with the spring, barrel, and fusee, the wheels and pinions, of a watch. But if we study the texture of animal bodies more curiously, and especially if we compare animals with each other—for example, the simple structure of the lower creatures with the complicated structure of those higher in the scale of existence—we shall see, that in the lowest links of the chain animals are so simple, that we should almost call them homogeneous; and yet in these we find life, sensibility, and motion. It is in the animals higher in the scale that we discover parts having distinct endowments, and exhibiting complex mechanical relations. The mechanical contrivances which are so obvious in man, for instance, are the provisions for the agency and dominion of an intellectual power over the materials around him.

"We mark this early, because there are authors who, looking upon this complexity of mechanism, confound it with the presence of life itself, and think it a necessary adjunct—nay, even that life proceeds from it: whereas the mechanism which we have to examine in the animal body is formed with reference to the necessity of acting upon or receiving impressions from, things external to the body—a necessary condition of our state of existence in a material world.

"Many have expressed their opinion very boldly on the necessary relation between organization and life, who have never extended their views to the system of nature. To place man, an intelligent and active being, in this world of matter, he must have properties bearing relation to that matter. The existence of matter implies an agency of certain forces;—the particles of bodies must suffer attraction and repulsion; and the bodies formed by the balance of these influences upon their atoms or particles must have weight or gravity, and possess mechanical properties. So must the living body, independently of its peculiar endowments, have similar composition and qualities, and have certain relations to the solids, fluids, gases, heat, light, electricity, or galvanism, which are around it.

"Without these, the intellectual principle could receive no impulse—could have no agency and no relation to the material world. The whole body must gravitate or have weight; without which it could neither stand securely, nor exert its powers on the bodies around it. But for this, muscular power itself, and all the appliances which are related to that power, would be useless. When, therefore, it is affirmed that organization or construction is necessary to life, we may at least pause in giving assent, under the certainty that we see another and a different reason for the construction of the body. Thus we perceive, that as the body must have weight to have power, so must it have mechanical contrivance, or arrangement of its parts. As it must have weight, so must it be sustained by a skeleton; and when we examine the bones, which give the body height and shape, we find each column (for in that sense a bone may be first taken) adjusted with the finest attention to the perpendicular weight that it has to bear, as well as to the lateral thrusts to which it is subject in the motions of the body."... Again p. 405, seq.

... "Mr. Hunter illustrated the subject thus:—Death is apparent or real. A man dragged out of the water, and to appearance dead, is, notwithstanding, alive, according to the definition we have given. The living endowments of the individual parts are not exhausted. The sensibility may be yet roused; the nerves which convey the impression may yet so far retain their property, that other motor nerves may be influenced through them; the muscles may be once more concatenated, and drawn into a simultaneous action. That vibratory motion which we have just said may be witnessed in a muscle recently cut out of the body, may be so excited in a class of muscles—for example, in the muscles of inspiration—that the apparently dead draws an inspiration. Here is the first of a series of vital motions which excites the others, and the heart beats, and the blood circulates, and the sensibilities are restored; and the mind, which was in the condition of one asleep, is roused into activity and volition, and all the common phenomena of life are resuscitated. Such is the series of phenomena which is presented in apparent death from suffocation; but, if the death has been from an injury of some vital part, the sensibilities and properties of action in the rest of the body, though resident for a time, have lost their relations, and there is a link wanting in that chain of vital actions which restores animation. Here, then, there can be no resuscitation; and the death of the individual parts of the body rapidly succeeds the apparent death of the body.

"We perceive now that our original conception of life and the terms we use respecting it, in common parlance, are but ill-adapted to this subject when philosophically considered. We early associate life and motion so intimately that the one stands for the other. If we then investigate by anatomy, we find a curious and minute mechanism in operation, an engine and tubes for circulation, and, in short, an internal motion of every particle of the frame; and the anatomist is also led into the error of associating in his mind life with motion and organization. But when we consider the subject more closely, and divest ourselves of habits and prejudices associated with words, we perceive that, without making any vain and even dangerous attempt at definition, life is first to be contemplated as the peculiarity distinguishing one of two classes into which all matter must be arranged; the one class, which embraces all living matter, is subject to a controlling influence which resists the chemical agents, and produces a series of revolutions, in an order and at periods prescribed; the other, dead matter, is subject to lapse and change under chemical agency and the common laws of matter.

"Let us examine the body of a perfect or a complicated animal. We find each organ possessed of a different power. But there is as yet no conventional language adapted to our discourse on this subject, and that is the source of many mistakes; for when a man even like Mr. Hunter had his mind illuminated upon this science, how was he to frame his language, when every word that he used had already a meaning which had no reference to the discovery he had made—to the distinct qualities which he had ascertained to belong to the living parts?...

"The difference between dead and living matter will appear to be, that in the one instance the particles are permanently arranged and continue to exhibit their proper character, as we term it, until by ingenuity and practice some means are found to withdraw the arranging or uniting influence; and then the matter is chemically dissolved: resolves into its elements, and forms new combinations: whilst the life continues, not simply to arrange the particles, and to give them the order or organization of the animal body, but to whirl them in a series of revolutions, during all which the material is passive, the law being in the life. The order and succession of these changes and their duration do not result from the material of the frame, which is the same in all animals, but from that influence which we term life, and which is superadded to the material." (Ibid. 408.)

Writing on Function Mr. Herbert Spencer discusses the following question. Its interest to our argument is unmistakable.

"Does Structure originate Function, or does Function originate Structure? is a question about which there has been disagreement. Using the word Function in its widest signification, as the totality of all vital actions, the question amounts to this—Does Life produce Organization, or does Organization produce Life?

"To answer this question is not easy, since we habitually find the two so associated that neither seems possible without the other; and they appear uniformly to increase and decrease together.... There is, however, one fact implying that Function must be regarded as taking precedence of Structure. Of the lowest Rhizopods, which present no distinctions of parts, and nevertheless feed and grow and move about, Prof. Huxley has remarked that they exhibit Life without Organization....

"It may be argued that on the hypothesis of Evolution, Life necessarily comes before organization. On this hypothesis, organic matter in a state of homogeneous aggregation, must precede organic matter in a state of heterogeneous aggregation. But since the passing from a structureless state to a structured state, is itself a vital process, it follows that vital activity must have existed while there was yet no structure: structure could not else arise. That function takes precedence of structure, seems also implied in the definition of Life. If Life consists of inner actions so adjusted as to balance outer actions—if the actions are the substance of Life, while the adjustment of them constitutes its form; then, may we not say that the actions to be formed must come before that which forms them—that the continuous change which is the basis of function, must come before the structure which brings function into shape? Or again, since throughout all phases of Life up to the highest, every advance is the effecting of some better adjustment of inner to outer actions; and since the accompanying new complexity of structure is simply a means of making possible this better adjustment; it follows that function is from beginning to end the determining cause of structure."— *Principles of Biology*, by Mr. Herbert Spencer, p. 153, seq.

We now return to Kant, from whom Dr. Whewell quoted the sentence—

"An organized product of nature is that in which all the parts are mutually ends and means."

Passing by a metaphysical paragraph expressed in a manner too technical for the general reader, Kant's practical comment on this sentence runs as follows:—

"Dass die Zergliederer der Gewächse und Thiere, um ihre Structur zu erforschen und die Gründe einsehen zu können, warum und zu welchem Ende solche Theile, warum eine solche Lage und Verbindung der Theile und gerade diese innere Form ihnen gegeben worden, jene Maxime: dass nichts in einem solchen Geschöpf UMSONST sey, als unumgänglich nothwendig annehmen und sie eben so, als den Grundsatz der allgemeinen Naturlehre: dass Nichts von ungefähr geschehe, geltend machen, ist bekannt. In der That können sie sich auch von diesem teleologischen Grundsatze eben so wenig lossagen, als dem allgemeinen physischen, weil, so wie bei Veranlassung des letzteren gar keine Erfahrung überhaupt, so bei der des ersteren Grundsatzes kein Leitfaden für die Beobachtung einer Art von Naturdinge, die wir einmal teleologisch unter dem Begriffe der Naturzwecke gedacht haben, übrig bleiben würde.

"Denn dieser Begriff führt die Vernunft in eine ganz andere Ordnung der Dinge, als die eines blossen Mechanism der Natur, der uns hier nicht mehr genug thun will. Eine Idee soll der Möglichkeit des Naturproducts zum Grunde liegen. Weil diese aber ein absolute Einheit der Vorstellung ist, statt dessen die Materie eine Vielheit der Dinge ist, die für sich keine bestimmte Einheit der Zusammensetzung an die Hand geben kann, so muss, wenn jene Einheit der Idee, sogar als Bestimmungsgrund a priori eines Naturgesetzes der Causalität einer solchen Form des Zusammengesetzten dienen soll, der Zweck der Natur auf ALLES, was in ihrem Producte liegt, erstreckt werden; weil, wenn wir einmal dergleichen Wirkung im Ganzen auf einen übersinnlichen Bestimmungsgrund über den blinden Mechanism der Natur hinaus beziehen, wir sie auch ganz nach diesem

Princip beurtheilen müssen und kein Grund da ist, die Form eines solchen Dinges noch zum Theil vom letzteren als abhängig anzunehmen, da alsdann bei der Vermischung ungleichartiger Principien, gar keine sichere Regel der Beurtheilung übrig bleiben würde." *Kritik der Urtheilskraft*, Section 65.

For the benefit of those who find Kant's German difficult we subjoin a neat French Translation from the pen of M. Barni.

"On sait que ceux qui dissèquent les plantes et les animaux pour en étudier la structure, et pouvoir reconnaître pourquoi et à quelle fin telles parties leur ont été données, pourquoi telle disposition et tel arrangement des parties, et précisément cette forme intérieure, admettent comme indispensablement nécessaire cette maxime que rien n'existe en vain dans ces créatures, et lui accordent une valeur égale à celle de ce principe de la physique générale, que rien n'arrive par hasard. Et en effet ils ne peuvent pas plus rejeter ce principe téléologique que le principe universel de la physique; car, de même qu'en l'absence de ce dernier il n'y aurait plus d'expérience possible en général, de même, sans le premier, il n'y aurait plus de fil conducteur pour l'observation d'une espèce de choses de la nature, que nous avons une fois conçues téléologiquement sous le concept des fins de la nature.

"En effet ce concept introduit la raison dans un tout autre ordre de choses que celui du pur mécanisme de la nature, qui ne peut plus ici nous satisfaire. Il faut qu'une idée serve de principe à la possibilité de la production de la nature. Mais comme une idée est une unité absolue de réprésentation, tandis que la matière est une pluralité de choses qui par elle-même ne peut fournir aucune unité déterminée de composition, si cette unité de l'idée doit servir, comme principe a priori, à déterminer une loi naturelle à la production d'une forme de ce genre, il faut que la fin de la nature s'étende à tout ce qui est contenu dans sa production. En effet, dès que pour expliquer un certain effet, nous cherchons, au-dessus de l'aveugle mécanisme de la nature, un principe supra-sensible et que nous l'y rapportons en général, nous devons le juger tout entier d'après ce principe; et il n'y a pas de raison pour regarder la forme de cette chose comme dépendant encore en partie de l'autre principe, car alors, dans le mélange de principes hétérogènes, il ne resterait plus de règle sûre pour le jugement." Critique du Jugement, Section 65.

Kant is not in any dress the easiest of thinkers to follow—a result possibly consequent upon the resemblance which his writings bear to trains of reasoning as they pass from the lips of one who thinks aloud. The following paragraph from another work of Dr. Whewell's may be useful to some minds as a comment upon this portion of Kant's teleology.

"There is yet one other Idea which I shall mention, though it is one about which difficulties have been raised, since the consideration of such difficulties may be instructive: the Idea of a purpose, or as it is often termed, a Final Cause, in organized bodies. It has been held, and rightly, that the assumption of a Final Cause of each part of animals and plants is as inevitable as the assumption of an efficient cause of every event. The maxim, that in organized bodies nothing is in vain, is as necessarily true as the maxim that nothing happens by chance. I have elsewhere shown fully that this Idea is not deduced from any special facts, but is assumed as a law governing all facts in organic nature, directing the researches and interpreting the observations of physiologists. I have also remarked that it is not at variance with that other law, that plants and that animals are constructed upon general plans, of which plans, it may be, we do not see the necessity, though we see how wide is their generality. This Idea of a purpose,—of a Final Cause,— then, thus supplied by our minds, is found to be applicable throughout the organic world. It is in virtue of this Idea that we conceive animals and plants as subject to disease; for disease takes place when the parts do not fully answer their purpose; when they do not do what they ought to do. How is it then that we thus find an Idea which is supplied by our own minds, but which is exemplified in every part of the organic world? Here perhaps the answer will be readily allowed. It is because this Idea is an Idea of the Divine Mind. There is a Final Cause in the constitution of these parts of the universe, and therefore we can interpret them by means of the Idea of Final Cause. We can see a purpose, because there is a purpose. Is it too presumptuous to suppose that we can thus enter into the Ends and Purposes of the Divine Mind? We willingly grant and declare that it would be presumptuous to suppose that we can enter into them to any but a very small degree. They doubtless go immeasurably beyond our mode of understanding or conceiving them. But to a certain extent we can go. We can go so far as to see that they are Ends and Purposes. It is not a vain presumption in us to suppose that we know that the eye was made for seeing and the ear for hearing. In this the most pious of men see nothing impious: the most cautious philosophers see nothing rash. And that we can see thus far into the designs of the Divine Mind, arises, we hold, from this:—that we have an Idea of Design and of Purpose which, so far as it is merely that, is true; and so far, is Design and Purpose in the same sense in the one case and in the other" [81].

It will be well worth while to close this present series of illustrations by a review of Professor Huxley's last published and best considered positions on Teleology. He printed, in 1871, an article on Haeckel's "Natürliche Schöpfungs Geschichte," and has now entitled it "The Genealogy of Animals," and included it in his recent volume of Critiques. We may therefore assume that we here find the distinguished Biologist's deliberate opinions. He says, p. 305,

"The Teleology which supposes that the eye, such as we see it in man or one of the higher Vertebrata [82], was made with the precise structure which it exhibits, for the purpose of enabling the animal which possesses it to see, has undoubtedly received its death-blow. Nevertheless it is necessary to remember that there is a wider Teleology, which is not touched by the doctrine of Evolution, but is actually based upon the fundamental proposition of Evolution. That proposition is, that the whole world, living and not living, is the result of the mutual interaction, according to definite laws, of the forces possessed by the molecules of which the primitive nebulosity of the universe was composed. If this be true, it is no less certain that the existing world lay, potentially, in the cosmic vapour; and that a sufficient intelligence could, from a knowledge of the properties of the molecules of that vapour, have predicted, say the state of the Fauna of Britain in 1869, with as much certainty as one can say what will happen to the vapour of the breath on a cold winter's day.

"Consider a kitchen clock, which ticks loudly, shows the hours, minutes, and seconds, strikes, cries 'cuckoo!' and perhaps shows the phases of the moon. When the clock is wound up, all the phenomena which it exhibits are potentially contained in its mechanism, and a clever clockmaker could predict all it will do after an examination of its structure.

"If the evolution theory is correct, the molecular structure of the cosmic gas stands in the same relation to the phenomena of the world as the structure of the clock to its phenomena."

Mr. Huxley's comparisons [83] are always amusing, partly because they are of an unlooked for description. They also keep up the attention of his readers or hearers. But they have one great fault—the fault we noticed in explaining the nature of analogical argument—they carry away the mind too far, and lead the reader often, sometimes the writer himself, into very serious oversights. Let us take notice how the Professor carries out his present similitude.

"Now let us suppose a death-watch, living in the clock-case, to be a learned and intelligent student of its works. He might say, 'I find here nothing but matter and force and pure mechanism from beginning to end,' and he would be quite right. But if he drew the conclusion that the clock was not contrived for a purpose, he would be quite wrong. On the other hand, imagine another death-watch of a different turn of mind. He, listening to the monotonous 'tick! tick!' so exactly like his own, might arrive at the conclusion that the clock was itself a monstrous sort of death-watch, and that its final cause and purpose was to tick. How easy to point to the clear relation of the whole mechanism to the pendulum, to the fact that the one thing the clock did always and without intermission was to tick, and that all the rest of its phenomena were intermittent and subordinate to ticking! For all this, it is certain that kitchen clocks are not contrived for the purpose of making a ticking noise.

"Thus the teleological theorist would be as wrong as the mechanical theorist, among our death- watches; and, probably, the only death-watch who would be right would be the one who should maintain that the sole thing death-watches could be sure about was the nature of the clock-works and the way they move; and that the purpose of the clock lay wholly beyond the purview of beetle faculties.

"Substitute 'cosmic vapour' for 'clock,' and 'molecules' for 'works,' and the application of the argument is obvious." (pp. 306, 7.)

One thing is very obvious here—and that is a flaw. State the case as a proposition thus— One or both of the two beetles is to the clock and its maker, as man is to the world and its Maker. A tremendous assumption—surely as sufficient to have startled Francis Bacon as the apparition of a new Idol. Is there any possible reason for elevating a death-watch—thinking in character as a death-watch—into a capable interpreter of clocks? Moreover, the ground principle of our human Teleology is that Man holds a lofty relation, not to the Universe only, but to its Maker likewise. He claims, in a word, the most sublime of all earthly kinships. The very fact that he can look with intelligent and admiring appreciation upon the works of God, justifies his belief that he has a real insight into their excellence, and is so far at least akin to the mind of God. If Mr. Huxley meant that a proportionate degree of insight into clock-making was possessed by his beetles, they would surely have been able to read the clock's dial-plate and understand the lesson conveyed by its pointers. The death-watch would at least say "labuntur horae"—and comprehend that time was being registered—although he might even then fall far short of our human belief "pereunt et imputantur," and fail of knowing that time registers itself in a record of moral good and evil.

The truth is that all mixing up manlike attributes with brute animality, and what seems ten times worse, with machines of wood and metal, can be nothing better than an attempt to produce a sound and prolific offspring from some ill-assorted and heterogeneous hybridism.

We have adverted to this peculiarity of style before and venture upon doing so again, because all admirers of Mr. Huxley's great powers (and who can read his writings without such admiration?) may surely be justified in wishing that he would discard it at once and for ever. Its practical effect is apparently to assume the real point at issue and to cover up the tacit assumption. That he is really no chance offender in this respect may be gathered from a few instances noted at random. We have just had a couple of philosophic death-watches [84] — one a Teleologist, the other a Mechanicist—the lucubrations of both being neither exactly human, nor yet Coleopterous. We observed before a righteous clock [85] —regularly moral if regularly wound up. He has besides a machine, undescribed but endued with a gift of ratiocination [86] —and more curious still a piano [87] which listens when it is played upon, and though possessed of only one sense (hearing) succeeds in building up "endless ideas" of a certain cast and cogency. From this self-educated instrument much may of course be looked for, and accordingly we find

"Its cogitative faculties immersed
In cogibundity of cogitation,"

till it evolves from the depth of its consciousness something like an idealistic theory of sound. This hypothesis, Mr. Huxley in reply to his piano, refutes, first by an appeal to the material substance of the instrument itself; and secondly to the existence of a musician who plays upon it. Will he permit us to accept in like manner the fact of our own nobler subsistence, and also the being of One Who attunes its secret heart-strings to notes of sublime melody?

The monsters aforecited irresistibly remind us of a repartee of Goldsmith's. He wittily said that Dr. Johnson would make little fishes talk like great whales. Had they done so it may be doubted whether the Doctor's idolatrous biographer would have discovered a minnowy mind beneath their Johnsonian utterances. And we confess to a difficulty of our own. The righteous clock is indeed genuinely Huxleian, but what shall we say of his mechanical logic, his piano, and his death- watches? By way of illustrating our perplexity let us suppose some rural sexton to mix up his own instincts with those of a biological burying beetle. The destiny of all flesh would naturally be determined in the first place by a decent covering of earth. But what about its final end? Would that be an aldermanic beetle feast or a Resurgam?

Think again how a member of the Society for the Prevention of Cruelty to Animals might breathe a benevolent spirit into a much employed dissecting knife. The sharp thing would certainly entertain a repugnance to the horrors of vivisection. There might also be a denial of its utility based on the scalpel's personal experience, or perhaps a moral doubt as to whether such means are justified by the ends proposed. Would Mr. Huxley listen to the remonstrance and undertake to lift up his powerful voice at Paris or at Berlin besides a few other remote places which need not be particularized?

Or finally what ear would he lend to a magnifying glass accustomed to habits of observation and possessed by the soul of Spurzheim. Suppose it should affirm that a slice of Destructiveness is recognizably different in structure from a section of Benevolence; and

Acquisitiveness in like manner distinguishable from Ideality! Yet a humanitarian scalpel or Spurzheim magnifying glass may be thought a Huxleian phenomenon.

A truce to such mongrel meditations. We gladly turn away from them and continue our quotations from the Professor's sentiments delivered in propria persona, recommencing at the place where our last extract broke off. (p. 307.)

> "The teleological and the mechanical views of nature, are not necessarily, mutually exclusive. On the contrary, the more purely a mechanist the speculator is, the more firmly does he assume primordial molecular arrangement, of which all the phenomena of the universe are the consequences; and the more completely is he thereby at the mercy of the teleologist who can always defy him to disprove that this primordial molecular arrangement was not intended to evolve the phenomena of the universe."

We quite agree with Mr. Huxley that Mechanism never can exclude final causes, and that a thorough-going theory of Evolution (taken apart from its excrescences) disables the theorist from all real disproof of intention or Design. As we said before, the question of how the theorist's primordial arrangement began, is left unprovided for. And if a beginning, so certainly an end. The more steadily the first state of the Universe conceivable by Science is contemplated, the wider and more determinate the view thus taken, the more evident it becomes that the ground occupied by Natural Theology is not fenced off by the iron pale of Mechanism. The fencer is (as Huxley says) "at the mercy of the Teleologist."

The Professor's next sentence deserves careful consideration—

> "On the other hand, if the teleologists assert that this, that, or the other result of the working of any part of the mechanism of the universe is its purpose and final cause, the mechanist can always inquire how he knows that it is more than an unessential incident— the mere ticking of the clock, which he mistakes for its function."

How far this criticism holds good of many well-meant treatises filled with special instances of Design is a question for candid consideration. Meantime the whole sentence amounts to this conclusion:—We must distinguish between such wide arguments as Baden Powell's, and the details of certain writers who have dealt with what they thought good examples and illustrations of a grand universal principle. And that such is Mr. Huxley's meaning we may perceive from another paragraph immediately preceding our first extract. (p. 305.)

> "In more than one place, Professor Haeckel enlarges upon the service which the Origin of Species has done, in favouring what he terms the 'causal or mechanical' view of living nature as opposed to the 'teleological or vitalistic' view. And no doubt it is quite true that the doctrine of Evolution is the most formidable opponent of all the commoner and coarser forms of Teleology. But perhaps the most remarkable service to the philosophy of Biology rendered by Mr. Darwin is the reconciliation of Teleology and Morphology, and the explanation of the facts of both which his views offer."

Now, such being the state of facts, we may refuse to say with Huxley that the following question (asked p. 307) is "not irrational." "Why trouble oneself about matters which are out of reach, when the working of the mechanism itself, which is of infinite practical importance, affords scope for all our energies?"

We cannot forego our trouble, for two reasons. First, according to the statements before quoted, Mr. Darwin's researches have improved the case for Teleology. Advocates of Design may therefore take courage, they have gained a potent alliance. Secondly, "the practical working of the Mechanism itself" is very far, we think, from being our All—so far, indeed, that it sinks into insignificance compared with the hope of Immortality. Our highest interest lies in gathering such information as we can regarding Him with Whom we have to do as the Arbiter of our future existence. Above all things, we desire Him to be our Father and our Friend. Perchance His attributes are not matters out of reach. He may be very near to every one of us, if we are indeed His Offspring.

Another opinion of Professor Huxley's is of great auxiliary value to the argument from Design. The structures mentioned have to some minds appeared as its most serious difficulties.

> "Professor Haeckel," he explains, "has invented a new and convenient name, 'Dysteleology,' for the study of the 'purposelessnesses' which are observable in living organisms—such as the multitudinous cases of rudimentary and apparently useless structures. I confess, however, that it has often appeared to me that the facts of Dysteleology cut two ways. If we are to assume, as evolutionists in general do, that useless organs atrophy, such cases as the existence of lateral rudiments of toes, in the foot of a horse, place us in a dilemma. For, either these rudiments are of no use to the animal, in which case, considering that the horse has existed in its present form since the Pliocene epoch, they surely ought to have disappeared; or they are of some use to the animal, in which case they are of no use as arguments against Teleology." (p. 307.)

It would be hard to overestimate the value of this opinion, still more hard to overrate its genuine and outspoken honesty.

Mr. Huxley places at the end of his recent volume a passage from Bishop Berkeley which we will venture to borrow by way of conclusion to this lengthy note:—

> "You see, Hylas, the water of yonder fountain, how it is forced upwards in a round column to a certain height, at which it breaks and falls back into the basin from whence it rose; its ascent as well as its descent proceeding from the same uniform law or principle of gravitation. Just so, the same principles which, at first view, lead to scepticism, pursued to a certain point, bring men back to common sense."

Adsit omen! May it be even thus with our large-minded Professor and with all other sovereign princes of Biology— Ἵλεως Ἀσκληπίος !

Chapter 3

CONDITIONS OF HUMAN KNOWLEDGE: ITS DISABILITIES AND FIRST PRINCIPLES— IDEALISM—POSITIVISM—MATERIALISM— WE MUST ACCEPT ULTIMATE TRUTHS

"The words which the great German poet put into the mouth of Mephistopheles when describing himself to Faust, afford perhaps the most concise and forcible statement of what we may call the anti-scientific spirit:—

'Ich bin der Geist der stets verneint,
Dem alles, was entsteht, zuwider ist.'

The true spirit of science is certainly affirmative, not negative; for, as I mentioned just now, its history teaches us that the development of our knowledge usually takes place through two or more simultaneous ideas of the same phenomenon, quite different from one another, both of which ultimately prove to be parts of some more general truth; so that a confident belief in one of those ideas does not involve or justify a denial of the others."— *Address of the President of the British Association*, 1873-4. p. 13.

"Philosophy is but wise and disciplined thought upon the subjects on which all men think. The minds of men, left to their own natural working, will never cease to think on these things; and if Philosophy should cease to attempt to think wisely on them, she abandons her position as a guide. She has been to blame for the carelessness of her procedure, for the over-weeningness of her pretensions. But the remedy is soberness, not scepticism. Is it, after all, an evil, that in some directions we fail to attain certainty by mere thinking?... As in nature, the picture you see is not broad light and dark, but a thousand tender tones and hues melting into each other, and vibrating together between the light and dark: so is the mind of man." Archbishop of York—*On the limits of Philosophical Inquiry*, pp. 25-26.

"To the knowledge of the most contemptible effect in nature, 'tis necessary to know the whole Syntax of Causes, and their particular circumstances, and modes of action. Nay, we know nothing, till we know ourselves, which are the summary of all the world without us, and the Index of the Creation." Glanvill, *Vanity of Dogmatizing*, Chap. xxii. Ed. 1. p. 217.

"A branching channel, with a mazy flood?
The purple stream that through my vessels glides,
Dull and unconscious flows, like common tides:
The pipes through which the circling juices stray,
Are not that thinking I, no more than they:
This frame compacted with transcendent skill,
Of moving joints obedient to my will,
Nurs'd from the fruitful glebe, like yonder tree,
Waxes and wastes; I call it mine, not me."
Dr. Arbuthnot.

"'To the eye of vulgar Logic,' says he, 'what is man? An omnivorous Biped that wears Clothes. To the eye of Pure Reason what is he? A soul, a Spirit, and divine Apparition. Round his mysterious Me, there lies, under all those wool-rags, a Garment of Flesh (or of Senses), contextured in the Loom of Heaven; whereby he is revealed to his like, and dwells with them in UNION and DIVISION; and sees and fashions for himself a Universe, with azure Starry Spaces, and long Thousands of Years. Deep-hidden is he under that strange Garment; amid Sounds and Colours and Forms, as it were, swathed in, and inextricably over-shrouded: yet it is skywoven, and worthy of a God. Stands he not thereby in the centre of Immensities, in the conflux of Eternities? He feels; power has been given him to Know, to Believe; nay does not the spirit of Love, free in its celestial primeval brightness, even here, though but for moments, look through? Well said Saint Chrysostom, with his lips of gold, "the true Shekinah is Man:" where else is the God's-Presence manifested not to our eyes only, but to our hearts, as in our fellow man?'"— Sartor Resartus, Chap. x. *Pure Reason.*

SYNOPSIS OF CHAPTER 3

This Chapter may be characterized as a parallel between the difficulties alleged to be fatal against Theism, and the difficulties attaching to very various departments of human knowledge, embracing its most necessary and its most certainly accepted kinds. From this parallel the conclusion becomes evident, that whoever accepts one set of truths cannot be debarred by these or similar difficulties from accepting the higher truth likewise. That such an acceptance is natural and valid appears further evident from the fact that a knowledge of God belongs to the class of Practical beliefs, and is enforced by the same reasonable necessity. This topic forms the transition to Chapter 4 on "Our Reasonable Beliefs."

The same inferences are also stated in a destructive form, e.g., Should a thinker choose to deny the possibility of Theism, he ought (if consistent) to deny all those truths which stand or fall by a parallel set of reasonings. But by doing this he lands himself in a state of doubt, so extreme and thorough, that the whole Universe becomes a rayless blank.

A corollary is added on Materialism.

Analysis —Man the interpreter of Nature. Nature gives by answering our interrogations; these must depend on our powers of assimilating knowledge. Some questions inevitable, e.g., What are the first grounds of Truth?

Has Man any faculty of apprehending the Infinite? Can we know our own Personality or that of others?—or any Thing in itself? Inference against Scepticism based on human ignorance.

Fallacy of the Unthinkable or Inconceivable. Ideas of Self and not-Self, inexplicable, yet undoubted. From things as they are, let us turn to things as they appear. How do we perceive, hear, see?

Perception as an instrument of Intelligence, inscrutable. We acknowledge the insoluble mystery but accept the fact.

Marvels of eyesight, and their problems. How much and what do we see? Comparison with Sound;—Form, Colour, Tone. Evidence on which we receive sense impressions. Comparison between healthy and diseased sensations,—between our organs of sense and those of animals. We soon arrive at a twilight territory of knowledge and can explain no more.

Imperfections in our powers of Verification. How great is the subjective Element in our perceptions? Idealism,—most difficult to answer when most extreme. Philosophic denial of all proof of external things as distinguished from Mind (e.g., by Mill). Fact-knowledge, and absurdities involved in the ordinary method of defining and alleging Facts. Polar tendencies of Phenomenalism which take the shapes of Idealism and Positivism, resulting in Nihilism or Indifferentism. The end of these things! Mr. Herbert Spencer on Theology, compared with Mr. Huxley, and criticized by Mr. J. Martineau, who denies that the Unknowable can be any object of religious feeling,—a protest strongly maintained by Mr. J. S. Mill.

The difficulties attending every kind of knowledge paralleled with the difficulties alleged against Theism. If the Inexplicable be also the Unknowable, there is an end to all knowledge. We cannot predicate veracity of our human Mind, we cannot even know that we know anything. Mr. J. S. Mill accepts Mind as an inexplicable Fact underlying all other Facts and Beliefs. We must accept ultimate Truths.

Transition to Chapter 4. on the affirmative evidence for our Reasonable Beliefs.

Corollary on Materialism. Far more difficult than its antithesis. Conclusion to be drawn from these difficulties.

Additional Notes and Illustrations

A. Account of some theories respecting our Personal Identity.
B. Helmholtz, Popular Lectures on Recent Progress of the Theory of Vision.
C. Helmholtz on Specialties of Sensibility.
D. Popular account of Pure Idealism with critical remarks.
E. On the Relations of Fact and Theory.
F. On the "Unknowable."
G. Mr. J. S. Mill as an Independent Moralist.

Additions to Corollary

Note:

H.   Archebiosis, or Spontaneous Generation.
I.   On Materialism.

CONDITIONS OF HUMAN KNOWLEDGE

Is the great Book of Nature—the world we live in—a closed or open book to Man? On this question all have thought often,—and many have written much,—students—men of science—religious teachers—poets, and philosophers.

We ask this question of ourselves variously circumstanced, and under various impulses. We ask it if, like AEschylus' watchman, we contemplate

> "The congress of the nightly stars
> Bright potentates, set proudly in the sky."

Or when we sail upon a sea made solemn by its vastness, dying in far distance, with no boundary except itself, as each swelling wave rises against the sky. We ask it, on some stately mountain top looking down over light and shadow,—over the rest and the motion of the landscape. More earnestly still, perhaps, while from the depth of a twilight valley we admire the sunset lingering upon inapproachable alpine snows;—rosy heights unveiling their loveliness, yet soon to be hidden till the Light of this lower world shall shine afresh amongst their clefts and pinnacles.

And who is not in earnest, as sunset and sunrise remind him how the majestic clock of Time moves on? Yonder glorious luminary has warmed with form and life countless organisms, scattered over mountain summits, in ocean depths, through wild savannahs and forests;—organisms throughout regions of earth, water, air, so remote and inaccessible that their wonderful excellence of beauty has never been beheld by Man's perishable eye. Knowing, as we cannot but know, how soon our own eyelids must close beneath the sun, we yearn within our soul, longing for a truer insight into the great Universe above and beyond us; and for a firmer feeling that we ourselves are an imperishable part of it. Somewhere in this Universe, must surely be contained things brighter and better than those we now possess. Else, why is it clothed so lavishly with half-revealed charms, adapted to touch our most delicate sympathies, to win us from our worse selves, and allure us on like willing captives to its loveliness? Awakened in our senses, awakened in our souls, we desire to know, to feel, and to attain;—these three impulses become our fixed and enduring aspirations.

But, how? We all remember that Undine sought a soul and found a sorrow;—a sorrow the more intolerable, because through its burden she first realized her hard-earned dower of coveted immortality. Yet, as she truly says, every creature cannot but strive after that which is naturally higher than itself.

One secret of progress we soon discover. What Nature can give us depends on what she can tell us. And here is a prevailing motive for the endeavour to unclose fair Nature's book.

Another step in thought is early taken in our day, though the civilized world was slow in reaching it. We soon perceive that Nature's answers must catch their tone and compass from our interrogations. In numerous sciences, this axiom carries the whole theory and practice of experiment;—that grand distinction between Bacon's inductive process, and the induction of the ancient world. In other walks of inquiry, intellectual and moral, the same truth has grown up and blossomed with a ruling idea of the crucial or prerogative question: slow in being framed, and difficult often in the asking, but, when asked, certain to elicit a reply.

A third postulate is also quickly apparent. Our inquiries must be subject, for utility's sake, to our power of assimilating knowledge. And thus our faculty for asking questions is governed by our faculties for apprehending answers.

The last and paramount requirement is forced upon us. Beyond and over all, comes the pressure of our own need and private anxiety. There are many truths which we discern afar off, like features of a smiling land of promise; and, knowing that they must become one day the heritage of mankind, we tend towards them without haste, yet without forgetfulness, and in this temper of mind wait contentedly. But, there are some truths for which we cannot afford to wait. They concern our destinies too closely; they are too near our hearts; too influential on our lives and happiness. The old question asked in the youth of human philosophy, is the one we all begin by asking in our first confidence and eagerness of pursuit. Ask it in what words we may, it always comes to much the same thing; and if we could answer it, we should answer all questions in one. For, though we clothe our query with various shapes, and seldom put it in the form following, its true meaning is, "what are the realities of the Universe, and what the essential ground of all we see and think?"

It is always worth a thinker's while to look this human problem more than once in the face. Suppose a faculty [88] for such insight granted, it must be different in kind, rather than degree, from our logic of ordinary life. It cannot proceed discursively, abstracting, generalizing, connecting, deducing. It must know—or look at its object directly, just as genius knows, images and conveys to other minds, not through a train of explanatory definition, but by kindling within them a spark of its own light. If there be such a faculty, it will work, (as Aristotle [89] says of the Supreme Intellect,) by what seems to us most like an act of touch; a figure half-shadowed out when we say we grasp or apprehend a truth; and much as St. Paul speaks, in bidding men to seek and feel after and find the Lord.

We are not all conscious of such a faculty. But if dim to some, is it certainly dim to all? Did Plato see farther than Herschel could when he burst the barriers of the sky? Did Schelling at any time behold what Hamilton pronounced invisible? [90]

Or again, if not actually ours now,—if those who have asserted it have spoken in error,—is there a hope that in the Future of Man individual or collective, he will ever grow up to it? The thought is not unknown to physicists as well as moralists. In both camps hopeful minds have conceived the possibility. And, then Mankind will look the secret of the Universe face to face.

Meanwhile, thinking men have laid siege to the absolute Truth by aid of such powers as they commonly call into action. For centuries past, the nature of things in themselves,—and along with (or perhaps above) all other natures, the "Self" within every man has been among the most fascinating of objects pursued by human thought. Yet, how far do we really know the life throbbing in every pulse? Can we tell the secret of our own individuality? We feel it every day;—it endues us with a separate existence, distinctly several, and apart from others, and so intensely vivid to ourselves, that we seem in our own eyes like small centres of the

Universe, with men and women,—nay, worlds and stars,—revolving round us [91]. Yet, strange to say, our bodies are at all times undergoing change, sufficient in a few years to eliminate their present frame, and remould a future compound of gradually assimilated elements. And it seems stranger still, that while the law of Change rules supreme in these fabrics,—(built to be continually dissolved and continually built again),—each rude mark and scar maintains its place; no old wound forgets to ache; no cicatrice even, nor superficial blemish, dies quite away. We are always changing, always being transformed; yet, to each of our bodies continues its one individual configuration; within each of our minds its self-collection, its memories, its expectations, and its individual consciousness [t].

Weighing these inconsistencies together, shall we say that, in any proper sense, we know our own selves? And, if not, can we expect truly to know the self of anything? May we not travel further, and inquire whether we can conceive a self-ness of any kind,—whether the very idea is not to us absolutely inconceivable? And, when this question is answered as it must be answered, need we feel surprised if we fall short of conceiving the self-subsistent God? At what value, therefore, shall we rate sceptical arguments drawn from our failure; and resting on the fallacious consequence, that the inconceivable (or unthinkable as some prefer to call it) is likewise the impossible? [u]

That a fallacy really lurks beneath these words,—that the contrary is true, we know as a matter of fact [92]. We entertain really no doubt whatever of our own continued sameness, and individual existence. We are quite sure that our self-ness has, gone on throughout the years of our natural life. How it first became clear to our inward sense, is a point confessedly disputable. Some suppose that it existed as a principle of consciousness,—a kind of primordial instinct in our minds. Others—that our internal impressions, one and all, formed a panoramic scene; impressions from without and impressions from within evenly painted on the retina of the mental eye. Time and comparison were needful to give us the true distinction. Those who think thus usually take another step; and add that resistance to our self-ness first informs us of its being. There is resistance to a muscular sense, somewhat akin to touch, but specialized to feel the kind of impact given by things impenetrable. There is also a resistance which thwarts our desires, endeavours, and determinations. Be this as it may, we never doubt our own identity of being; we never doubt the other-ness and outer-ness of beings like ourselves, and of objects beyond number. Yet, that which makes ourselves and them, what we and they are,— our self-ness and their self-ness—raises a question we cannot answer; here is, we feel, a something which overpasses our means of investigation. Men, however, do not stay to discuss such questions, or to test the origin and limits of intellectual conceptions before accepting the fact. They do not even ask whether Philosophical victory sits on the banner of Idealism, pure or constructive; Realism materialistic or natural;—or whether it crowns any other imaginable variety of cosmological theorem. We are perfectly sure of our facts; and no array of possible difficulties whatsoever can prevail to shake our assurance.

Let us leave for the present, in its native shadows, the central point of our own self; the original centre of our earliest apparent universe. Yet, if we cannot know this first growing-point of our individual life, it may be useful to inquire what can we know about it? can we learn, for example, how that inner vitality, once begun, is maintained and fed?—By a process of receiving into itself, (we are told), the aliment which flows through our senses. We are also told, (as appeared in the last chapter), how very requisite is a knowledge of natural processes. Let us, then, look at this process of sense-alimentation, narrowing the problem as much as possible. We have already cut off one end of it—the germ-point of the self -stimulated; and will now cut off another piece—the assimilation of mental ideas when elaborated. We simply ask how does this food from without, get into us? The widest avenue of entrance is proverbially our sense of eyesight. Its information, (as people in general agree, from Horace down to Mr. Mill), being gathered through many definite impressions, and received from all distances, is at once the most significant, and the most commanding. The first step is clear. We see by impinging rays of light,—movements in a luminiferous ether, making images on the sensitive network of the eye; a circumstance ascertained by the same sense of sight which receives the image. From this delicate surface, begins a second series of movements;—they take place this time in an organized nerve-material, and are carried, like telegraph-currents, to the Sensory. Arrived there, we may next suppose that they excite some new motions, or corpuscular changes. Do we know— can we know any more? Is the grammar or dictionary written which translates them into the language of the mind; or teaches us how we have, since our infancy, worked a perpetual miracle of speech respecting each of them? The eye, as an optical instrument [v], is a marvel of science displayed; the eye as an instrument of intelligence, especially of human intelligence, is a marvel of inscrutable mystery.

The mysteries of every-day life are the last things dreamed of in every-day philosophy. When we wake up to their existence, it is astonishing to find how continually, without being able to explain things, we can feel, and know them;—know them that is in the sense of acting intelligently (without theorizing) upon them.

The example we have taken, teaches us several good and important lessons. There is in it much we can understand; much that we cannot understand; and a twilight territory between the intelligible and the non-intelligible. All three are, of course, mixed together when we speak of sight,—in itself, a matter of every-day experience. So far as the mechanical construction of an optical chamber goes, everything seems obvious. We can, likewise, perceive how well contrived is the apparatus for washing and wiping the outside transparent surface. Also, the value of its arched hedge against irritants dropping upon the eyeball from above; and of the arrangements for altering both axis and focus instantaneously. But what does this instrument enable us to see? Not the rays of light themselves,—only objects which they illuminate. The space traversed by rays from all suns and all stars, remains itself unseen. The ether which fills space is invisible,—yet its motions make the light of the world [93]. Then, too, the nervous screen on which these ray movements are received, is not sensitive to all transmitted undulations. Red excites the optic nerve by striking it with four hundred and seventy-four millions of millions of wave-impacts in a single second. Violet strikes it in the same time with six hundred and ninety-nine millions of millions of impulses [94]. These two colours are the extremes of the light octave. In an octave of sound, the highest note vibrates twice as quickly as the lowest. So too, the shortest wave of violet is half the length of the longest red wave, and its motion is twice as rapid. But the curious point is that the human ear receives eleven octaves in the scale of sound; [95] —the human eye has a range over only one octave in the scale of light.

Our remarks have carried us over the borders of the twilight territory,—a circumstance we may ascertain by putting into words what we think we know, and our reasons for thinking that we know it. If the eye be in focus, (but not otherwise), a line of light—that is to say moving imponderable matter of extreme tenuity—so passes through its transparent liquids as to strike a sensitive spot, and there produce what is called an image. We apprehend in our minds this image-producing function as a relation between light and the effect realized. A relation definite and exact,—in scientific language a "constant"; which we can formulate into optical laws, and thus express with useful nicety. Taking advantage of the laws thus obtained, and employing that light-power which everywhere blesses our world, we reproduce the like, image upon a screen. Its likeness we gather from comparison, by looking into an eye from without. Both images, thus seen by us, are in point of fact similar sensations.

A philosophic reader may at once perceive what the Idealist will infer respecting this act of comparison. Neither image—on retina or on screen—exists apart from the eye. So far as we know, if there were no eyes there would be no images; and some writers (e.g., Schleiden) have positively affirmed that without eyes all would be, not only to us, but in itself, darkness;—the world absolutely void of Light. But the truth may be summed in a sentence. Light is not for the eye in the same sense that the eye is for light. Light is for other things besides. It exerts its activity on life, animal and vegetable;—on inorganic substances;—and in other ways likewise.—Going no further than our screen, we can so manage matters as to engrave and otherwise fix the image thrown upon it;—in other words our moving line of imponderable matter will produce further effects, chemical and mechanical, visible and palpable.

Proceeding to a cross-examination of the knowledge with which we have credited ourselves, our next business is to try whether we can verify the objectivity of our optical image. Now it impresses sight in two respects,—as superficial form—and as colour. The family of forms is, we are aware widely connected. Sound evokes them. Draw a violin bow across a string stretched over finely silted sand, and the different notes will be correlated by a diversity of shapes [96], into which the sand will arrange itself. Therefore, we ought to find means of verifying Form without much difficulty. Indeed we do so every day satisfactorily; our hands are perpetually demonstrating the general accuracy of our eyes, and even those delicate instruments our finger-ends, do not always add much to the information sight has given us.

But about colour? Distinct colour-waves have (as we said before) distinct velocities, and are therefore objectively distinguished even in the inorganic universe. They also act differently upon the growth of animals and plants,—and other distinctions might be added. The sensation is, however, our point,—the special thing called colour both by careful speakers and in child parlance,—what do we really know about this? Little indeed except as an impression received by sight. The man born in complete blindness taking a piece of red cloth to examine, described the fabric minutely; but, when asked if he could say anything about its redness, likened that "hue angry and brave" to the sound of a trumpet. A simile most conclusive,—suggested probably by his having often heard of certain "scarlet-coated gentry";—and proving beyond doubt that colour is non-existent in the sensory of a person affected from birth by a deep-seated lesion. To one less thoroughly blind, spectra are possible, and red light may be produced under pressure. It thus appears, that colour must be perceived by a nervous substratum, called the rod and cone layer; and hence we explain our power of distinctly seeing the blood-vessels of the retina lying immediately before that structure [97].

These curiosities, of vision shew that our powers of verifying shape are superior to our powers of verifying colour [98]; add, too, that the latter sensation, (as an idealist might maintain,) is known to be sometimes unreal, since it occurs without a coloured object. We can produce it, for instance, by gazing at the sun—a phenomenon mentioned by Aristotle. But then, this ideal sense-affection ranges with a variety of others, which taken together constitute a very much wider law. Not to mention many superinduced mental states, we see light under the influence of a touch or blow,—of electricity,—of chemicals, such as narcotic medicines, which attack the nervous system. We hear sound under like appliances stimulating the auditory nerve. And the whole of these affections are to be explained by another Aristotelian doctrine, extended and pushed to its consequences. Special senses have their own proper faculties, and when called into action each exerts its power within its special province. Had Aristotle dissected out nerve-fibres, he might have discovered the larger empire of specialty now known to our anatomists [99].

Idealism easily widens its doubt, to correspond with the dimensions of the wider nervous law. Does not an aptitude for special impressions, so stringently determined as to translate the antecedent "blow" into the consequent, "light" or "sound," disqualify our senses for giving evidence respecting supposed facts of the outer world? As for the "distinctive impressibility of the eye," as Mr. Bain [100] describes colour, it need not be held real except for our own sensorium, [w] and if colour be a questionable reality, other alleged realities become questionable too. The world we live in, may be a totally different world from what we are taught, generation after generation, to believe it. Who can lay down the limits of what our minds create for themselves outside us? [101]. The mental disease of the madman causes his eye to see that which is not. Guilt and sickness fill bedchambers with unreal spectres. Putting disease aside, and taking the case of healthy eye and healthy mind, it is confessedly difficult to define the exact province of each. A boy couched by Cheselden [102] saw all things in one plane; there was no perspective, and objects in the room seemed to touch his eyeballs. The mind creates perspective, how much then may it not create? The mind also refuses to surrender its own associations at the bidding of optical laws. Mr, Wheatstone's ingenious instrument called the Pseudoscope, brings into play laws which reverse the impressions of solidity and hollowness. A person looking through it steadily at the face of a statue sees a hollow mask. The convexity of feature is gone, and a concave set of features (representing the bust reversed) is perceived in its stead. But, let the same person gaze through his pseudoscope ever so long at the face of a human being, and he will look for a like reversal in vain. The flesh and blood features refuse to change;—in other words, the mind refuses to yield its long-accustomed impression [103]. If these things and others like them are fairly considered, what becomes of our readings in the unclosed book of Nature? The nature we see is our own thought reflected back again. Nature's answers take not only tone and compass, but meaning and utterance from our own interrogations. We think that we are assimilating knowledge, when we are actually engaged in manufacturing aliments to suit our own intellectual digestions. The most inward of all things,—our essential self,—at once retired into shadow when we pursued it; and now, in trying to show how self is fed by substance from without, we have learned to suspect that all its food is unsubstantial [x].

We may henceforth consider ourselves face to face with Sphinx; and it is well to take the true measure of her lineaments. If the above reasoning be sound, to know, is to make a mirror and reflect ourselves back from it. To verify, is to put ourselves in new postures before our infallible mirror. Each fresh item of induction, is a freshly reflected phantom. At all events, the contrary position will never be established. Ignorant as we are, respecting the true centre of our mental firmament, we must necessarily be always more ignorant respecting all possibilities which seemingly outlie its glowing horizon. No one who rationally weighs the worth of a fact, or who decomposes it into its elementary constituents, will ever be absurd enough to imagine that he can disprove the ideal theory by proving the truth of its opposite.

The strongest strain of Idealism comes upon the last sentence. Some years ago, English philosophers had agreed in the conclusion that all debates must for the future be settled by an appeal to facts. Could there be a more happily chosen ground for arbitration?—or one better suited to the calibre of everybody concerning whose business-like reflections we might say, with King Henry,—

> "His thinkings are below the moon"?

Some inquiring spirits preferred "law," but then they agreed with all others, (except transcendentalists,) that a law to be valid must also be a fact.

A belief in this settlement still pervades most non-philosophic circles. A fact is now-a-days an infallible remedy for the disturbed mind; just as once

> "the sovereign'st thing on earth
> Was parmaceti for an inward bruise."

A mind too disturbed to abstain from logical litigation when this receipt is administered, must certainly be afflicted with monomania. Nobody, of course, (whether Idealist or Transcendentalist,) need feel much aggrieved by being called mad. At some time or other, it is the common lot of all, from a murderer proud of being caught red-handed in our day, to a Jewish Pharisee and the son of a Pharisee, long ago departed to his rest. Besides, some madnesses are so fortunate as to justify themselves, an event now happening to Idealists [104]. In Germany, France and England, the persuasion gains ground that no tasks are so difficult as first to define, and secondly to establish a fact.

Now the task of a Natural Theologian, is to establish, (if he can), the greatest and most solemn of all facts. In order to do his work honestly, he must ascertain as far as possible the conditions of proof, the ground on which fact-knowledge reposes. And it will be admitted that the problem of evidence raised by Idealism, is difficult, crucial, and underlies all other problems. "The most fundamental questions in philosophy," says Mr. Mill, "are those which seek to determine what we are able to know of external objects, and by what evidence we know it" [105].

This field of inquiry is therefore of the most supreme interest to us. Idealism possesses an additional attraction for anyone who argues under a belief in the final victory of truth. Both sides of the argument may be placed in high relief, without incurring the imputation of bad faith, or worse morality; and thus Idealism furnishes what used to be sought for during the days of tournaments,—a strictly neutral, ground.

In this ordeal let no one think a single effort directed

> "To crush a butterfly or brain a gnat."

Reasoners on "hard texts" seldom commit any error between premises and conclusion;—granted the former, the other will surely follow. Most oversights occur—or are slipped in—over the first postulates [106]. These generally appear very simple and very true, and pass unquestioned. Yet, no primary truth can ever be very simple to man, else why so many conscientious doubters?

What indeed can seem more simply true than the admission of a fact? Yet facts are often inspissated theories, while many theories are merely explained facts. One of the greatest authorities on Inductive Philosophy writes thus (Whewell's *Philosophy of the Inductive Sciences*. Ed. 2. Vol. I. p. 45)—

"We are often told that such a thing is a Fact; A Fact and not a Theory, with all the emphasis which, in speaking or writing, tone or italics or capitals can give. We see from what has been said, that when this is urged, before we can estimate the truth, or the value of the assertion, we must ask to whom is it a Fact? what habits of thought, what previous information, what Ideas does it imply, to conceive the Fact as a Fact? Does not the apprehension of the Fact imply assumptions which may with equal justice be called Theory and which are perhaps false Theory? in which case, the Fact is no Fact. Did not the ancients assert it as a Fact, that the earth stood still, and the stars moved? and can any Fact have stronger apparent evidence to justify persons in asserting it emphatically than this had?"

The generality of English jurymen might be expected to give an affirmative verdict. For have they not seen with their own eyes the Sun rise up in the East, ascend to the top of the sky, and go down in the West? And is not seeing, believing?

The question, what elements are required to yield the product of trustworthy perception, phenomenon, or fact, is investigated by Dr. Whewell through several pages preceding the one from which we have quoted. After discussing it at length, he writes (p. 42):

"And thus, we have an intelligible distinction of Fact and Theory, if we consider Theory as a conscious, and Fact as an unconscious inference, from the phenomena which are presented to our senses."

The subject is in itself so singularly interesting that a few more extracts are added in our Additional Notes [y]. Let the reader, while perusing them, remember that Idealism once so sovereign in its empire, is only the other pole of a line of thought which just now happens to be in the ascendant. Both poles strongly resemble half-truths. And what is more delusive in evidence than a half-truth, or more perilously sophisticating to the mind of him who utters it?

The thorough-paced Idealist deals with the presentations of his inner consciousness, precisely as the Positivist deals with the presentations of his outer senses. They are his phenomena, his facts. Beyond the circumstances of their inward occurrence and succession he knows and can know nothing. You may arrange them into series of antecedents and consequents,—and then the observation becomes a law,—a law of association, uniform order, or necessary connection: whichever you may choose to call it. In one respect, he has an advantage over the Positivist. No thinker equidistant from both, is likely to deny that primary facts are for every man, the phenomena most immediately apparent to his own consciousness.

Amongst ordinary men, however, the reasoning Idealist seldom appears; the Idealist in feeling and temper is by no means rare. A man weary and worn by sorrow or old age, thinks and speaks of his life as very like a dream. And numbers who have exhausted the strength of self-controlling will, loiter along their way, regardless whether a moving panorama on each hand is or is not, an unreality. Like travel-tired travellers down the Danube, or the Rhine, they interweave scenes bright and dark, as they float by, in one endless train of dimly felt reverie.

The same characteristic holds good in regard to many a Positivist. Very few people have ever examined those iron wheels, on which the conclusions of Positively-inclined writers seem to run so rapidly. They may be flawed—they may be true—hardly any one has thought of sounding them. But common life has its Positivism, as well as its Chemistry; and the Positivism of common life is everywhere. It saves labour,—you may take facts as you find them. It troubles no one,—a Pyrrhonic posture is the easiest of attitudes. It frees busy people from moral anxieties, ideal terrors, the shadows of futurity. In short, to men of the world it is neither more nor less than Indifferentism.

The comparison between these two Nihilistic tendencies might be pushed farther, but it has been carried far enough for our purpose. Both sorts, when viewed as principles of practical life, coincide in yielding the conclusion we now wish to deduce. It is folly to be deterred from the pursuit of ultimate truth, by any amount of speculative difficulty whatsoever. And the reason is plain. Practical truths—the beliefs which affect our hearts and lives—are always ultimate truths. To give them up, is to give up our highest and best,—perhaps our all. It is worse than useless to quail before intellectual obstacles. The Difficult soon begins to appear the Impossible.

And soon the result ensues, which might naturally be expected. Is it possible to imagine any discouragement heavier, than the feeling that we can effect little to acquire a knowledge of truth, goodness, and God;—a feeling, that do what we will, all we want most—all that is truly Divine—must remain to us a darkness or a dream? Let any man think in his heart, that what ought to rule his life, and raise him higher than his lower self, is a secret unknowable, and he loses the fear of doing wrong;—for how can he help it?—and the hope of a brighter and better future;—for how shall he attain it? Then, he sits down to wrap himself in cynical self-sufficingness. Inevitable ignorance is soon developed into intellectual Pessimism. The death of hope and fear, makes the man himself a moral Pessimist. Our conscience, sympathy, devotion, happiness in higher and in lower things alike,—if unstirred by vivid emotions—must become dull and blunted. Next follows

"The waveless calm, the slumber of the dead;"—

a state of suspended animation, broken only by fierce stimulants—the galvanisms of, our lower life. These are succeeded, in due course, by spasmodic susceptibilities, which demand at no distant day the anodyne and the narcotic. And—

"Oh, that way madness lies!"—

Therefore we repeat it,—and it cannot too often or too earnestly be repeated,—let no man excuse himself from the pursuit of practical truth [z] by any amount of speculative difficulty whatsoever. It would be a false optimism to say there is no difficulty in thinking truly;—to represent its difficulties as trifles;—or to forget the painful fact that they beset our age of cold erudite criticism, like pitfalls in the Valley of the Shadow of Death. But, must not all things really great and good be toilsome to men who are neither very good nor very great? And have we not, every one of us, who tries to be good, our proper fields of hard yet repaying work? The bee gathers honey where one idle schoolboy sees only thorns and briers—and where another sucks poison.

In our days, Doubt is thorough. So thorough, that it soon ceases to be doubt, and the mind passes quickly from its dim twilight to a rayless blank. Mr. Herbert Spencer puts the case of Theology as follows (*First Principles* p. 43):

"Criticising the essential conceptions involved in the different orders of beliefs, we find no one of them to be logically defensible. Passing over the consideration of credibility, and confining ourselves to that of conceivability, we see that Atheism, Pantheism, and Theism, when rigorously analysed, severally prove to be absolutely unthinkable."

These three conceptions the writer does in fact analyse after his own fashion,—briefly first, pp. 30-36,—and further on argues the whole question in extenso. The result, of course, is that all three "beliefs" must finally be abandoned. What then becomes of the Absolute ground, or First Cause of all things? Spencer is too clear-sighted not to acknowledge that there must in reason be a First, and an Absolute.

"M. Herbert Spencer," says Ravaisson [107], "en proclamant la grande maxime que nous ne connaissons rien que de relatif, a fait cependant une réserve importante. L'idée même du relatif, remarque-t-il, ne saurait se comprendre sans celle à laquelle elle est opposée. Et nous concevons, en effet, au delà de toutes les relations de phé nomènes, l'absolu: c'est ce quelque chose qui est placé au delà de toute science, et qui est l'objet de la religion; quelque chose seulement de mystérieux, d'obscur, sur quoi on ne peut avoir, selon M. Spencer, aucune lumière."

The last negative clause is amply justified on p. 113 of "First Principles."

"By continually seeking to know, and being continually thrown back with a deepened conviction of the impossibility of knowing, we may keep alive the consciousness that it is alike our highest wisdom and our highest duty to regard that through which all things exist as The Unknowable."

And this closing word becomes with Spencer, the constant name of a Power, the consciousness, of which is "manifested to us through all phenomena" [108].

Such a position, maintained by such a writer, has of course met with ample consideration. Mr. Huxley appears to have arrived at a somewhat similar conclusion. Of Religion he says [109],

"Arising, like all other kinds of knowledge, out of the action and interaction of man's mind, with that which is not man's mind, it has taken the intellectual coverings of Fetishism or Polytheism; of Theism or Atheism; of Superstition or Rationalism. With these, and their relative merits and demerits, I have nothing to do; but this it is needful for my purpose to say, that if the religion of the present differs from that of the past, it is because the theology of the present has become more scientific than that of the past; because it has not only renounced idols of wood and idols of stone, but begins to see the necessity of breaking in pieces the idols built up of books and traditions and fine-spun ecclesiastical cobwebs, and of cherishing the noblest and most human of man's emotions, by worship 'for the most part of the silent sort' at the altar of the Unknown and Unknowable."

Concerning this general idea (or negation of Idea) Mr. J. Martineau has made antagonistic observations, by way of criticism on Mr. Spencer's book.

"To say," he writes [110], "that the First Cause is wholly removed from our apprehension is not simply a disclaimer of faculty on our part; it is a charge of inability against the First Cause too.... And in the very act of declaring the First Cause incognizable, you do not permit it to remain unknown. For that only is unknown, of which you can neither affirm nor deny any predicate; here you deny the power of self-disclosure to the 'Absolute,' of which therefore something is known;—viz., that nothing can be known,"

And again with much force [111],

"You cannot constitute a religion out of mystery alone, any more than out of knowledge alone; nor can you measure the relation of doctrines to humility and piety by the mere amount of conscious darkness which they leave. All worship, being directed to what is above us and transcends our comprehension, stands in presence of a mystery. But not all that stands before a mystery is worship" [aa].

Mr. Mill (doing battle with another antagonist) denies every attribute claiming faith and worship, to the idea of a morally Unknowable God. The passage occurs in his Examination of Hamilton, pp. 123-4.

"If, instead of the 'glad tidings' that there exists a Being in whom all the excellences which the highest human mind can conceive, exist in a degree inconceivable to us, I am informed that the world is ruled by a being whose attributes are infinite, but what they are we cannot learn, nor what are the principles of his government, except that 'the highest human morality which we are capable of conceiving' does not sanction them; convince me of it, and I will bear my fate as I may. But when I am told that I must believe this, and at the same time call this being by the names which express and affirm the highest human morality, I say in plain terms that I will not. Whatever power such a being may have over me, there is one thing which he shall not do: he shall not compel me to worship him" [ab].

Now, suppose that instead of siding on this occasion with Mill and Martineau, we were to accept the alternative offered by Spencer and Huxley. Would this surrender of Natural Theology—or rather of all Theology—necessitate in reason any other vast surrender also? We have already answered in the affirmative. The surrender would penetrate every field of knowledge and of thought. We have already shewn this. For, the thread binding the present section into a connected whole runs thus: Survey the conditions of interrogating, first, nature; secondly, our own highest nature; next, our senses; finally, our consciousness; and add to them the enormous difficulties which attend every step taken in compliance with those indispensable conditions. Indispensable, that is, to our knowing anything, of any sort, in any way whatsoever. You have, then, no right to isolate Theism. It is false logic, to speak of the intellectual difficulties attaching to our apprehension of the Deity, as if they were substantial objections. In this respect, Theism stands within the same category of speculative perplexity, and reasonable necessity, as do other supreme truths [112].

Put the case to the judgment of Reason, once for all. If we agreed to accept Herbert Spencer's position, we should consent to deny that anything can be known of an Absolute. And the denial would proceed upon this maxim:—"whatsoever is inexplicable is also unknowable." Consider, now, what other ultimate truths would fall into the same tomb-like Category. We must silence all human utterance respecting all first grounds;—our own individuality;—and every object of reason which becomes inconceivable, when we attempt to define it by the processes of ordinary logic. All utterance respecting our own senses and sensations;—our own existence, as beings distinct from a world of beings and things really existing outside us.

In fine, we could never know that we know either anything or nothing; for, we should have silenced the deepest of all utterances,— the one upon which all truth and reason depend. We should have relegated our Mind along with our God, to the same abysmal gulf of the Unknowable. Henceforth, we could predicate of Mind nothing essential to purposes of knowledge,—and least of all essentials,—Veracity.

Mr. Mill closes his laborious endeavours to explain our natural belief in Mind as follows:

"The truth is, that we are here face to face with that final inexplicability, at which, as Sir W. Hamilton observes, we inevitably arrive when we reach ultimate facts; and in general, one mode of stating it only appears more incomprehensible than another, because the whole of human language is accommodated to the one, and is so incongruous with the other, that it cannot be expressed in any terms which do not deny its truth. The real stumbling-block is perhaps not in any theory of the fact, but in the fact itself. The true incomprehensibility perhaps is, that something which has ceased, or is not yet in existence, can still be in a manner, present: that a series of feelings, the infinitely greater part of which is past or future, can be gathered up, as it were, into a single present conception, accompanied by a belief of reality. I think, by far the wisest thing we can do, is to accept the inexplicable fact, without any theory of how it takes place; and when we are obliged to speak of it in terms which assume a theory, to use them with a reservation as to their meaning" [113].

Two pages further he ingenuously adds:

"I do not profess to have adequately accounted for the belief in Mind."

In other words, the perplexities remain on Mill's system as they do on all systems. But the Belief and the Fact remain likewise.

It is the same with our belief of other ultimate facts. We live an individual life,—we know not what. We see and perceive,—we know not how. Yet such are the facts, and we thoroughly believe and act upon them.

The pivot on which these and similar beliefs turn is a subject of the greatest interest and importance. On this same pivot turns our primary affirmative Argument for Natural Theism. To establish it will be the purpose of the next Chapter, and a succession of affirmative arguments, separate but convergent, will occupy the remainder of this Essay.

Corollary:—If any reader of these pages has felt the fascination of some one among the many materializing hypotheses now in vogue, let him remember that, in fair debate, Materialism can never have the slightest chance against Idealism.

All materializing theories labour under an enormous weight of unverified postulates. They set out from neither the most natural, nor yet the surest, sources of our knowledge.

Naturally, we start from self-ness, and learn to put outer things and beings in opposition to our own primary self- consciousness.

In after life, when we ask why we are sure of any kind of knowledge; the primary truths upon which all our reasonings proceed, are always the presentations of our own mind.

If we proceed to analyse accepted relativities, we soon perceive that Mind enters into our facts, and also into our sense-presentations. In particular, an examination of the noblest of all senses—the sense of sight—will convince any careful analyst that such is undeniably the case. The reader may recal Mr. Mill's words [114], —"I do not believe that the real externality to us of anything, except other minds, is capable of proof." "For ourselves," says Professor Fraser, "we can conceive only—(1) An externality to our present and transient experience in our own possible experience past and future, and (2) An externality to our own conscious experience, in the contemporaneous, as well as in the past or future experience of other minds" [115]. In this view Mr. Mill (who quotes Fraser), entirely acquiesces, and in this same spirit he writes, "Matter may be defined, a Permanent Possibility of Sensation" [116]; —and adds that he can accept no other definition.

Whether the reader can or cannot define Matter otherwise; he will, at all events, perceive that the Materialist assumes as his primary postulate, that which is by no means the primary fact accepted by Mankind. He starts with taking Matter for granted;—but, if he inquires, he will discover that Matter is known to him in the second place only; he really first knew Mind. When he questions sensation, or consciousness, he questions Mind; and, throughout his whole life, theoretical as well as practical, Mind is nearer to him, and more strongly evidenced, than any other "Possibility" whatsoever.

Such, then, is the first heavy burden of unauthorized postulation, which the Materialist's theory binds upon him. But, in the task of postulating without authority from Nature, it seems impossible to stop short. Mind, being an absolute necessity, must be got in some way—(from Matter of course)—evolved, correlated, secreted. No account is given how Matter could have been thus transformed and glorified. Yet, in default of such account, it is impossible to divine why that primary postulate ever existed at all.

The highest attenuation of Matter can no more help to explain Life or Mind, than to say that brain, (deprived of its vitality,) is composed of cerebrin, lecythin, and cholesterin, explains its sensibility, and other vital and intellectual endowments. And we encounter the same unbridged gulf at every turn of the materialistic hypothesis. There is a wide gap between the inorganic world and all organisms, vegetable or animal. We are, however, told that when certain inorganic elements are combined, under certain conditions, they form protoplasm,—a substance manifesting phenomena of vitality. The elements are known,—the conditions are unknown,—and until protoplasm has been produced by a chemical experi menter, instead of within a living laboratory, we may safely believe that the unknown conditions form the essential cause of the production. And we are given to understand by Professor Huxley [117], that on this subject speculation has been premature.

The gap between Body and Mind is wider still. Body has its known properties,—measurable figure, weight, and other like specialties. Mind has its properties also,—such as intelligence, emotion, reason, will. Thinking has never been shown to be a property of Body; nor have weight and measure been applied to Mind. The laws of each differ as decisively as their properties. Body obeys gravitation, cohesion, and chemical affinity. Mind has its laws of reasoning, mathematically, logically, analogically. Now, what resemblance is here visible [118]? Body cannot compel Will,—but is moved by it; and there is no more verisimilitude known to us of Body to Will, than there exists between the noble thought of a high-souled Man and the paving-stone he walks upon. The foregoing is, as every honest materialist will acknowledge, but a slight specimen of the many difficulties of Materialism. So little does any materializing process of "resolution" really resolve anything, that any —even the most plausible—can only be pronounced an abortive attempt to bring something near and familiar to us, out of something unknowably remote.

The materialist's allegation is generally, that he wishes to accept as little as possible. But the accusation of the natural Theologian against Materialism, is that it accepts far too much. Mind being a necessary and indispensable fact, the one fact underlying all other facts,— whoever is bent on simplifying his beliefs, had better begin by believing in his own Soul. And if further bent on viewing all things as "resolvable," his surest wisdom will be to resolve Matter into Mind. It is really the easier alternative, and has a double merit,—it starts from the best-known fact, and it satisfies his desire for "simplification."

At all events, the consequences resulting from Materialism, are too serious to permit a disregard of Probability. We must, surely, find and follow the very best guide we can:—

> "These are no school-points; nice philosophy
> May tolerate unlikely arguments,
> But heaven admits no jests."

Mr. Huxley [119], who sees advantages (simplicity and unification) in employing a materialistic terminology, adds the very striking caution—"But the man of science, who, forgetting the limits of philosophical inquiry, slides from these" (materialistic) "formulae and symbols into what is commonly understood by materialism, seems to me to place himself on a level with the mathematician, who should mistake the x's and y's, with which he works his problems, for real entities —and with this further disadvantage, as compared with the mathematician, that the blunders of the latter are of no practical consequence, while the errors of systematic materialism may paralyse the energies and destroy the beauty of a life."

The words italicized are remarkable. The materializing façons de parler do not embody a knowledge of "real entities" after all. And such is the language of one [120] who stands in the foremost rank of European Biologists.

ADDITIONAL NOTES AND ILLUSTRATIONS TO CHAPTER 3

A. Account of Some Theories Respecting Our Personal Identity

In a sentence worthy of the pen of Glanvill or of Sir T. Browne, Locke remarked

> "The Ideas, as well as Children of our Youth, often die before us: And our Minds represent to us those Tombs, to which we are approaching; where, though the Brass and Marble remain, yet the Inscriptions are effaced by Time, and the Imagery moulders away. The Pictures drawn in our Minds, are laid in fading Colours, and if not sometimes refreshed, vanish and disappear." *On Retention*, B. II., chap. x. 5.

This truly human feeling did not hinder Locke from writing (chap, xxvii.) on the subject of Self-ness in a manner which appeared to imply that Consciousness, or Consciousness plus Memory "made" Personal Identity;—or to use Reid's words "whatever hath the consciousness of present and past actions, is the same person to whom they belong."

Bishop Butler's strictures on the topic are known to most students: but, as Sir William Hamilton observes (*Foot-note on Reid*, pp. 350, 351),

"Long before Butler, to whom the merit is usually ascribed, Locke's doctrine of Personal Identity had been attacked and refuted. This was done even by his earliest critic, John Sergeant, whose words, as he is an author wholly unknown to all historians of philosophy, and his works of the rarest, I shall quote. He thus argues:—'The former distinction forelaid, he (Locke) proceeds to make personal identity in man to consist in the consciousness that we are the same thinking thing in different times and places. He proves it, because consciousness is inseparable from thinking, and, as it seems to him, essential to it.... But, to speak to the point: Consciousness of any action or other accident we have now, or have had, is nothing but our knowledge that it belonged to us; and, since we both agree that we have no innate knowledges, it follows, that all, both actual and habitual knowledges, which we have, are acquired or accidental to the subject or knower. Wherefore, the man, or that thing which is to be the knower, must have had individuality or personality, from other principles, antecedently to this knowledge, called consciousness: and, consequently, he will retain his identity, or continue the same man, or (which is equivalent) the same person, as long as he has those individuating principles.... It being then most evident, that a man must be the same, ere he can know or be conscious that he is the same, all his laborious descants and extravagant consequences which are built upon this supposition, that consciousness individuates the person, can need no farther refutation.'

"The same objection was also made by Leibnitz in his strictures on Locke's Essay....

"For the best criticism of Locke's doctrine of Personal Identity, I may, however, refer the reader to M. Cousin's ' Cours de Philosophie.'"

One of Locke's arguments is worthy of attention from its oddity. He says (chap. xxvii. 20),

"But if it be possible for the same Man to have distinct incommunicable Consciousnesses at different Times, it is past doubt the same Man would at different Times make different Persons; which, we see, is the Sense of Mankind in the solemnest Declaration of their Opinions, Human Laws not punishing the Mad Man for the Sober Man's Actions, nor the Sober Man for what the Mad Man did, thereby making them two Persons; which is somewhat explained by our Way of speaking in English, when we say, such a one is not himself, or is besides himself; in which Phrases it is insinuated, as if those who now, or at least, first used them, thought that Self was changed, the self same Person was no longer in that Man."

It appears strange that so acute a writer should not have perceived the true consequences to be deduced from his observation. We never really treat a man who goes mad as becoming another personage. But if he has lost his self-control from causes by himself uncontrollable, we do not punish his criminalities, and we do divest him of his social powers; he can neither vote for Parliament, bequeath property, nor do many other acts, during the period of his affliction. But we use all means for his cure, and rejoice at his return to health and society. If a man "beside himself" were "a different person," then "tipsy he" would certainly not be "ipse he."—Yet the father of ethical science decided that the criminal drunkard deserves double meed of punishment.

To Locke's theory of Personal Identity Hamilton dedicates one more note. He gives (Reid, p. 353), an extract from Lord Kames (Essays on the Principles of Morality and Natural Religion), who pronounces his own opinion and appends some unpublished remarks of Dr. Reid.

> "Mr. Locke, writing on personal identity, has fallen short of his usual accuracy. He inadvertently jumbles together the identity that is nature's work, with our knowledge of it. Nay, he expresses himself sometimes as if identity had no other foundation than that knowledge. I am favoured by Dr. Reid with the following thoughts on personal identity:—
>
> "'All men agree that personality is indivisible; a part of a person is an absurdity. A man who loses his estate, his health, an arm, or a leg, continues still to be the same person. My personal identity, therefore, is the continued existence of that indivisible thing which I call myself. I am not thought; I am not action; I am not feeling; but I think, and act, and feel. Thoughts, actions, feelings, change every moment; but self, to which they belong, is permanent. If it be asked how I know that it is permanent, the answer is, that I know it from memory. Everything I remember to have seen, or heard, or done, or suffered, convinces me that I existed at the time remembered. But, though it is from memory that I have the knowledge of my personal identity, yet personal identity must exist in nature, independent of memory; otherwise, I should only be the same person as far as my memory serves me; and what would become of my existence during the intervals wherein my memory has failed me? My remembrance of any of my actions does not make me to be the person who did the action, but only makes me know that I was the person who did it. And yet it was Mr. Locke's opinion, that my remembrance of an action is what makes me to be the person who did it; a pregnant instance that even men of the greatest genius may sometimes fall into an absurdity. Is it not an obvious corollary, from Mr. Locke's opinion, that he never was born? He could not remember his birth; and, therefore, was not the person born at such a place and at such a time.'"

When we come to Hume, the case is considerably altered. He opens the question after his own manner by asking how the fact commonly stated can be; and using the difficulty of explaining this "how" as a sufficient objection against the fact asserted. "There are some philosophers," he writes (*Treatise*, B. I., Part iv., Sect. 6), "who imagine we are every moment intimately conscious of what we call our self; that we feel its existence and its continuance in existence; and are certain, beyond the evidence of a demonstration, both of its perfect identity and simplicity....

> "Unluckily all these positive assertions are contrary to that very experience, which is pleaded for them, nor have we any idea of self, after the manner it is here explained. For from what impression could this idea be derived?... If any impression gives rise to the idea of self, that impression must continue invariably the same, through the whole course of our lives; since self is supposed to exist after that manner. But there is no impression

constant and invariable. Pain and pleasure, grief and joy, passions and sensations succeed each other, and never all exist at the same time. It cannot therefore be from any of these impressions, or from any other, that the idea of self is derived; and consequently there is no such idea.... For my part, when I enter most intimately into what I call myself, I always stumble on some particular perception or other, of heat or cold, light or shade, love or hatred, pain or pleasure. I never can catch myself at any time without a perception, and never can observe anything but the perception.... The mind is a kind of theatre, where several perceptions successively make their appearance; pass, re-pass, glide away, and mingle in an infinite variety of postures and situations. There is properly no simplicity in it at one time, nor identity in different; whatever natural propension we may have to imagine that simplicity and identity. The comparison of the theatre must not mislead us. They are the successive perceptions only, that constitute the mind; nor have we the most distant notion of the place, where these scenes are represented, or of the materials, of which it is composed."

It is curious that Hume wishing to represent Mind as a melting mist of successive perceptions, should be driven into the use of a word which implied a something continuing and permanent as affording the stage on which all passing scenes called "impressions" are enacted.

Hume next discusses the laws of association; and then proceeds (same Section sub fin.)

"As memory alone acquaints us with the continuance and extent of this succession of perceptions, 'tis to be considered, upon that account chiefly, as the source of personal identity. Had we no memory, we never should have any notion of causation, nor consequently of that chain of causes and effects, which constitute our self or person. But having once acquired this notion of causation from the memory, we can extend the same chain of causes, and consequently the identity of our persons beyond our memory, and can comprehend times, and circumstances, and actions, which we have entirely forgot, but suppose in general to have existed. For how few of our past actions are there, of which we have any memory? Who can tell me, for instance, what were his thoughts and actions on the first of January, 1715, the eleventh of March, 1719, and the third of August, 1733? Or will he affirm, because he has entirely forgot the incidents of these days, that the present self is not the same person with the self of that time; and by that means overturn all the most established notions of personal identity? In this view therefore memory does not so much produce as discover personal identity, by shewing us the relation of cause and effect among our different perceptions. 'Twill be incumbent on those who affirm that memory produces entirely our personal identity, to give a reason why we can thus extend our identity beyond our memory.

"The whole of this doctrine leads us to a conclusion, which is of great importance in the present affair, viz., that all the nice and subtle questions concerning personal identity can never possibly be decided, and are to be regarded rather as grammatical than as philosophical difficulties. Identity depends on the relations of ideas; and these relations produce identity, by means of that easy transition they occasion. But as the relations, and the easiness of the transition may diminish by insensible degrees, we have no just standard by which we can decide any dispute concerning the time, when they acquire or lose a title to the name of identity. All the disputes concerning the identity of connected objects are merely verbal, except so far as the relation of parts gives rise to some fiction or imaginary principle of union, as we have already observed."

If any one feels dissatisfied with these conclusions our author is ready with his apology—

"The intense view of these manifold contradictions and imperfections in human reason has so wrought upon me, and heated my brain, that I am ready to reject all belief and reasoning, and can look upon no opinion even as more probable or likely than another. Where am I, or what? From what causes do I derive my existence, and to what condition shall I return? Whose favour shall I court, and whose anger must I dread? What beings surround me? and on whom have I any influence, or who have any influence on me? I am confounded with all these questions, and begin to fancy myself in the most deplorable condition imaginable, environed with the deepest darkness, and utterly deprived of the use of every member and faculty.

"Most fortunately it happens, that since reason is incapable of dispelling these clouds, nature herself suffices to that purpose, and cures me of this philosophical melancholy and delirium, either by relaxing this bent of mind, or by some avocation, and lively impression of my senses, which obliterate all these chimeras. I dine, I play a game of back-gammon, I converse, and am merry with my friends; and when after three or four hours' amusement, I would return to these speculations, they appear so cold, and strained, and ridiculous, that I cannot find in my heart to enter into them any farther." (Part iv., Section 7.)

Is not this good-humoured? Is it not a piece of pleasant bantering, to be equalled only by certain French philosophers? The real conclusion, however, winds up his First Book and runs as follows:—

"A true sceptic will be diffident of his philosophical doubts, as well as of his philosophical conviction; and will never refuse any innocent satisfaction, which offers itself, upon account of either of them.

"Nor is it only proper we should in general indulge our inclination in the most elaborate philosophical researches, notwithstanding our sceptical principles, but also that we should yield (sic) to that propensity, which inclines us to be positive and certain in particular points, according to the light, in which we survey them in any particular instant. 'Tis easier to forbear all examination and inquiry, than to check ourselves in so natural a propensity, and guard against that assurance, which always arises from an exact and full survey of an object. On such an occasion we are apt not only to forget our scepticism, but even our modesty too; and make use of such terms as these, 'tis evident, 'tis certain, 'tis undeniable; which a due deference to the public ought, perhaps, to prevent. I may have fallen into this fault after the example of others; but I here enter a caveat against any objections, which may be offered on that head; and declare that such expressions were extorted from me by the present view of the object, and imply no dogmatical spirit, nor conceited idea of my own judgment, which are sentiments that I am sensible can become nobody, and a sceptic still less than any other [121]."

It is obvious to remark that no amount of easiness would maintain most minds in this balanced position of the pleasant know-nothing man. The general tendency would be to acknowledge the negative side alone. And it would be well if an absence of serious convictions, seriously asserted, and acted on, did not gradually weaken the sense of Responsibility by making Truth appear indifferent because unattainable.

We, however, are just now more concerned with two other equally obvious comments. One, that Hume appears to take for granted the point at issue. Suppose it for argument's sake to be true that impressions and ideas (as described by him) make up our whole ordinary consciousness; does this shew that no latent power or entity exists by which we become conscious of those passing trains? When impressed by colours, are we conscious of an optic nerve, retina, crystalline lens and other instrumental powers of vision? Can we, if we try, perceive by sense the nerve-currents brainwards, or the sensory which receives and compares them? In both cases (eye and inward eye) pathology affords an evidence of consciousness which happy health refuses us. The brainsick sense sees colours and phantoms which are not—the disordered mind dwells on impressions and ideas absolutely unreal, and acts on them as stern realities. And thus our own purely subjective states reveal to us our own subjectivity. 'Tis so in fevers, in lunacies, in vices—'tis so to the drowning or the desperate man. These mournful changes which pass over ourselves issue from an interior activity of self-ness and form one of its commonest verifications. This first comment admits of extension. If we endeavour to introduce experiment (as well as experience) into Mental Science, must we not ask a previous question:—Shall this or that experiment be tried? In other words, by what inner law shall we shape our inquiries so as to gain useful facts for our intended induction?—Nay, we may further ask: What inner Being is to settle the questions, criticize them, and judge the final issue? And if we seem to see our way on these topics, we may feel pretty sure that whenever our psychology comes to practical trial, we proceed as being sure of a Self, more or less self-conscious of Self, and are quite confident that its self-ness will continue during the whole time of our investigations.

Our second comment may be simply summed, but the consideration given to it ought to be minute and careful. Suppose instead of successive perceptions, impressions, or ideas, we substitute a succession of phenomena, and then apply to them Hume's line of thought, we have an acute statement of the modern teachings which relegate the noblest part of our Nature, our reasonings and our beliefs to the territory of the Unknowable. In a word, all knowledge thus seems to be gained by "looking on," none by "looking in." Truth within ourselves especially if it manifests a Truth above ourselves is made to appear hopeless. And so far does the process of Elimination extend, that principles involved even in our "looking on" must not be drawn out of their latency, for fear they should become accepted parts of knowledge. Let any thinker repeat with this substitution the Personal Identity argument in his own mind, and he will soon see what a shadow is cast over an infinitely wider world of thought [122].

The same process of repetition ought in fairness to produce another effect. Are not these philosophic argutiae, these Pyrrhonic subtilties closely akin to the difficulties raised against all first principles; and more particularly all Theistic principles? But does anybody on their account doubt his own Self-ness or Identity? Or does any one refuse to act on the supposition of other-ness, and outer-ness, or ignore his world of fellow-men and hard objectivities which press upon him from every side? Why then should anybody ignore on their account the great First-Cause?

In the text of Chapter 3, the elements of our reasonable belief in our own Personal self-ness and sameness have been shortly mentioned;—of such work-day belief, that is to say, as suffices for actual life, and gains from it, and throughout it, a perpetual verification. If any one wishes to go deeper than this, he must inquire upon what evidence first principles are accepted by reasoning men; what difficulties attach to such principles; and under what conditions these difficulties are held to be nugatory. This inquiry is troublesome but promises real satisfaction. We have not, therefore, declined it, as may be seen in the ensuing Chapter. One fact is manifest beforehand—that whatever evidence is presupposed valid by those first principles of every-day knowledge, may be safely presupposed, accepted, and reasoned upon, in the ground-work of Natural Theology.

It was Hume's object to push his scepticism to its most extreme verge. Thus pushed, it "so wrought upon" him that he was "ready to reject all belief and reasoning" till a return to every-day life made his speculations appear in his own eyes "cold and strained and ridiculous." What then was the inference Hume himself intended? Which was really groundless—every-day belief or scepticism? Will his useful dilemma induce the reader to receive Kant's excuse for the celebrated doubter, when he bids us let the man alone because he is but trying the strength of human reason? At all events, Hume's way of stating his case seems to justify the old remark, that, while Superstition is refuted by Reason, Nature itself refutes the Sceptic.

B. Extracts from Popular Lectures, by Professor Helmholtz, on the Recent Progress of the Theory of Vision

"If now we compare the eye with other optical instruments, we observe the advantage it has over them in its very large field of vision. This for each eye separately is 160° (nearly two right angles) laterally, and 120° vertically, and for both together somewhat more than two right angles from right to left. The field of view of instruments made by art is usually very small, and becomes smaller with the increased size of the image.

"But we must also admit, that we are accustomed to expect in these instruments complete precision of the image in its entire extent, while it is only necessary for the image on the retina to be exact over a very small surface, namely, that of the yellow spot. The diameter of the central pit corresponds in the field of vision to an angular magnitude which can be covered by the nail of one's forefinger when the hand is stretched out as far as possible. In this small part of the field our power of vision is so accurate that it can distinguish the distance between two points, of only one minute angular magnitude, i.e., a distance equal to the sixtieth part of the diameter of the finger- nail. This distance corresponds to the width of one of the cones of the retina. All the other parts of the retinal image are seen imperfectly, and the more so the nearer to the limit of the retina they fall. So that the image which we receive by the eye is like a picture, minutely and elaborately finished in the centre, but only roughly sketched in at the borders. But although at each instant we only see a very small part of the field of vision accurately, we see this in combination with what surrounds it, and enough of this outer and larger part of the field, to notice any striking object, and particularly any change that takes place in it. All of this is unattainable in a telescope.

"But if the objects are too small, we cannot discern them at all with the greater part of the retina.

'When, lost in boundless blue on high,
The lark pours forth his thrilling song,'

the 'ethereal minstrel' is lost until we can bring her image to a focus upon the central pit of our retina. Then only are we able to see her.

"To look at anything means to place the eye in such a position that the image of the object falls on the small region of perfectly clear vision. This we may call direct vision, applying the term indirect to that exercised with the lateral parts of the retina—indeed with all except the yellow spot.

"The defects which result from the inexactness of vision and the smaller number of cones in the greater part of the retina are compensated by the rapidity with which we can turn the eye to one point after another of the field of vision, and it is this rapidity of movement which really constitutes the chief advantage of the eye over other optical instruments....

"A great part of the importance of the eye as an organ of expression depends on the same fact; for the movements of the eyeball—its glances—are among the most direct signs of the movement of the attention, of the movements of the mind, of the person who is looking at us." Popular Lectures on Scientific Subjects, pp. 212-214.

The great German next proceeds to catalogue some principal defects of the Eye. 1. Chromatic aberration connected with 2. spherical aberration and defective centering of the cornea and lens, together producing the imperfection known as astigmatism, and 3. irregular radiation round the images of illuminated points.

"Now," adds Helmholtz, "it is not too much to say that if an optician wanted to sell me an instrument which had all these defects, I should think myself quite justified in blaming his carelessness in the strongest terms, and giving him back his instrument. Of course, I shall not do this with my eyes, and shall be only too glad to keep them as long as I can—defects and all. Still, the fact that, however bad they may be, I can get no others, does not at all diminish their defects, so long as I maintain the narrow but indisputable position of a critic on purely optical grounds." (p. 219.)

He then goes on to other faults. 4. Defective transparency. 5. Floating corpuscules (Muscae Volitantes). 6. The "blind spot" with other gaps in the field of vision.

"So much," he concludes, "for the physical properties of the Eye. If I am asked why I have spent so much time in explaining its imperfection to my readers, I answer, as I said at first, that I have not done so in order to depreciate the performances of this wonderful organ, or to diminish our admiration of its construction. It was my object to make the reader understand, at the first step of our inquiry, that it is not any mechanical perfection of the organs of our senses which secures for us such wonder fully true and exact impressions of the outer world. The next section of this inquiry will introduce much bolder and more paradoxical conclusions than any I have yet stated. We have now seen that the eye in itself is not by any means so complete an optical instrument as it first appears: its extraordinary value depends upon the way in which we use it: its perfection is practical, not absolute.... Wherever we scrutinise the construction of physiological organs, we find the same character of practical adaptation to the wants of the organism; although, perhaps, there is no instance which we can follow out so minutely as that of the eye.

"For the eye has every possible defect that can be found in an optical instrument, and even some which are peculiar to itself; but they are all so counteracted, that the inexactness of the image which results from their presence very little exceeds, under ordinary conditions of illumination, the limits which are set to the delicacy of sensation by the dimensions of the retinal cones....

"The adaptation of the eye to its function is, therefore, most complete, and is seen in the very limits which are set to its defects. Here the result which may be reached by innumerable generations working under the Darwinian law of inheritance, coincides with what the wisest Wisdom may have devised beforehand. A sensible man will not cut firewood with a razor, and so we may assume that each step in the elaboration of the eye must have made the organ more vulnerable and more slow in its development. We must also bear in mind that soft, watery animal textures must always be unfavourable and difficult material for an instrument of the mind....

"But, apparently, we are not yet come much nearer to understanding sight. We have only made one step: we have learnt how the optical arrangement of the eye renders it possible to separate the rays of light which come in from all parts of the field of vision, and to bring together again all those that have proceeded from a single point, so that they may produce their effect upon a single fibre of the optic nerve.

"Let us see, therefore, how much we know of the sensations of the eye, and how far this will bring us towards the solution of the problem." P. 226, seq.

From the Professor's mention of "much bolder and more paradoxical conclusions," the final result of his next inquiry may be anticipated. Sensation is so far from making evident the truth of our visual knowledge that it increases our perplexities tenfold.

"The inaccuracies," he tells us, "and imperfections of the eye as an optical instrument, and those which belong to the image on the retina, now appear insignificant in comparison with the incongruities which we have met with in the field of sensation. One might almost believe that Nature had here contradicted herself on purpose, in order to destroy any dream of a pre-existing harmony between the outer and the inner world.

"And what progress have we made in our task of explaining Sight? It might seem that we are farther off than ever; the riddle only more complicated, and less hope than ever of finding out the answer. The reader may perhaps feel inclined to reproach Science with only knowing how to break up with fruitless criticism the fair world presented to us by our senses, in order to annihilate the fragments." (p. 269.)

How triumphant does Idealism now appear! How little trustworthy that boasted sense of which mankind have constantly said, "seeing is believing," although an apostle and philosophers innumerable have put the two in opposition!

Perhaps, however, instead of leading to a "triumph of Idealism," the paradoxes and incongruities—in a word, the vast accumulation of the Unknowable—belonging to eyesight considered as a Sensation, must be allowed to land us on the shore of a far-stretching Scepticism illimitable to the mind's eye. And this seems to be the eminent writer's own final opinion [123]. So, too, it will always appear when the case is fairly argued out; and that for the reasons adduced in our text. The course of argument there pursued was adopted before the Professor's book came to hand; but we have now added some extracts from his pages in the shape of footnotes, and have given references to other interesting topics touched upon by him.

For our purpose, however, it is necessary in some degree to disregard the variety of those topics, and fix our attention upon the conclusive issue. It is plain, that respecting our senses, as well as our other primary sources of information, the limits of what we can completely explain are very narrow. Yet each for himself and all of us for our race must needs every day accept and act upon this limited and imperfect kind of knowledge about what most essentially concerns our actions as well as our speculations.

Several strong examples of such incompleteness are given by Helmholtz in his scientific inquiry into the rationale of the visual sense-impressions. We observe, for instance, in his chapter on Sensation (p. 236 seq.) that all light-waves are the same in kind of movement, but differ in size as widely as the ripples on a sea-beach (round which happy children play) differ from the vast Atlantic ship-engulfing billows sixty or a hundred feet apart. All these undulations are similar in respect of reflection, refraction, interference, diffraction, and polarisation, as well as in their production of heat [124]. Now, it is the interpretation of such movements into its own language by which our eye gives us the sensation of colour. Yet this power of interpretation is curiously limited—it does not appreciate the gentler ripples of the light-waves—it does not reach to their mightier undulations. Consequently, there may be tender colour-delicacies adorning the Universe, completely incognisable by us, and there may be also glows and intensities of light-beams magnificently resplendent, and unspeakably grand in tone, of which we can through our visual apparatus form no possible conception. Thus, our eye translates some waves into a language which we call colour, but its scholarship is limited. A certain number of signs it catches and interprets, the rest lie altogether outside its ken. The Sun's softer light-harmonies, and his most awful emanations of beauty remain equally unknown.

And another limitation has been imposed upon our optical apparatus. For a perception of heating powers belonging to colour-waves the eye refers us to the skin;—and as to their chemical powers we are only just now discovering the instruments fitted for their true appreciation.

Skilful, too, and yet at the same time very skill-less, is the divination into sunlight given us by our human eyes;—sunlight, that is to say, as a general resultant in its whiteness. For, if our eyes, keen and susceptible to us perfect clearness, attempt to analyze white light into its factors and elements, their resolving faculty manifests still more blank inabilities. And they fail also in examining certain colours:—

"The most striking difference," writes Helmholtz, "between the mixture of pigments and that of coloured light is, that while painters make green by mixing blue and yellow pigments, the union of blue and yellow rays of light, produces white.... In general, then, light, which consists of undulations of different wave-lengths, produces different impressions upon our eye, namely, those of different colours. But the number of hues which we can recognise is much smaller than that of the various possible combinations of rays with different wave-lengths which external objects can convey to our eyes. The retina cannot distinguish between the white which is produced by the union of scarlet and bluish-green light, and that which is composed of yellowish-green and violet, or of yellow and ultramarine blue, or of red, green, and violet, or of all the colours of the spectrum united. All these combinations appear identically as white; and yet, from a physical point of view, they are very different. In fact, the only resemblance between the several combinations just mentioned is, that they are indistinguishable to the human eye. For instance, a surface illuminated with red and bluish-green light would come out black in a photograph; while another lighted with yellowish-green and violet would appear very bright, although both surfaces alike seem to the eye to be simply white. Again, if we successively illuminate coloured objects with white beams of light of various composition, they will appear differently coloured. And whenever we decompose two such beams by a prism, or look at them through a coloured glass, the difference between them at once becomes evident.

"Other colours, also, especially when they are not strongly pronounced, may, like pure white light, be composed of very different mixtures, and yet appear indistinguishable to the eye, while in every other property, physical or chemical, they are entirely distinct." (pp. 239-241.)

We may speak of visual Sensation, then, as a limited power of translating light. And what relation does visual Perception bear to this Power? Probably the simplest way of expressing it, is to say that it is neither more nor less than the translation of a translation. The mind thus construes to itself what the visual sense is every moment busied with expressing in its own special language—the interpretation of movement, into colour, light and shadow. And from these data—these colours, lights and shadows, the mind draws its own inferences.

Now these inferences thus drawn from preceding Sense inferences,—limited in range, as we have seen, and defective in analytic power;—these inferences, such as they are, constitute the boasted certainty of eyesight; and of all things apprehended by its means,—all

—quae sunt oculis subjecta fidelibus et quae
Ipse sibi tradit spectator.

It needs but a statement of the mode in which our final mind-interpretations are constructed,—of these translated translations,—obscure in grammar and imperfect in vocabulary—to prove how very difficult is the position of the Realist. In view of this Empire of the Unknowable proclaimed by Science over the surest of our perceiving powers, the firmest foundations of our experimental knowledge, Helmholtz suggests that his reader "may feel determined to stick fast to the 'sound common sense' of mankind, and believe his own senses more than physiology." (p. 270.)

And such, no doubt, is the conclusion of the matter to the greater part of mankind. But we will in the first place prefer hearing the last word of the physiologist. From page 270 to page 313 of his work, he argues out the great question of how we perceive under the full impression of its vast importance to psychology, metaphysics, and the first principles upon which all science and all reasonings repose.

"We have," he says (p. 281), "already learned enough to see that the questions which have here to be decided are of fundamental importance, not only for the physiology of sight, but for a correct understanding of the true nature and limits of human knowledge generally."

The Physiologist's last word is this—Sense impressions are signs, the meaning of which we learn inductively by a process of self education.

"Illusions obviously depend upon mental processes which may be described as false inductions.... There appears to me to be in reality only a superficial difference between the 'conclusions' of logicians and those inductive conclusions of which we recognise the result in the conceptions we gain of the outer world through our sensations. The difference chiefly depends upon the former conclusions being capable of expression in words, while the latter are not; because, instead of words, they only deal with sensations and the memory of sensations. Indeed, it is just the impossibility of describing sensations, whether actual or remembered, in words, which makes it so difficult to discuss this department of psychology at all." (pp. 307, 8.)

And again (p. 314),

"There is a most striking analogy between the entire range of processes which we have been discussing, and another System of Signs, which is not given by nature but arbitrarily chosen, and which must undoubtedly be learned before it is understood. I mean the words of our mother tongue.

"Learning how to speak is obviously a much more difficult task than acquiring a foreign language in after-life. First, the child has to guess that the sounds it hears are intended to be signs at all; next, the meaning of each separate sound must be found out, by the same kind of induction as the meaning of the sensations of sight or touch; and yet we see children by the end of their first year already understanding certain words and phrases, even if they are not yet able to repeat them. We may sometimes observe the same in dogs.

"Now this connection between Names and Objects, which demonstrably must be learnt, becomes just as firm and indestructible as that between Sensations and the Objects which produce them. We cannot help thinking of the usual signification of a word, even when it is used exceptionally in some other sense; we cannot help feeling the mental emotions which a fictitious narrative calls forth, even when we know that it is not true; just in the same way as we cannot get rid of the normal signification of the sensations produced by any illusion of the senses, even when we know that they are not real.

"There is one other point of comparison which is worth notice. The elementary signs of language are only twenty-six letters, and yet what wonderfully varied meanings can we express and communicate by their combination! Consider, in comparison with this, the enormous number of elementary signs with which the machinery of sight is provided. We may take the number of fibres in the optic nerves as two hundred and fifty thousand. Each of these is capable of innumerable different degrees of sensation of one, two, or three primary colours. It follows that it is possible to construct an immeasurably greater number of combinations here than with the few letters which build up our words. Nor must we forget the extremely rapid changes of which the images of sight are capable. No wonder, then, if our senses speak to us in language which can express far more delicate distinctions and richer varieties than can be conveyed by words."

Finally (pp. 315, 16),

"The correspondence, therefore, between the external world and the Perceptions of Sight rests, either in whole or in part, upon the same foundation as all our knowledge of the actual world,—on experience, and on constant verification of its accuracy by experiments which we perform with every movement of our body. It follows, of course, that we are only warranted in accepting the reality of this correspondence so far as these means of verification extend, which is really as far as for practical purposes we need.

"Beyond these limits, as, for example, in the region of Qualities, we are in some instances able to prove conclusively that there is no correspondence at all between sensations and their objects.

"Only the relations of time, of space, of equality, and those which are derived from them, of number, size, regularity of co-existence and of sequence—'mathematical relations' in short, are common to the outer and the inner world, and here we may indeed look for a complete correspondence between our conceptions and the objects which excite them.

"But it seems to me that we should not quarrel with the bounty of nature because the greatness, and also the emptiness, of these abstract relations have been concealed from us by the manifold brilliance of a system of signs; since thus they can be the more easily surveyed and used for practical ends, while yet traces enough remain visible to guide the philosophical spirit aright, in its search after the meaning of sensible Images and Signs."

Let therefore this account of visual Perception be accepted by us, as it will probably be by three- fourths of scientific men throughout Europe. And, next, let us ask, as every real thinker will proceed to ask, on what grounds of certitude rests our assurance as regards the daily and hourly information received through this avenue of perception, reasoned and acted upon with unswerving confidence by us all?

For an examination of the ground principle of Induction, the reader must be referred to our next chapter. But it is at once clear that no human experience can possess the attribute of universality, otherwise it would cease to be human. We have then in this present appeal to the veracity of Experience, no absolute knowledge to deal with, only knowledge as relative to mankind. Nay, we must go a little further still in our limitation, and say to the generality of mankind. For our eyes do not all see perfectly alike—a North-American Indian sees what a Cockney cannot discover; the trained eye discerns differently from the untrained. On the differences of power in eye and ear rest the differences in many kinds of theorising—amongst which art-perceptions yield an obvious and familiar set of examples. And if we try for a more precise estimate of the value of our limited human relativity, and proceed by way of comparison between our own diverse endowments, who shall venture to say that the eye of our body interpreted by our understanding, tells our inmost self more truly than the eye of our human soul, informing us directly of the facts of its intuitive vision? So far as our actual means of valuing these two modes of beholding can go, there is no knowledge so perfect as the product of pure intuition, the glorious fabric of Mathematical Science. And to pure Science it matters not whether the requisite Schematism is drawn upon a sheet of white paper or on the clear tablet of the imagining faculty of a philosopher. The purely inward view is in truth generally the farthest reaching, and the most unclouded. When, therefore, it is, and has been for centuries, apparent to the inmost eye of the generality of our race that there really exists a spiritual world within themselves—above them, and in the far distant future beyond us all, permanent while we change, and the evidence of our own ultimate permanency,—such knowledge may undeniably be human, the very flower and distinction of our human nature; and it may on that account be received by us as true.

If, again, our ordinary human soul is so far a Christian as to exclaim with Tertullian, "O good God," by what logical process shall we confute its utterance, while we maintain the utterance of our commonest sense-perceptions?

That we all see in frames, that we all think in frames, no rational thinker or perceiver will deny. If, however, any of us chooses to be an Idealist or Nihilist, let him at least be consistent;—if he will assert the necessity of Doubt, let him maintain its empire by doubting his own assertion. But let no man think that Doubt leads him any whither except to an abnegation of thought, a mistrust alike of Sense and Soul, and an abdication of every human prerogative:—

> "Thy hand, great Anarch, lets the curtain fall,
> And universal Darkness buries all."

So sang the witty rhymer, but we may add in prose that Doubt if thoroughly real, invariably commits suicide, and becomes first doubtful, after that, a non-entity at last.

C. Helmholtz on Specialties of Sensibility

The following passages from this interesting writer will be found in his Chapter "on the Sensations of Sight," between pp. 232 and 236. They will, it is hoped, be thoroughly intelligible if read in connection with the part of our last Chapter (pp. 158, 9) where a reference to this note was made.

"The nerve-fibres have been often compared with telegraphic wires traversing a country, and the comparison is well fitted to illustrate this striking and important peculiarity of their mode of action. In the network of telegraphs we find everywhere the same copper or iron wires carrying the same kind of movement, a stream of electricity, but producing the most different results in the various stations according to the auxiliary apparatus with which they are connected. At one station the effect is the ringing of a bell, at another a signal is moved, and at a third a recording instrument is set to work.... Nerve-fibres and telegraphic wires are equally striking examples to illustrate the doctrine that the same causes may, under different conditions, produce different results.... As motor nerves, when irritated, produce movement, because they are connected with muscles, and glandular nerves secretion, because they lead to glands, so do sensitive nerves, when they are irritated, produce sensation, because they are connected with sensitive organs.... Whether by the irritation of a nerve we produce a muscular movement, a secretion or a sensation depends upon whether we are handling a motor, a glandular, or a sensitive nerve, and not at all upon what means of irritation we may use. It may be an electrical shock, or tearing the nerve, or cutting it through, or moistening it with a solution of salt, or touching it with a hot wire. In the same way (and this great step in advance was due to Johannes Müller) the kind of sensation which will ensue when we irritate a sensitive nerve, whether an impression of light, or of sound, or of feeling, or of smell, or of taste, will be produced, depends entirely upon which sense the excited nerve subserves, and not at all upon the method of excitation we adopt.

"Let us now apply this to the optic nerve, which is the object of our present enquiry. In the first place, we know that no kind of action upon any part of the body except the eye and the nerve which belongs to it, can ever produce the sensation of light. The stories of somnambulists, which are the only arguments that can be adduced against this belief, we may be allowed to disbelieve. But, on the other hand, it is not light alone which can produce the sensation of light upon the eye, but also any other power which can excite the optic nerve. If the weakest electrical currents are passed through the eye they produce flashes of light. A blow, or even a slight pressure made upon the side of the eyeball with the finger, makes an impression of light in the darkest room, and, under favourable circumstances, this may become intense. In these cases it is important to remember that there is no objective light produced in the retina, as some of the older physiologists assumed, for the sensation of light may be so strong that a second observer could not fail to see through the pupil the illumination of the retina which would follow, if the sensation were really produced by an actual development of light within the eye. But nothing of the sort has ever been seen. Pressure or the electric current excites the optic nerve, and therefore, according to Müller's law, a sensation of light results, but under these circumstances, at least, there is not the smallest spark of actual light.

"In the same way, increased pressure of blood, its abnormal constitution in fevers, or its contamination with intoxicating or narcotic drugs, can produce sensations of light to which no actual light corresponds. Even in cases in which an eye is entirely lost by accident or by an operation, the irritation of the stump of the optic nerve while it is healing is capable of producing similar subjective effects. It follows from these facts that the peculiarity in kind which distinguishes the sensation of light from all others, does not depend upon any peculiar qualities of light itself. Every action which is capable of exciting the optic nerve is capable of producing the impression of light; and the purely subjective sensation thus produced is so precisely similar to that caused by external light, that persons unacquainted with these phenomena readily suppose that the rays they see are real objective beams.

"Thus we see that external light produces no other effects in the optic nerve than other agents of an entirely different nature. In one respect only does light differ from the other causes which are capable of exciting this nerve: namely, that the retina, being placed at the back of the firm globe of the eye, and further protected by the bony orbit, is almost entirely withdrawn from other exciting agents, and is thus only exceptionally affected by them, while it is continually receiving the rays of light which stream in upon it through the transparent media of the eye.

"On the other hand, the optic nerve, by reason of the peculiar structures in connection with the ends of its fibres, the rods and cones of the retina, is incomparably more sensitive to rays of light than any other nervous apparatus of the body, since the rest can only be affected by rays which are concentrated enough to produce noticeable elevation of temperature.

"This explains why the sensations of the optic nerve are for us the ordinary sensible sign of the presence of light in the field of vision, and why we always connect the sensation of light with light itself, even where they are really unconnected. But we must never forget that a survey of all the facts in their natural connection puts it beyond doubt that external light is only one of the exciting causes capable of bringing the optic nerve into functional activity, and therefore that there is no exclusive relation between the sensation of light and light itself."

Some of the quotations just made direct attention to illusions of Sight which (as we have seen in our last note) Helmholtz elsewhere calls "false inductions." Now one curious fact relative to these impressions is that in many instances the objective consequent is due to a subjective antecedent. Some readers may like to peruse a short account of five variously caused sight-illusions taken from an Oration on Positivism delivered by the present writer at

St. George's Hall in May 1871. The particulars here given of the fifth illusion should be compared with the foot-note on page 158 ante.

"I will mention five instances in which people believe they see something, and do not see it; in other words, the objective antecedent is wanting, and the impression is produced partly by the sensory apparatus, partly by the mind itself. As I describe these instances one by one, let my hearers ask themselves, How does this illusion come about? Is it produced by our optic instrument or by our mental activity?

"First, then, Take a lighted stick, and whirl it rapidly round and round. You believe you see a circle of sparks—in reality it is no more than a simple train, and on a like illusion the Catherine-wheel is constructed. Again, put yourself in the hands of an optically inclined friend, and let him operate upon you thus. He shall place a cardboard down the middle axis of your face, quite close against your nose—one side of his board, say the right, coloured a brilliant red, the left a vivid green. After an instant or two let him suddenly substitute another board, white on both sides. Do my young friends guess what will follow? Your right eye will see green, your left red—the reverse of what they saw before; yet neither will see correctly, for both eyes are looking at uncoloured surfaces.

"Thirdly, Watch the full moon rising—how large and round she looks, resting as it were upon that eastern hill, and seen amidst the tops of its forest trees! How much larger and broader than when she hangs aloft in upper sky! Has every one here learned the true reason why? If not, look at her through a slit in a card, and her diameter will be the same.

"Fourthly, A schoolboy is crossing his bedroom in the deep dark night, anxiously hoping that his head may not come into collision with the bed-post. Though carefully and successfully avoiding it, he imagines of a sudden that the blow is imminent. Quick as thought he stops to save his head, and, behold, the room is as quickly filled with sparks or flames of fire. Another moment, and all becomes dark once more. I have heard many a schoolboy exclaim over this phenomenon, but never knew one who could explain it. Finally, did you ever, on opening your eyes in a morning, close them quickly again, and keep them shut, directing them as if to look straight forwards? Most persons of active nervous power, after a few trials—say a dozen, or a score—are surprised to see colours appear and flit before the sight. Some years ago, Germany's greatest poet tried, at the suggestion of her greatest physiologist, a series of experiments on these coloured images. He found that by an effort of will he could cause them to come and go, govern their movement, march, and succession. And this took place under no conditions of impaired sensation, nor any hallucination of a diseased mind. A thoroughly healthy will succeeded in impressing itself upon physical instruments, controlling their law, and creating at its own pleasure an unfailingly bright phantasmagoria.

"Some here may, others may not, have apprehended the distinctions between our five cases. The first two are due to the sensory apparatus, its optical laws of continued impression and complementary colour. In the latter three, mind intervenes. The enlarged size of the moon occurs through rapid comparison, the fiery lights in a dark room through instinctive apprehension, both influences of mind on the sensory system. The fifth and most interesting of all is no bad example of interference between moral and material law. The will truly causative (you may remark) overrules the natural process of physical impression, alters it, and creates a designed effect. I wish I could induce my young friends to devise a number of experiments on similar mixed cases, and, having tried them, to dissect out their real laws. These sharpenings of the critical faculty are exceedingly useful—they cultivate clearness; and most people know that two-thirds among our mistakes in life are caused by confusion of thought.

"Besides all other uses, such lessons teach at once the necessity, as we said before, of observing your own observations. And as, first, the real witness of every observation is our mind; every fact which comes through our bodily senses being to us a mental impression, it seems but common sense to hear above all things what mind has to say for and about itself. Then, secondly, where would be the benefit derived from our observations, if we could not reason upon them, or could place no confidence in our own reasonings? Yet the art of reasoning is so purely a mental process, that it can be represented by symbols as abstract and free from material meaning as if they were bare algebraic signs. Thirdly, in the most accurate of sciences mind extends our knowledge far beyond the circle of observation, and gives us axiomatic assurance of its own accuracy. Who ever saw, or ever can see, all straight lines in all conceivable positions, yet who doubts that throughout the whole universe no two straight lines ever did inclose or can inclose a space? And, fourthly, can it be a matter of indifference to any of us what evidence the mind offers concerning its own moral nature, and what is the value of that evidence, and the laws deducible therefrom? How true it thus appears that 'know thyself' lies at the root of all knowledge, and that the man who receives no witness from within can know nothing as he ought to know it!"

D. Popular Account of Pure Idealism with Critical Remarks

"A classification of systems of philosophy according to the cosmological conceptions governing them has actually been made. It is founded on a consideration of the differences among philosophers as to what that totality of existence is which is to be accepted as really vouched for by Mind. All agree, as we have said, that Mind is the sole voucher for anything; but philosophers are divisible into schools according to the various views they have taken of the constitution of that phenomenal Universe, that Cosmos, that total round of things, of which we have a recurring assurance in every act of perception, and which is orbed forth more or less fully for each man in his wider contemplations.

"The popular or habitual conception of mankind in general is that there are two distinct worlds mixed up in the phenomenal Cosmos—a world of Mind, consisting of multitudes of individual minds, and a world of Matter, consisting of all the extended immensity and variety of material objects. Neither of these worlds is thought of as begotten of the other, but each of them as existing independently in its own proper nature and within its own definite bounds, though they traffic with each other at present. Sweep away all existing minds, and the deserted Earth would continue to spin round all the same, still whirling its rocks, trees, clouds, and all the rest of its material pomp and garniture, alternately in the sunshine and in the depths of the starry stillness. Though no eye should behold, and no ear should hear, there would be evenings of silver moonlight on the ocean- marge, and the waves would roar as they broke and retired. On the other hand, suppose the entire fabric of the material Universe abolished and dissolved, and the dishoused population of spirits would still somehow survive in the imaginable vacancy. If this second notion is not so easy or common as the first, it still virtually belongs to the popular conception of the contents or constitution of the Cosmos. The conception is that of a Natural Dualism, or of the contact in every act of perception of two distinct spheres, one an internal perceiving mind, and the other an external world composed of the actual and identical objects which this mind perceives.

"On the first exercise of philosophic thought, however, this conception is blurred. An immense quantity of what we all instinctively think of as really existing out of ourselves turns out, on investigation, not to exist at all as we fancy it existing, but to consist only of affections of the perceiving mind. The redness of the rose is not a real external thing, immutably the same in itself; it is only a certain peculiar action on my physiology which the presence of an external cause or object seems to determine. Were my physiology different, the action would be different, though the cause or object remained the same. Indeed, there are persons in whom the presence of a rose occasions no sensation of redness such as is known to me, but a much vaguer sensation, not distinguishable from what I should at once distinguish as greenness. And, as colour is thus at once detected as no external independently-existing reality, but only a recurring physiological affection of myself and other sentient beings like myself, so with a thousand other things which, by habit or instinct, I suppose as externally and independently existing. When I imagine the depopulated Earth still wheeling its inanimate rotundity through the daily sunshine and the nocturnal shadow, or one of its bays still resonant in moonlit evenings with the roar of the breaking waves, it is because, in spite of myself, I intrude into the fancy the supposition of a listening ear, and a beholding eye analogous to my own. It is only by a strong effort that I can realize that a great deal at least of what I thus think of as the goings-on of things by themselves is not and cannot be their goings-on by themselves, but consists at the utmost of effects interbred between them and a particular sentiency in the midst of them. But the effort may be made; and, when it is made repeatedly, in a great many directions, and with reference to a great many of the so-called properties of matter, the inevitable result for the philosophic mind is that the popularly-imagined substance of a real external world finds itself eaten away or corroded, at least to a certain depth. So far philosophers are agreed. It is when they proceed to consider to what depth the popularly-imagined substance of the real external world is thus eaten away, or accounted for, that they begin to differ.

"Some philosophers, departing as little as may be from the popular judgment, suppose that, however much of the apparent external world may be resolved into affections of the subjective sentiency, there still remains an objective residue of such primary qualities as extension, figure, divisibility, mobility, etc., belonging to external matter itself, and by the direct and immediate cognizance of which the mind is brought face to face with external substance, and knows something of its real goings-on. Philosophers of this school are known generally as Realists. More numerous, however, are those who, not allowing an objective and independent reality even to the so-called primary qualities of matter, but believing them as well as colour, odour, or savour, to be only affections of the sentiency, deny that the mind is in any sense brought face to face with real external things such as they seem in the act of perception. To thinkers of this school there has been given the general name of Idealists. This broad distinction of Philosophers cosmologically into Realists and Idealists is so far convenient enough. Cosmologically, or in respect of this present Universe of ours, with its dualism of Mind and Matter, every man must declare himself either a Realist or an Idealist, if he understands the meanings attached to these terms. The distinction has reference solely to his notion of the so-called external or material world in its relations to the perceiving mind. If he abides, though only in part, by the popular conception, and regards the material world as a substantial reality independent of the perceiving mind, and which the mind, according to its powers, presses against and directly apprehends in every act of perception, then he is a Realist. If, on the other hand, he cannot see that there need be asserted any external material world with such characters as we attribute to it, but supposes that our unanimous agreement in the imagination of such an external world is merely a habit of our own sentiency, projecting its own ideas or affections outwards, and giving them a body, then he is an Idealist."

Masson, "Recent British Philosophy," pp. 58-64. Again p. 69, seq.,

"There is the system of Constructive Idealism. It may be so called to distinguish it from the more developed and extreme Idealism presently to be spoken of. According to this system, we do not perceive the real external world immediately, but only mediately—that is, the objects which we take as the things actually perceived are not the real objects at all, but only vicarious assurances, representatives, or nuntii of real unknown objects. The hills, the rocks, the trees, the stars, all the choir of heaven and earth, are not, in any of their qualities, primary, secondary, or whatever we choose to call them, the actual existences out of us, but only the addresses of a 'something' to our physiology, or educations by our physiology out of a 'something.' They are all Thoughts or Ideas, with only this peculiarity involved in them, that they will not rest in themselves, but compel a reference to objects out of self, with which, by some arrangement or other, they stand in relation. Difficult as this system may be to understand, and violently as it wrenches the popular common sense, it is yet the system into which the great majority of philosophers in all ages and countries hitherto are seen, more or less distinctly, to have been carried by their speculations. While the Natural Realists among philosophers have been very few, and even these have been Realists in a sense unintelligible to the popular mind, quite a host of philosophers have been Constructive Idealists. These might be farther subdivided according to particular variations in the form of their Idealism. Thus, there have been many Constructive Idealists who have regarded the objects rising to the mind in external perception, and taken to be representative of real unknown objects, as something more than modifications of the mind itself—as having their origin without. Among these have been reckoned Malebranche, Berkeley, Clarke, Sir Isaac Newton, Tucker, and possibly Locke. But there have been other Constructive Idealists, who have supposed the objects rising in the mind in external perception to be only modifications of the mind itself, but yet, by some arrangement, vicarious of real unknown objects, and intimating their existence. Among such have been reckoned Descartes, Leibnitz, Condillac, Kant, and most Platonists. The general name 'Idealists' it will be seen properly enough includes both the classes as distinct from the Natural Realists, inasmuch as both classes hold that what the mind is directly cognizant of in external perception is only ideas. But, inasmuch as these ideas are held by both classes, though under divers hypotheses, to refer to real existences beyond themselves, and distinct from the perceiving mind, the thinkers in question may also properly enough be called Realists or Dualists, though not 'Natural' Realists or Dualists. They occupy a midway place between the Natural Realists and the philosophers next to be mentioned.

"There is the system of Pure Idealism, which abolishes matter as a distinct or independent existence in any sense, and resolves it completely into mind. Though this system is named in the scheme, for the sake of symmetry, and as the exact antithesis to Materialism, it is difficult to cite representatives that could be certainly discriminated from the merely Constructive Idealists just mentioned on the one hand, and from the school of philosophers next following on the other. Fichte is, perhaps, the purest example." Ibid. pp. 69-72.

For perfect clearness we must put together two other passages from Professor Masson's interesting volume:—

"There is the system of Nihilism, or, as it may be better called, Non-Substantialism. According to this system, the Phaenomenal Cosmos, whether regarded as consisting of two parallel successions of phaenomena (Mind and Matter), or of only one (Mind or Matter), resolves itself, on analysis, into an absolute Nothingness,—mere appearances with no credible substratum of Reality; a play of phantasms in a void. If there have been no positive or dogmatic Nihilists, yet both Hume for one purpose, and Fichte for another, have propounded Nihilism as the ultimate issue of all reasoning that does not start with some à priori postulate."

Masson, "Recent British Philosophy," p. 66.... If any one could assert

"There is no Absolute," surely it might be the Nihilist, who has analysed away both Matter and Thought, and attenuated the Cosmos into vapour and non- significance. Yet, from the abyss of a speculatively reasoned Nihilism more void than Hume's, Fichte returned, by a convulsive act of soul,—which he termed faith —an intense, a burning, a blazing Ontologist. Ibid. p. 81" [125].

This is certainly an eloquent account of philosophic Idealism as it may in its various phases be represented to the world of general readers. It turns, as every such speculation must turn, on the great principle, that our Sensations are so many series of signs and symbols [126]. They may be preordained, and our apprehension of them innate;—they may be arbitrary, and their interpretation the work of man's intelligence. To decide this question, is to decide something as to the extent of their relativity; but will any one pronounce their information absolutely true?

At this point occurs a wide divergence between two great schools of Idealism—the Psychological, and the Theological thinkers. These schools inosculate in respect of some of their arguments, and of their objections against ordinary modes of thought. They disagree, however, in their aims—the ports at which they land themselves and their disciples.

Psychological Idealism is best known to most readers through Mr. J. S. Mill. The Theological view, so far as this country goes, seems to have made scant progress beyond Berkeley and a few of his clever followers. For ordinary Englishmen, a reference to continental writers on this question seems useless;—Theology being discussed by them in so ab extrâ a manner as to put them out of court with even the most metaphysical of our theologians.

Regarding the subject in a psychological light, Mr. O'Hanlon made the following common-sense remarks amongst others of a more abstract nature: [127] —

"To come now to Mr. Mill's Idealism. He, as all the world of thinkers knows, following the steps of Berkeley and Hume, claims, by means of his power of analysis, and by the aid of the formidable psychological instrument furnished him by the doctrine of the Association of Ideas, to have got rid of all other existences save and except states of consciousness, actual and possible.... I propose to try and answer his arguments" (i.e., within certain expressed limitations)— "Let A = all my sensations. "B = the group of sensations and of permanent possibilities of sensation I call my body." C = the group of permanent possibilities of sensation I call my friend Smith.

"Now I find B always related to A in a very peculiar manner. B has in perpetual conjunction with it a long series of manifold states of consciousness, A. C resembles B in very many particulars, but it is not so related to A. I hence conclude, if I follow Mr. Mill, that C is so related to some other A, that is, to some other consciousness. In drawing this conclusion, in extending to C, which so closely resembles B, my experience of B, I, according to Mr. Mill, do but extend the principles of inductive evidence, which experience shews hold good of my states of consciousness, to a sphere without my consciousness."

The italicized words sound simple enough to the ordinary reader, but argument upon them involves (as Mr. O'Hanlon observes) two serious postulates.

"(a) That there is a sphere beyond my consciousness; the very thing to be proved, (b) That the laws, which obtain in my consciousness, also obtain in the sphere beyond it."

But;—

"'Such an inference'" he goes on to quote from Mill "'would only be warrantable if we could know à priori that we must have been created capable of conceiving whatever is capable of existing: that the universe of thought and that of reality, the microcosm and the macrocosm (as they once were called) must have been framed in complete correspondence with one another. That this is really the case has been laid down expressly by some systems of philosophy, by implication in more, and is the foundation (among others) of the systems of Schelling and Hegel; but an assumption more destitute of evidence could scarcely be made, nor can one easily imagine any evidence that could prove it unless it were revealed from above.'" Mill on Hamilton, chap. VI. p. 65.

The reader will probably see at once where the abstract difficulty lies, and how it runs up into the higher metaphysics.

Now, as Mr. O'Hanlon puts the case, taking all this for granted;

"A boy cuts his finger and screams.... Yet if I was not by, the boy, the knife, the blood, the scream, would only exist potentially."

Or on the other hand if I sacrifice consistency and substitute 'actually' for 'potentially,' "I thereby reject the validity of the Psychological method" which asserts "that the belief in an external cause of our sensations" is not original but "generated 'so early as to have become inseparable from our consciousness before the time at which memory commences.' ... Nevertheless, it afterwards admits that the belief in the case of persons, has an external cause. Hereby the method commits suicide, falsus in uno, falsus in omnibus."

Finally, he remarks,

"the psychological method professes very little regard for our natural beliefs. Now I can, by a vigorous effort, regard matter as mere states or possible states of my consciousness (at least I can do so for the moment), but I can also look on other persons in the same light. Why should one natural belief be treated more tenderly than another?... In short, if I refuse to postulate a non ego, and if I hold that, supposing the states of consciousness I call the ego can be shewn capable of producing the notion of the non ego, then they did produce it, and if I hold that they can be shewn to be so capable, such a theory is equally applicable to external consciousnesses as to external matter. In both cases, I cannot get out of the sphere of my own feelings; there may be something beyond or there may not, but if there is, it is at all events incognisable by me, and to all intents and purposes I am alone in the universe" [128].

In drift and true meaning Bishop Berkeley's Idealism differed toto caelo from Mill's, as well as from Hume's idealistic Scepticism. His belief in a world outside us all was as firm as that of the firmest Realist, and by a world outside us he meant a world which neither we nor our conceptions can alter. His reasoning was also of the most common-sense description. Sensation is (as before said) a sign between us and things outside. But the sign tells us nothing of any substratum on which the things signified depend for their sign-giving powers. Matter (as commonly understood [129]) is a figment devised by certain philosophers;—the true subsistence of the outward world is in and for mind, and apart from thought it does not subsist at all. But my mind, nay the human mind, is limited. There is One whose thoughts are not as our thoughts;—in Him the world subsists, and in Him we also have our Being continually. The world is what it is to us, in and through Him, and it appeals not to our so-called material frames but to our minds.

Berkeley's argument was simply this. Take away gross matter—and the world is still perfectly

Real. It is real because God is real. Real for us, real in Him; and by this we know His Reality [130].

By comparing this phase of Idealism with the modern doctrine of what is called the "Conditioned," its Theological interest becomes still more obvious. Suppose we naturally know only what is conditioned (i.e., dependent on some Absolute reality to us unknown), what ought, asks Dr. Mansel, to be the inference? The right inference is that the Divine Absolute did not leave our world in ignorance, but did really reveal Himself to Man.

The fate of arguments framed in special interests, however noble those interests may be, is usually the same. Some clever antagonist allows their destructive force, but refuses their affirmative conclusions. Berkeley's denial of the unknown substratum called matter was approved by sceptics, who scoffed at his unknown God. His idealism was pronounced unanswerable, his divinity needed no answer. There fore, the Reason remained without satisfaction of any kind,

"Most of the writings" says Hume "of that very ingenious author form the best lessons of scepticism which are to be found either among the ancient or modern philosophers, Bayle not excepted. He professes, however, in his title-page (and undoubtedly with great truth,) to have composed his book against the sceptics as well as against the atheists and freethinkers. But that all his arguments, though otherwise intended, are, in reality, merely sceptical, appears from this, that they admit of no answer, and produce no conviction." (*Inquiry Concerning the Human Understanding*. Section XII.)

And be it remarked that this final clause forms a skilled definition of Scepticism—its essential notion—given by an expert. Dean Mansel himself who left at his death an unfinished article upon Berkeley, suffered under a charge of promoting what he desired to discourage. So dangerous is it to deal with wide questions by narrowing their sweep to a point; yet on the other hand how few students are prepared to read and think widely?

Shall we attribute to a growing width of Thought, the increased breadth of view under which Idealism has of late years been represented? The German Philosopher, with whom Schwegler closes his philosophic history writes "This ideality or non-substantiality of the finite is the chief maxim of philosophy; and for that reason every true philosophy is idealistic" (Idealismus) [131]. In England Mr. Green of Balliol signalises Berkeley's "true proposition—there is nothing real apart from thought—" and carefully distinguishes it from the one so often substituted for it—the fatal flaw of the Berkeleian argument [132]. Another influential thinker, Mr. Herbert Spencer,—who, like Professor Huxley, uses materialistic symbols treating them as symbols only,—has been for some time labouring after a "reconciliation of Realism and Idealism," which again is considered by an able critic, Mr. Henry Sidgwick, "an impossible compromise."—Mr. Spencer's answer to Mr. Sidgwick, on this particular point, will be found in his recently published volume of "Essays" (III. 282 seq.). A very instructive sentence occurs on p. 290.

> "Should it be said that this regarding of everything constituting experience and thought as symbolic, has a very shadowy aspect; I reply that these which I speak of as symbols, are real relatively to our consciousness; and are symbolic only in their relation to the Ultimate Reality."

So much then for a question which in a variety of shapes has exercised the human intellect throughout countless generations, and in all countries from India to the United States. It has also pervaded all spheres of Thought from physical science, (on which compare further, Additional Note I., and our next chapter), to the great philosophico-theological domain as we have already seen in certain specimens of Western thought. It would be easy to illustrate its empire far more extensively from those wonderful Eastern systems brought home to English readers thirty-six years ago by the translation of Ritters' Ancient Philosophy, but very imperfectly comprehended even now, notwithstanding the agreeable reception which Professor Max Müller has provided for them. To his writings we will gladly refer the curious student.

E. On the Relations of Fact and Theory

> "The distinction between Theory (that is, true Theory) and Fact is this: that in Theory the Ideas are considered as distinct from the Facts: in Facts, though Ideas may be involved, they are not, in our apprehension, separated from the sensations. In a Fact, the Ideas are applied so readily and familiarly, and incorporated with the sensations so entirely, that we do not see them, we see through them. A person who carefully notes the

motion of a star all night, sees the circle which it describes as he sees the star, though the circle is, in fact a result of his own Ideas. A person who has in his mind the measures of different lines and countries on the earth's surface, and who can put them together into one conception, finds that they can make no figure but a globular one: to him, the earth's globular form is a Fact, as much as the square form of his chamber. A person to whom the grounds of believing the earth to travel round the sun are as familiar as the grounds for believing the movements of the mail coaches in this country, looks upon the former event as a Fact, just as he looks upon the latter events as Facts. And a person who, knowing the Fact of the earth's annual motion, refers it distinctly to its mechanical cause, conceives the sun's attraction as a Fact, just as he conceives as a Fact, the action of the wind which turns the sails of a mill. He cannot see the force in either case; he supplies it out of his own Ideas. And thus, a true Theory is a Fact; a Fact is a familiar Theory. That which is a Fact under one aspect, is a Theory under another. The most recondite Theories when firmly established are Facts; the simplest Facts involve something of the nature of Theory. Theory and Fact correspond, in a certain degree, with Ideas and Sensations, as to the nature of their opposition. But the Facts are Facts, so far as the Ideas have been combined with the Sensations and absorbed in them: the Theories are Theories, so far as the Ideas are kept distinct from the Sensations, and so far as it is considered still a question whether those can be made to agree with these.

"We may, as I have said, illustrate this matter by considering man as interpreting the phenomena which he sees. He often interprets without being aware that he does so. Thus when we see the needle move towards the magnet, we assert that the magnet exercises an attractive force on the needle. But it is only by an interpretative act of our own minds that we ascribe this motion to attraction. That, in this case, a force is exerted—something of the nature of the pull which we could apply by our own volition—is our interpretation of the phenomena; although we may be conscious of the act of interpretation, and may then regard the attraction as a Fact.

"Nor is it in such cases only that we interpret phenomena in our own way, without being conscious of what we do. We see a tree at a distance, and judge it to be a chestnut or a lime; yet this is only an inference from the colour or form of the mass according to preconceived classifications of our own. Our lives are full of such unconscious interpretations. The farmer recognizes a good or a bad soil; the artist a picture of a favourite master; the geologist a rock of a known locality, as we recognize the faces and voices of our friends; that is, by judgments formed on what we see and hear; but judgments in which we do not analyze the steps, or distinguish the inference from the appearance. And in these mixtures of observation and inference, we speak of the judgment thus formed, as a Fact directly observed.

"Even in the case in which our perceptions appear to be most direct, and least to involve any interpretations of our own,—in the simple process of seeing,—who does not know how much we, by an act of the mind, add to that which our senses receive? Does any one fancy that he sees a solid cube? It is easy to show that the solidity of the figure, the relative position of its faces and edges to each other, are inferences of the spectator; no more conveyed to his conviction by the eye alone, than they would be if he were looking at a painted representation of a cube. The scene of nature is a picture without depth of substance, no less than the scene of art; and in the one case as in the other, it is the mind which, by an act of its own, discovers that colour and shape denote distance and solidity. Most men are unconscious of this perpetual habit of reading the language of the external world, and translating as they read. The draughtsman, indeed, is compelled, for his purposes, to return back in thought from the solid bodies which he has inferred, to the shapes of surface which he really sees. He knows that there is a mask of theory over the whole face of nature, if it be theory to infer more than we see. But other men, unaware of this masquerade, hold it to be a fact that they see cubes and spheres, spacious apartments and winding avenues. And these things are facts to them, because they are unconscious of the mental operation by which they have penetrated nature's disguise.

"And thus, we still have an intelligible distinction of Fact and Theory, if we consider Theory as a conscious, and Fact as an unconscious inference, from the phenomena which are presented to our senses."—Whewell, *Philosophy of the Inductive Sciences*, B. I. Chap. ii. Sect. 10.

F. On the "Unknowable"

If the word which heads this note could be accepted in the sense understood by Mr. Spencer's American critic, as a truthful and in all respects complete description of the First Ground of all things, there must of course be an end of all Theology, natural, and supernatural; Theism, Pantheism, and Atheism, would together become what Comte thought them,—equally unfounded, equally unmeaning, and therefore equally to be opposed, condemned, and ostracized. Between Humanity and all that is Superhuman the gulf would appear hopelessly impassable.

"To be consistent," says the Editor of the *American Index*, "Empiricism must utterly sink the soul in its material surroundings...." Mr. Spencer makes his election in Empiricism, but shrinks from the acceptance of its necessary implications, and thereby forfeits his title to rank among the great leaders of philosophy. Teaching that every faculty of the mind is the effect of impressions made by the Environment upon the Organism, he should also teach that the mind is nothing distinct from the organism, and that the mind's faculties will perish at the disintegration of the organism; that, as fire is a mere phenomenon of chemical combination, ceasing with it, so life is a mere phenomenon of organic "re-arrangement of parts," and will cease when the Dissolution which is the converse and sequel of Evolution has become complete; and that the "theory of a 'soul' is as completely exploded as the theory of 'phlogiston.'"

Such is the opinion of an unsympathising reviewer, who calls himself a Positivist of the latest development. He despises Comte, praises Hamilton, and preaches the truth of Dualism. "If," he writes, "physical science sneeringly objects that mental science proceeds on a sheer assumption of mind, the retort is crushing and cogent that physical science proceeds on the sheer assumption of matter. Who ever yet demonstrated the existence of either?... Only by admitting what can neither be demonstrated without a begging of the question, nor doubted without a reductio ad absurdum of all intelligence,—namely, the natural veracity of the intuitive and cognitive powers,—is a truly positive science possible." From this dualistic Positivism he predicts the rise of a new Theology. "We believe that Theism must be re-theologized on the basis of pure Positivism, as the absolute condition of its future growth." From the same point of view, Mr. Spencer's "reconciliation of Science and Religion" is "pretended"; and his "philosophy is chiefly valuable as indicating the rapid spread of the true spirit of Positivism," but, "like Comtism, it possesses little or no value as an exposition of Positivism in the highest departments of science."

This censure of Spencer was combated in a subsequ``ent number of the Index, by a writer signing himself "Evolutionist." The Editor prints his letter, and replies to it briefly:—

"1. The 'unknowable' must be an absolute blank to every intelligence. It surely cannot be held legitimate to make any predicate of it whatever, as Mr. Spencer himself admits. Yet he does make predicates of it which are 'derived from our own natures' and thus violates his own principle. 'Omnipresence' is simply presence throughout all space; and what do we know of 'presence' at all but by our own experience? Mr. Spencer does the very thing he forbids us to do, in making this predication.

"2. The difference between him and us is briefly this. He denies that we know anything of Force; we affirm that we know it just so far as it perceptibly acts. The Cause of Nature we maintain to be known in its effects. Hence Force is not to us the 'Unknowable,' but is rather the 'God of Science,' known just so far as Nature is known."

Here follow some stringent criticisms of the distinction between phenomena and noumena accepted by Mill as well as Spencer, which we pass over as being somewhat unintelligible without a longer discussion than can here be given to them.

On the subject of our first quotation—Empiricism—many readers may like to peruse the opinion of a writer far removed from Mr. Abbott in philosophy. The following is Hegel's dictum:—

"In Empiricism lies the great principle that whatever is true must be in the actual world and present to sensation.... Touching this principle it has been justly observed that, in what we call Experience, as distinct from the individual sensation of individual facts, there are two elements. First, there is the infinitely complex matter, which so far as itself is concerned is individualised: secondly, there is the form, as seen in the characteristics of universality and necessity. Empiricism no doubt can point to many, almost innumerable, similar perceptions: but, after all, no multitude, however great, can be the same thing as universality. Similarly, Empiricism reaches so far as the perception of changes in succession and of objects in juxtaposition or co-existence; but it presents no necessary connexion. If sensation, therefore, is to maintain its claim to be the sole basis of what men hold for truth, universality and necessity can have no right to exist: they become an accident of our minds, a mere custom, the content of which might be otherwise constituted than it is.

"It is an important corollary of this theory, that in the empirical mode of treatment the truths and rules of justice and morality, as well as the body of religion, are exhibited as the work of chance, and stripped of their objective character and inner truth" [133].

Considering how far Hegel confirms the American Positivist's opinion respecting the inevitable conclusions of consistent Empiricism, Mr. Spencer may with reason be congratulated on his very happy inconsistency.

The subject of quotation No. 2—Spencer's position in regard of the Unknowable—contains a censure which unites in alliance many widely differing authorities on this side the Atlantic. Some of these assail it from an extremely hostile point of view; but the criticism of others is conceived in a half-friendly, half-indifferent spirit. Mr. Spencer has very lately published a third volume of "Essays," and devotes Articles X and XI to his reviewers [134]. It need hardly be said that these pages will repay perusal. We shall here venture on giving a brief account of his defence as it presents itself to our own understanding.

The most salient difference between him and his critics generally, seems to lie in this circumstance;—they begin by taking the word "Unknowable" in its strict (i.e., its proper) signification. Hence they appear to assume that by "Absolute" he means—or ought to mean even when seeming to say the contrary—" absolutely abstract." Now of a mere, that is, a pure and complete abstraction, nothing can be predicated, because the idea is perfectly empty. It is in fact a Nothingness.

But suppose we say of this Absolute, (as Spencer does), it exists;—we have predicated something already;—something which destroys its complete emptiness. And again, if we are asked or, (what is better), ask ourselves how we know that an Absolute does exist, and proceed to reply, as Spencer himself replies, because it must exist; we shall have made respecting our Absolute this highest of all possible predications. It is not only Being, but necessary Being, or, in other words, it is a Self-Existent. Still more, since it is so in contradistinction from the universe of relativities, it is The Self-Existent, a totally different idea from that which the American editor dissects.

But now comes the question, who or what is answerable for the Reviewer's misconception,—Spencer or his critics? Is it the poverty of language, or the law of controversial sequency,—a law under which every thought arises as antagonistic to some other thought, and afterwards, when arisen and firmly established so as to become the subject of analysis, is found to yield more than was at first conceived. Then, of course, another antithesis arises respecting it, and we have to decide how much and what is truly meant, a question which often comes before us in this shape:—Is our thought merely the not so and so, or is it a real substantive idea? In the former case it is one-sided and negative; in the latter it is many-sided and affirmative.

At the first blush, it seems natural to blame Mr. Herbert Spencer. Everyone must feel astonished to find how much he himself knows of the Unknowable. The following sentences, however, contain a good account of one amongst his principal explanations of this apparent incongruity. Speaking of Mr. Martineau's conception of the Creator [135], he writes (*Essays*, Vol. III. p. 299):—

"Finding, as just shewn, that it leaves the essential mystery unsolved; I do not see that it has an advantage over the doctrine of the Unknowable in its unqualified shape. There cannot, I think, be more than temporary rest in a proximate solution which takes for its basis the ultimately insoluble. Just as thought cannot be prevented from passing beyond Appearance, and trying to conceive the Cause behind; so, following out the interpretation Mr. Martineau offers, thought cannot be prevented from asking what Cause it is which restricts the Cause he assigns. And if we must admit that the question under this eventual form cannot be answered, may we not as well confess that the question under its immediate form cannot be answered? Is it not better candidly to acknowledge the incompetence of our intelligence, rather than to persist in calling that an explanation which does but disguise the inexplicable? Whatever answer each may give to this question, he cannot rightly blame those who, finding in themselves an indestructible consciousness of an ultimate Cause, whence proceed alike what we call the Material Universe and what we call Mind, refrain from affirming anything respecting it; because they find it as inscrutable in nature, as it is inconceivable in extent and duration."

There will be to many people much force in this plea for leaving inscrutables amidst their primary obscurities. But it is open to a rejoinder suggested by Mr. Spencer himself,—you cannot prevent the Mind from inquiring; and, in point of fact, Spencer in person leads the way. He places before us the ultimate idea of a self-existent First Cause. Now surely he might reflect that such an Idea not only permits but invites analysis;—it is no empty abstraction, but a substantive thought and a full one. But he bars analysis to his own satisfaction, by saying that the Idea is in its own Nature inscrutable. Respecting this position two questions arise. First, if inscrutable as to its ultimate nature—its highest essence, and deepest thought,—is it so in its attributes? Next, if Spencer's special walk in philosophy ends with the bare positing of this Idea, must all Philosophy do the same? Suppose the Physicist says—"Here I learn to know the Fact of a self-existent universal First Cause," may not the investigator of our Practical human Reason try to discover whether an Ethical view ought or ought not to be taken of this Self-Existent? To answer "No," is either to make physical philosophy the sole philosophy; or it is to dismember and disjoint the universal Body of Truth into departmental carcase-fragments;—a process which never can begin till all Life has been effectually crushed out of the Whole [136]. For every one who takes wide views of Philosophy;—for every inquirer into First Principles;—above all, if Mr. Spencer will permit us to say so, for every Encyclopaedic writer like himself, a question must arise the answer to which it is incumbent on all and each to ascertain, "Can we have any conscious idea whatever of a First Cause without including that very fact of Personality from which Spencer appears to shrink?" Nay we may rather put the point thus: "Is not our idea and definition of Causality derived from Personal existence, and apart from this source of derivation, does not the derived idea perish?"—If so, to speak of a non-personal First Cause both of the outside world and of mind itself is to use words to which no thinker can consciously attach any real meaning. There must, says Mr. Spencer, be Power behind Appearance;—in other words, Phenomena imply a Cause behind them,—but to add that this Power or Cause is conceivably impersonal, seems nothing better than to imagine (Hibernicè) at the beginning of the phenomenal chain, a prior phenomenon which in its own nature and ex vi verborum cannot account for a Beginning [137] at all;—cannot, to use Mr. Spencer's expression, be "ultimate"; and, in short, requires to be accounted for, itself.

The truth is, that such ideas as First, Ultimate, Power accounting for appearance, or Cause underlying phenomena, cannot be spoken of as altogether Unknowable; because they imply and contain within themselves certain knowable and strongly defined characteristics. Pressed by his critics, Mr. Spencer becomes painfully aware of this truth; and is fearful of being driven by logic and philosophical consistency to plead guilty of believing in a Personal Author of the Universe, and of making Theism the ultimate word of Science. We see on pp. 292 and 302 of Vol. III. how he manifests a preference for the phrase non-relative, vice Absolute; meaning thereby (if he means anything new) to replace an affirmative idea by a negational abstract, empty enough to land him at once in American Positivism. For, if the non-relative means more than to say that he is unable to predicate relativity of the whole Universe of things—if it means more than an avowal of Positivist ignorance—it really does mean a true Absolute after all; and very few students of Mr. Spencer will doubt that in the sense of an Absolute (not necessarily Hegelian), this ground idea of his must be accepted.

As courteous antagonists, we will endeavour to abstain from joining with Mr. Sidgwick in the severest censure which has yet befallen Mr. Spencer,—the imputation of a "mazy inconsistency," a "fundamental incoherence," and an "inability to harmonize different lines of thought." We rather wish to congratulate him on presenting such an appearance before the eye of a critic so accomplished, and so equitable; it is a sign that we have not as yet heard Mr. Spencer's final utterance. He is, we are quite sure, divided by a wide tract of thought from the American Positivists;—but we are not sure that he may not ultimately be found amid the ranks of Scientific Theists. This at the present moment appears the most natural development of the thoughts maintained in his recently published volume. That the nature of God, considered as the "ultimate cause of what we call the material universe and what we call mind," is to us at present inscrutable;—that clouds and darkness are round about Him;—that His ways are not as our ways, nor His thoughts as our thoughts, no meditative Theist will deny. But, though the Heavens are higher than the Earth, though beatified spirits worship in humble adoration of the Incomprehensible, yet the measureless distance does not hinder us from knowing Him as a Spirit, and therefore as a Person; nor yet from confidently affirming that Righteousness and Judgment are the habitation of His throne.

G. Mr. J. S. Mill as an Independent Moralist

Few passages of Mr. Mill's writings are better worth reading than pages 123, 4, of his "Examination of Sir W. Hamilton's Philosophy." In these pages the eminent writer asserts his own strong moral sentiments, and throws to the winds that inconsistent Utilitarianism with which he had trained his mind to associate them. He will worship no Unknowable Being whose supreme moral nature does not affirm our human morality. "Why is this?" an opponent might fairly ask; "is it not useful so to do? is not such worship conducive to that noblest final end, the interest of mankind?" By saying "No" you affirm two things: one, the dissociation of Religion from Utility; a second, the indivisible association of Religion with absolute Morality.

Some antagonists may consider the first of these two propositions inadmissible, the second objectionable, or at all events, exceedingly doubtful. Everyone who maintains that Natural Theology has, in addition to its other elements, a firm and moral ground, will accept with ready assent the second proposition, and will say that the truth or falsehood of the first depends on the meaning attached to an ambiguous word. We are equally sure that "Godliness is profitable for all things," and that "Honesty is the best policy." But then we are quite sure also, that the final cause of Godliness is not profit, nor its essential nature a love of gain; and that policy is not a true description of honesty, nor the being politic the true and proper aim of the honest man. And Mr. Mill, when his moral sentiments asserted themselves, felt these certainties as elements of his inner life. Rather than worship a Being whose unknown moral attributes fell beneath, not the dictates of Utility, but the purest instincts of his own inmost morality, Mr. Mill goes on to declare that he is willing to suffer the horrors of Eternal death [138]. Hell is better than a violation of his own moral nature. Can this be a declaration deduced from the supreme law of Interest,—is it not rather a foundation maxim of independent morality? Violate such foundation maxims, says the independent moralist, and you need not even speak of "Going to hell," hell will come to you. Sooner or later you will find its undying torments within you.

In an article on the death of Mr. Mill, the Pall Mall Gazette expresses its perception of his leading inconsistency as follows:—

"It is impossible to read Mr. Mill's works with any attention, and in particular to look with intelligence on the later part of his career, without seeing that by temperament he was essentially religious, but that as far as positive doctrine went his mind was an absolute blank. We believe that it was this sharp contrast between theory and feeling which drove him into the schemes for the improvement of the world which have been exposed to so many, and, in some respects, to such well-founded objections. Having to love something, and being, as it were, chained down by his own logic to this world and this life, past, present, and future, he struggled to make a sort of religion out of man as he might come to be after centuries or millenniums. Humanity, progress, a realization of all the ideals at which his theories pointed—these were his divinities, for he was a man who could not do without some divinity, and he could find no other. We do not think that his life or his thoughts were triumphant. If he had consistently followed out his own views, if he had carried out his Benthamism with perfect consistency, the result would have been too hard, too grim, too dismal for his eager and sensitive heart. Hence came the faltering, the inconsistency, the romance of his later days. It is a spectacle which may well humble everyone who looks on it with intelligence and sympathy. From us, at least, it shall never draw one word of sarcasm, or one thought which is not full of deep respect, regret, and pity. He bore a burden common to many. If he bent under it, it was not because his strength was less, but because his sensibility was greater. When he died one of the tenderest and most passionate hearts that ever set to work an intellect of iron was laid to rest. May he rest in peace, and find, if it be possible, that his knowledge was less complete than he perhaps supposed, and that there was more to be known than was acknowledged in his philosophy." (Pall Mall Gazette, *Saturday*, May, 10, 1873.)

A little earlier in the same article we find another paragraph worthy of careful consideration:—

"No succession of writers ever exercised greater power over the fortunes of this nation, we might say of any nation, than Locke, Hume, Adam Smith, Bentham, and Mr. Mill. What may be described as the theory of modern life has been thought out by them, and translated into its practical equivalents with a persistency, a precision, a degree of method and calmness unequalled in the history of thought. We do not say that their results are complete, but we do say that their teaching has been successful to an unexampled degree; and that, however unpopular it may be with ardent and enthusiastic persons, it is impossible to believe that it could have done what it has done without possessing a very strong hold on human nature."

Viewing this extract by the light of the one before cited, we cannot help asking what side of human nature is it to which the Benthamite doctrines attach themselves? Shall we not regret that the hard, the grim, and the dismal, should characterize our 19th century philosophy? Philosophy that is falsely so called; for the true is "not harsh and crabbed as dull fools suppose."

The text of this Essay and its earlier notes were completed while Mr. Mill was in the ripeness of his powers, and when the present writer never expected to outlive him. Death softens our view of one who has passed away—the bygone life becomes like a moonlighted landscape—asperities hidden in shadow, and a soft radiance poured over each grander eminence. So may it be felt by the critic of every great departed! If, indeed, it prove otherwise with Mr. Mill, the preventing cause will probably be found in certain pages of his published "Autobiography."

H. Archebiosis, or Spontaneous Generation

The origin of Life is a question that naturally excites much interest, and consequently has been much discussed. It is obviously a problem that presents difficulties of no ordinary kind, and therefore it is by no means astonishing that many theories have been started and statements made which have in turn been quickly contradicted.

It is now known that the whole cycle of phenomena—collectively denoted by the term "Life,"—is manifested by a substance possessing definite physical and chemical properties, and by no other. This substance constitutes the entire organism of the lower forms of life, whether animal or vegetable, and also of the higher in their earliest stage, while from it by various metamorphoses are developed the different histological elements composing the complex tissues of higher animals and plants. Its name Protoplasm is in consequence exceedingly apt, when properly understood.

As to the origin of Protoplasm (or apparent Life) it is clear from a little consideration that two questions may be asked: first, how did Protoplasm arise? and secondly, when once this substance had come into being are we to suppose that from that time to this all Protoplasm has been derived by unbroken descent from the first Protoplasm, or does fresh Protoplasm even now arise in the same way as did the first?—in other words, does the transition from the inorganic to the organic, from what has never lived to what is living, still take place as it must have taken place at some period or another?

To neither of these questions can Physical Science return a perfectly certain and definite answer. And it must be confessed that as far as our knowledge of Nature goes, those have the best of it who maintain first, that all existing Protoplasm implies pre-existing Protoplasm; secondly, that as to the method, the conditions of the real origin of Protoplasm nothing whatsoever is known; and thirdly, that, notwithstanding all assertions and experiments to the contrary, the origin of living things from dead and decaying organic matter (i.e., matter that has lived), or from inorganic matter under given conditions (spontaneous generation, generatio aequivoca, archebiosis) has never been proved and demonstrated in such a manner as to allow us no room for hesitation, no place for doubt.

The difficulties and dangers besetting this thorny and much-vexed subject will be better understood if we institute a short examination into the history and present condition of the doctrine of Spontaneous Generation.

It is certain from the results of astronomical and geological investigation, that at an exceedingly remote epoch, estimated by untold millions of years, the earth's surface was absolutely unfitted for the presence of life; nay, more, that even the laws of chemical combination were suspended, and in abeyance. After the glowing spheroid cooled down, and various chemical compounds were formed, life as a matter of fact made its appearance on the earth. Throughout the inorganic world the continuity is unbroken—the present is truly the child of the past. But in the organic world it is not so. Whether life arose in the natural course of universal law, or how it did arise, we cannot tell, scientifically, that is to say; no assertion, one way or the other, admits either of proof or disproof. There are absolutely no data to proceed upon. The very first organic remains discovered belong to a comparatively high type.

It is as though in a garden every plant and bush burst at once into full flower, and never showed the flower in the bud.

These points are very well put in a passage of Littré [139]:

"Jusqu'à ce moment, nous avons cheminé de phénomènes en phénomènes qui se passaient tous sous le régime des lois chimiques et physiques. Leur succession ne présentait aucune solution de continuité; les degrés tenaient l'un à l'autre; et c'est cette déduction qui satisfait l'esprit humain, et qu'il nomme explication. Une fois que l'on reconnaît une dissémination première, dans l'espace, d'une matière douée de gravitation et de mouvement, tout en ignorant absolument d'où vient cette matière and d'où procèdent son mouvement et sa dissémination, le reste s'ensuit. Des amas qu'on appelle soleils se forment par condensation; cette condensation développe une immense chaleur; le refroidissement graduel sépare les amas primordiaux en amas secondaires et plus petits qui se meuvent comme lui, se refroidissent comme lui, et représentent nos planètes, nos satellites, et en particulier notre terre. On a l'univers, on passe au monde, et du monde au globe terrestre.

"Mais là, sur le monde terrestre, un hiatus se présente. Un phénomène nouveau, une force nouvelle apparaît, et la vie se développe en végétalité et animalité. Ce phénomène nouveau, cette force nouvelle, cette vie ne succèdent point par une action continue aux actions continues dont le soleil et la terre sont le théâtre; du moins, en l'état actuel de nos connaissances, la continuité nous échappe. On conçoit, grâce à des faits expérimentaux recueillis de toutes parts et transformés en lois, comment notre globe se refroidit, comment, en se refroidissant, il prend sa forme, comment l'atmosphère, les continents, la mer se constituent; mais on ne conçoit plus comment la vie y parait à un moment donné. Et ce fut bien à un moment donné: pendant des millions de siècles, la terre, vu son incandescence, fut impropre à toute vie. Quand la température y eut baissé au degré compatible avec les existences vivantes, ces existences se montrèrent; mais comment? par quel procédé?

"Il ne faut pourtant pas faire valoir outre mesure cette discontinuité. Une discontinuité, autre que celle qui appartient à l'apparition de la vie, est survenue dans le cours du développement de la terre. Quand les particules qui la composent, étaient animées d'une immense chaleur, une dissociation complète y régnait; elles n'obéissaient qu'aux lois du mouvement, de la gravitation, de la chaleur et de la lumière; les lois chimiques, c'est-à-dire de combinaison et de décombinaison, n'y étaient qu'à l'état virtuel. Elles passèrent à l'état effectif, dès que l'abaissement de la température le permit. Je sais bien qu'une différence considérable existe entre ces deux discontinuités: en effet, depuis lors, il a toujours été possible de reproduire à volonté les faits chimiques; et, toutes les fois que nous en avons besoin, nous répétons le phénomène d'origine qui se produisit dans les combinaisons et décombinaisons. Pour la vie, c'est autre chose; elle a été une fois émise, et, depuis le phénomène d'origine, elle ne se propage que par génération. Un être vivant est necessaire pour produire un être vivant; et, ni par les procédés de la nature, ni par ceux de la science, ce qui se fit au moment créateur ne se refait. Malgré cette considerable différence, il demeure que la terre a possédé des forces virtuelles qui sont entrées en action, quand les conditions générales, se modifiant graduellement, l'ont permis."

A little further on he continues:—

"Au point de vue d'origine, on abandonnera la question comme toutes les questions qui impliquent une cause première. La philosophie positive s'exprime là- dessus comme elle s'exprime touchant toutes les choses hyperphysiques, c'est-à-dire placées au delà de l'expérience. Quand elle entend les matérialistes prononcer que la vie est le résultat des forces physiques et chimiques dont on connaît l'action, elle refuse d'accepter une solution qui dépasse les prémisses. Mais elle n'écarte pas la solution matérialiste au profit de la solution théologique; l'intervention d'un Dieu créateur est également invérifiable par l'expérience, et, partant, atteinte de la même fin de non-recevoir. Maintenant, si on demande à la philosophie positive quelle est, à elle, sa solution entre la génération matérialiste et la création surnaturelle, elle répond qu'elle n'a aucune solution à proposer, que rien ne peut la forcer à croire ce qui n'est pas démontré, et qu'elle accepte, avec autant de fermeté que d'humilité, une ignorance invincible sur tout ce qui est indemontrable."

In the first passage certain salient points are strikingly brought out, above all the vast difference between the worlds organic and inorganic; but, next, how much soever a Positivist may be pleased to believe only that which admits of phenomenal verification, it is not every one, especially if given to thought, who would willingly endorse the second paragraph. If we know only what we can verify, many beliefs must needs be abandoned, and amongst them some which have received the almost universal assent of mankind. Knowledge (in the sense of verifiable knowledge) and Belief may appear two widely different things; but it should never be forgotten that we often accept the one as surely as the other.

The ancients held that living things arose from the earth at any time, engendered by the warmth of the sun and moisture. Absurd as it may seem, the belief that blue-bottle flies, etc., were a natural result of the decay of meat and other organic matter obtained credence even in comparatively modern times. Redi, an eminent Italian, first demonstrated experimentally the falsehood of this doctrine, and for some time the hypothesis of spontaneous generation appeared to have received a death-blow. And by degrees the conviction that every living thing proceeded from a germ gained strength, and was confirmed by the rapidly extending use of the microscope. Yet in the eighteenth century certain experiments of Needham seemed to establish the fact that in boiled infusions where presumably all germs were destroyed, small Infusoria made their appearance even when means were taken to exclude the entrance of fresh germs. Buffon lent the authority of his great name. These experiments were repeated by the Abbé Spallanzani, who showed by more careful methods the fallacy of the conclusions drawn. A passage in Sir B. Brodie [140] which alludes to these facts may be worth quoting:—

"Crites. Then am I to understand that you would reject altogether the hypothesis of equivocal generation, which supposes that under certain circumstances, even at the present time, particles of inorganic matter are brought together, and so united as to become endowed with organization and life?

"Eubulus. The question is one of great interest, and I will refer you to Ergates for an answer, knowing at the same time pretty well what that answer will be.

"Ergates. Of course Crites refers to the production of those minute creatures, known by the name of Infusoria, in the experiments of Walter Needham, and some others.

"It is true that in these experiments certain vegetable and animal infusions, after no very long period of time, when examined by the microscope, are found to contain a multitude of minute creatures, of various forms, exhibiting signs of spontaneous motion, and multiplying their species in the usual manner. Some of these are even of a complicated structure, much beyond what might, à priori, be expected as the result of the first attempt of inorganic matter to enter into the realms of organic life. The subject has been so frequently discussed, that I need not trouble you with the details of the arguments which have led the most eminent naturalists to believe that these creatures are not really spontaneously engendered, but that they are derived from minute ova which are present in the air, and which, when placed under circumstances favourable to their development, burst into life: in the same way as the egg undergoes those changes which convert its contents into a bird, when placed under the influence of the animal heat of the parent. But even if this view of the matter be not correct, the case is not really altered; for, after all, the Infusoria are never detected except in vegetable and animal infusions, which necessarily presuppose the existence of organic life."

But it is one thing to demolish the theory and statements of an antagonist, and another to erect a structure in their place. However completely Spallanzani had demonstrated the faults and untrustworthiness of Needham's results, he had not established the opposite doctrine, and to many it seemed that the very conditions under which his experimentation was conducted, were sufficient to prevent the development of life. But the work begun by Schulze and Schwann and ended by Pasteur apparently has supplied what was wanting in Spallanzani's researches. The evidence is thus admirably summed by Professor Huxley: [141] —

"It is demonstrable, that a fluid eminently fit for the development of the lowest forms of life, but which contains neither germs, nor any protein compound, gives rise to living things in great abundance, if it is exposed to ordinary air; while no such development takes place, if the air with which it is in contact is mechanically freed from the solid particles, which ordinarily float in it and which maybe made visible by appropriate means.

"It is demonstrable, that the great majority of these particles are destructible by heat, and that some of them are germs, or living particles, capable of giving rise to the same forms of life as those which appear when the fluid is exposed to unpurified air.

"It is demonstrable, that inoculation of the experimental fluid with a drop of liquid known to contain living particles, gives rise to the same phenomena as exposure to unpurified air.

"And it is further certain that these living particles are so minute that the assumption of their suspension in ordinary air presents not the slightest difficulty. On the contrary, considering their lightness and the wide diffusion of the organisms which produce them, it is impossible to conceive that they should not be suspended in the atmosphere in myriads."

The experimental means by which these facts are proved may be briefly stated:—

I.   The air contains solid particles. Professor Tyndall has shown, as all who have read "Dust and Disease" know to their own discomfort, that the purest common air, when submitted to a beam of electric light, renders the track of that beam visible. Ergo, it must contain solid particles capable of scattering light.

II.   These particles are mostly destructible by heat, or may be mechanically strained off. He has shown this by the fact that common air which has passed through a red-hot tube, or through a filter of cotton-wool, will no longer render the track of the electric beam visible.

III.   Many of these particles are germs. Schulze and Schwann proved that when air is passed through red-hot tubes, then through a fluid which is capable of affording a nidus to the germs, if present, no development of life takes place. Similarly Schroeder established the same fact by using a strainer of cotton-wool. Further, Pasteur gave an additional proof by microscopical examination, as well as by a direct experiment. He passed air through gun-cotton, dissolved this in ether; and in the collodion germs were clearly recognizable. Also he plunged a piece of cotton-wool through which air had been strained into an experimental fluid. This fluid soon swarmed with forms of life.

IV.   The experimental fluid may be inoculated by simple exposure to air as well as by any fluids known to contain living forms; e.g., if the fluid be placed in an open vessel, living forms soon make their appearance. Yet supposing the aperture of the vessel, instead of pointing vertically upwards, be turned obliquely or downwards, the fluid will remain clear for an indefinite time. Similarly a drop of an infusion containing living forms added to the experimental fluid soon causes it to swarm with life. The forms that appear are the same in either case.

V.   The experimental fluid cannot give rise itself to these forms. It is known as Pasteur's solution, and consists of water, ammonium, tartrate, sugar, and yeast ash. Hence there is no organic matter in it. If proper care be taken, it may be kept for an indefinite time.

VI.   The germs are so minute that in many cases, even when known to be present, they are scarcely visible to the highest microscopic powers. They must be universally diffused, as any organic infusion left exposed soon swarms with the forms to which they give rise.

Such an array of facts, proved experimentally over and over again, must convince the most tenacious sceptic, and he may feel inclined to agree with the opinion expressed in the following passage from Sir B. Brodie: [142] —

> "Crites. Then, if I understand you rightly, you have arrived at these conclusions. First, that there was a time when this earth was not in a fit state for the maintenance of either animal or vegetable life. Secondly, that in its present condition there is no evidence of any law being in operation which would account for any living beings being called into existence except as the offspring of other living beings which previously existed; and that from these premises we cannot fail to arrive at this further conclusion, that the first introduction of life on earth must have been by some special act of the creative power, of which we have no experience at present.
>
> "Eubulus. I suspect that this, really and truly, is all we actually know on the subject."

Notwithstanding this apparently irresistible amount of evidence, the question of abiogenesis has recently been revived by Dr. C. Bastian in a well-known book, "The Beginnings of Life." Dr. Bastian believes that he has demonstrated the origin of living organisms from organic infusions as well as from solutions of salts containing no organic matter: nay, even more wonderful facts than these which it is unnecessary to specify. His experiments are so numerous, his assertions and figures so clear and definite, and his reputation for previous good scientific work once so high, that the book has caused no small stir and discussion. Could Dr. Bastian's facts be only established, they would inevitably revolutionize the whole science of Biology.

However, the same fate which has overtaken his predecessors has befallen Dr. Bastian himself. A nearly universal verdict of "Not proven" has been returned: and not only is the accuracy of his experimentation denied, but even worse accusations have been brought. To enter into details of his experiments would require too much space, but it may not be uninteresting to detail some of the peculiarities and difficulties which attend on the investigation of such a subject as Spontaneous Generation.

At the very threshold of the inquiry stands a grand difficulty. Strange as it may seem, it is nevertheless true, that notwithstanding the many years, the immense labour bestowed by illustrious men on this subject, next to nothing is known of the relations existing between the lowest forms of life, animal or vegetable (especially the latter), as well as their germs, and varying physical and chemical conditions. Heat, light, cold and darkness, alkalies and acids with other chemical compounds, one would imagine to be not without their influence. Yet what this influence may be in a given case, none can tell. Enough is known in the way of a few detached facts to make it certain that these agents have very decided effects. It might be thought that anyone who wished to attack the problem of Spontaneous Generation anew would first try to obtain some connected knowledge on this point. Indeed, until it has been cleared up somewhat, it is not very evident what good Experimentation on Heterogenesis can do. It is much as if a chemist were to throw a handful of stuff (what he knew not) into a crucible, and then expect a valuable result. It can scarcely be doubted that many of these lower organisms live and grow under conditions which à priori might seem incompatible with vitality.

It is clear also that the work of one experimenter ought to be such as may admit of repetition by another with the same result. Now no one who attempts the study of this subject of Spontaneous Generation, can fail to be struck with the immense mass of conflicting evidence. Some mischievous spirit appears to have purposely thrown confusion over the whole. Facts are alternately stated and denied. It is very hard to be sure of the right road, even for an experienced person.

Another point relates to the value of the evidence when obtained. It can scarcely be doubted that out of a given number of experiments undertaken to establish a case of Heterogenesis or Archebiosis, great value should be attached to the negative evidence afforded by those that disprove the supposed fact. A little consideration will show the reason. The precautions to be taken against the intrusion of germs are innumerable: a slight exposure to the air, accidental contact of an unheated rod or tube, or neglect of some other particulars may inoculate the experimental fluid. Hence even with care the chances are many in favour of some such accidental intrusion, and great caution should always be exercised before an affirmative result can be regarded as firmly established.

And further there is the experimentalist himself to be taken into account. The task requires an intimate knowledge of many minute organisms, and the different forms they assume; an acquaintance, wide and accurate, with various experimental methods; a clear view of the end and the various precautions required to attain that end; a mind ready to contrive, prone to doubt and to hesitate, rather than to be convinced. Men vary much in the amount of what is scientifically termed their personal equation, and one difficulty in accepting the results of a piece of work is the danger of misplaced confidence.

As was said before, Dr. Bastian's attempt to demonstrate the reality of Spontaneous Generation has been a failure. His experiments have been repeated, and failed to give the like results in the hands of competent men. Witness the following quotation from a careful review of his book in the *Microscopical Journal* [143]. It relates to the now celebrated cheese and turnip solution.

"Nevertheless in consequence of the interest which Dr. Bastian's work has excited, we have made the experiment (and that repeatedly) as directed by him. This is not the occasion on which to give the details of the experiments in question. It will, however, perhaps add some value to the remarks which it has been our duty to make when we state that, carefully following Dr. Bastian's directions, using at the same time great care as to cleanliness and due boiling, we have obtained results which in every single instance, out of more than forty tubes closed on four separate occasions, simply contradict Dr. Bastian. We believe, then, that Dr. Bastian's last dogma in archebiosis,—his belief in turnip solution with a fragment of cheese—must be placed in the same category as his colloidal urea, his spontaneously generated bog-moss, his fungi born in crystals, his unmistakable processes of heterogenesis, and his 'watching' and 'experimentation' in general."

The reviewer proceeds to question whether Dr. Bastian has even the knowledge requisite for so delicate an investigation. It would be supposed that he was intimately acquainted with various microscopical structures; but we read [144],

"Professor Huxley gives a contribution towards the determination of the personal value in Dr. Bastian's researches. He (Dr. Bastian) will recollect that he wrote to me asking permission to bring for my examination certain preparations of organic structures, which he declared he had clear and positive evidence to prove to have been developed in his closed and digested tubes. Dr. Bastian will remember that when the first of these wonderful specimens was put under my microscope I told him at once that it was nothing but a fragment of the leaf of the common bog-moss (Sphagnum), and he will recollect that I had to fetch Schacht's book "Die Pflanzenzelle" and show him a figure which fitted very well with what we had under the microscope before I could get him to listen to my suggestion, and that only actual comparison with Sphagnum, after he had left my house, forced him to admit the astounding blunder which he had made.'

"Of these three pieces of evidence, the last is the most important, for, whilst it places us on our guard with regard to Dr. Bastian's accuracy generally, it at the same time furnishes a key to the explanation of a number of his experiments in which, according to that precipitate discoverer, 'organisms' were found on opening tubes containing infusions which had been boiled and sealed hermetically."

How then are we to sum up the case? for or against Dr. Bastian? Can any thoughtful person admit the conclusions of one apparently so unfit for his task? The best answer is in the words of his Reviewer [145].

"Briefly it is to be said that the chapters in this book on heterogenesis, contain a reckless attempt to revolutionize biological doctrine without a single demonstration of fact to justify it, even if it be admitted that the observations and drawings cited are accurate. Revolution in science as in politics can only be justified by success—a wanton attempt in either sphere must deserve the severest condemnation. Dr. Bastian by his exhibition of himself in dealing with heterogenesis writes himself down as incapable—as inadmissible in the character of a witness in a scientific investigation. The Sphagnum delusion is now explained, for it becomes evident that we have to deal with an individual with whom such delusions are no rare exceptions.

"We should indeed be sorry to believe that Dr. Bastian is himself aware of the injury which he is doing to the cause of science, by promulgating these rash assertions as to the beginnings and changes of living things; we altogether decline to entertain the notion that he is himself conscious of the baselessness and flimsy character of his startling discoveries, and is nevertheless willing at the expense of injury to the cause of intellectual progress, to obtain for himself a temporary notoriety. On the contrary, we believe that he is under the influence of a delusion, similar to those which from time to time obtain notoriety in the case of 'spiritualists,' 'circle-squarers,' and such victims of belief in the marvellous. The origin and mode of growth of such delusions form a very interesting psychological study, and it is only when we have obtained a proper conception of Dr. Bastian as an abnormal psychological phenomenon that we can hope rightly to appreciate the whole of the statements made in his book.

"Delusion and self-deception are much commoner than the world is generally accustomed to consider them. In a very well-known and often quoted remark we have a recognition of the wide- spread occurrence of delusions and an attempt to explain their origin; the saying to which we allude is, 'The wish was father to the thought.' There cannot be the least doubt that men are unconsciously hindered or misdirected in their estimate of fact by previously formed desires. Such a desire acts on the mind like the suggestion of the mesmerist to an individual who has allowed himself to be brought into the hypnotic condition. In this way many misconceptions and strange contradictions of testimony are to be explained."

The importance of the subject is sufficient apology for so long a quotation. But our quotations allow us to draw one conclusion; that so far as Spontaneous Generation is concerned human knowledge is exactly in status quo. Up to this time there is no evidence, worth consideration, that establishes a single good case of heterogenesis; nay, rather all evidence points to the conclusion that Protoplasm is invariably derived from pre-existing Protoplasm, at least under existing conditions. Then too there is no fact known which enables us to say how Protoplasm arose in the first instance. On this point we are in the darkness of complete scientific ignorance. The whole discussion may be well closed by a striking passage from Professor Huxley's before quoted address [146].

"But though I cannot express this conviction of mine too strongly, I must carefully guard myself against the supposition that I intend to suggest that no such thing as abiogenesis ever has taken place in the past, or ever will take place in the future. With organic chemistry, molecular physics, and physiology yet in their infancy, and every day making prodigious strides, I think it would be the height of presumption for any man to say that the conditions under which matter assumes the properties we call 'vital' may not, some day, be artificially brought together. All I feel justified in affirming is, that I see no reason for believing that the feat has been performed yet.

"And, looking back through the prodigious vista of the past, I find no record of the commencement of life, and therefore I am devoid of any means of forming a definite conclusion as to the conditions of its appearance. Belief, in the scientific sense of the word, is a serious matter, and needs strong foundations. To say, therefore, in the admitted absence of evidence, that I have any belief as to the mode in which the existing forms of life have originated, would be using words in a wrong sense. But expectation is permissible where belief is not; and if it were given me to look beyond the abyss of geologically recorded time to the still more remote period when the earth was passing through physical and chemical conditions, which it can no more see again than a man can recal his infancy, I should expect to be a witness of the evolution of living protoplasm from not living matter. I should expect to see it appear under forms of great simplicity, endowed, like existing Fungi, with the power of determining the formation of new protoplasm from such matters as ammonium carbonates, oxalates and tartrates, alkaline and earthy phosphates, and water, without the aid of light. That is the expectation to which analogical reasoning leads me; but I beg you once more to recollect that I have no right to call my opinion anything but an act of philosophical faith."

Obviously, as Professor Huxley points out, between philosophical faith and philosophical knowledge there is a chasm to be bridged over. But should the hypothesis ever be verified, it would make no difference to the reasonings of the Natural Theologian—since the concurrence of conditions necessary for the production of the phaenomenon would manifestly ensue upon some definite though recondite law, at present beyond our ken.

I. On Materialism

The ambiguities attaching to this term were mentioned in a foot-note on our very first page. Since that note was written, the tendency of scientific men has been to increase the number of hypotheses respecting the nature and laws of the material world, and by consequence to multiply the shades of signification conveyed by the word Materialism.

So long as such distinctions are confined to the territory of pure science, whether that of the Physicist or of the Biologist, they do not in themselves affect the religious (or ethico-religious) position of any thinker; and need not, therefore, occasion any trouble to the Natural Theologian. But it is worthwhile to observe how rashly, on account of some such scientific discussion, a writer is said to be a Materialist or no Materialist, by persons who (understanding little or nothing of science themselves) drag the unhappy author outside the pale of his own domain, and affix to him some religious or irreligious epithet which he has neither desired nor deserved.

The philosophic idealist often escapes; he is pronounced "no Materialist," because he doubts the substantive existence of Matter, yet he may and often does hold that the ideal thing he calls his soul, has a life inextricably bound up with that other ideal thing he calls his body, and must perish with it, never to live again.

We may add the useful remark that so far as Ethico-religious Materialism is concerned it is much more easily tested by the Doctrine of Soul than the Doctrine of Body. For example, consistent Materializers will always maintain that the reasoning human soul differs from the animal soul of brutes, not in quality, but in quantity. Dr. L. Büchner (sometimes called a "crass Materialist") makes this assertion repeatedly, and explains it by adding—

> "Man has no absolute advantage above the animal; his mental superiority being merely relative. There is not one intellectual faculty which belongs to man exclusively; his superiority is merely the result of the greater intensity, and the proper combination, of his capacities. The enlarged human faculties are, as we have already seen, the natural and necessary result of the higher and more perfect development of his material organ of thought" [147].

Turning to a more refined species of Materialism, we find a similar value always placed on the dogma that whatever differences exist between man and brute, they amount to a distinction not of kind, but only of degree. The consequences hence deduced are of the very greatest importance, and they run much as follows. No one will venture to assert that the power of what has been hastily called Volition is, or can be, an endowment of mere animal nature. We do not lay upon the tiger (as we do popularly lay upon the tyrant) a moral responsibility on account of his savage appetites. Their indulgence does not flow from any reasoning faculty of Will. His cruelty is the movement of automatic instincts, governed by laws like those which rule over the inanimate world; more complicated probably, but no-ways different in their essence. The fall of a stone, and the spring of a tiger, are both consequences of determining laws inherent in their several modes of existence, and moving both as machinery is moved by a steam engine. Now, a difference in degree only, argues no difference in those essential laws which rule equally the greater and the less. The giant and the dwarf are alike subject to the same laws of body and mind; and man is (as we have seen) but a mentally taller brute. The tyrant, therefore, resembles the tiger; the human animal is moved as the other animals are moved, and, like them, is subject to the determining law, just as the lifeless world is so subjected. In plain words, then, this human machine is moved like other machines. What we call Reason, spontaneity, volition, are, when analysed, no exceptions to the law-governed mechanism of the world we live in. Our motives make us, not we our motives. The faculty we exercise under the name of Choice, is really neither more nor less than a determined, unalterable, impulsion; the result of a mechanical law. And this law has formed and now constitutes the Universe [148].

Refined Materialism proceeds to ask in the next place, what more do we know of Matter than its rigid undeviating reign of Law?—The great Globe itself obeys the same Laws as the falling stone: they pervade and direct the mechanism of the starry heavens. Life does not exempt either vegetable or animal from the same rule of law. We have just seen that Mankind is not so made to differ, as to permit a plea of exemption from the same empire. Ascend from Protoplasm to the highest human intelligence,—one heritage devolves through brute to man. The same mechanical law accounts for the "Psychogeny" of both. Mechanical Law, in its ramifications, is (as has been said) all we really know of Matter. It now turns out that all Mind has been developed by this same ever-ramifying law; may be analyzed back into its elements; is most truly expressed by its symbols; and can never be exempted from its determinations. Mind, therefore, and Matter are resolvable into this sole unity—the Law of ultimate mechanical movement and impulsion.

We have called this system a refined Materialism; but another name for one of its most influential shapes has appeared and made considerable progress, particularly on the continent of Europe. This name is Monism; and is intended to declare that every other belief must be at best a Dualism.

What then is the true human meaning of this Monistic creed? Our souls (if we have souls), possess the image, not of Absolute Being and Personality, but of abstract Fate, and rayless, eyeless Necessity. We live machines; those supposed moralities we commonly miscall our Volitions, spring out from beneath the moving wheels. We die, as machines go to pieces when the wheels get out of gear; and no other account need be asked of the broken clock-work. Here lies a man, close beside him moulders a dog. They are now what they always were,—copartners in the same inexorable destiny.

Inexorable:—yes; for, standing beside these two graves, we see where our higher Philosophy and our religious hopes alike lie buried. What is Mechanical Law to us? The antithesis of Providence; therefore, with the edict which proclaims its sway, all our prayers are ended. And what is Man, compared with the equal dog who bears him company? One event befals them both; yet we may ask whether before or after that one event, Man has or can have any preeminence above the beast? Let him be spoken of as statesman, warrior, orator, poet, painter, sculptor, musician; none of these epithets convey any truth. He may possibly be a speaking, striking, weaving, drawing, colouring, sound-producing machine. But the Designer of the Universe and the human artist have disappeared together. What we took for the author of immortal works, an original genius, an inspired hero of his kind, "a man and a leader of men," was a piece of wheel-work driven by unalterable law. There was the same "must be" to him as to his dog. There never was and never could have been, nor yet ever will be any essential difference; two spirits are gone downwards to the earth.

Man has not even the sad preeminence of Sin. Where can he find or make room for wrong-doing, when impelling Mechanism determines all? And where Sin is not, Repentance cannot come.

Hope is shut out along with Remorse and its unmeaning pains. Man has no ladder of ascent left him; and why should he wish to climb? If there were such a ladder as Jacob dreamed, its base must rest on lifeless Law, and at its summit there would only be this same Law, enthroned and Deified.

Thus, when the primaeval Nebula arose in Space (how or why it arose is not told us), its vapoury Law contained all that is, and all that can be:—Plato and Shakespeare, Moses and St. John glimmered in its tremulous twilight. Worlds inanimate and animate scintillated from its fires. What we call Heaven and Earth are its dumb children, its law-determined Evolutions. Thou and I, O reader, have harboured strange fancies;—let them go;—we are but parts of the Whole; and the Whole is a mechanical Unity. Now that we find ourselves disabused and illuminated, our great difficulty may perhaps be to fall down, Strauss-like, and worship this Universum. Can such worship, or such an object of worship, bless and satisfy our high aspiring race? Eyes that have watched for Righteousness, hearts that have yearned after it, let the answer come from you! In this answer lives or dies the twofold belief of the Natural Theologian, the twofold hope resulting to Mankind. The belief, that is to say, in a personal Immortality, the belief in a personal God.

It may now seem plain that the readiest test of moral or religious Materialism is its doctrine, not of Body but of Soul. There is no charm in such a word as Matter to differentiate the character of a philosophy. Looking at the material world, any thinker may be a Natural Realist or a Pure Idealist; yet being either or neither, he may materialize, or the reverse, so far as Morals and Religion are concerned. The simple question ought rather to be; Is man mechanically governed by the Law which rules the world of Abiology (the lifeless inorganic world), or is he, can he become, a Law unto himself? [150]

It would be unfair to omit impressing upon the reader's mind that physical science per se is by no means answerable for ethico-religious Materialism. As a question of fact, it does not seem established that students of Nature, whether physicists or biologists, have, as such, been the chief offenders. On the contrary, for every single instance of the kind, it seems quite probable that at least two metaphysical writers might be found guilty. Obviously, some such large proportion may reasonably be expected, when we consider that Determinism, (the word Mill and others prefer to Necessity), is a theory involving a certain kind of metaphysics.

But the really largest crop of materializers arises from a Debateable Land. There is a hybrid class of "thinkers," concerning whom the best physical-science authorities allege that "such nebulous rascals are mere metaphysicians," while metaphysical speculators, pure and simple, feel quite sure that "though under a cloud, the gentlemen must be Physicists" [151].

So far as Biology [152] is concerned, let the reader compare Mr. Herbert Spencer's latest utterances already referred to, (in *Essays*, Vol. III. sub. fin., especially pp. 249-50), with the following passages from Mr. Huxley.

"I suppose if there be an 'iron' law, it is that of gravitation; and if there be a physical necessity, it is that a stone, unsupported, must fall to the ground. But what is all we really know and can know about the latter phenomenon? Simply, that, in all human experience, stones have fallen to the ground under these conditions; that we have not the smallest reason for believing that any stone so circumstanced will not fall to the ground; and that we have, on the contrary, every reason to believe that it will so fall. It is very convenient to indicate that all the conditions of belief have been fulfilled in this case, by calling the statement that unsupported stones will fall to the ground, 'a law of nature.' But when, as commonly happens, we change will into must, we introduce an idea of necessity which most assuredly does not lie in the observed facts, and has no warranty that I can discover elsewhere. For my part, I utterly repudiate and anathematize the intruder. Fact I know; and Law I know; but what is this Necessity, save an empty shadow of my own mind's throwing? But if it is certain that we can have no knowledge of the nature of either matter or spirit, and that the notion of necessity is something illegitimately thrust into the perfectly legitimate conception of law, the materialistic position that there is nothing in the world but matter, force, and necessity, is as utterly devoid of justification as the most baseless of theological dogmas." ("On the Physical Basis of Life," Lay Sermons, pp. 157-8.)

And again (pp. 159-60):—

"We live in a world which is full of misery and ignorance, and the plain duty of each and all of us is to try to make the little corner he can influence somewhat less miserable and somewhat less ignorant than it was before he entered it. To do this effectually it is necessary to be fully possessed of only two beliefs: the first, that the order of nature is ascertainable by our faculties to an extent which is practically unlimited; the second, that our volition counts for something as a condition of the course of events.

"Each of these beliefs can be verified experimentally, as often as we like to try. Each, therefore, stands upon the strongest foundation upon which any belief can rest, and forms one of our highest truths. If we find that the ascertainment of the order of nature is facilitated by using one terminology, or one set of symbols, rather than another, it is our clear duty to use the former; and no harm can accrue, so long as we bear in mind, that we are dealing merely with terms and symbols."

Symbols, are to the true philosopher like old-fashioned copper "tokens," privately impressed with letters and devices, but lacking the Royal image and superscription. They are, as Spencer and Huxley agree, "unknown quantities;"—relativities not entities. They are employable enough where they suit [153], provided Mr. Huxley's caveat (p. 161) is steadily kept in mind. "The errors of systematic materialism may paralyze the energies and destroy the beauty of a life."

The reader may be pleased to put the subject of Materialism before himself in a compendious shape as follows:—If the question asked be, "What is Matter?" the answer appears little likely to be of moment to morals or Natural Theology, except so far as human ignorance is made a plea for Scepticism. But, if it is inquired, "whether the Mechanical Laws of Matter are the laws of Universal Nature, including human nature? the issue becomes most momentous. The reply made, answers another question of the deepest interest:—"Are there any conditions under which a Science of Natural Theology is possible?" If Mechanism be the law of the Universe, Natural Theology is plainly impossible.

Chapter 4

BELIEFS OF REASON: PRINCIPLE OF INDUCTION—THEISM—CONFIRMATION AND ILLUSTRATIONS

"While we indulge to the Sensitive or Plantal Life, our delights are common to us with the creatures below us: and 'tis likely, they exceed us as much in them, as in the senses their subjects; and that's a poor happiness for Man to aim at, in which Beasts are his Superiours. But those Mercurial spirits which were only lent the Earth to shew Men their folly in admiring it; possess delights of a nobler make and nature, which as it were antedate Immortality; and, at an humble distance, resemble the joyes of the world of Light and Glory. The Sun and Stars, are not the world's Eyes, but These: the Celestial Argus cannot glory in such an universal view. These out-travel theirs, and their Monarch's beams: passing into Vortexes beyond their Light and Influence; and with an easie twinkle of an Intellectual Eye look into the Centre, which is obscur'd from the upper Luminaries. This is somewhat like the Image of Omnipresence. And what the Hermetical Philosophy saith of God, is in a sense verifiable of the thus ennobled soul, That its Centre is every where, but its circumference no where ....

" ... And yet there's an higher degree, to which Philosophy sublimes us. For, as it teacheth a generous contempt of what the grovelling desires of creeping Mortals Idolize and dote on: so it raiseth us to love and admire an Object, that is as much above terrestrial, as Infinite can make it. If Plutarch may have credit, the observation of Nature's Harmony in the Celestial Motions was one of the first inducements to the belief of a God. And a greater then he affirms, that the visible things of the Creation declare him, that made them. What knowledge we have of them, we have in a sense of their Authour. His face cannot be beheld by Creature-Opticks, without the allay of a reflexion; and Nature is one of those mirrors, that represents him to us. And now, the more we know of him the more we love him, the more we are like him, the more we admire him. 'Tis here that knowledge wonders; and there's an Admiration, that's not the Daughter of Ignorance. This indeed stupidly gazeth at the unwonted effect. But the Philosophical passion truly admires and adores the supreme Efficient ....

".... And from this last article, I think I may conclude the charge, which hot-brained folly layes in against Philosophy; that it leads to Irreligion, frivolous and vain. I dare say, next after the divine Word, it's one of the best friends to Piety. Neither is it any more justly accountable for the impious irregularities of some, that have paid an homage to its shrine; than Religion itself for the extravagancies both opinionative and practick of high pretenders to it. It is a vulgar conceit, that Philosophy holds a confederacy with Atheism itself, but most injurious: for nothing can better antidote us against it: and they may as well say, that Physitians are the only murtherers. A Philosophick Atheist, is as good sense as a Divine one."— Glanvill's *Apology for Philosophy*, at end of *Scepsis Scientifica*, Ed. I. p. 177, seq.

Ἔστι γὰρ ἀπαιδευσία τὸ μὴ γιγνώσκειν τίνων δεῖ ζητεῖν ἀπόδειξιν καὶ τίνων οὐ δεῖ Ὅλως μὲν γὰρ ἀπάντων ἀδύνατον ἀπόδειξιν εἶναι· εἰς ἄπειρον γὰρ ἂν βαδίζοι, ὥστε μηδ' οὕτως εἶναι ἀπόδειξιν. Arist. *Metaph*. IV. (Γ) cap. 4.

The following is the translation of MM. Pierron et Zévort:

"C'est de l'ignorance de ne pas savoir distinguer ce qui a besoin de démonstration de ce qui n'en a pas besoin. Il est absolument impossible de tout démontrer: il faudrait pour cela aller à l'infini; de sorte qu'il n'y aurait même pas de démonstration." *Métaphysique* d'Aristote, Tome I. p. 116.

"Man's higher Instinct leads to lofty aspiration,
To generous sentiment, and boundless desire,
Till he seeks and finds the Author of his Soul.
In seeking for him he perfects his virtue,
By finding him he is made strong within,
And being strong he strengthens his brethren."

"Light is natural to the Eye, and the Eye improves under Light,
So Truth is natural to the Mind, and the Mind improves under Truth.
But the student of Goodness must himself become good,
So far at least as to choose Goodness for his best portion.
If base passion or worldliness is allowed to domineer,
No man can gaze steadily at Purity and at God.
And then perhaps he despairs of religious truth,
And moralizes on Man's feebleness and limited faculties,
So unfitted to fathom the Divine and to know the Eternal!"
F. Newman. *Theism*, pp. 2 and 12.

"The world offers just now the spectacle, humiliating to us in many ways, of millions of people clinging to their old idolatrous religions, and refusing to change them even for a higher form; whilst in Christian Europe thousands of the most cultivated class are beginning to consider atheism a permissible, or even a desirable thing. The very instincts of the savage rebuke us. But just when we seem in danger of losing all, may come the moment of awakening to the dangers of our loss. A world where thought is a secretion of the brain-gland, where free-will is the dream of a madman that thinks he is an emperor though naked and in chains, where God is not, or at least not knowable, such is not the world as we learnt it, on which great lives have been lived out, great self-sacrifices dared, great piety and devotion have been bent to soften the sin, the ignorance, and the misery. It is a world from which the sun is withdrawn, and with it all light and life. But this is not our world as it was, not the world of our fathers. To live is to think and to will. To think is to see the chain of facts in creation, and passing along its golden links, to find the hand of God at its beginning, as we saw His handiwork in its course. And to will is to be able to know good and evil; and to will aright is to submit the will entirely to a will higher than ours. So that with God alone can we find true knowledge and true rest, the vaunted fruits of philosophy."— *Limits of Philosophical Inquiry.* By the Archbishop of York, p. 24.

"The mind of man becomes
A thousand times more beautiful than the earth
On which he dwells, above this frame of things

In beauty exalted, as it is itself
Of quality and fabric more divine."
Wordsworth. *The Prelude*, sub. fin.

"Religion, Poetry is not dead; it will never die. Its dwelling and birth place is in the soul of man, and it is eternal as the being of man. In any point of space, in any section of Time, let there be a living Man; and there is an Infinitude above him and beneath him, and an Eternity encompasses him on this hand and on that; and tones of Sphere-music, and tidings from loftier worlds, will flit round him, if he can but listen, and visit him with holy influences, even in the thickest press of trivialities, or the din of busiest life. Happy the man, happy the nation, that can hear these tidings; that has them written in fit characters, legible to every eye, and the solemn import of them present at all moments to every heart! That there is, in these days, no nation so happy, is too clear; but that all nations, and ourselves in the van, are, with more or less discernment of its nature, struggling towards this happiness, is the hope and the glory of our time. To us, as to others, success, at a distant or a nearer day, cannot be uncertain. Meanwhile, the first condition of success is, that, in striving honestly ourselves, we honestly acknowledge the striving of our neighbour; that with a will unwearied in seeking Truth, we have a sense open for it wheresoever and howsoever it may arise."— Carlyle. *Miscellanies*, p. 99, Last Edition.

SYNOPSIS OF CHAPTER 4

With the last Chapter closes what may be termed the more critical part of this Essay. The remainder is occupied with a series of affirmative arguments.

The preparation for these arguments having been minutely made, explanatory additions become less necessary.

The main object of the present chapter is to establish a tenable Theory respecting those Human Beliefs among which is included our primary Belief in Theism. Their nature and validity not having as yet been sufficiently investigated (see footnote (b) p. 256 post), some extent of discussion attends the inquiry. To many readers the territory opened out will appear new. It ought however to be traversed by all careful students of Psychology.

Analysis:—Tendencies of the Human Mind resulting in certain concrete Beliefs. The Inductive Principle, or Law of Uniformity, investigated. Various explanations of its origin examined and rejected; particularly the hypothesis which resolves it into Laws of Association. Shewn to be a primary Belief; at first pre-rational, afterwards limited and established by

Reason. The latter process separates by a strong line of demarcation the realm of Humanity from that of the lower creation.

Animal instincts, some improvable, some "survivals." Human instincts transformed by Reason. Certain primary Beliefs peculiar to Man. Hence his special culture.

Theism. Fallacies from confusion between Tests of Speculative and of Practical Truth. Lesson of Mathematics. Speculative truths tested by analytic process; Practical by synthetic; their work becomes their ever-growing verification. Application of this test to two practical beliefs; our natural belief in externalities, and our belief in the Supernatural. Speculative difficulties intruded into the practical sphere become apparently insuperable. Both spheres essentially Human. Natural Realism compared with Realistic Theism.

Formation and growth of Belief in the Supernatural as a Belief of Reason. Absurdities attaching to its rejection. Ennobling influences of its acceptance explained and exemplified. Ideal of Humanity, crowned by the Ideal of God, to Whom both the Natural and the Moral world bear witness.

BELIEFS OF REASON

In the last section, we have examined a number of intellectual perplexities, running closely parallel to certain primâ-facie objections commonly alleged against Natural Theism. We have seen that they are, in reality, difficulties arising from the impotence of the Human Mind, whenever it is directed to the contemplation of first or supreme, Principles. In all reason therefore, they cease to be objections. We are, in fact, constantly finding ourselves obliged to accept as an undeniable truth, or a real existence, what when placed objectively before our mental vision, appears inexplicable, self-contradictory, or absolutely unthinkable.

The power which compels us to many an admission of this kind is the mind itself, asserting a strength of insight, in-born and inalienable, notwithstanding the symptoms of weakness, which (psychologically speaking) may have seemed threatening to overcloud and disable it [ac].

Hence, we are led to suspect that some at least of those symptomatic weaknesses, are mistakes in diagnosis. This suspicion will be shared by most persons tolerably acquainted with the present state of psychology, and particularly with the manner in which foregone theories are supported by over-refined analysis. At all events, the reactionary strength of the mind is best shown in the concrete beliefs resulting from its own simplest activities.

Our simplest mental activities are naturally our earliest. Amongst them, none are more distinctly marked than our impulses to believe and act upon certain definite pre-suppositions. These differ from the vague and purposeless dreams of childhood, by gradually becoming clear, practical, and expansive. One of the most vigorous, permanent, and prevailing, amongst them all, is our human belief in the existence of supernatural power. Upon another presupposition (not originally the clearest), seems to rest, in the first degree, that principle which gives validity to all the inductive sciences. We will carefully examine this latter belief, with the object of drawing from the process certain aids for an examination of the former [ad].

Induction is defined as the legitimate inference of the more general, from the less general;—the general from the particular;—and (with more startling distinctness) of the

Unknown from the Known. It is at once evident that, whatever may be the logical form into which this mode of inferring is thrown, there must in the nature of things be some ulterior principle to give it legitimacy. This principle, when raised to the rank and dignity of a philosophic postulate, is commonly known as the Law of Natural Uniformity. A law claiming such extensive dominion that one cannot help asking in what code, human or Divine, of reason or of experience, it was originally found written.

Let us have recourse to the code of reason first. Euclid gives admirable instances of things true by necessity of reason. The moment we understand what right lines are, we see at once and for all time that two straight lines, infinitely prolonged, can never inclose a space. No one ever did see a mathematical line of any kind ("length without thickness"),—no one ever saw or conceived any real or ideal thing of infinite extent, neither can we think infinity at all. Yet the terms of the geometrical proposition carry their own evidence. We may sum the case, as Euler the mathematician put it. He finished a demonstration upon Arches by saying, "All experience is contrary to this, but that is no reason for doubting its truth."

Now, there appears nothing in the least resembling this case, in the conception of Natural Uniformity. No thinker can predicate substantial impossibility of the idea that Nature should ever be otherwise than Uniform.

Suppose, then, we consider the code of Experience. Where shall we find the experience required? Ours is far short of universal, either in an absolute or an approximate sense. We are the children of to-day—yet the law wanted must be to all intents universal. It has been answered to this obvious requirement, that we enjoy the results of an experience constant and uniform, "coextensive not with the life of the single individual who employs them, but with the entire history of the human race" [154]. But in what history is any such experience written? History in its letter, is full of events which contradict Nature's uniformity, of interruptions, marvels, miracles. For cattle to speak, is quite a common occurrence in Livy. An ordinary Roman would have been perplexed by the absence of signs and wonders; he would have felt it something to be accounted for. History tells us on every written page to believe in what seems impossible; and some writers on historical evidence, claim for it a greater amount of credibility whenever it testifies to the greater number of improbable incidents. For, do not writers of fiction deal in probabilities [155]?

Another method of giving force to the principle of natural Uniformity, is based on our alleged sense of personal subjection to the chain of events;—the outer world is said to penetrate the inner by an impression of its unvarying sequence, its laws of unbroken continuity. But does the lesson of life really go this way? Most men, when meditating over their own lives, think rather of the causation they have themselves exercised, or might have exercised, than of any iron links of causality in nature. So strongly do they feel their causal power, that, whereas one man boasts of being the architect of his own fortunes, another blames himself because he has been foolish enough to let things take their chance. What people chiefly realize and act upon, is the relation between Man and Nature—or, else between Man and Man;—relations prolific in consequences which we shall have to consider by-and-bye.

A more summary mode of explaining our human impression of natural Uniformity, is by resolving it into certain laws of Association. We see antecedent and consequent every day, and get to consider them as indissolubly associated. If we see a present antecedent, we expect a coming consequent. The event and its futurity, are thus fused in a common solvent. Yet, one palpable objection lies against this theory, and it is fatal. Fatal against it, and against all theories which rest our belief upon experience, or upon any process of reasoning, inductive or demonstrated. The objection consists in the plain fact, that this belief resembles animal instinct [156] in one definite particular—it exists previously to all observation or exercise of intelligence on the subject.

We see it in all young creatures. The instinct of children is to act upon a supposition that the thing they have enjoyed or suffered shall recur regularly and without interruption. The darling brought down to dessert every day for a week, feels injured by a breach of the custom, just as the cat or dog fed from their masters' table expects the same hand to continue always kind. Child, kitten, and puppy, need no second scalding to look askance at the tea-kettle. Grown people's confidence in the stability of Empires often reposes on no much stronger foundation. Most men rest satisfied with an indefinite and unreasoning presumption all their lives long. They desire no further explanation—a happy circumstance, perhaps, considering the theories they might have to investigate.

Mr. James Mill in his "Analysis of the Human Mind" made great and continual use of the laws of Association. He applied them (amongst other ways) to our belief in the uniform futurities of Nature.

"There can" he writes "be no idea of the Future; because strictly speaking the Future is a non- entity—of nothing there can be no idea.... Our whole lives are but a series of changes, that is, of antecedents and consequents. The conjunction, therefore, is incessant; and, of course, the union of the ideas perfectly inseparable." (Vol. I. pp. 362-3.)

And again, (p. 367,)

"But I am told, that we have not only the idea of to-morrow, but the belief of to-morrow; and I am asked what that belief is. I answer, that you have not only the idea of to-morrow, but have it inseparably. It will also appear, that wherever the name belief is applied, there is a case of the indissoluble association of ideas. It will further appear, that, in instances without number, the name belief is applied to a mere case of indissoluble association; and no instance can be adduced in which anything besides an indissoluble association can be shewn in belief. It would seem to follow from this, with abundant evidence, that the whole of my notion of to-morrow, belief included, is nothing but a case of the inevitable sequence of ideas."

This theory Mr. Bain (no hostile critic) annotates as follows.

"The case that is most thoroughly opposed to the theory of indissoluble association is our belief in the Uniformity of Nature. Our overweening tendency to anticipate the future from the past is shown prior to all association; the first effect of experience is to abridge and modify a strong primitive urgency. There is, no doubt, a certain stage when association co-operates to justify the believing state. After our headlong instinct has, by a series of reverses, been humbled and toned down, and after we have discovered that the Uniformity, at first imposed by the mind upon everything, applies to some things and not to others, we are confirmed by our experience in the cases where the uniformity prevails; and the intellectual growth of association counts for a small part of the believing impetus. Still, the efficacy of experience is perhaps negative rather than positive; it saves, in certain cases, the primitive force of anticipation from the attacks made upon it in the other cases where it is contradicted by the facts. It does not make belief, it conserves a pre- existing belief."

In Mr. Bain's comment it is worthy of particular remark that he considers experience less as a foundation, than a test always,—a limit sometimes,—of that law which gives life to all the experimental sciences. "The uniformity imposed by the mind," he observes, "applies to some things but not to others." His view, therefore, places the principle itself in the light of a generality given by the mind and apprehended as a leading maxim. Its field is sometimes reasserted,—sometimes contracted,—by experience; but in both cases the effect is a process of discrimination.

In support of this view, it may be fairly urged that a child calculates on the uniformity of human character and conduct, to an extent not justified in after life. Any child correctly expects a stone to fall when thrown into the air, without the least idea of that special reason for its fall, which can be mathematically extended to the stars. In like manner, our very earliest belief in the reality of men and objects outside us, confuses persons and things as resisting antagonists which ought to be punished and overcome. Experience, therefore, brings discrimination. Thus, too, the natural apprehension of a power above nature, occupies a more defined sphere in our own old age than the first radiant glimpses of our wondering upward-springing childhood. And the same may be said of the world's several eras of religious thinking. Yet, if some eminent writers are correct in contending that the belief in a Supreme "Heaven-Father," (so strong in the Aryan [157] family,) was of extreme antiquity, we must admit that our race's infancy cherished a more truly Theistic faith, than many intervening ages of moral degeneracy retained [158]. But, side by side with this admission, we ought to place two notable facts,— first that our sense of the supernatural has really educated the great heart of Man; teaching him from the love of God to love his neighbour likewise.— Next,—that the awful impression has, on the whole, grown with his growth, and strengthened with his strength; acquiring fresh light and beauty with every fresh access to his noblest illumination. Exactly in proportion, as man increasingly learns to love and live for his neighbour, he has always increased the depth and earnestness with which he lives for and loves his God. In these two facts is bound up the secret of our Western civilization.

We must return, however, for a few paragraphs to the general consideration of what may be called our pre-rational beliefs [ae]. That they are pre-rational (account for them as we will), is evident since from them spring our first tendencies to reason in special directions, and our first ability to receive and assimilate such mental food as may be afforded us. "The primary facts of intelligence,"—says Sir W. Hamilton, "the facts which precede, as they afford the conditions of, all knowledge,—would not be original were they revealed to us under any other form than that of natural or necessary beliefs" [159]. A central point this; and one most essential for the Psychologist! Indeed, every one who explains such beliefs into laws of association, commits the oversight of refining away the chief fact involved in those laws themselves. For, the very idea of association presupposes a guiding impulse. How can we classify without a standard of classification, arrange or connect without threads of connection or arrangement? Laws of association must cluster round an associating principle, just as translucent halos encircle the Sun. Laws of association do not make principles; but an operative principle evokes associations, and manifests itself in their law.

Oversights like this, and the one before noted by Mr. Bain, are examples of the paralogism incident to all attempts at explaining the inexplicable. In his eagerness, the metaphysical refiner subtilizes away the truth under analysis. Even so, in days of old, Alchemists used to sublimate the gold intended for transmuting inferior metals, till it flew off in elastic vapour, and all that had been precious, vanished from the eager speculative man. A frequent issue this, to searchers after our true philosopher's stone.

The catalogue of pre-rational beliefs or impulses to believe, is considerable, and might easily be enlarged. But there is much to hinder a full enumeration. In the first place, they emerge from a border-land between the brute and the man; and border territories are proverbially fertile in disputes. Next, they have to be sought out and examined in the birthplace of intelligence; and the beginnings of knowledge like the beginnings of history are overshadowed by a twilight haze. Then, too, amongst the painters of human nature, (who after all are but men,) there prevails a disinclination to confess how largely our human life is cradled under the rule of unreason and impulsiveness. Most of us hardly know why we act, yet, every one likes to believe himself reasoning and reasonable. Finally, some religious minds shrink back from realizing the idea of an instinctive belief in the moral antithesis of Right and Wrong, or in a Supreme First Cause and Judge of all men. They feel as if to admit it were almost degrading to Faith,—forgetful that the philosophic Apostle took this view and expressed it with the utmost boldness [160]. Forgetful, also, that from whatever source Man's reason sprang, from the same welled forth every bright stream of practical activity,— impelling him to work in spheres as yet unconquered by the force of his own understanding.

The hindrances now described are, after all, grounded on an inadequate conception of the true distinction between the Animal and the Man. Apart from the fact that ultimate objects of instinct differ as widely as the idea of a future life differs from the poorest enjoyments of the brute world,—quite apart from all consideration of aims and ends,—the impulses themselves are in their own activities very far indeed from occupying the same level. There are instincts of the utmost importance to all self support and self protection, and to the sustenance and care of others, which appear in their own nature simple and unalterable;—unerring within their direct line, but beyond it helpless and narrow in their field of operation. Other instincts again,—such, for example, as impel animals to construction, and human beings to art,—are evidently influenced and enlarged by intelligence. Beavers adapt their dams, birds their nests, and the bee her comb, to all kinds of circumstances, so far as they can command the means of adaptation. Their intelligence also delights itself in different kinds of adornment [161]. But the power of meeting exigencies, is manifestly limited throughout the lower creation. The bee has, for ages, worked upon marvellously accurate principles, unintelligible to mathematicians before the calculus was invented, and only fully explained of late years. She always erects one effectual and skilful kind of barricade [162] against hostile swarms, as well as that dreaded assailant, the Death's head moth. Furthermore, she evinces readiness in fitting all her material structures to place, occasion, and circumstance. Yet, observe the same bee exhausting herself by vain struggles against the sloping roof of a greenhouse, of which every window is thrown wide open. She perseveres, hour after hour, in unavailing endeavours to escape by her one accustomed upward track of flight, unable to conceive the possibility of transparent but impenetrable glass; and incapable of learning the fact by her repeated disappointments. In this way, hundreds of bees, butterflies, and other winged insects, perish miserably every summer. So, too, the highly educated and intelligent dog, will try to scratch holes in hard flag stones, and, after trials innumerable, still scratches on without seeming to discover that he never succeeds in making a single hole. Thus, also, birds in captivity keep up the perpetual motion of their heads—(useful to the poor prisoner no longer!) and generations after generations of captives maintain the instinctive practice. Numberless instances might easily be adduced to the same effect. But no similar observation holds good of man. The child soon discontinues its efforts to thrust an arm through a glass window; and every day learns some new lesson in the properties of material objects. The engineer builds dams as well as the beaver;—but, beside dams, what marvels innumerable does he achieve with his earthworks, his timbers, and his stones! Speaking generally, we perceive that man has an instinctive tendency to lay hold of a practical fact, idea, and law of action, as a concrete whole; [163] — seizing it, at first, as the animal does without being able to analyze, recompound, or extend it. But reason holds the candle to instinct [af]. The impulse deepens and widens,—becomes distinguished by boldness and comprehensive breadth;—and it is difficult, if not impossible, to fix boundaries to its ultimate expansion. An expansion coextensive with the completed destinies of mankind.

We say thus much of our lower instincts, transformed and made glorious by reason shining through them; just as the setting sun transforms and glorifies the clouds floating high overhead, or the half-translucent foliage of the grove in which we walk. But there belong exclusively to Man, instinctive beliefs, impulses, and ideas, which possess a glory of their own;—raise him, first above the brutes,— next above himself as he now exists,—and make him know that he may aspire to become the denizen of a brighter world than this. Among them, is the feeling that Nature herself is (like the tree or cloud illumined by the sun), everywhere penetrated by a beauty and a power streaming through her;—compared with the reality of which she is but a filmy veil,—or it may be an illusive image. The sun himself, the light and life of the lower world, symbolizes an existence more truly kindling and ensouling, which animates and makes brilliant the blue arch of sky. Such thoughts as these haunted the first utterances of our race,—and it needed but another step to make us feel that this living light shines within ourselves,—and that, go where we will, a strength and Majesty go with us, which are not of the earth, earthy. Thus, the consciousness grew upon Man that his inner being glows with a radiance more sparkling than the stars, to which he lifts his bodily eyes. By-and-bye, he learned to think of the heaven within him, as symbolic also;—and to cherish a trembling trust that, when he dies, its brightness will grow pale, and vanish away only by reason of a glory which excelleth.

The Apostle beloved of his Master, told us of a true Light that lighteth every man. Yet, we might have been slow to realize the purer splendours over-arching our human soul, if they had not autotyped themselves on the language we commonly speak. Perhaps, a more convincing proof still to some of us, is what every now and then becomes incidentally known;—the God-ward impulses of a happily developed childhood, under circumstances favourable to the growth of "natural piety." In the heart of a child, feelings like those we have described, dwell untutored, as in their native and appropriate home. An awe and dread accompany them amongst the world of men, but to the child they are never overpowering or oppressive. His finely-strung imagination works painlessly. The voices he hears when no human voice speaks, cause him no fear;—they call to him from a region towards which his young soul springs up. They soothe him with sensations of hope and peace and love unutterable. This yearning affection for things unseen, makes the deepest joy of a happy childhood; it is a reason why Christ said, "Of such is the kingdom of Heaven."

A beautiful childhood is a very beautiful reality. Partly because of the exquisite simplicity which tones down and harmonizes all its impulses. But, very often, its beauty is only known in its loss;—and we mourn in after years over hope, love, and peace, broken down by life's attrition;—yet fair to look upon, even in their ruins [ag].

No one is likely to doubt that the belief we have been describing, is peculiar to and characteristic of Man. A more subtle question would be this;—Suppose it could be taken away, how nearly would Man and brute approach each other [164]? A question deserving the attention of every one, who lives

"In self-adoring pride securely mailed."

Probably, the proudest of mankind little think how deeply their culture, art, and refinement, are indebted to a faith shared by the lowliest. One point, at least, seems clear,—if Morality did not perish in the wreck, a true and independent moral sense would bring us back to a belief in our own souls, their immortality, and their God.

Another question more essential to our purpose has been buried under heaps of fallacy and misconception. Theists are often told that the ideas of a Deity,—a future life,—and generally all that is conceived as supernatural, have no absolute trustworthiness;—they are not self-evident axioms, and they cannot be demonstrated. One answer to these alleged difficulties has been implicitly given in the last Chapter. If such objections are valid at all, they are valid against every practical first-truth therein considered. They are valid against all primary practical truths, looked at from the theoretical side, and tested by the rules proper to what is called pure Reason;—Reason, that is to say, not applied, but speculative. But, then, it is from this very employment of tests upon truth not in pari materia, that the first stage of fallacy begins. The second step in error follows naturally from the first. Compared with the clearness and definition of mathematics, all other axioms and proofs appear dim and dubious. The consequence is, that our minds fall into trains of false comparison on the all-important subject of certitude. Errors of that kind are always growing mischiefs; our tongues follow the lead of our thoughts, and hazy thinking becomes hazy speaking. Not only so, but words develope themselves into the leaders of thought; and hazy speaking engenders a hazier thinking still. People take mathematical certainty to be the sole type of all true and valuable certainties. Practical maxims are spoken of, as merely probable, Right and Wrong as the efflux of moral sentiments [165]. Few seem to be aware how the philosophical arrangements of first-truths ought to be applied. They should be applied to discriminate the processes, by which various kinds of truths are discoverable;—they stamp a character upon them, when discovered; but they do not determine the intrinsic worth and validity of the discoveries.

Why, let us ask, does Mathematical truth occupy so lofty a position? Because, first, the constitution of our nature obliges us to accept its axioms, and by consequence each successive step in its impregnable demonstrations. Next, because we can verify so many of its theorems objectively. We apply them to remote planetary and stellar spheres beyond our own reach; where our own minds can neither alter nor colour anything. What then ought to be the fair and legitimate inference from an issue magnificently tried throughout the celestial universe? Surely this, and no other. It confirms, in the very highest possible degree, the truth-telling power of our own human nature. Whatsoever our mental constitution clearly compels us to accept, that same we ought to hold true, and maintain unswervingly.

Henceforth, therefore, we ought to look upon our Reason as having been put upon its conclusive trial. Every year that passes renders the verdict if possible more triumphant. We ought, henceforth, to make our assent absolute and unhesitating in the case of those other truths, which, while things continue as they now are, can never be tried and confirmed by an appeal of the same description.

It is not difficult to see how opposite would have been the issue from an employment of improper tests;—the test, for instance, of the Unthinkable. The universe, we should then have said, must be thought of as finite or as infinite. Either way it is inconceivable;—therefore the Universe cannot exist objectively at all.

Vicious as such a process would be, it is not so faulty as that of confounding the proper methods and attestations of speculative and practical truth [166]. Our human consciousness must in both cases give our data. We have to ask and obtain its answers,—but, in the two different spheres of knowledge, we must frame our interrogatories differently, and expect assurances differing not in degree of certainty, but in kind;—in value to human action;—and in the mode of their deliverance. We inquire into Speculative truth by analysing it, until we arrive at undemonstrable axioms which assert their own validity. We assure ourselves that Practical principles are true by following them in their synthetic growth. Do they spring from a maxim we find ourselves urged by our own nature to accept,—and the opposite of which we cannot but broadly reject;—and do they really work in the world,—exert an ennobling influence within their own domain, and intertwine themselves with the other truths and activities of our human life? If so, we may be assured of their vitality and their certitude. We know them, in short, by their stringency,—and by a happy experience of their power. Consequently, our knowledge ought to grow and strengthen, as our human age and the world's age both roll on. Practical truth, thus tried and acknowledged, is indeed the silver thread which leads us always. Some shrink from trusting it when stretched across the grave; yet, without it, all beyond is lost in haze, and our present life becomes enigmatical and self-contradictory.

Let us then apply the tests (found valid in their own practical sphere) to the case of our belief in a Supernatural and supreme Power. But, that we may do so with more evident effect, it will be well to place in juxtaposition with it another powerful belief, and our progress will be rendered easier if we fix upon one which has already been, in part at least, under discussion. Nothing seems better fitted for this purpose, than what Professor Masson calls "the paramount fact," resulting alike to Hamilton and to Mill,—the universal persuasion in men of their own existence, as beings distinct from, but related to, an external world around them. It will be observed that, thus described, the fact is of a most concrete sort,—our inner reality in relation to an outer reality,—just as believing in a Supreme Being we believe in a Power that holds solemn relations to our individual selves and to our common Humanity.

We have therefore to observe the impression made upon our human endowment of practical Reason, when looking face to face at these two fact-beliefs, which for brevity's sake we shall call the Natural and the Supernatural.

Did the uninstructed and stammering childhood of our race, separate, in thought, the Supernatural from surrounding nature? Can we absolutely say either yes or no to this inquiry? The "Heaven- Father" of pre-historic [ah] day would seem if fully considered to make the separation clear. The type-idea, thus outlined, is drawn, not from symbolizing and personified Nature, but from an actual, living, fatherly, Man. And the tendency of primitive Man might rather be to raise natural objects into living beings, than to lower persons into things.

It is so, we are sure, with our children's apprehension of the Natural. They know a world of persons and things antagonistic to their own wills and efforts, but they begin by making the things into persons. A thwarted baby-boy beats the table, his kitten, and his nurse indifferently. So far as observation has been extended to the religious apprehensions of the very young, they would seem to spiritualize the material universe;—to behold unseen powers in the changing clouds, and hear them in the sighing of the wind. Wordsworth's "Ode on Immortality" is a picture as full of childlike human truth, as it is of unearthly beauty.

But, as regards both principles, the human train of thought is nearly similar in its first rise, and grows in definiteness and expansion by a nearly similar process. A true Man sets each principle to work, and from its working gathers its real value and verification.

If the world outside him were a phantastic shadow, the practical conclusion fairly inferred would be quietism. Bolingbroke said to King Richard—

"The shadow of your sorrow hath destroyed
The shadow of your face."

But, suppose both face and sorrow were themselves only shadows? What worth in Man's body then,—what worth in his soaring mind? The natural issue would be to drift down the shadowy [167] stream into a darker abyss of Nothingness.

Speculation [168] must lay down its arms, as powerless against such a supposition. The evidence of our senses [169] themselves is resolvable into shadows.

It was not by speculation that our strong Western will encountered the ideal enigmas of every day life. Act upon externalities, and they will re act upon you. As a matter of fact, it is necessary to commence by admitting that the souls of others are as impenetrable to us, as the material things into which we cannot force our way. But, things and persons react upon us differently; and we act upon them in widely different ways. By an exertion of our will, we can change or stop a natural tide of inorganic antecedents and consequents and direct it to our own purposes. Beings like ourselves, we must allure, manage, inform, and persuade. Soon we find, by experience, that other human beings are very like ourselves; and the higher animals nearer to us than stocks and stones. We find this through the exercise of our own causal activities upon them.

The idea of the Supernatural marches along no very dissimilar route. The strong man subjects Nature, but the Supernatural is above both it, and him. He cannot even possess the thought of the Supreme. Whether he will or no, it possesses him. To his reason, Nature cannot subsist, as the true and independent ground of anything;—her laws are the servants of his volition;—and her chain of antecedent and consequent hangs between a First and a Last, without giving any sufficient account of either. If the Universe began in a shining Nebula, the question remains unsolved,—what first brought the thin cloud into being? The practical Reason, confirmed by experience, distinctly perceives that productive nature transforms all things,—but originates nothing;—that, contrariwise, when human nature wills to commit a wrong,—it really originates the crime. A disputant may assert that Man's will originates no act;—the criminal is never guilty,—and the judge and jury who try him are not answerable for their own decision. The same disputant may add that the Court in which, they sit is unreal, and their bodily persons only shadows. The one set of suppositions is as tenable as the other, and precisely as unpractical.

In the common course of Nature, then, Mankind has learned to maintain, as a truth of reason, that the Supernatural Power is a Will,—that is a Personality. In other words Man becomes a Theist.

As in Natural Realism, so in realistic Theism, we try how our principles will work. Realists in thought, we treat men and things as natural realities; diverse when compared together, but alike in outsideness as they stand related to ourselves. Action and reaction then go on as are to be expected. Life seems to us one long verification of the truth we began by accepting.—And so, too, it is with our belief in a Being Supernatural and Divine. If we succeed in figuring to ourselves a world of adaptation, order, law, progress, unity, we have but to open our eyes, and it appears spread out before us. If we think that the world's creation would blend all physical needs into pleasurable pursuits and satisfactions, we may look and see the union accomplished. If we frame a scheme of trial and moral discipline, to raise the feeble and confirm the strong, its realization is not wanting amongst us. From our own feelings, we can imagine how a Father's eye would look pityingly down upon fear and sorrow, and all the strains incidental to moving laws; the attrition of other wills, the tumults, failures, ill doings, and perversities of our sensitive and social existence. How a Father's hand would bind up all that is weak, wild, and wilful in his children, with threads of rainbow coloured hope and joyful anticipation; bidding them believe that ere long the uncertain dimness, which is as morning spread upon the mountains, shall brighten into steady splendour, shining on to a perfect and unclouded day.

We find as a matter of fact that this hope is no stranger to the human breast; that numbers live in it; numbers have died for it; and pre-eminently those of whom the world was not worthy.

The growth of thought from a bare idea of the Supernatural to a belief in a pure and sublime Theism,—and the sufficient account it renders of the world, ourselves, and our destinies, must be looked upon as matters of fact in the work-day history of mankind. Practical human reason has really travelled by this track, and, from day to day, perceives new truths to verify the old conclusion. Every attempt to adapt other theories to the working facts become, by their unfitness for the purpose, indirect evidence for Theism. How short a time has passed since Campbell lamented over—

"The hopeless dark Idolater of Chance;"

and since the authors of "Rejected Addresses" ridiculed a system which made the universe an accident [170]. — Now, chance sounds as strangely in scientific ears as Fate did to our strong- willed forefathers. Next, came that unintelligible contradictory phrase, a "blind intelligence;" a thing called a mind, that goes it knows not whither, and moves it knows not why. From this thing, immersed in the darkest ignorance, and unconscious even of its own existence, we were asked to believe that arrangement, harmony, excellence, beauty, were the productions. No wonder if men soon concluded that a moving force,—material and soulless,—would equally fulfil the same exalted functions. And, surely, one thing is an account of the Universe as reasonable and as sufficient as the other.

If we place a non-theistic theory in relation to our human inner nature, there ensues the same monstrous incongruity. The plenitude of loveliness, which overflows creation, as it were with multitudinous waves of light, we are asked to think of as the work of blind non-being. But, there is a greater plenitude of loveliness, in the good and noble acts, words, and thoughts of one bright soul of heaven-aspiring Man. Must we, then, believe that truth, sincerity, justice, rightness, goodness, purity, are all the offspring of a something infinitely lower than our weakest human will? [171] —Is that unknown something to be also the beacon of our hopes, the refuge of each forlorn and shipwrecked brother, the happiness giving itself to satisfy the unsatisfied aspirations of our long-enduring hearts?

Surely, the mockery of madness could go no further. What can the morally impotent or the morally imperfect do for us? Even to the careless eye of common sense, it is clear at a glance, that with the Impersonal our distinctive spiritual life can have no possible relations. If this be so, the very first idea of Supernatural Power is not advanced.—Contrariwise, it is distorted, frustrated, nullified. And with it is destroyed our trust in our own conscious nature. The instinct of immortality lives and moves within us only to betray.—Man,—whose being is the highest reason for the world's whole being,—is henceforth a palpable inconsistency. There cannot in the dreams of fiction be found a stranger tissue of more startling,—or one might venture to say,—more revolting moral absurdities. And a moral absurdity contradicts the constitution of Man's mind, quite as thoroughly as an absurdity purely intellectual. It is, in reality, the most self-condemned of all conceivable contradictions.

Let us place side by side with this issue, first, the commonly conceived relation between a Personal supreme Being and his creation;— secondly, the apprehension of Theistic truth within the soul, as it comes to us substantiated by religious men. We shall, at all events, gain the advantage of a strong contrast between Theism and non-Theism;—and strong contrast with shadows is often a strong enlightenment.

First, then, to consider the idea of Creation as the work not of a blind thing, but a supremely wise and powerful Being. It is plain that (to say the very least) this idea is encompassed with slighter and fewer difficulties. If a doubter is not convinced by the ordinary argument from Design, he cannot avoid admitting the fact of its possibility;—that it is applicable, and has been applied, argued, and reargued, without any overwhelming rejoinder or refutation. And there are two obvious reasons why it has never been successfully refuted. One—the evident truth that, whatever rival theories [172] might or might not be expected to do, this theory explains the world. Next—that no other attempted explanations have ever found a First ground for any existing thing. In the theory of Design it continues an open question how far we may conceive the Creator's first act as a grand finality,—the launch of a vast assemblage of worlds formed,—or, being formed;—so built upon law and guided by far-stretching wisdom, that the Universe sails gloriously through the Ocean of Space like a thing of Life; each breath of Force, each wave of Time wafting it securely on. But, let any idea of a true creation be admitted, and no belief in existing laws of any kind, will ever banish the great and good God from the world which He has created and made. His presence adds glory to its fabric, and, when we walk in its garden of delights, we feel that He walks and speaks there too [173].

The argument from Creation to Creator forms the subject of the next Chapters. Therefore, we press it no farther here.

The point to be remembered now, is that this line of reasoning has alone offered a tenable explanation of the world's existence. And a like remark holds good of Natural Realism as opposed to Speculative Idealism. It is impossible (as we have seen), to prove or disprove either by bare argumentative abstractions. But, as a question of practical reason, the Natural Realist explains the outer world of individual existences, and his explanation tallies both with its phenomena and our own relations to them. Our material progress (that antithesis of oriental quietism), depends upon activities we should never have exerted had we not fully believed in a world of working energy within ourselves, and an outside world of reacting forces for us to work upon.

From mere material progress, let us turn our eyes to the nobler civilization of Mankind. A respect for human life because it is human,—honour paid to all men, inasmuch as manhood possesses an intrinsic title to honour,—the desire to do justice and love mercy,—sympathy with privation, suffering, and aberration, both moral and intellectual,—these are the true elements that soften and improve our race. And they are pre-eminently the dowry of nations believing in Theism. Theism is to these spiritual powers what Realism has been to material powers. Human beings are, by these two agencies, brought into contact with both the outer and the inner work of life. And as regards life's central work, the lesson of history is now what it always has been. To move man from a lower to a higher sphere, his soul must first be deeply stirred. And a spiritual stir and movement is the applied strength of a spiritual power [ai].

We propose, then, to see by example, what Theism may be to mankind. Many examples will not be needed, provided those selected are typical. We shall therefore choose some two or three distinctive types.

The task of selection reminds us to protest, once for all, against the weak and cynical way of illustrating human nature which threatens to become prevalent. If we want to see what a true man is, we must not seek his fossil effigies, by delving into the scanty and disputable records of primaeval savagery [aj], and unearthing the crumbled seeds of better things, which died before coming to perfection. It is like estimating the Oak from a mouldy Acorn. It is worse!—Barbarism tends to distortion and degeneracy. We might as wisely pronounce a maimed dwarf with carefully flattened forehead, the beau ideal of human strength and beauty, as seek to know the mind of man amid its wrecks and perversities. We must rather look at our race in its strongest and noblest development. The healthy acorn grows into a spreading oak;—the truly human child becomes, not a crooked dwarf, but an upright intellectual giant. The investigation of maimed deformities may have its interest for comparative purposes, but no ancient Greek nor Hebrew, no modern European nor American, ought to be painted with lineaments which are revolting to his higher nature. Let us help the savage by every means we can, except by asking him to sit for a model of Humanity. When we do this, we have assuredly lost our very best reason for helping him at all.

The examples following, no one will doubt to be types of true and highly developed men. The first, is intended to shew how Theism stands out before the apprehension of a Man engaged in searching out abstract truth.

The Philosophy of Sir W. Hamilton has become familiar to most people, so far as his theory of "the Conditioned" is concerned. They are aware that his mind dwelt on the speculative difficulties surrounding a knowledge of the Absolute, the self-subsisting First Cause, and true Ground of all things. Yet, to the veracity of God he appeals for the veraciousness of our primary beliefs. Over against a whole school of Idealists, he places, as the one fatal objection, this same veracity—"Either maintaining the veracity of God, they must surrender their hypothesis;—or, maintaining their hypothesis, they must surrender the veracity of God" [174]. And, if the existence of a Deity is known, there can be no doubt that His truth is amongst the highest and clearest to us, of all His essential attributes. We cannot (as Sir William says) "suppose that we are created capable of intelligence, in order to be made the victims of delusion; that God is a deceiver, and the root of our nature a lie" [175]. Therefore, he drew a wide distinction between, on the one hand, knowing the Absolute and the Supreme so as to examine and explain His nature, and, on the other hand, believing that He truly is, so as to affirm the fact of His being, and the necessary consequences of His existence. "When I deny," he writes, "that the Infinite can by us be known, I am far from denying that by us it is, must, and ought to be, believed!" [176] —In this belief, Sir William saw a sufficient reason for accepting, as Mr. Mill advises all to accept, "the inexplicable fact." And indeed the problem of truth perpetually does come, (evade the conclusion as we will), in one shape or another, to this same necessity of final acceptance. Mr. Coleridge's Friend is one long investigation into this necessity, and he fairly closes his argument by saying that always,—start from whatever point we may,—"reason will find a chasm, which the moral being only, which the spirit and religion of man alone can fill up" [177].

3 For Sir W. Hamilton, Theism bridged the vast abyss! No one could more strongly estimate its vastness, and the poverty of our visual powers when we stand beside it;—the dim feeling which makes us shrink back from its awful verge. But Theism became to him the strength of a noble life;—a life of much self-sacrifice, and meagre earthly recompense [ak].

The next typical thinker we shall quote is one pre-eminent for his careful study of the constitution of Man, the course, the aims, and aptitudes of his moral existence. It seems hardly necessary to add the name of Bishop Butler. The reader will find pleasure and instruction, if he peruses Butler's two sermons on the Love of God, from the second of which the following passages are cited:—

"Nothing is more certain, than that an infinite Being may himself be, if he pleases, the supply to all the capacities of our nature. All the common enjoyments of life are from the faculties he hath endued us with, and the objects he hath made suitable to them. He may himself be to us infinitely more than all these: he may be to us all that we want. As our understanding can contemplate itself, and our affections be exercised upon themselves by reflection, so may each be employed in the same manner upon any other mind; and since the supreme Mind, the Author and Cause of all things, is the highest possible object to himself, he may be an adequate supply to all the faculties of our souls; a subject to our understanding, and an object to our affections.

"Consider then: when we shall have put off this mortal body, when we shall be divested of sensual appetites, and those possessions which are now the means of gratification shall be of no avail; when this restless scene of business and vain pleasures, which now diverts us from ourselves, shall be all over; we, our proper self, shall still remain; we shall still continue the same creatures we are, with wants to be supplied, and capacities of happiness. We must have faculties of perception, though not sensitive ones; and pleasure or uneasiness from our perceptions, as now we have.

"There are certain ideas, which we express by the words, order, harmony, proportion, beauty, the furthest removed from anything sensual. Now, what is there in those intellectual images, forms, or ideas, which begets that approbation, love, delight, and even rapture, which is seen in some persons' faces upon having those objects present to their minds?—'Mere enthusiasm!'—Be it what it will: there are objects, works of nature and of art, which all mankind have delight from, quite distinct from their affording gratification to sensual appetites; and from quite another view of them, than as being for their interest and further advantage. The faculties from which we are capable of these pleasures, and the pleasures themselves, are as natural, and as much to be accounted for, as any sensual appetite whatever, and the pleasure from its gratification. Words to be sure are wanting upon this subject: to say, that everything of grace and beauty throughout the whole of nature, everything excellent and amiable shared in differently lower degrees by the whole creation, meet in the Author and Cause of all things; this is an inadequate and perhaps improper way of speaking of the divine nature; but it is manifest that absolute rectitude, the perfection of being, must be in all senses, and in every respect, the highest object to the mind....

".... Now, as our capacities of perception improve, we shall have, perhaps by some faculty entirely new, a perception of God's presence with us in a nearer and stricter way; since it is certain he is more intimately present with us than anything else can be. Proof of the existence and presence of any being is quite different from the immediate perception, the consciousness of it. What then will be the joy of heart, which his presence, and the light of his countenance, who is the life of the universe, will inspire good men with, when they shall have a sensation, that he is the sustainer of their being, that they exist in him; when they shall feel his influence to cheer and enliven and support their frame, in a manner of which we have now no conception? He will be in a literal sense their strength and their portion for ever" [178].

Of the last writer here adduced, it is needless to say more than that amongst living authors, he is rarely equalled in his subtle analysis of the tender and emotional side of humanity.

"The personal relation sought, is discerned and felt. The Soul understands and knows that God is her God; dwelling with her more closely than any creature can; yea, neither Stars, nor Sea, nor smiling Nature hold God so intimately as the bosom of the Soul. What is He to it? what, but the Soul of the soul? It no longer seems profane to say, 'God is my bosom friend: God is for me, and I am for Him.' So Joy bursts out into Praise, and all things look brilliant; and hardship seems easy, and duty becomes delight, and contempt is not felt, and every morsel of bread is sweet....

".... But Oh philosopher, is all this a contemptible dream? thou canst explain it all? or thou scornest it all? Whatever theory thou may'st form concerning it, it is not the less a fact of human nature: one of some age too: for David thirsted after God and exceedingly rejoiced in Him, and so did Paul; and the feelings which they describe are reproduced in the present day. To despise wide-spread enduring facts is not philosophic; and when they conduce to power of goodness and inward happiness, it might be wise to learn the phenomena by personal experience, before theorizing about them. It was not a proud thing of Paul to say, but a simple truth, that the spiritual cannot be judged by the unspiritual.

"The single thought, 'God is for my soul, and my soul is for Him,' suffices to fill a universe of feeling, and gives rise to a hundred metaphors. Spiritual persons have exhausted human relationships in the vain attempt to express their full feeling of what God (or Christ) is to them. Father, Brother, Friend, King, Master, Shepherd, Guide, are common titles. In other figures, God is their Tower, their Glory, their Rock, their Shield, their Sun, their Star, their Joy, their Portion, their Hope, their Trust, their Life" [179].

Such is Theism, penetrating the head and heart of Man; appealing to his intellect, his conscience, and his affections. Such is Theism; sending upwards, out of Man's spirit, aspirations which "dumb driven cattle" cannot breathe—often the sole sweet incense from Earth to Heaven. It is possible that, to some readers, the passages extracted will sound like the accents of a foreign tongue. Of such it may properly be asked, whether any man has a right so to call in question another sane man's honest consciousness, as to deny its reality, worth, and excellence? There are ears on which the music of Shakespeare's words, or Mozart's notes, fall tuneless and unmeaning. Yet, who on that account would deny the true sense and delight of poetry, rhythm, and melody? We cannot, in reason, forget that even from ordinary men a small amount of affirmation, if conscientious, unselfish, and collected, outweighs and annihilates a host of perplexing doubts. But, every great Man's thought is at least a grand fact; every expression of it a benefaction to his fellow-men. And, as respects the mighty power with which Theism stirs and impels the soul, we may rest absolutely assured that, where one human being is found to give it utterance, thousands have felt the movement, and have silently governed their life's work by it. Happily, the brightest gifts of our existence are also the commonest;—the sunshine of the world, and the sunshine of the Soul.

Countless numbers have, indeed, professed to discern by an inward sense the reflected reality of a Supreme Being. They who feel it most deeply, do not attempt to explain the Substance of which an imperfect copy exists within themselves, acknowledged, yet inexplicable; at once the greatest enigma, and the noblest fact of their essential being. They are content to look upwards to the Supreme Mind they have found;—to treasure such knowledge as they have; and adore its object. Many of those who have thus believed and acted are amongst the most excellent and perfect of our race.

Has any theory of the Universe which ignores the original of an image discovered within ourselves, accounted for what we perceive through our senses, our consciousness, and our moral insight,—so well as that theory which acknowledges and reverences a God?

Chapter 5

PRODUCTION AND ITS LAW: CONDITIONS OF ACTIVITY—WILL AND REASON IN CONTRAST WITH MATERIALISM AND MECHANISM—CREATIVE MIND CHARACTERISED BY VISIBLE PRODUCTS

" Πολλὰ τὰ δεινά, κοὐδὲν ἀνθρώπου δεινότερον πέλει. " Sophocles, Antigone.

"These be the two parts of natural philosophy,—the inquisition of causes, and the production of effects; speculative, and operative; natural science, and natural prudence." Bacon's *Advancement of Learning*. Book II.

"The perception of real affinities between events (that is to say, of ideal affinities, for those only are real), enables the poet to make free with the most imposing forms and phenomena of the world, and to assert the predominance of the soul.

"Whilst thus the poet animates nature with his own thoughts, he differs from the philosopher only herein, that the one proposes Beauty as his main end; the other Truth," Emerson. Idealism.

"The question of questions for mankind—the problem which underlies all others, and is more deeply interesting than any other—is the ascertainment of the place which Man occupies in nature and of his relations to the universe of things. Whence our race has come; what are the limits of our power over nature, and of nature's power over us; to what goal we are tending; are the problems which present themselves anew and with undiminished interest to every man born into the world." Huxley. *Man's Place in Nature*, p. 57.

"Der Mensch ist das einzige Geschöpf, das erzogen werden muss. Unter der Erziehung nämlich verstehen wir die Wartung (Verpflegung, Unterhaltung), Disciplin (Zucht) und Unterweisung nebst der Bildung. Dem zufolge ist der Mensch Säugling,—Zögling—und Lehrling." Kant. *Pädagogik*, Einleitung.

"Man's Intellectual Progress consists in the Idealization of Facts, and man's Moral Progress consists in the Realization of Ideas." Whewell's *Moral Philosophy*, Additional Lectures, p. 129.

"Say! when the world was new and fresh from the hand of its Maker,
Ere the first modelled frame thrilled with the tremors of life,....
.... Forms of transcendent might—Beauty with Majesty joined,
None to behold, and none to enjoy, and none to interpret?
Say! was the Work wrought out! Say was the Glory complete?
What could reflect, though dimly and faint, the Ineffable Purpose
Which from chaotic powers, Order and Harmony drew?
What but the reasoning spirit, the thought and the faith and the feeling?
What, but the grateful sense, conscious of love and design?
Man sprang forth at the final behest. His intelligent worship
Filled up the void that was left. Nature at length had a Soul."
Sir J. Herschel. *Essays*, etc., p. 737.

"Wär ein verständiger Sinn auch mir doch beschieden gewesen!
Aber es täuschte mich trügrischer Pfad, hieher mich, dann dorthin
Lockend. Nun bin ich bejahrt und doch unbefriedigt von allem
Forschen. Denn wo ich den Geist hinwende, da löst sich mir alles
Auf in Eins und Dasselbe: da alles Seyende, allzeit
Allwärts angezogen, in ähnliche, eine Natur tritt."
Jacobi. Werke, *Vorrede zu David Hume*, p. 103.

"Throughout all future time, as now, the human mind may occupy itself, not only with ascertained phenomena and their relations, but also with that unascertained something which phenomena and their relations imply. Hence if knowledge cannot monopolize consciousness—if it must always continue possible for the mind to dwell upon that which transcends knowledge; then there can never cease to be a place for something of the nature of Religion; since Religion under all its forms is distinguished from everything else in this, that its subject matter is that which passes the sphere of experience." Herbert Spencer. *First Principles*, p. 17.

SYNOPSIS OF CHAPTER 5

The argument of this chapter turns upon the analysis of concrete processes carried on throughout human life; together with their correlations or correspondent factors visible in rerum naturâ. All these being complex activities, resolve themselves into series of simpler activities, which, though separable in thought, follow each other inseparably as real working elements of human or natural productions,—or of both.

In each productive process of Mankind, we perceive:— 1. A purpose conceived,—(the end or final cause.) 2. A power or force which has to be (a.) discovered and (b.) fitted to this human purpose. 2. (a.) This implies that the object in quest exists, or is capable of being evoked into active existence, as a Force or operative Law capable of producing real effects. Otherwise, it would be no auxiliary to Man. Viewed per se, and apart from its being fitted to his special purpose, it must therefore be a natural power or law, and answers to what Bacon calls a Form or Formal cause [180].

(It is plain that human production requires some particular utilization of a producing force, wider in itself than this or any other ancillary application of its energies. Compare

Bacon's philosophic observation [181] that the operative Form "deduces the given nature from some source of being which is inherent in more natures.")

2. (b.) A number of such powers, forces, laws, forms, present themselves to the intellectual eye of an inventor or producer. Possible fitness, (adaptability)—must therefore next be determined. And here the power is no longer considered separately, but in relation to some Formation.

In 2, therefore, we have (a) a simple fact or general law of Force;—and (b) a correlated fact, or specialized law of Production.

3. Finally, for operative activity, there must be an efficient cause putting in movement the productive law, over and above its intelligent apprehension just presupposed. This efficient Cause, as seen always in human Production, is a Will.

Now each several step in this series comes before us as an act of Mind. But out of this number one only needs to be examined here;—because

Purpose (1) has been treated of in Chapter 2. Will (3) occupies the close of this Essay.

No. 2, therefore, (divisible into a and b,) makes the proper subject-matter of the present Chapter. It has been written to meet the difficulties felt by a certain number of reasoners respecting the argument from Design. They are very often indisposed to accept that argument, because its analogical nature makes it appear circuitous; and because they hesitate when attempting to appreciate its exact value: compare p. 53 ante. There is also a lurking dread of that spectral shadow called Anthropomorphism, haunting some minds with a pertinacity, which may be estimated from p. 54 seq. By such reasoners let the present Chapter,—which proceeds not by way of analogy, but through a direct analysis of acknowledged facts—be read as a substitute for Chapter 2. Or, they may if they please, consider the present and two following Chapters as a Treatise entirely distinct from the rest of the volume; this present Chapter serving as a brief statement of the case for physico- theology; while the two arguments ensuing sketch out Ethico- or Moral Theology; on which complementary modes of thought see p. 107 ante, together with text and notes now about to follow. Finally, by all those who accept the reasoning from Design as already explained, let both it and our other various lines of argument be treated as separate evidences of Natural Theology, each resting on its own grounds, but all consilient at last.

Analysis. —Advance and Retrogression of Discovery and of Civilization. Progress dependent on realizing the relativity between Power and Function. This condition of success is examined at length.

Perception of existing Relations, and creation of new ones by human Reason and Will. Illustrations from histories of Invention, Art, Education, and Self-Education.

Production of Change within ourselves. Self conquest, Self formation, and Re-formation. Inability of animals arises from domination of motives unalterable by themselves and instinctively apprehended. Training relative to motor instincts of various sorts. Self-training requires freedom from the domination of any single unbalanced or unalterable impulse. It implies the power of using motives as counterpoises, and of introducing new elements into the sphere of our ideals.

Influence of human presence upon the education of animals; influence of the Divine Idea upon Man.

Transition from the sphere of Intellect to that of Will in relation to the World. The Spring of Production a movement of Will; the Idea of Production an insight into the Mind of Nature; discovered not logically, but as shewn in operation in Nature. Law and Idea, Intelligence and

Matter. Manifold Forces imply a central Unity. Putting aside the analogical inference from apparent Purpose, the question of operative Law (Force, Form, Mind,) is examined in its many activities, their correlations and their underlying Oneness.

Natural Law in action: hypothesis of limited intelligence. Case of Unreason, Creation by Chance. Breadth of Law seen in its general fitnesses, and grander unities. Exceptional effects in "Functioning."

Character of Mind in Nature. Law, type, idea. Adaptation even if purposed is not Arbitrary. A Supreme Will must be a sovereign Reason.

Perfection of Mind in Nature estimated from convergent fitnesses and correlations, as exemplified by Sight and Hearing. Also by their effects in producing Beauty, Happiness, and a sense of sympathy. Mind in Nature not bare intelligence, but possessing emotional attributes, not harsh nor unlovely, but tender and loveable.

Additional Note

On the Doctrine of Chances applied to the structural Development of of the Eye, by Professor Pritchard.

PRODUCTION AND ITS LAW

"Life," said Dr. Johnson, "has not many things better than this:"—"we were," Boswell explains, "driving rapidly along in a post-chaise." But what if the two men, congratulating themselves upon their speed, could have read (with some approach to second-sight) Dr. Darwin's lines—

> "Soon shall thy arm, unconquer'd steam! afar
> Drag the slow barge, or drive the rapid car.
> Or on wide-waving wings expanded bear
> The flying chariot through the fields of air."

The slow barge now traverses the wide Atlantic as fast as even fast-living America can desire. The rapid car whirls across England in a few brief hours. With what half-envious astonishment, might Dr. Johnson have computed the arrowy flight of these iron creations over land or water;—with what sententious wisdom might he not have dilated on the uncontrolled dissemination, Sir, of books, knowledge, and civility;—to say nothing of vile whiggism or possible rebellion!

No wide-waving wings have as yet wafted us over rivers and mountains. But some inventors still cherish a hope of applying steam steerage, and perhaps steam propulsion, to very large balloons.

It is curious to think of the many centuries, during which men saw elastic vapour lifting their kettle lids, without catching the idea of steam power, or reflecting on the movement it produced. Curious, too, to remember how slowly the idea grew, after the Marquis of Worcester had explained the relation between the power and its movement-producing func tion. His "fire-water-work" (as he called it), "drove up water by fire," at a rate of 1250 lbs.

through one foot, to the consumption of 1 lb. of coal. This is about 200 times the waste of a good modern engine. But the principle was there. Water flowed without intermission, at a height of forty feet, driven only by the elastic force of steam. The introduction of atmospheric pressure half obscured the original conception; steam- power seemed in danger of losing its proper functions. Passing by Papin and Savery [182], the descent of Newcomen's piston depended on the production of a vacuum beneath it; at much cost of heat and labour, much waste of fuel and force. Strange, that for so many years nobody thought of introducing steam-power above the piston, as well as below it.

The retrograde path which science sometimes treads, is also clearly shewn in the long-delayed invention of the paddlewheel steam-boat. The first patent was taken out by Jonathan Hulls in 1736, and his rare pamphlet may be seen at the British Museum, or in Mr. Partington's reprint [183]. Strange, that so good a thing should have continued so long neglected;—up to the days of the first Napoleon, and, (fortunately perhaps for civilization,) under the Conqueror's imperial rule. The same fate, however, befel Trevithick's "walking engine" made in 1802. He applied high- pressure steam-power to a railway locomotive which really travelled (1805) at Merthyr Tydvil. Every one knows how slowly this invention has grown up into the useful goods-train or the luxurious roll of the express.

The relation between a power so well tested, and propulsion, was thus long in being fitted with perfect mechanism, and presented to the eyes of mankind as a familiar every day phenomenon. But the idea of propelling carriages by other means than animal sinews, had been working the reverse way; and a desirable end suggested a search for means. Men tried to fit other powers to the function; the problem gave rise to wind-driven chariots, and other curious contrivances for travelling by land, which are graphically described by Lovell Edgeworth and several of his contemporaries. Then, too, came the desire to sail against the wind, and independently of water currents. A vignette in the first Edition of *Bewick's Birds* (vol. 1, p. 257), published in 1797, shews us a ferry-boat crossing a river by means of a windmill which turns paddle wheels [184]. The engraver has marked by a ripple at the vessel's bows the strength and swiftness with which she stems the stream.

The history of these machines carries with it a very useful moral. It furnishes an apt similitude to the delays and retrogressions which are found in the onward march of mankind, in the gains and triumphs of civilization. These sometimes occur to nations through error, violence, and wrong. Compulsory celibacy, forced upon the most cultured men, was, according to Mr. Darwin, one cause why Spain, notwithstanding her great generals, navigators, and inventors [185], has been distanced by freer nations. Then, too, as he adds, "the holy Inquisition selected with extreme care the freest and boldest men in order to burn or imprison them.—In Spain alone, some of the best men ... were eliminated during three centuries at the rate of a thousand a year [186]. The streams of both invention and human improvement resemble, in this respect, the current of a mighty river. We always encounter—and always ought to expect—whirlpools, back-waters, and other sinuosities, as we descend the flowing tide.

Very frequently, civilization is retarded by another kind of difficulty, also besetting the inventive arts. Like them, Progress depends upon its capacity for happily realizing the relativity [al] between Power and Function. The philan thropist sometimes,—the craftsman often,—has only to think of the function required, and to grasp a relation pre-existing in the laws of the natural world,—fit it to its own purposes, and usefully employ the adaptation. This was the case when elastic vapours of many kinds were examined relatively to their power of producing movement. Each deeper investigation brings a clearer insight into a more deeply-hidden law. The apprehension of "Heat as a mode of Motion," [am] is an instance in point.

Sometimes—in human affairs oftenest—the mind originates a new relation between Power and Function, and launches it, like an unimagined locomotive, whirling and dashing onwards throughout the world of men. The will of a powerful king or conqueror, statesman or missionary, evokes a new power; gives it life and motive energy, and sends it out to perform its intended function amongst millions of mankind, and for many generations. Hence, Kant said there were two things which filled him with awe: one, the starry heavens, that mightiest example of mighty powers orderly performing their appropriate functions; the other, Man's Will, a power less mighty in one sense, but belonging to a sphere where mass and measurement are not, and performing functions signalized too frequently by wrongful determination. Functions which, whether rightly or wrongly performed, involve a mightier Something than all the inorganic worlds ever displayed, a Something we define by that deepest of ideas and most awful of truths,—Responsibility.

The whole subject admits of extensive illustration. The relativities of Power and Function are infinitely varied in Nature, Art, and Thought; in the unity of the whole world, and in the disunited world of Humanity. But, however varied in their sphere of operation, all relations between Power and Function coincide in one characteristic. They appeal to mind alone, and by mind alone can be apprehended so as to become operative. Those that belong to the human sphere of activity are in part the perceptions of Mind; in part they are evidenced to our consciousness as its own creations.

If we look at the inorganic world, Man apprehends such a relativity as that between steam-power and propulsion, and applies it. In the realm of pure mathematics, there are powers of another sort, which (when applied) require allowances to be made in "functioning" them. Provided metal, timber, friction, and cross-circumstances have their proper margin given, those abstract entities [187], absolute in truth, become realized in practice. When we come to organization, particularly higher organisms, the functions of the biological kingdom are more complex. Yet the trainer of animals knows how to combine and modify old powers so as to produce new ones. The pointer, the greyhound, the racehorse, and the hunter are all examples. Then, too, men manipulate men. See how the face of all Europe is covered with training establishments of every description [an]. Youths are fitted for army, navy, bar, parliament, politics. The powers of attention, memory, habit, are all pressed into service, just as the inventor of locomotives calculates the strength and tenacity of iron, brass, copper, and other materials, fits each pipe, crank, and wheel, to its intended function, and ends by speeding his fellows past the doors of their fellow-men. Now, the manipulation of these materials is a calculable process, and succeeds at last. But there is one disappointment often awaiting the manipulator of mankind. His failure arises from the fact that the moral purpose, which he must take for granted, is very commonly wanting among those he undertakes to educate.

Another inventor of the highest sort, an artist, conceives a majestic thought. It becomes to him the work of his life, the function he ardently desires to realize. To the true Art-man, his conception is a noble ideal, and some instinct, or proclivity of his own nature, teaches him how to adapt it to the ears and eyes, the intellect and feelings of his race. There are sounds which die in their newborn sensations of delight, yet haunt the memory while consciousness remains. There are colours appealing to one single organ of perception, and, through it, penetrating the soul with images that rise again and again in nightly and daily dreams. And there are words, the forms and creations of our distinctive human mind, through which it exercises its sublimest powers, and which are (in themselves) among the most sublime. They have their proper functions. Age after age, from country to country, from nation to nation [188], they have moved the souls of readers to emotion, reasoning, will, activity. Noble words, expressing ideas unknown to all intelligences below man, and called into existence by him, prolong their own lives by extending his intellectual and affective life. They burn like incense within the temple of his spirit, but, unlike incense, survive undyingly in the immortal flame which kindles them.

There is a still loftier and more solemn function we all exercise—or ought to exercise—in or upon the sphere of our own souls. To us is committed the task, our human task,—morally imperative on no sentient beings inferior to ourselves,—of transforming and reforming, that is (to all intents and purposes) truly forming our own inward nature. We have not, at present, to consider how near heaven may and does draw to earth, in this highest of works known to us who dwell beneath the sky. But the absolutely human part of it belongs to this place.

Every one has learned how hard it is to break through even one bad habit. The evil has in most cases enchained body as well as mind. A drunkard's hand is naturally reached out to lift the cups it has been used to lift. His thirst, too, recurs at the accustomed hour;—and the readers of "Elia" know something of what happens when it is left unslaked. A tingling and straining of the palate is associated with the sight of the eye; the drunkard's throat burns when he sees the draught before him; his frustrated desire is followed by the most frightful sufferings throughout his disorganized nervous system. The same is true of other like habituations; as may be read in De Quincey's *Opium Eater*, and in the last book of Charles Dickens, left behind him an unfinished fragment. It is true, also, of countless smaller customs which prevent many a man from achieving what Hooker calls "great masteries." Every muscle, fibre, and organ of our frame, performs easily the functions it has been used to perform, but undergoes a strain if put out of its usual course.

The mind (as well as the body), has its laws of habit and association. We perceive this fact most readily in the less perfect intelligence of the animal kingdom, of untutored man, and of people who are more inured to action than to reflection. The more rudimentary the mind, the more real is its state of subservience to association and habit, which may then be properly termed its governing laws. But it would be improper to apply this word "governing" to the same laws in connection with higher natures. In a man whose reason and will have attained their manly majority, such laws have ceased to be governors;—their province is simply administrative. Deposed from their rule over his existence, they become his ministers, servants, instruments. There is, thus, a compensatory constitution of human nature, whereby the light within us, which lighteth every man, may be said to make us free [189]. It exempts us, that is, from the sway of customary laws which guide and reduce to subjection the merely animal intelligence.

A habit broken is a customary law broken. And any one who breaks through a customary law already inwoven with the fibres of his own life, is a man par excellence. And the deeper that inweaving,—the greater the laceration of living fibres,—if he rends them in obedience to duty, and because to do otherwise would be to do wrong, the more truly and emphatically he is a Man. Again, if we proceed to ask by what means he breaks the bonds of custom, the Manhood of his act appears still more distinctly. His purpose may be, and often is, accomplished by setting a higher law of his being over against a lower;—putting a more really human power in movement to tame and quell some animal propensity. But then, what is that secret strength which apprehends and evokes the higher law? What is the central spring that moves the strictly human power, and converts it from a sleeping capacity for good, into an acting and living energy? Clearly, it is the Man's truest humanity;—the endowment which makes him Man.

There are lives of men plainly told, and undoubted, where re -formation,—that is self - formation,—appears like a flash of electric fire. The Will in such men has energized, just as intellect flashes out in its noblest condition of genius; and can best be described by the poet or the seer who knows what it is to create, and new create. These lives more than realize Caesar's boast;—the truly human soul came to itself,—saw itself,—and overcame. The conqueror did a deed which, (truly done,) was done for ever, and yielded him the presage of perpetual peace. Histories of self-conquest do, however, remarkably differ in respect of the time employed upon the work. Some victories are, as we have said, rapid and brilliant as the march of Alexander,—others slow and embarrassed, like the weary path of a pilgrim through deserts of rolling sand. But no pilgrim who is in earnest need despair. Putting aside all consideration of supernatural aid, he may take courage from the essential greatness of his own human being, when contrasted with the being of all creatures below mankind.

The comparison sets out from this question:—What can merely animal nature do to raise itself? Man, we know, can train certain brutes—he can entrap all;—but no brute can in any wise deliver himself from the snare of a single appetite. The weakness, as well as the strength, of animal intelligence lies in the vividness of its instincts. Animals appear conscious of the working of powers within themselves; and they apprehend those functions, with the performances of which their powers are correlated. Hence, in part at least, the pleasure of a bird in nest-building; a bee in storing her comb, or a predacious creature in its successful pursuit of prey. But the relation between animal power and function appears so nearly fixed, as to be hedged round by narrow limits; and only in a very small degree susceptible of modification. So far as we can discover, the brute is deficient in the means of self-education, for three distinct reasons. One, because he cannot escape fulfilling the normal functions of his unreasoning impulse. In the second place, because he is unable to overcome the urgency of one innate power, by opposing to it the claims and vigour of another. Thirdly, he can never introduce anything new into the relativity between power and function. He can command no spring of high aim or creative thought, which might give new purpose to his better powers, or open out some further sphere of activity before unknown.—Were this possible, he might lift the functions of his common life above their old destinies, and above themselves.—And this would be a work of self-education.

To pursue our comparison,—we must remember that the ability for self-education and the capacity for being educated, are correlatives; and we may measure the one by the other. The animal world has never shewn strength enough to raise itself very high;—it has never ceased to be distinctly animal. But, has it ever possessed latent powers for which opportunity was always wanting? Mankind, for their own purposes, have (we know) continually been testing [ao] the endowments of inferior creatures. How high, then, can man by his endeavours raise the animal race?—He can generally train them to a greater quickness in the exercise and nicety of their own instinctive powers, and a more enduring performance of their instinctively presented functions. By reward and punishment, he can inure them to some degree of self-restraint; and he takes advantage of a thousand pretty impulses and fondnesses of animal nature, to call into being attachment,—nay, often passionate devotion,—towards himself. In this sense, Man has been styled the God of his domestic brute—his horse, his dog, his elephant. It would be a curious subject of reflection, to inquire what effect might possibly be produced upon the human mind by the visible presence, and incessant influence, of beings, as much higher than men, as men are higher than brutes? The moment we start this idea in our minds, it is difficult to evade an impression that Man must be a desolate creature, if he can never in some way see the Invisible [ap].

To leave this curious point. Nothing appears more really conclusive against all supposed capacity for great development, than the history of what are called "learned animals";—of the mechanical means necessarily employed for teaching them, and the mechanical results obtained. There is indeed no better word to describe the true state of the case; than the term "mechanical," as opposed to everything that is ideal, or truly creative [aq]. If a brute could idealize the laws of outward nature,—or the laws connecting his own powers with their proper functions, he might see them as a Man does, and give them a fresh existence within his own intelligence. He would then be able to invent an alphabet, conceive a picture, and view the properties of outward objects as universals inwardly apprehended. In this way, he would acquire exemption from the reign of mechanism, and live a really creative life. Possible conceptions—ideal functions—would require new powers to realize them;—and these powers would be searched for and found. Or, vice versâ, an idealized power,—a power seen, (not as it is, but as it may be)—would lead to the discovery of fresh functions,—new fields of enterprise,—new realms of imagination.

It is manifest at a glance, how far in fact these conquests are from the world of creatures, by us, therefore, called unreasoning. Art, letters, and abstract thought, are no visitants of the animal sphere. Words cannot come where thoughts are not; and therefore language, in the human meaning of language, is unknown to brutes [190]. And no effort made by Man has ever been successful in sharing with his humble companions any one—(much less all) of these attainments. His artistic sense of Beauty, and power of giving it varied expression, find no Echo beneath himself; he can in no wise teach by historical record, poetry, abstract calculation, or abstract thought. Neither can he impart the true secret of social sympathy,—and forbid the stricken deer to weep and die alone. Intelligence without imagination, cannot conceive a sorrow so lonely or unseen. Therefore, it knows little of deep sorrow,—for even the mortally-wounded bird will strive to hide its wound [191].

Now, in each and all of these respects, every human being devoted to self-education starts from the plain fact, that Man is educable:—

"Parents first season us,—then schoolmasters."

The master of many a middle-school has frequent occasion to say with Horace;

——"At ingenium ingens
Inculto latet hoc sub corpore."—

And the schoolmaster, also, knows that a little spark will often light into fire some vast store of emotional as well as intellectual elements lying asleep within [192].

We therefore speak (if we speak correctly), of educating an animal in a totally different sense from educating a boy. For, facts are as we have stated them, whatever theories may be.

There is one more point of contrast to stimulate and encourage the self-educating portion of Mankind; and this point is the most characteristic endowment essential to Humanity. A man is not creative by virtue of his ideals alone, however bright and beautiful those visions of his intellect may be. He calls into existence that, which as yet is not, by virtue of his Will. We know this, although inexplicable, to be true;—partly from the evidence of our own Consciousness,—which asserts that it is so, and partly from the evidence of Morality,—which says that it must necessarily be so. Were it otherwise, no amount of Criminality could make a Criminal responsible. And this truth of responsibility is one which may occasion serious reflection to us all; to some of us sad remembrances.

Man, considered as causal or creative mind, cannot but act upon the world without, as well as the world within himself. And perhaps the nearest idea we are able to form of the process of production, is the inter -action of power and function, evoked by a Will, (that is a Cause); and continuing operative by aid of ordinary laws and relativities of nature [ar]. One man resolves to construct a steam engine, and on steam-power he concentrates his thought. He conceives the relation between watery vapour and propulsion;—and by using arbitrary signs, formulates and measures it. Then, he considers the laws and properties of metals, fits each contrivance into place and produces his machine. Another determines to commit a murder. He wavers—debates—wills the deed, and says,—

> "I am settled, and bend up
> Each corporal agent to this terrible feat."

Every reader of Macbeth sees displayed before his eyes the airy dagger; the human muscle strained to clutch the shadow first,—afterwards, the reality;—the time, place, circumstances, all combined, followed up—worked out, till the murderous man has chained all conditions of success to his behest;—fulfilled his slowly-matured purpose,—and become, as in Will, so in act, a murderer. A third human being endeavours to invent a method for teaching the deaf and dumb;—spends a life in labouring among his silent tomb-like pupils, and succeeds to his joy and their inestimable benefit at last. He awakens powers lost in the shadow of death, and incites them to the performance of those true and appropriate functions, from which they had been incapacitated by a dwarfed and thwarted development. Before he aroused them, all such powers were only possibilities, visible to his hopeful eye. Now, they are utilized and happy activities; and, like impulses down a long electric chain, perpetuate themselves for generations after the benevolent inventor is taken from the race he had loved and educated.

There are two features in which all these productive men resemble each other. One, the creative influence of a purely human will, which not only sees what is not as though it is,—but also determines that it shall be. The other, a way of looking at, or rather, through Nature, as something more than an assemblage of facts or phenomena;—of penetrating to the mind of Nature,—her ideal laws legible by the intellectual eye of Man;—and finally, of putting each required law into motion,—that is to say, converting an idea into a force, by the movement of the producer's Will.

And the same is true of every useful producer, from the man who grows corn and wine, to the politician by whose foresight is arranged a treaty which gives Europe the blessing of half a century's peace. There is, probably, no example of production more definite than the work of a real statesman. A gifted human mind determines to pursue the thing that is just and right and good; sees where the means to be utilized may be found and enforced; touches the right spring of activity and power, and leads his fellow-men into a path of precedent or constitution for which ages may consecrate his memory.—But, let us suppose that he or any other true producer falls short of realizing his idea. Then, the act of Will would be in its essence as noble a reality as the deed itself. Yet the work intended,—the production must needs be lost. Creative will, as an efficient cause, would have moved within the moral sphere; but beyond, and into the outside world of men and things, its activity must have failed to penetrate.

When the case comes before us in this manner and is fairly weighed, we see that the man who wills a good choice, reflects to his fellows the image we are accustomed to call Divine. And that the man who produces a good act reflects to his fellows the further likeness and idea of a Creator. The will of man reflects a supreme will, when it refuses the evil and chooses the good;—the creative energy of man reflects a supreme energy, when it produces actual good; working and remaining effectual in the world. These human reflections may be feeble shadows, and far away from the Supreme;—as distant as earth and stars asunder, but they are typical images nevertheless. Man, in whom the Theist finds the impress of God, is by his power of Causality, as far raised beyond the laws of material existence, as animal life and movement are superior to the clods of soil on which the living creature walks, with a consciousness of being exalted above what he treads upon.

If these far away reflections, so striking to a Theist, are, by an unbeliever, pronounced insufficient proofs of Theism,—they remain still of very great value to the argument—Who shall, in the teeth of them, assert a reign of law in opposition to a reign of Causation, when we perceive that Causality is the grand endowment underlying the highest intelligence in this world, and distinguishing man from every inferior creature? A large class of objections dies in the fact that there is known to us a power which can truly originate actions;—a clear spring of volitional creativeness. And, as we have already seen, it is this human power which endows us with the faculty of self-education, and, at the same time, lays upon us the burden of responsibility. It exempts Man from what would otherwise be an iron chain of antecedents and consequents, linked together by mere mechanical laws. Man, we are sure, may interpolate in this chain; he may commence a new series within and over-riding it. The non-Theist would (if consistent), describe such an act of will as a miracle. Nevertheless, it is true to every-day life, and each guilty person, justly condemned, is a living example of this truth.

Any reader who has been deterred from admitting the arguments for Theism by the strength of objections apparently unanswerable, may feel, if he will thoughtfully reperuse this chapter, that many very formidable difficulties have melted away. He may also be inclined to admit that, if facts are to be considered the best grounds for reasoning with probability from the known to the unknown, the facts of nature, (including human nature,) make not against, but for, the conclusions of Natural Theology. And they do so all the more stringently, because they coincide with the higher and more spiritual tendencies of Man's being,—with the beliefs and aspirations of the most nobly endowed among his race.

Many readers will go further than this. They will perceive in the constitution of our distinctive nature, and more particularly in the movement of Volition, a really probable though far away similitude with the producing Cause of all things. At all events they will say that no other similitude or illustration has ever been conceived with so much probability. To such minds the argument would appear sufficiently convincing if shaped as a very wide application of the analogous reasoning stated in our Chapter on Design. The limitations there laid down should in this case be carefully observed; above all as regards the pivot on which such an argument must turn.

A larger class of readers may prefer to leave the field of this inviting analogy untouched; and remain content with having noted its resources in passing. They will thus prefer to pursue the more direct line of thought already adopted, especially since it has the merit of avoiding even the most shadowy apparent assumption of the principle invidiously termed Anthropomorphism. We therefore continue to place Man's causative nature side by side with external Force, and to set the powers he exercises as an inventor, artist, and producer, over against those natural powers we see elicited and brought to light by his activities. This is the aspect of the world to which the Relativity between Power and Function most obviously conducts us. Surveyed from this aspect it becomes plain that Nature is not entirely a soulless mechanism;—but that the Mind of Man finds something which corresponds to his human Thought, and which answers the touch of his idealizing impulse by implicitly obeying it. He is able, in this manner, to distinguish Nature's Mind from Nature's raw material.

Most of us are so accustomed to look at the world *ab extrâ*, and place ourselves in antithetical opposition to it, that we experience a kind of embarrassment in changing our point of view, and considering how much Nature and human nature correspond and harmonize together. There is something strange to many persons, in the thought that law is an idea put into operation [as]; that, when we speak of the dynamic agencies and living forces of nature, the dynamism is derived from intelligence; the life springs from mind. This is one of the puzzles and perplexities which hang a veil between God, who is pure Reason, and this outside world. No doubt there is much that appears dark and enigmatic in every attempted explanation of the subject. Yet it is clear that, whatever our conception of matter and mind may be, one of these two must be resolvably consequent upon the other; and the efforts of physicists have been strained for many years to diminish the distance between them. With these efforts, however, we have nothing to do beyond very distinctly adducing them [at] in order to shew where this particular difficulty really lies, and that it is by no means a special question of Natural Theology. The point for us, is rather to see how much we can discern respecting the action of Mind in and upon Nature. To see, that is, how many facts the realities of Production teach us. And throughout the whole realm of Productiveness (commencing from the steam-engine and ending with human self-formation), there is a certain sameness of procedure and of principle transparently discernible. And this truth, fairly examined, yields more than one kind of argument for Theism.

At the first blush of the subject, it is evident that the scientific producer when he begins to move, starts from the Causal power of mind. He moves through ideas or impulses of which he is internally conscious, and which present to him a chosen aim to be realized, a goal to be attained. It is equally evident that, when his aim is to make or effect something external to himself, he next proceeds to discover or accept one or more principles, existing for Mind alone [193], but operative in Nature. Such principles yield to his reason the requisite proportionate relation of Power employed, to Function designed. Upon this intelligent perception of intelligible laws, he acts;—it works well, and succeeds;—and from this experience of working and success, he finds for his productive intelligence a daily and hourly verification.

It is well to place this subject in various lights before reasoning upon it. We may illustrate the relativities or laws, through which Intelligence acts, by saying that they are to the fabric of the world, what the motory nervous system is to a highly-developed living organism. And, putting aside for a moment the intellectual agency of man, and applying our similitude to illustrate natural production alone, we may say that, just as the mandatory nerves imply some volitional centre, so these intelligent laws presuppose a mind in Nature. And we may not only make this clearer, but also evidence it more certainly, by pointing to the fact that amidst Nature's almost infinite manifoldness, we see everywhere harmony, symmetry, order. Forces, like lines of light, traverse the world, illuminating, (so to speak), the moving scenes of its magnificent transparency. And the one electric lamp that sends forth those illuminating rays, typifies the Unity from which emanate all cosmical Forces, and which shines visibly through them all [au].

There is nothing imaginative or metaphysical involved in this statement. It amounts to no more than what many very eminent physicists lay down, as implicitly contained in their sciences. On this very ground, Professor Baden Powell holds the validity of the argument from Design, as was mentioned in a former chapter. He puts the case into a few words thus:— "In the present state of knowledge, law and order, physical causation and uniformity of action, are the elevated manifestations of Divinity, creation and providence" [194]. A few passages further on, he repudiates with scorn the vulgar supposition that physical science can be confined to the circle of outward experience alone [195]; it includes within itself the principle of directing intelligence. According to Comte himself, "un fait s'explique par un fait d'un ordre supérieur, dont la perfection est sa raison, dont l'action qu'elle renferme est sa cause" [196].

It does indeed seem as impossible to deny the existence and operation of Mind in Nature, as it is to deny the existence and consciousness of our own minds. No tenable reason can ever be assigned why, when we look forth into the world surround ing us, we should be able to ascertain the fact of corporeal existence by means of our bodily senses, and be, at the same time, unable to ascertain the fact of existing intelligence by means of our mental intuitions. Each kind of existence has its appropriate evidence, and both sorts of evidence claim our belief by appealing to the veracity of our human consciousness.

If, therefore, it were possible to say with certitude "There is no God," the certainty would not, because it could not, eliminate Mind from the Universe. The law of production exists in, and for the Mind,—and so far as we can know, Mind in some shape or other works through the intelligible law [av]. Suppose we frame a crucial case for investigation.

Without speculating upon the first origin of things natural—without taking into the inquiry any preconception of a Divine personality—let us inquire what the world of Nature as it now exists can teach any man respecting the kind, degree, or condition of Mind, which regulates and moulds it? We are obliged to say "moulds it";—for Nature is not presented to us as an inert mass. We see movement, change, and activity everywhere. And this fact makes a vast difference to the present question.

Let us, then, suppose the inquirer setting out from an attempt to conceive mind as immersed in matter; either being identical with it [aw], or pervading it, like a subtle fluid, or imponderable force. Let some such conception be supposed his starting point. What sort of a Power must he finally determine this mind to be?

Could he possibly commence with a mundane intelligence inferior to the mind of Man?—The bee can build a cell, the beaver a dam—but the bee cannot construct a dam, nor the beaver a cell. The same is true universally. Animal intelligence acts in single right lines. We should, therefore, be obliged to conceive as many minds immanent in nature, or as many modifications of mind, as there are varieties of production. And if this were true, what would become of the order and harmony of the Universe? We call it by that name, because we know that, (notwithstanding its marvellous diversity and manifoldness,) it forms a grand united whole. It would become necessary, next, to admit a governing intelligence, able to control the countless species of intelligent power employed in producing all sorts of effects. And it really seems easier, at once to conceive a supreme Mind, framing its ideas into intelligible laws, and launching the forces of the Universe in moving might along them.

There are many obvious reasons why, after all, this would be the easiest [197], and therefore the preferable, conception. One lies in the immeasurable width and extent of that relativity between power and function, which we have seen to underlie every known production,—and conceivable possibility of ruling or moulding Nature. Now, under power we class forces such as those which hold corpuscles in cohesion, balance the orbs of heaven, or control the growth of a crystal. Such as those, again, which make Life the counterbalance of dissolution and decay; and enable the animal frame to resist decomposing influences; to feed, to grow, to energize, and move freely on earth, in water, or in air. Such as those, finally, which yield us the pabulum of sensation, thought, emotion; and subserve our efforts to attain whatever is highest or noblest in our human world.

We know what sorts of intelligence are required to apprehend, and to do no more than apprehend, the rationale of many among these natural movements, forces, and processes. Some of them can be explained only by a very great mathematician, other some by an equally great chemist, biologist, or psychologist. And in some, Man of the 19th century is as much a tyro and disciple,—as ignorant and as tentative—as his forefathers were two thousand years ago. What a complexity of Minds, or what a majestic supremacy of one Mind becomes thus discernible by the eye of Reason! Of Reason we say, meaning thereby the reason of a human being who looks facts in the face, puts them together and draws the inevitable conclusion. Were this drawn, it would amount to something very like a re-affirmation of Theism. At present, however, we will not press these topics further; since our object is to put an opposite conception on its complete trial, so as to see what is eventually implied in it.

Suppose, for instance, a merely sensitive intelligence to represent the character of mind administering the Universe. Conceive, if you choose, the world to be like an animal as some old philosophies conceived it. The way in which a human being sees Power and Function is altogether different from the way in which they would be viewed by the supposed mundane intelligence. We do not see them as two entities separately existing, and the relation which is of such vital consequence to all inventors and producers, as something which ensues between them. To us, the causal essence of the Power lies in the relativity itself, and we often actually recognize the Power passing over into its Function, and becoming lost in it. An example in point, lies in the active combination of uncombined atoms and molecules;—the relativity (or, as in such a case it is termed, the attraction) is the immediate cause of the production.

"Thus" says Dr. Tyndall [198] "we can get power out of oxygen and hydrogen by the act of their union, but once they are combined, and once the motion consequent on their combination has been expended, no further power can be got out of the mutual attraction of oxygen and hydrogen. As dynamic agents they are dead."

We can, in this manner, produce from the combustion of coal, light, heat, and propulsive force; but coal and oxygen are consumed in the producing process. Yet in this process, what and how much would have come within the grasp of a merely sensitive intelligence? Simply the object coal,—the brilliant light,—the pleasant heat,—and the actual movement of an incomprehensible machine. Let Mundane Mind be thus conceived and Nature would necessarily be administered by an intelligence which never got below the surface. The result, as we may certainly perceive, must have always lain between either an unchanging sameness, or the instability of chance misdirection. A state of things which compared with our actual world would seem most unsatisfactory; but which never has in fact been realized, for a reason at once apparent to the reader's sagacity.

Take another instance of change. The chemical elements of a Galvanic battery disappear in performing their function of causing a current, and the current may in turn disappear in the decomposition of water. But what merely sensitive intelligence could discern the invisible agency,—or measure the conversion of force, where nothing is visible except loss? Besides, in this latter example do we not see how truly correlative these two terms Power and Function are? We may intelligently think and speak of the chemical constituents of the battery, as conjoint Power;—and of their accomplishing their Function in the Current. But we may also speak of the current as a Power, accomplishing its Function by evolving from water two elementary gases. In other words, the ideas of Power and Function, definite enough to the eye of reason, are in all other respects, fluent. They are neither things, nor phenomenal attributes of things. They are power and function by virtue of a relation existing between them, and this relation is a fact not of the bare impressible sense, but of our purely reasoning intellect.

The same consequence appears, (in a shape which to some minds may be easier,) from viewing in another light the very same example of a galvanic battery, applied to decompose water. At each end of the chain there are palpable materials, visible to corporeal sense. But, between them runs the true force;—and this is absolutely impalpable. We theorize upon this force, but, whatever our theories may be, we accept its reality as a fact clear to our human mind. And we also clearly see that no lower mind could possibly apprehend it.

And here arises a curious question well worth a brief consideration. It is this:—To any kind of mind, the faculties of which are bound up in sense, what would appear to be the realities, and what the unrealities of the Universe? Galvanic wires or chains are perceptible to our bodily senses, but the traversing force is imperceptible. Hence, in our common speech, we are easily led to talk of the polar elements or objects (whatever they are) as realities par excellence;—but without in the least meaning to imply that the nexus or relativity between them is any less real; or less a fact. What we do mean, is, that this reality is a fact to another, and a finer, faculty. But what would it be if the finer faculty were wanting?—Reality would in that case become phenomenal;—and phenomena (according to Dr. Whewell and other inductive philosophers), would at the same time cease to be facts.

So far, therefore, as we know,—and we still limit this discussion to what we really do know,—were Reason wanting, all the nobler part of the Universe—its highest realities,—as understood by us, could not be held real. They would fade like an insubstantial pageant—or the baseless fabric of a dream. For, be it repeated,— we do not see as a merely sensitive mind must see. Principles and laws, sustaining and administering the universal mechanism, are the visible realities of intellect; and are visible to intellect alone. Thus, no one ever saw the principle of the arch except by an act of intellectual sight, and yet in the strength of it all arches stand firm. So, too, an architect knows that the stability and beauty of his structure depend on much that is hidden from the uninstructed human eye. What meaner eye, then, could ever succeed in piercing the secret architecture of the Universe? To the mundane mind, if less than human, the most real would become unreal,—and the shadow appear to be the substance. No supposition can possibly seem more absurd! Yet, when people speak of a "blind intelligence" in Nature, they must mean something less than Reason by that strange contradictory appellation.

The case for Unreason can never be improved by saying that 'The world, as it exists, is a system of accordant forces; tending to fulfil their functions through a kind of self-evolving movement, excited and controlled by correlation and correspondence, action and interaction. The products prevail, where they do prevail, through the completeness of their harmony with their surroundings. By virtue of this acquired excellence which becomes intrinsic, each finally develops itself into a permanent and integrated unit.' Here, obviously, the question of Intelligence recurs. If Mind were a necessary postulate before, how much more stringent the necessity now! From hosts of uncounted relativities we infer an Absolute;—surveying their rhythmical stir and onward strivings what shall we predicate respecting it? The world might have been a discord;—Whence came its first symphonious movement?—its after-waves of sphere-music majestically sweet to understanding ears;—its deeper and still deeper accordances;—

"The Diapason ending full in Man,"

that is to say, thus ending so far as the solemn march has been played out! What shall be hereafter, we know not now. But most marvellous of all as yet, is that first chord which struck the key-note of the whole harmonious performance [199].

It is evident that the answers to these inquiries, must have the effect of infinitely elevating our own idea of the intelligence discoverable in natural productions;—because they will add to our perception of its wonderful insight, a still more wonderful impression of fore sight,—a foresight extending over illimitable periods of time; and causing effects, for the calculation of which no power of intellect actually known to us, would have any adequate sufficiency.

The only apparent evasion of this consequence, is to deny arrangement altogether. But, then, how great are the resulting difficulties! In the first place, it would seem at once to restore covertly, if not openly, that very ancient Divine principle, Chance; whose banishment has long been agreed upon by reflective men. In the next place, it is not clear how, looking at the scientific doctrine of Chances [ax], they would, when calculated, yield any probability whatever of production;—or even (what appears a less thing), of development from a rudimentary or less perfect structure already existing. The consequence is, that one or more principles besides Chance must soon be postulated, and "blind laws" are held insufficient because not unlikely to become guilty of incidental misdirection. This need of auxiliary postulates has determined some very staunch advocates of Evolution to maintain that the circle of evolving laws or forces must certainly be ruled by some Intelligence, either inherent and immanent (mind and movement identical),—or else separate, transcendental, and probably personal, superintending and superior to them all [ay]. Indeed the affirmation of Mind in Nature as a positively perceived Fact appears to be the sure direction of our human understanding, if allowed to observe and judge in a common-sense way. And the reason of the thing is obvious. Whenever we perceive anything by bodily vision and touch, or other material instruments, we unhesitatingly attribute to it a material existence. We derive our impression from a material antecedent, and say here is a corporeal substance,—in a word,— body. So, on the other hand, whenever material instruments are dispensed with, (because inadequate and unsuitable), and when Mind alone is used as our medium of perception, we are quite sure that what we perceive is not Body but Mind. In this manner, we know what to say of arrangement, counterbalance, superior excellence, (which means superior fitness), tendency to a function, (that is fitness in movement), or of a system of relation and correlation transcending the highest flight of human imagination. We say at once, here is Mind. We do not think it necessary to employ a periphrasis, and reason on the properties of intelligence, any more than we should, when receiving information from our senses, commence a syllogism on the properties of Matter. We simply say in the two several cases,—here is body,—here is mind. And, as regards both propositions, we are in all likelihood equally safe in saying so.

The real question, therefore, remains just as we before stated it. We then derived our statement from the process of production,—first by analyzing it, and next, by shewing that the analysis was verified in experience. We have since run some risk of repetition, in order to look at the whole subject of Mind in Nature from various points of view. The effect has been to confirm for us, the issue above raised as being the right and true question. We must not ask, "Is there Mind in the natural world?" but "What kind and degree of Intelligence do we, from our observation of facts, attribute to the Mind evidenced in the Universe?"

It is in answering this question that the fitnesses of organized structures yield so many important considerations. We are not however obliged to follow the chain of the Design argument, liken these structures to objects of human art, and say, here is Design implying a Designer. We may quite as easily look at them in the light of the great productive Law we have been investigating. Fitness consists in the nicety of the manner in which Function is correlated with Power. Throughout the realm of organisms, vegetable and animal, the most beautiful examples of such correlation meet us at every turn [az]. When therefore we put our query, what character may here be ascribed to the Mundane Intelligence, the reply cannot seem doubtful. Instances of pre-eminent Fitness (such as those adduced further on) need not be understood in any other sense than this, in order to accomplish the purpose for which they are described. Neither need such words as adaptation or design, used for brevity's sake, be taken as references to the analogical argument discussed in our second Chapter. Mr. Darwin himself has frequently employed the expressions "contrivance," "purpose," etc., without intending any such reference,—nay, rather with the full intention of arguing for a different account of the "contrivances" he specifies.

From such wonderful examples of Fitness, many minds will choose at once to read the broad lesson of Teleology. Be it observed then that if this is done, the larger the generality under which the principle of Design is conceived, the better for its force in reasoning. As an argument, the idea has suffered from the imagination of readers dwelling upon the specialities recounted in many valuable books to the exclusion of wider and more universal conceptions. There is a vast difference [ba], between the assertion of a grand Unity, (in subservience to which all other things have their several determinate purposes,) and the being able to say in each smaller instance, here is the design or intended relation between this individual structure or condition, and this sole and definite finality. A good specimen of the difficulty thus occasioned, is an objection of Littré's against the idea of Divinely beneficent adaptation. Why, he asks, should the bite of a mad dog have been allowed to produce hydrophobia? Why, that is, should the dog's saliva have been so contrived, as to convey so virulent a blood poison? The true answer, of course, must be that this effect is but one operation of a much more extensive physiological law;—a law producing results, often of the most beneficial character. We must also, (as the same writer allows), draw a strong distinction between every law, and what is technically termed its "functioning" [200]. Littré views Nature as a moving panorama of antecedents and consequents;—but he is obliged to confess that the nexus is not invariable. There are, indeed, variations, for which he employs this same "functioning," as a kind of apology. The necessity of such an apology is in itself a remarkable fact; since it shews how little rigorous is the common argument used by many physicists against the probability of Miracles. The necessity of natural sequence is, after all, no adamantine fatality; and therefore Testimony to an event contrary to our experience and expectation, may have a most decisive value [201].

We have already shewn that to see a law in Nature, is to see an actual instance of wide intelligence. Now, so seen, it is known as existing in rerum naturâ —active—energizing—productive. But, suppose we for a moment conceive the intelligible law, as existing only in the intelligence itself,—a thought prior to its realization. The law is then what writers on natural history often call a type;—or, as it is termed in the older philosophical language, an idea. The readers of S. T. Coleridge will not easily forget his chapter reconciling the Platonic and Baconian [bb] methods of Philo sophy. It turns, in great part, upon the essential identity of idea with law. (*Friend*, Vol. III. Essay ix.)

If, therefore, we perceive in anything creative, or any system whatsoever, a harmony of power with function, we call it fitness, or even adaptation when describing the actual matter of our own observations. But, if we speak of the same harmony as an act of mind, we call it intelligent adaptation. And, this at least, is what careful writers on Natural Theology mean by the word Design. Yet, certain careless objectors have misconceived the plain meaning, so far as to assert that if we would speak of any production as designed, it must first be proved not only intentional but arbitrary. This misconception—(the very opposite of our meaning)—seems to turn upon the mixture of two distinct notions,—the design of reason and the determination of caprice. If Natural Theologians wished to prove that the Designer of the Universe was always doing wrong,—and was always right because he did wrong,—it would be necessary to argue that design and caprice are one and the same thing. But Natural Theology endeavours to shew the exact contradictory. Its idea is, above all things, the Idea of a Sovereign Reason manifest in universal Law.

The rejoinder has been made that at all events a Will is implied in Design;—and that he who wills acts arbitrarily. Of course, there is a certain sense in which this may be true. A Sovereign will could at pleasure refuse the Right and choose the Wrong, but then it would cease to be a Sovereign Reason. That is, it would cease to be Sovereign at all, in any true Theology. And we may, likewise, add that the ordinary instances and illustrations of Design never aim at proving Will directly;—their immediate object is to shew Intelligence, foreseeing ends or functions, and purposing their attainment. It is clear that Will must indirectly be implied in such an argument. But, then, it is so implied, partly because all Reason is per se identical with Will, and partly because (as we shall endeavour to shew), Causation necessarily emanates from Will. The reader must, however, assign each conclusion to its proper argument, and keep each argument to its proper conclusion;—a rule which those who dispute for victory, and not for truth, frequently fail to observe.

The use we are now making of fitness and adaptation is less to prove the existence of Mind in the Universe, than its grandeur, grasp, and comprehensiveness. For this purpose our clearest evidence arises from the coincidence of several diverse conditions, tending to one sovereign finality of function. And indeed, this argument from coincidence, is generally the most convincing;—the greater the convergence of separate conditions,—the stronger is our assurance that Mind determined the result [bc]. Our sense of sight has always been a favourite subject in Natural Theology. It is familiar, and, so far as a broad outline of the function is concerned, may be easily studied by any common-sense person. It is, also, evidently one Function; yet, even cursory observation shews a great diversity of powers contributing to produce it. How diverse they are, may be perceived by supposing first one and then another element of eyesight to be absent, and considering what the effect of each deficiency must be.

Suppose, there were no light. The eye then, however beautiful and perfect in structure, would not be a means serving any purpose of perception. It is clear thus that the eye is an optical instrument.

Suppose, again, light and optical arrangement both in existence, but, also, that the eye had no power of adjusting itself to the direction of objects and other circumstances; evidently its function of vision would be very much restricted.

In relation to this end, the eye is a mechanical [202] instrument.

We might, further, suppose the optical apparatus to work well, its adjustment also to be perfect,—and the picture on the retina no less so. But, with this perfect picture, suppose all ended. The function of eyesight would be as irretrievably gone as in our first case.

This shews us that the eye does not really see. It is the servant of an impressible Power,— and this impressible power uses it, and sees through it.

Suppose, finally, that the picture on the retina set vibratory nerves in movement—each microscopic stroke producing its effect of vibration. Let something be seen by the impressible Power, but not apprehended as an object of common perception. Let there be no comparison with other sensations; no transcript into sense-language, of what is at once seen, touched, heard, smelled, or tasted. Consider, how barren and unproductive the result! Eyesight is reduced to a play of coloured images. There can be no malleable material for Intelligence to work up. Nothing to be cast into any universal mould;—no possibility of a greedy Mind feeding eagerly through the quick perceiving eye.

In the absence of information given, or thought stimulated, we must pronounce such sight unintelligent;—and the Eye an unintelligible phenomenon. But why? The anatomical structure remains perfect. It is the adaptation that has been lost along with the finality, and this loss is fatal. Hence the paramount importance of finality.

Any student may pursue this ruling idea of "adaptation to a functional end," through a vast range of the Animal kingdom. There are eyes fitted to long distances—almost telescopic;—eyes so contrived as to be absolutely microscopical. Then, as the refraction of water differs from that of air, the optical lenses of fishes become rounded almost like little balls. And, the observer who passes into the tribes of Invertebrata, will acquaint himself with eyes mounted upon footstalks [203], and eyes multiplied and placed in different situations. Few natural objects are more wonderful than the contrivance of a compound eye. The many hexagonal tubes, which may be reckoned by the thousand, are cemented together on one expanded and swollen nervous disk, reminding us of the thalamus in the great plant order of Compositae, (Syngenesia),—in the Elecampagne for instance, the Bur Marigold, Thistle, and Centaurea. A compound eye has a range of vision extending over about 180 degrees, (half a circle), and must from its structure be endowed with specializing distinctness. Mind in the

Universe, is thus presented to us, as in the New Testament,—wide as the whole arch of heaven, but cognizant of a sparrow or a lily.

A creature with diminished vision—such as the Mole—or the Amblyopsis, is a curiously interesting study in itself;—still more so as an example of adaptation.

In old times, the Mole was accounted blind. Aristotle [204] observed that a structural eye exists, but that a skin is drawn over it, and this skin deprives the animal of sight. His observation has made work for commentators, from Simplicius downwards. Trendelenburg (on the De Anima) confines himself to criticism. Torstrik makes a kind of apology for not excising "quae loco ἀτοπωτάτῳ de talpâ dicuntur." Cardinal Tolet accepts the observation, and thinks the Mole's eyes thus admirably protected from the bad effects of a sudden access of light, when he rushes violently into appearance overground. Naturalists during many centuries, made the whole history of the mole a piece of guesswork, and no creature except the Sloth or the Earwig has ever been more generally misrepresented. Perhaps our familiar old English "Moldwarp" (West of England "Want"), might have remained a puzzle to this day had not a French courtier [205] fled from the Paris Revolution, and devoted his attention to Moles. The fact that the eye of our Western Mole is not completely closed, may be proved by throwing a living specimen into a pond. But, in the South and East of Europe the "blind mole" does really exist [206], as has been shown by Erhard and the Prince of Musignano. In more than one species, the skin passes over the eyeball without any loss of hair.

This diminution of eyesight is a case of what has been called "retrogression." Now the Mole is a highly developed Mammal, and his position in the animal kingdom entitles him to the best of eyes. But, they would not suit his habits. The same is true of the Blind-fish of Kentucky (Amblyopsis Spelaeus). For such a creature, not the distinct vision of objects,—but a sensation of light,—was the desirable possession,—and the creature has it [207].

It does not in the least matter, as a question of Fitness, whether this retrograde condition of the eye was brought about by natural laws slowly acting upon the animal frame, or produced in some more rapid way. The fitness is the same; and, as we are at present engaged, not on proving the existence of Mind, but in illustrating the greatness of a confessedly existing mind, these instances of far reaching adaptation are very strongly in point.

Of the cavernous life and habits of the Amblyopsis there is not much to be said; though the idea of a happy existence amidst depths of sepulchral gloom, naturally excites our imagination. But "the little gentleman in black" whose health used to be enthusiastically drunk a century and a half ago, is a perfect study [208] in himself. We are interested by his fairy-like gift of hearing (noted by Shakespeare); his gluttony; his fleetness of foot; his combativeness; and his castle-building! As a civil and military engineer, he far surpasses the beaver, though dwelling in dark places, and with only a dubious pair of eyes in his scheming quick-conceiving head.

Probably, the sense we should all least wish to lose is our eyesight. Its perpetual delight, and its capacity for improvement by training are powerful motives for treasuring its possession. The savage and the microscopist, the artist and the astronomer, all train their faculty of vision; and how differently do these four classes of eyes see!—The difference is, we know, in exact proportion to the intelligence which employs and educates them. And, conversely, how the nobly-governed eye informs and educates the Mind! What a world of hope, then, as well as beauty, seems to die when we conceive the blind man in his dim solitude! Yet the contentment of its sightless inmates, is one of the most salient comforts of every blind asylum. Most likely, their cheerfulness depends on the great use of finger-dexterity, and the exquisite susceptibility of the ear. And these delicate endowments, which make our several senses inlets of happiness, are amongst the most fascinating illustrations of the Universal Mind with which we have to do.

The structure of the ear is far less commonly dwelt upon by most writers, than the structure of the eye. Indeed, its organization seems to less certainty explained, the problem being, of course, to trace the transmission of sound to the auditory nerve. But, as in ancient Egypt, so in modern England, the treatment of disease in special organs has been divided amongst special therapeutists; and the ear does not fail to benefit by being better understood. There is, even now, room for hypothesis in some parts of the process of sonorous transmission,—and beyond that process, science does not pretend to go. Modern views, however, as Dr. Tyndall truly says, "present the phenomena in a connected and intelligible form, and should they be doomed to displacement by a more correct or comprehensive theory, it will assuredly be found that the wonder is not diminished by the substitution of the truth." No one has put the wonder into a more intelligible shape than this well known writer, at the close of his book upon Sound [209].

Employing instances of Design for the purpose, to us most relevant, and gleaning a few among hosts of shining illustrations, there is nothing more alluring than the spectacle of the organic world, considered as a source, not of life only, nor of information only, but of emotional pleasure and never failing enjoyment. No kind of existence can be more depressing to our highly-strung human nervous-system, than the shut up occupations which overgrown cities necessitate. Yet, with what unrepressed vigour of delight does the artizan, the physician, the schoolmaster, or the curate of a town parish, look upon the open world beyond! And, never has there existed any human being more truly impressible by Nature's loveliness, or more skilled in conveying the impression to the minds of others, than a genuine British Naturalist. For the holiday-maker to walk with such a lover of Nature through field and forest, over moor and mountain, by rivulet, lake or sea, is to gain a new sense of wonder and admiration;—new perceptions of excellence, symmetry, and unity; while freshened emotions of religious awe and trust keep springing upwards from them all. It is with outward nature, as it is with individual natures; the regard of a loving eye is the true revealer of hidden secrets. For in reality we see, not only with our bodily sense and our contemplative reason, but also with the strength and insight of affection. And thus many a weary Man perpetually finds the aspect of the visible universe indescribably soothing amidst his own confusions and disappointments. He may feel, at times, that his human heart can penetrate beyond what eye and head have taught him; and, while thoughtfully observing the footprints of creative mind, he can feel within his bosom a sense of superhuman tenderness, like the warm breath of his living Creator.

The very fact that highly-endowed and deeply thoughtful men [210] have so felt and spoken, ought not to be without its influence. There is much conveyed—very much indeed—by the truth that the world is beautiful. If, when we examine natural production, intelligent operation is seen to imply an operative intelligence, is it not also true that realized beauty implies an ideal beauty, intelligently preconceived in a Mind itself beautiful? Had there been nothing in earth or sky to soothe, elevate, and make happy, with what different feelings, should we have attempted to picture productive Mind at work through an unlovely Universe!

ADDITIONAL NOTE: ON THE DOCTRINE OF CHANCES APPLIED TO THE STRUCTURAL DEVELOPMENT OF THE EYE

The present Savilian Professor of Astronomy at Oxford wrote, in 1867, as follows:—

"The chances of any accidental variation in such an instrument being an improvement are small indeed. Suppose, for instance, one of the surfaces of the crystalline lens of the eye of a creature, possessing a crystalline and cornea, to be accidentally altered, then I say, that unless the form of the other surface is simultaneously altered, in one only way out of millions of possible ways, the eye would not be optically improved. An alteration also in the two surfaces of the crystalline lens, whether accidental or otherwise, would involve a definite alteration in the form of the cornea, or in the distance of its surface from the centre of the crystalline lens, in order that the eye may be optically better. All these alterations must be simultaneous and definite in amount, and these definite amounts must coexist in obedience to an extremely complicated law. To my apprehension then, that so complex an instrument as an eye should undergo a succession of millions of improvements, by means of a succession of millions of accidental alterations, is not less improbable, than if all the letters in the 'Origin of Species' were placed in a box, and on being shaken and poured out millions on millions of times, they should at last come out together in the order in which they occur in that fascinating and, in general, highly philosophical work.

"But my objections do not stop here. The improvement of an organ must be an improvement relative to the new circumstances by which the organ is surrounded. Suppose, then, that an eye is altered for the better in relation to one set of circumstances under which it is placed. By-and-bye there arise a second set of circumstances, and the eye is again, by Natural Selection, altered and improved relatively to the second set of circumstances. What is there to make the second set of circumstances such that the second improvement (relative to them) shall be an improvement or progress in the direction of the ultimate goal of the human eye? Why should not the second improvement be a retrogression away from the ultimate organ now possessed by man, and necessary to his well-being? But all this suiting of the succession of circumstances is to go on, not once or twice, but millions on millions of times. If this be so, then not only must there be a Bias in the order of the succession of the circumstances, or, at all events, in the vast outnumbering of the unfavourable circumstances by the favourable, but so strong a bias, as to remove the whole process from the accidental to the intentional. The bias implies the existence of a Law, a Mind, a Will. The process becomes one not of Natural Selection, but of Selection by an Intelligent Will." *Analogies in the Progress of Nature and Grace*, (being the *Hulsean Lectures for 1867*,) Appendix A, p. 125 seq.

The whole article should be carefully studied by the reader.

Chapter 6

CAUSATION: LIMITS OF PHYSICAL LAW— THE BEGINNING—CAUSE AND WILL—MIRACLES

"Chidhar, the Prophet ever-young
Thus loosed the bridle of his tongue.
"I journeyed by a goodly Town,
Beset with many a garden fair,
And asked of one who gathered down
Large fruit, 'how long the Town was there
He spoke, nor chose his hand to stay,
'The town has stood for many a day,
And will be here for ever and aye.'

"A thousand years passed by and then
I went the self-same road again.

"No vestige of that Town I traced,—
But one poor swain his horn employed,—
His sheep unconscious browsed and grazed,
I asked 'when was that Town destroyed?'
He spoke, nor would his horn lay by,
'One thing may grow and another die,
But I know nothing of Towns—not I.'

"A thousand years went on and then
I passed the self-same place again.

"There in the deep of waters cast
His nets one lonely fisherman,
And as he drew them up at last
I asked him 'how that Lake began?'
He looked at me and laughed to say,
'The waters spring for ever and aye,
And fish is plenty every day.'

"A thousand years passed by and then
I went the self-same road again.

"I found a country wild and rude,
And, axe in hand, beside a tree,
The Hermit of that Solitude,—
I asked 'how old that Wood might be?'
He spoke, 'I count not time at all,
A tree may rise, a tree may fall,
The Forest overlives us all,'

"A thousand years went on and then
I passed the self-same place again.

"And there a glorious City stood,
And 'mid tumultuous market-cry,
I asked 'Where rose the Town? where Wood
Pasture and Lake forgotten lie?'
They heard me not, and little blame,—
For them the world is as it came,
And all things must be still the same.

"A thousand years shall pass, and then
I mean to try that road again."
Lord Houghton, after Rückert.

"What a modern talks of by the name, Forces of Nature, Laws of Nature; and does not figure as a divine thing; not even as one thing at all, but as a set of things, undivine enough,—saleable, curious, good for propelling steam-ships! With our Sciences and Cyclopaedias, we are apt to forget the divineness, in those laboratories of ours. We ought not to forget it! That once well forgotten, I know not what else were worth remembering."—Carlyle. *Heroes*.

"Two worlds, the one intellectual, the other sensual, were equally given to us from the beginning, and all attempts to deduce them from one principle (except the Deity) have failed."—*Von Feuchtersleben*.

"What am I? how produced? and for what end?
Whence drew I being? to what period tend?
Am I th' abandon'd orphan of blind chance?
Dropped by wild atoms in disorder'd dance?
Or from an endless chain of causes wrought,
And of unthinking substance, born with thought?
By motion which began without a Cause,
Supremely wise, without design or laws."—Arbuthnot.

"Pouvoir c'est vouloir."— Guesses at Truth.

"If only once weird Time had rent asunder
The curtain of the Clouds, and shown us Night
Climbing into the awful Infinite
Those stairs whose steps are worlds, above and under,
Glory on glory, wonder upon wonder!...

"Ah! sure the heart of Man, too strongly tried
By Godlike Presences so vast and fair,
Withering with dread, or sick with love's despair,
Had wept for ever, and to Heaven cried,
Or struck with lightnings of delight had died!

"But he, though heir of Immortality,
With mortal dust too feeble for the sight,
Draws thro' a veil God's overwhelming light;
Use arms the Soul—anon there moveth by
A more majestic Angel—and we die!"
Frederick Tennyson.

SYNOPSIS OF CHAPTER 6

The two last Chapters are intended to be read consecutively, but are formally separated in order to mark the transition of Argument. If this is borne in mind, and the line of thought pursued continuously, there will appear to be little need for further elucidation.

The main object of the present Chapter is to distinguish the physical chain of Sequency from Causation properly so termed. In other words to divide the World, as we see it, into two spheres; the Mechanical and the Personal.

The former is characterized by invariable Sequence. The latter by Causation, and by causal interference with the mechanical chain of antecedent and consequent.

Inferences are drawn from these contrasted facts.

Analysis. —Causation not explained by any of the empirical sciences. Time accounts for nothing. Explicit statements of scientific men on the subject. "Inquire elsewhere." This is one good reason for the study of Natural Theology.

Only one kind of true Cause known to us by Experience. Distinction between a true Cause and the invariable antecedent of an invariable consequent. Antecedent enters Chain of natural sequence; Cause does not. Cause must account for the several links of Chain, for the connection between those links, and for the entire Chain considered as a Whole and Unity in Nature. This position illustrated and investigated. How grasped by the young mind. Its verification.

Known facts of Causation result in the Unknowable; a condition which attaches to the most certain of all truths. Personality a case in point. Another case that of alterations caused by Volition in chains of Natural Sequence. Common-sense allowances made for this last fact.

Application à fortiori to the Divine Personality. Presumption for miracles; its nature and limits. Intervention does not destroy Order and Unity. Hence we distinguish two possible kinds of Evidence, from,—

1.   General Order of World.
2.   Occasional variation.

Both leading up to a Supreme causal Personality.

CAUSATION

This sixth Chapter occupies a totally different sphere of Thought from the one preceding it. Instead of examining the world as it now is, we shall inquire what its present existence necessarily presupposes. Time, in the ordinary meaning of the word, is no factor in our calculation. We have to deal with Time's antecedents.

These words sound like a long farewell to our companion and auxiliary,—Natural Science! Geology, Palaeontology, Astronomy, are unanimous in telling us of periods immeasurably remote. But, they are all silent on two more distant and profound subjects—a Beginning and an Eternity. In the world best known to us, vast cycles—each comprehending many ages of life—- point back to preceding cycles made up of ages more numerous still, during which the world was absolutely void of life. Upon that primaeval fabric, are graved long records of changes beyond the reach of Thought. A single epoch,—the era when our globe, an incandescent mass of matter, was cooling in its flight,—is alone sufficient to exhaust all our imaginative powers. Did water first surround the glowing orb as a heated vapour? Did clouds first descend upon it like a fiery rain-storm? Suppose some sentient creature floating through ether to look upon the unformed world,—how wild, how weird must have been the spectacle! How different from what earth and ocean may appear to any similar Intelligence now.

Science discoursing upon such topics is more poetical than the most sublime poetry. And the science that does speak of them is the widest of all sciences, After certain cycles of ages, the Biologist hands us over to the Mineralogist and the Chemist. After certain other cycles, we give up those guides in turn; and gauge nature by measuring mass, speed, force, comparing our own orb with kindred orbs, and trying to collect what the comparison can say respecting the earliest conditions of the Universe. But, all this is no answer to our proposed question concerning Time's antecedents. "The territory of physics" says a well-known physicist, "is wide, but it has its limits from which we look with vacant gaze into the region beyond" [211]. And these words are evidently true. Time serves, in this respect, as the index of our incapacity. We travel back from the period of Man to the period of a ferny coal field, a trilobite or an Eozoon, and from thence to the period when nebulous light-masses shone out through illimitable space. No doubt, when we have learned to contemplate such vapoury states of attenuated matter, we have learned a great deal. Modern analysis finds in them the elementary constituents of our own planetary system; the same elements which glow with greater apparent brilliancy in our Sun. But this is not all. To the sober eye of science, those fires, which burned before stars were kindled, display in their splendours materials entering into the composition of our transitory frames; materials required continually by our bodies and by our productive arts. We live, if modern science may be trusted, by the assimilation of elements now shining in the celestial sphere; elements which glittered there through long cycles of ages before our Earth was. And we employ the same elements in the common industries of civilisation [212]. This bewildering thought seems to link us with that Sun, which is the glory of our day, with those wandering lamps which make night beautiful; and with all the hosts of heaven, which have always fascinated the upward gaze of man, and have sometimes won his heart to worship them.

The more overwhelming these thoughts appear, the grander is the emphasis of our yet unanswered question. We have seen that we are able to travel backwards—not in fancy, but in reason—from era to era, however incalculable the measurement of each era may be; and, when our travels have reached their utmost goal, we find the marvellous Continuity of Nature still unbroken. And this very fact, is, in itself, a sufficient proof that we have not approached Time's antecedents. What we have really done, is to carry the Present with us into an immeasurably distant Past. We know not yet what is presupposed by both,—we cannot say what went before them.

It is very important for us to be thoroughly clear upon the result. For there is a sort of unreflecting idea afloat, that if vast periods of Time are conceived, the whole Universe is conceived also. All seems explained, since everything may come to pass in Time! So it may, in one sense. Time gives opportunity; but then there must be a moving power [213] to work in the opportunity. Let it therefore be distinctly borne in mind, that Time causes nothing. To dispense with a spring of action, is to imagine that Time will stop the river's flow, or that the river will stop without a cause in time:—

"Rusticus expectat, dum defluat amnis; at ille
Labitur et labetur in omne volubilis aevum."

In reality, Time accounts neither for good nor for evil, neither for the end nor yet for the beginning of any single work.

And the same is true respecting any chain, however long, made up of antecedents and consequents, however numerous. We see in them movements propagating movements; but then we are obliged to ask, what moved the first of them? The reader may remember Professor Huxley's picture of a cosmic vapour, from a knowledge of which a sufficient Intelligence might have predicted our present world. Looking further, we find this cosmic vapour to be composed (as he says) of molecules possessing forces or properties; in other words, what he really described was a potential Universe; not a Cause, but an already caused production. What, then, caused it?

It was not the Professor's business,—nor is it the business of any Physiologist or of any Physicist, to explain what lies beyond the territories of his science. Consequently he does not account for the existence of this "primitive nebulosity." The "sufficient Intelligence" is only spoken of a possible interpreter or prophet. And Professor Huxley is right and wise in his reticence.

Professor Tyndall is equally wise and right in telling us that

"Science knows much of this intermediate phase of things that we call nature, of which it is the product; but science knows nothing of the origin or destiny of nature" [214].

There is always a rightness and wisdom in stating a limit, and an issue, distinctly. No one endowed with clearness of vision, will think the Universe as likely to be adequately accounted for by an eternal nebula, as by an eternity of Mind. No one will exactly state to himself, the meaning of such words as Chance, Time, Law, and others of a like description; and, with those meanings in remembrance, pronounce that any or all of them can explain the origin of anything. But by popular lecturers and article-makers, immeasurable series of conditions are sometimes mentioned in a manner which almost implies that, because immeasurable, the speaker or writer supposes that such conditions may possibly be creative.

Any reader of current literature will scarcely need reminding, that most modern savants usually acquiesce in, and feel burdened by, a sense of "the Inscrutable." And therefore, when summing up the results of scientific truth, they honestly and consistently reduce their disciples to an alternative,—an alternative of which no disciple of any special science ought reasonably to complain. Choose, they tell him, between confessing, "here is the Incomprehensible—here I rest;" or, if you please, endeavouring to "find other means of knowledge, which we do not pretend to furnish." This is no more than to say, and say fairly, "Be satisfied with such information as we can give,—or, if you please, inquire elsewhere." And this seems reasonable; for who would assert that a Professor of Poetry ought to give competent instruction in the Calculus?

We may assume that every student of Natural Theology has made up his mind to "inquire elsewhere." And it is the part of an earnest man so to do. Were not the Future linked to the Present, we all might feel less earnest, less persevering, less anxious for inquiry. Yet, if there be a Future beyond our Present, we at once perceive a weight of reason beyond all powers of estimate, why such a connecting chain must certainly exist. All our experience, every argument from analogy, and all morality, fall into one and the same scale. But of this, more hereafter. There is no doubt that our wisdom and our duty coincide with our natural instincts, in bringing us to this resolution. We may not be able to learn all we could wish of that Future which follows our present; but what we can truly learn is to us a treasure beyond price. Let us, therefore, proceed as fellow- pilgrims in the search.

It is an undeniable fact—one amongst the hard and actual facts which life teaches—that, in the whole of our experience, we never know of more than one kind of cause,—a cause, that is, in the true sense of originating any event or series of events. Nothing can be more certain as respects our knowledge of the material world. From this point of view, Sir J. Herschel describes Brown's book on "Cause and Effect" as

> "a work of great acuteness and subtlety of reasoning on some points, but in which the whole train of argument is vitiated by one enormous oversight; the omission, namely, of a distinct and immediate personal consciousness of causation in his enumeration of that sequence of events, by which the volition of the mind is made to terminate in the motion of material objects. I mean the consciousness of effort, accompanied with intention thereby to accomplish an end, as a thing entirely distinct from mere desire or volition on the one hand, and from mere spasmodic contraction of muscles on the other" [215].

This causation we experience continually. A heavy stone falls from a wall, and kills a man. No one threw it. We say it fell—or, as a physicist might express it, obeyed the law of gravitation. But we may remember that from the tower of Thebez "a certain woman cast a piece of a millstone upon Abimelech's head and all to break his scull." We form quite a different opinion of this event. We say, here is a case in which "the volition of the mind is made to terminate in the motion of a material object." Some might accuse, others excuse, the woman of Thebez; but all would argue that she caused the death of Abimelech.

Your boy wants to beat a chair which has fallen upon him; you tell him why he must not, and all you say is sound philosophy. He also wants to kill his cat for devouring his canary bird; and again you philosophize correctly. But, suppose your young philosopher for his own pleasure wrings his canary bird's neck? The chair fell by mechanical law—the cat obeyed the law of her hungry instinct—but your boy is culpable. He was the true cause of his own cruel act,—in a word he was responsible. And this same truth of Causation, involved in Responsibility, and constituting one of its necessary factors, is like Mind in Mr. Mill,—a truth which we must accept—inexplicable, but unquestionably real. We know that Will is a Cause,—and we do not actually know of any other cause in the wide Universe. The fact comes home to us in a variety of ways. Was Thurtell the cause or the physical antecedent of Weare's death? If not the cause, we ought never to think him, or any murderer, slaver, torturer, or tyrant, at all in the wrong; neither can we hold them in any manner responsible.

Let the reader put this case to himself in as many different shapes as he can. The result will always come to the same issue. We may suppose a Nebula, Law, Force, so arranged as to be the physical antecedent of a world. And nothing can be more marvellous than the idea of such an arrangement! But we cannot imagine any existence really causing an effect, save one,—a Will. Therefore, if we wish to go beyond Nebula, Law, or Force, which are merely physical antecedents,—and ask what caused one or all of them, we are obliged (so far as we are disciples of experience) to say their Cause was a Will. And when we say this, we allege a sufficient reason.

A few paragraphs back, we availed ourselves of the authoritative verdict pronounced by scientific thinkers, on the question of what is, and what is not, from their point of view, knowable. And we saw where physics terminated,—that is, in a Nebula. This is their limit.

Yet, there is nothing to hinder a physicist from becoming also a Natural Theologian. It is not every man who will rest in a negative conclusion. Professor Baden Powell was among the malcontents in this respect; and we desire now to quote from his writings some passages referred to in the argument of a former Chapter.

But before doing so, it would be unfair to conceal that a tribute of gratitude appears due to writers who mark the boundary of their own thought, however little we ourselves desire to stay acquiescently within its limitations. There is honesty in their act;—there is an incitement for other men to try out their lines of thinking also. Finally, all such writers are unexceptionable witnesses to the interest and reality belonging to a separate science of Natural Theology. In all these respects, they occupy a totally different position from the indifferentist or sneering sceptic; and it would be injustice to confound such broad distinctions of moral aspect. With this acknowledgment let us return to Baden Powell.

In his "Connexion of Natural and Divine Truth" [216] he writes thus:—

"The study of physical causes (understood in the simple meaning which we have before endeavoured to fix,) while it supplies the unassailable evidence of design and adjustment, as unavoidably carries us thence onward to the idea of an Intelligence from which that design emanated, and of an agency by which that adjustment was produced. It brings us, in a word, to recognise an influence of another kind, of an order different from, and far above that of physical causes or material action:—to acknowledge a sublime moral cause, the universally operating source of creative power and providential wisdom.

[bd] ... We have already noticed, in other cases, the ambiguities arising from the diversity of meaning attached to the same term "cause." Here, then, it becomes more peculiarly necessary if we adopt the popular expression, "the First Cause," to recur carefully to the distinction, if we would preserve any clearness of reasoning.

"We refer to senses of the term absolutely distinct in kind. Nor is it a term of mere verbal difference. It is of importance, whether in guarding against fallacies in evidence or in answering the cavils of scepticism.... When we ascend to the contemplation of creative intelligence, the distinction is not between a prior and a subsequent train of material action, but between physical order and moral volition. It will thus be apparent that the metaphor so often used of the chain of natural causes whose last and highest link is its immediate connexion with the Deity;—the very phrase of a succession of secondary causes traced up to a first cause,—and the like, (so commonly employed,) are founded on a totally mistaken analogy.

"If we retain such metaphorical language at all, it would be a more just mode of speaking to describe the Deity as the Divine artificer of the whole chain,—not to connect Him with its links;—to represent the secondary causes as combined into joint operation by His power and will,—but not to make Him one of them." And again;—"If we require the aid of metaphor in attempting to give utterance to those vast conceptions with which the mind is overpowered, instead of speaking of the first and secondary links in a chain of causation, and the like, let us rather recur to the analogy of the arch (before introduced,) and we shall be adopting at once a more just and expressive figure, and shall here run no risk of speaking as if we confounded the stones with the builder,—their mutually supporting force with the skill of the architect who adjusted them" [217].

What Baden Powell called "physical causation," is now more commonly known as invariable antecedency, or invariable succession. Antecedents and consequents are phenomena of the natural world,—and the connection between them is their Law.

Now, suppose we take the Alphabet to represent a series of these antecedents and consequents, the latter invariably following the former; it does not, (as far as argument goes,) in the least signify what the series really is, any more than when we calculate algebraically. But to make things plain, let the Alphabet represent 26 cycles of succession; each cycle containing as many millions of years, or ages, as you choose to grant for the duration of the Natural Universe. We may state the problem thus,—the law of succession being assumed in our series as constant.

If we have Z, there certainly must have been Y, and conversely;— If there were no Y, there cannot possibly be Z. We go on,—

If Y, then certainly X;

If no X, then Y is impossible.

As we know Z in fact, we get back to Y; and, as we find Y, we retrogress to X. And the retrogression continues, say till we reach B,—

If B, certainly A;

If no A, then B is impossible. But, what are we to say of A? If A then certainly— what?

If no what?—then A is impossible.

It does not signify how far the chain of physical law may extend. From its very essence and definition, you must arrive finally at a first link. Or, in other words, the Continuity of Nature may go back through Time immeasurable,—Time will after all lead you to Time's antecedents. And when you have arrived at your first link, and inquire what must necessarily have preceded Time, it is well to consider the sort of account which alone you can accept, because it alone will sufficiently satisfy your reason.

You want, then, something which properly accounts first for A; next for the link between A and B; and thirdly, by consequence, for the whole Alphabet.

If, with this statement in mind, the reader turns back to the extracts made from Powell, he will see the force of several points strongly put by the Professor. He will see, for example, how inevitably physical causation carries us back to another, and very diverse Causation,—diverse in kind —not simply different in degree. Also, how the idea of Cause in this latter sense, takes us quite out of the physical nexus. And, further, that the only admissible Conception of a First Universal Cause, must be a conception of something which will not only bring about A, but likewise account for the entire series, linked together and consecutive, into one resulting Whole. For the Whole itself; in brief for the Many and the One.

We have now to ask further, what Facts can tell us respecting these two kinds of Causation. And let us again employ our letters, but rather in a different way.

Suppose P stands for a fact, which may also be described as a natural phenomenon. To account for P we go back to O, retrogress to N, M, and so on, as shewn already.

Again, suppose another fact which cannot be described as a natural phenomenon. Let us try whether P may, with equal propriety, stand for a human production or performance. That is—whether, instead of being a mere phenomenal fact, it may also be spoken of as an act.

We want then to account for P, thus considered. A striking circumstance appears at once evident, that to find the "why" of human activity we do not look to any antecedent;—we look to a consequent, or a series of consequences. The question we ask is,—with what view P became an act? In other words, we try to account for P, not by O, N, M, etc., but by Q, R, S, etc. For example: let P represent a murder. The crime was done for the sake of money, and for things which money will purchase; that is, the consequents,— Q, R, S, and so on, forming a series designed;—gains and purposes, long or short. But, no one would say that another series foregoing (O, N, M) ne cessitated the act;—that they were the certain antecedents of a necessary consequent (P) the murder. If it were so, we should have to congratulate the murderer for having been forced into so profitable a performance, and we should also have to leave him in the peaceable enjoyment of his profits.

Acts, therefore,—or volitional facts—move forwards through a series of consequents; while phenomena—that is, physical facts—run backwards through a series of antecedents.

If pressed to find a Cause for an act, we are never in a position to say,— If P, then certainly O;

If no O, then P is impossible.

We say, on the contrary, that the Cause of the act was Volitional,—that is, it was done by an agent or person acting. And further, that the consequents (Q, R, S, etc.) represent the purpose of the actor or agent, and that he is responsible for having adopted them as his prevalent motives or inducements.

But from these necessities of thought which hold alike as abstract truths, and in practical experience, several inferences follow:—

A volitional cause or agent, may stand before a series of consequents;—but cannot be ranged after such a series.

Our series represented by the Alphabet, was taken to be a series of invariable sequency. That is, each factor (letter) presupposed antecedents, which necessitated every factor in succession. Therefore we cannot represent any agent or volitional Cause, by an element (or letter) of that series at all. Nor yet his act. It follows on no such chain of antecedents. It is done in view of certain consequents.

If, therefore, we ask what can be conceived respecting the causation of the Universe,—its cause must (as Powell says), be placed absolutely outside and prior to the whole series. In other words,—a volitional or First cause can never belong to the physical chain of antecedent and consequent, bound together by natural law. And the reason is plain: in no true sense can such Cause ever be a necessary consequent at all. Such a Cause calls into existence, not only A, but the whole consecutive alphabet, representing cycles of millions of ages. Not the world's primaeval state alone,—- but the whole law-connected Universe. Thus, First Cause, and Secondary cause, apply not to difference of sequence alone,—but to an intrinsic and essential distinction. And, this distinction is so vast, that between the World's First Cause, and any given Secondary cause, there is fixed a gulf of separation as wide as the whole potential Universe.

Another way of looking at the subject of Causation may appear simpler to some minds.

Let the reader recal the problems of Idealism and Realism already discussed. He will also remember what Mr. Masson calls "the paramount result" to Mill and Hamilton alike;—the inevitable persuasion all men have of their own distinctness from an external world of things and persons surrounding them.

With this accepted result in remembrance, let the reader ask himself the further question, how he became originally impressed with the grand division of that world of objectivity,—how he first separated Persons from Things? He will account for the conception in some such way as this:—As a child, he was injured both by his nurse and his nursery table. He discovered that the table had been placed where it stood; but that his nurse struck him with a passionate intention of compelling him to obey her, against his own will. And, thus, in the succession of little troubles and events perpetually going on, he learned to distinguish them all into two broad classes: events dependent on previous circumstances, such as the position of the table; and events productive of intentional consequences, such as the ill temper of his nurse. The first class of events he could control by a change of outside conditions;—he could either move the table or keep his body out of its way. But, the nurse he had to humour and conciliate; and he soon found, to his cost, that very often his efforts to win her favour were unavailing, because her temper was so very, very bad. And this whole process of Childish reasoning became confirmed in after life by his practical reason, and verified by finding it work well every day. The child who thus ceases to blame the table for hurting him, but blames the temper of the nurse, is the "father of the Man," who praises or blames only when he discovers a true cause; and steadily ascribes Causation to a Will. And, employ what words we choose, this causative power is the grand tenable distinction between Persons and Things. And no amount of refined theory will ever induce us to act upon any other supposition. We remain fixed in our belief that a true Cause must, without exception, be always a true Personality.

It is worth while observing, likewise, with what emphasis of words, mankind marks its sense of this fact. We all say that we see such and such a cause,—or such and such a will at work. And the energy of expression is justified by analysis. For, when we see an orange or a cathedral, what we really perceive through our eye, may be summed as coloured surface, outline, light and shade. And seeing this, we say that we see the solid;—that is, seeing effects, we maintain that we see the cause. Moreover, this is true, if we remember that seeing is a compound process; the eye of the mind looking through the eye of the body. And we ventured to use the same language in our last chapter, and also to justify it, when we spoke of seeing the Intelligible. The man, therefore, is not far wrong who says that he sees God everywhere.

Look at the subject in whatever point of view we will,—as an abstract question—as a calculable problem—or an affair of plain common sense,—the result must finally come to one and the same thing. There can be no Cause,—no First to stand before (not in) the series of sequences, except a Being, Will, Personality.

Now as a matter of truth, there must necessarily exist some sufficient account of the Universe. Physical Science is right to speak of it as unknowable [218] by Physical investigation. It cannot lie in the physical series,—it must stand prior to the whole. It admits of no antecedent; but the sum of all existence is its consequent. Therefore, the sufficient account is a first Being, Will, and Personality. We must accept the result and acknowledge its truth, because it is an inevitable fact, if the question is argued upon the ground of other facts practically known, and not of theory, conjecture, or supposed possibilities. But it involves theoretical difficulties which we must acknowledge to be inexplicable. We cannot, however, forget that many other truths and matters of fact are inexplicable also [219].

A circumstance equally true, and equally incapable of theoretical explanation, may be stated as follows. If we revert, once more, to our representative letters of the alphabet, it will be recollected that the letter P was taken to represent a crime,—a murder for the sake of gain. P had for its consequents Q, R, S, but did not depend on the antecedents O, N, M; it was introduced extraneously into the series. In other words, the crime entailed a number of effects, which had in reality been premeditated by the murderer; while, in itself, it was to be accounted for only as the act of a Volitional Cause or Agent. And the remarkable point to us now, is the circumstance that such a designed series of events can thus be introduced into the order of nature by man's spontaneous choice. These determinations are in fact alterations in the ordinary course of Nature; and contradictions of its absolutely invariable sequency [be]. This fact, again, appears to be theoretically inexplicable, yet is practically true; and we verify its truth by determinations of the deepest interest and importance to our individual selves. Sometimes, men almost stand aghast at the consequences of choosing obstinately; and, through years of sorrow, accuse their own, and their friends' pertinacity.

Possibly, the difficulty in theory may be in some degree softened by the admissions of physical philosophers,—inventors and craftsmen of all sorts,—respecting the considerable allowance to be made for "functioning" their abstract calculations. The necessity of such allowance distinctly proves, that, even in the most exact of applied sciences, pure theory and practical result do not commonly coincide. And, when we look to the concerns of human society, it must be confessed that no amount of sovereign power, insight of statesmen, or experience grounded on precedent or on knowledge of mankind, does away with the absolute necessity of allowing what is called a "margin" for the actual working of any law, scheme, contrivance, or political constitution.

Speculative people are apt to find this truth verified to their cost and disappointment; and, perhaps, one reason for the general success of English administrators in government and colonization, is their habit of making very large allowances throughout all the practical arrangements. In managing the world, they consider the non-calculable element of Will,—and allow for the way in which it breaks in, with sometimes tremendous effect, upon the otherwise regular current of affairs.

But if this be true of the human Will, what ought to be said of the Divine? If we, with our limited power and understanding, can thus interrupt many series of events in our world, what shall we say concerning the Volitional Cause of the whole Universe? Concerning a Personality, which was before the chain of phenomenal antecedent and consequent began, and Which (as we have shewn must hold true of a First Cause), actually willed the whole as a whole, and arranged the end from the beginning? Recurring to our selected figure of the Alphabet, this primary Will, this incomprehensible Person is, in our view, the Alpha and Omega, the Beginning and the End, and beside Him there is none other [220].

So far, therefore, as a consideration of the world goes, and of mankind as existing in the world, arguments from analogy would lead to some positive expectation of Miracles. Our belief in the Uniformity of Nature does not exclude them; and our practical experience gives rise to a probability of their occurrence. When, however, we lift up our eyes to the Divine Mind as Supreme Reason, Miracles appear to us inconceivable without an adequate occasion. For we ourselves strive to act on true, fitting, and reasonable grounds of purpose; and shall we think less of Him, "Who teacheth Man knowledge"? But to pursue this last topic as it deserves, would carry us away from the domain of Natural Theology, and into that of Theology true and proper.

Our business has lain with the Natural world, human nature itself included. And in examining the successional chain, we have perceived that it is not forged of Adamant. Yet there is so much connection and unity running throughout it, that we may with the greatest justice speak of the order and course of nature. And, perhaps the highest kind of evidence to the being and attributes of God conceivable by us, lies in the concurrence of two separate kinds of proof; both resting on the reality of Divine causation viewed relatively to the World we inhabit. The one,—when we trace (as in this Chapter we have shewn that men ought to trace), the chain of natural sequence up to a Personal First Cause. The other,—when we find reason to believe that the First Cause and Creator of the world, has seen fit to interfere with its orderly course in a manner which distinguishes His intervention from our common every-day experience.

For such intervention, we could probably conceive no greater fitness, no nobler occasion, than the purpose of raising Men above themselves, and assuring them that there are more things in Heaven and Earth than are dreamed of in their Philosophies. And what human dream, vision, or philosophy, could ever have foreseen the things which God hath prepared for them that love Him?

Chapter 7

RESPONSIBILITY: RIGHT AND WRONG— A FUTURE STATE—SUPREME WILL AND PERSONALITY—POSSIBLE RELATIONS OF THE DIVINE BEING WITH MANKIND—EXPECTATION OF SUPERNATURAL AIDS TO KNOWLEDGE AND PRACTICE—THE BALANCE—L'ENVOY

"The astronomers said, 'Give us matter, and a little motion, and we will construct the universe. It is not enough that we should have matter, we must also have a single impulse, one shove to launch the mass, and generate the harmony of the centrifugal and centripetal forces. Once heave the ball from the hand, and we can show how all this mighty order grew.'"—Emerson. *Nature*.

"The essence of the Scandinavian, as indeed of all Pagan Mythologies, we found to be recognition of the divineness of Nature; sincere communion of man with the mysterious invisible Powers visibly seen at work in the world round him.... Such recognition of Nature one finds to be the chief element of Paganism: recognition of Man, and his Moral Duty, though this too is not wanting, comes to be the chief element only in purer forms of religion. Here, indeed, is a great distinction and epoch in Human Beliefs; a great landmark in the religious development of Mankind. Man first puts himself in relation with Nature and her Powers, wonders and worships over those; not till a later epoch does he discern that all Power is Moral, that the grand point is the distinction for him of Good and Evil, of Thou shalt and Thou shalt not."—Carlyle. *Heroes*.

"Our Religion is not yet a horrible restless Doubt, still less a far horribler composed Cant; but a great heaven-high Unquestionability, encompassing, interpenetrating the whole of Life. Imperfect as we may be, we are here, to testify incessantly and indisputably to every heart, That this Earthly Life, and its riches and possessions, and good and evil hap, are not intrinsically a reality at all, but are a shadow of realities eternal, infinite; that this Time-world, as an air-image, fearfully emblematic, plays and flickers in the grand still mirror of Eternity; and man's little Life has Duties that are great, that are alone great."—Carlyle. *Past and Present*.

"Goodness and greatness are not means but ends.
Hath he not always treasures, always friends,
The good great man?—Three treasures, life and light,
And calm thoughts, regular as infant's breath;
And three firm friends, more sure than day and night—
Himself, his Maker, and the Angel Death."
S. T. Coleridge.

"Omnia terrena
Per vices sunt aliena:
nescio sunt cuius;
mea nunc, cras huius et huius.
Dic, homo, quid speres,
si mundo totus adheres;
nulla tecum feres,
licet tu solus haberes."
From "This World is false and vain," lines 41-48.

"Threefold is the march of Time,
The Future, lame and lingering, totters on;
Swift as a dart the Present hurries by;
The Past stands fixed in mute Eternity.

"To urge his slow advancing pace
Impatience nought avails,
Nor fear, nor doubt, can check his race,
As fleetly past he sails.
No spell, no deep remorseful throes
Can move him from his stern repose.

"Mortal! they bid thee read this rule sublime:
Take for thy councillor the lingering one;
Make not the flying visitor thy friend,
Nor choose thy foe in him that standeth without end."
After Confucius, by Sir. J. Herschel.

"The world that I regard is myself; it is the microcosm of mine own frame that I cast mine eye on; for the other, I use it but like my globe, and turn it round sometimes for my recreation. Men that look upon my outside, perusing only my condition and fortunes, do err in my altitude; for I am above Atlas his shoulders. The earth is a point not only in respect of the heavens above us, but of that heavenly and celestial part within us: that mass of flesh that circumscribes me, limits not my mind: that surface that tells the heavens it hath an end, cannot persuade me I have any: I take my circle to be above three hundred and sixty; though the number of the arc do measure my body, it comprehendeth not my mind: whilst I study to find how I am a microcosm, or little world, I find myself something more than the great. There is surely a piece of divinity in us, something that was before the elements, and owes no homage unto the sun."
Sir. T. Browne. *Religio Medici*.

ἴσον δὲ νύκτεσσιν αἰεί,
ἴσα δ' ἐν ἀμέραις ἄλιον ἔχοντες ἀπονέστερον
ἐσλοὶ δεδόρκαντι βίον, οὐ χθόνα ταράσσοντες ἐν χερὸς ἀκμᾷ οὐδὲ πόντιον ὕδωρ
κεινὰν παρὰ δίαιταν· ἀλλὰ παρὰ μὲν τιμίοις
θεῶν, οἵτινες ἔχαιρον εὐορκίαις, ἄδακρυν νέμονται

αἰῶνα·....
..... ἔνθα μακάρων

νᾶσος ὠκεανίδες
αὖραι περιπνέοισιν, ἄνθεμα δὲ χρυσοῦ φλέγει,
τὰ μὲν χερσόθεν ἀπ' ἀγλαῶν δενδρέων, ὕδωρ δ' ἄλλα φέρβει

ὅρμοισι τῶν χέρας ἀναπλέκοντι καὶ κεφαλὰς. Pindar. Olymp. II.

"Stern Daughter of the Voice of God!
O Duty! if that name thou love
Who art a Light to guide, a Rod
To check the erring, and reprove;
Thou who art victory and law
 When empty terrors overawe;
From vain temptations dost set free;
From strife and from despair; a glorious ministry.

"I, loving freedom, and untried;
No sport of every random gust,
Yet being to myself a guide,
Too blindly have reposed my trust:
Resolved that nothing e'er should press
Upon my present happiness,
I shoved unwelcome tasks away;
But thee I now would serve more strictly, if I may.

"Through no disturbance of my soul,
Or strong compunction in me wrought,
I supplicate for thy controul;
But in the quietness of thought:
Me this uncharter'd freedom tires;
I feel the weight of chance desires:
My hopes no more must change their name,
I long for a repose which ever is the same.

"Yet not the less would I throughout
Still act according to the voice
Of my own wish; and feel past doubt
That my submissiveness was choice:
Not seeking in the school of pride
For 'precepts over dignified,'

Denial and restraint I prize
No farther than they breed a second
Will more wise.

"Stern Lawgiver! yet thou dost wear
The Godhead's most benignant grace:
Nor know we anything so fair
As is the smile upon thy face;
Flowers laugh before thee on their beds;
And Fragrance in thy footing treads;
Thou dost preserve the
Stars from wrong;
And the most ancient Heavens through
Thee are fresh and strong.

"To humbler functions, awful
Power! I call thee: I myself commend
Unto thy guidance from this hour;
Oh! let my weakness have an end!
Give unto me, made lowly wise,
The spirit of self-sacrifice;
The confidence of reason give;
And in the light of truth thy Bondman let me live!"
Wordsworth. *Poems*, 1807.

SYNOPSIS OF CHAPTER 7

The object of this Chapter is to shew that the universally enforced maxim of Responsibility unites in itself two factors.

(1.) A true power of Causation, as explained in Chapter 6. (2.) A moral distinction of Right and Wrong.

This second element of Responsibility is next investigated, and the Moral antithesis shewn to be inalienable. Right can never be Wrong, nor Wrong ever Right. Justice must certainly prevail at last.

From the connection of Morality with Causation, it may be inferred that the moral Law has its ultimate existence in a Supreme Personality—a just and sovereign God. This conclusion is verified. Human life and Human death read us the same lesson.

Corollary. —If the conclusion just drawn be accepted, and to know God be Life Eternal, we may also infer an à priori probability of some Supernatural assistances, intended to strengthen our human weaknesses and diminish our ignorance. This latter purpose would seem likely to include a better aid to happiness, and a more complete code of Moral Maxims.

Analysis. —As a social fact, Responsibility is universal, and accounted inalienable by any individual man. Responsibility involves Causation in the highest sense, together with Moral Sensibility.

Attempts to refine away ethical Rightness. An appeal to consciousness proposed:— Distinctness of moral feeling;—and its Permanence. Antithesis of Right and Wrong an irreconcileable Antagonism. Contrasted with correlation of Power and Function; this antithesis never fluent, but rigorous, immutable, imperishable, absolute. Ultimate coincidence of Happiness with Virtue is a necessary result of Independent Morality.

Moral Law exists conceivably in and by a Will alone; as— 1. Its cause and spring of movement. 2. Its source of expression and practical authority.

Being supreme, it exists in and by a Supreme Moral Will or Personality. That is to say, in and by God.

This conception verified. World inexplicable without Man. Man inexplicable without God; Whom to know is Life Eternal.

Corollary. —Supernatural assistance apparently to be expected when Moral Law is viewed as a human endowment proceeding from God. Thus Man is made for God, and God has not made Man in vain.

Confirmation from—

1. Image of Divine Love in Nature. 2. Nature of religious Trust as a Belief of Reason. 3. Incompleteness of our ethical knowledge apart from such assistance. 4. Universal expectation of Mankind.

L'Envoy.

RESPONSIBILITY

Responsibility is the most serious fact of our whole human world. The affairs of life could not go on for a single day if there were no Responsibility. We never release any man from its burden, without incapacitating him, at the same time, alike from business and from enjoyment. We lay it upon childhood, as soon as the child is able to reflect upon his own actions and to choose deliberately;—we do not take it away from a collected and self-controlled age. And every reasonable Man who stands by an open grave, or knows that he is rapidly approaching his own, feels, (above all other pressures,) the unending prospect of Responsibility. Looking at this prospect, we look into our deepest solitude;—

"Since all alone, so Heaven has willed, we die."

None of our fellows, the dear companions of our Soul, can carry our burden then. And though they walk by our side in life, and cheer us with their love, they cannot really bear that burden now. And, thus, in the most serious and solemn fact of our existence, we are always isolated and alone.

But Responsibility is something better to every one of us than a burden;—it is also an incalculable benefit. A man who has no true sense of responsibility, is an unformed human being;—and, in proportion as we feel it inwardly, and express the feeling by consideration and self-control, we make progress in real manliness. On this account, Responsibility may be pronounced our chief aid in the formation of a manly character. And, probably, among all the sources of human happiness, none yields a more unbroken serenity, than the habitual consciousness of being enabled to act up to the single mark of our responsibilities.

When a man has attained such practical wisdom, it "maketh his face to shine." His daily endeavour to do right, instead of causing him anxiety and disquietude, gives a buoyancy to the spirit; which shows itself in a peculiar brightness of countenance, unlike every other cheerful glance and aspect. The beaming faces, with which early Italian artists painted their good men and saintly women, are excellent illustrations of this expressional beauty.

Let us consider, through one chapter more, what Natural Theology has to say upon this subject. Responsibility has been shewn to involve, as one of its constituent principles, an idea of Causation. It is, also, clear that to hold a man responsible, he must be supposed to possess some power of distinguishing Right from Wrong. In our last chapter, we drew from the principle of Causation certain conclusions regarding the Universal First Cause. We have now to examine the principle of Moral Sensibility.

Every one at all acquainted with modern controversy, is aware that few questions have been more keenly mooted, than the origin of moral distinctions among mankind. The debate respecting them has run, for a great part of its course, parallel with that on the origin of our primary intellectual beliefs, alluded to in a former chapter. Neither of these controversies concerns us beyond a certain point. Our business lies with the facts of human nature, rather than with theories concerning any supposed possibilities as to their growth and accretion. But, one caution we suggested respecting the case of intellect, holds good and is important to every moral inquirer. Let the analyst beware of his alembic! There is nothing more easy than to vaporize reality altogether, by way of exalting a philosophy [221]. And in Morality, the result is far worse than in speculation. The distinctive character of our Moral Consciousness is the "essence" which lends to a right action its peculiar fragrance and beauty. Invaluable per se, it will surely be found of a nature so delicate and fugitive as to escape the tests of analytic psychologists. Yet when this is fled, the residuum must be worthless to Moral philosophy.

The "essence" just mentioned, merits a few minutes' attention. Men have been known to assert that their feeling of appreciation in respect of a very lovely woman, was precisely similar to their appreciation of a handsome horse. No doubt, the right answer is to tell such a man that he is utterly blind to the true loveliness of woman; and does not deserve to call a creature so excellent, his wife. You may, also, point out to him the various distinctive characters of female excellence,—refinement, purity, depth of feeling, self devotion, the noblest heroism, and so on. But if the man has put all his perceptions of diverse excellences into a private alembic, and sublimated them into one of the lowest among aesthetic susceptibilities; no argument will really convince him. The truly bright aesthetic eye—the grander imaginative powers are wanting,—the man is mentally colour-blind.

The same truth holds good of theorists who tell us dogmatically that our Moral Sensibility is nothing better than an accretion of baser materials which may be stripped off from each other in the reverse order of their growth, just like the coats of a stalactite or a tulip-root. As may readily be surmised, there is great difference of dogma, when judgment comes to be pronounced on the moral core and centre of the whole. Some are for the needs of society,—some utility in general,—the greater part for individual advantage. Others take theoretically polar directions; and with them, rightness consists either in quietism, or else in self-immolation. Self-approving feelings, (each advocate tells us,) have clustered round his pet growing point; and the clustering has endowed us with all the moral sense we happen to possess. Here again, it is doubtful whether a right answer will convince the experimentalist, bent on turning lead into gold. Yet whether convincing or not, most honest hearts would prompt an indignant rejoinder. The world at large, however, is likely to prove a more successful arbiter. The utilitarian will find that he excites little sympathy even when general utility forms his moral kernel;—and, when it is no more than a personal gain of worldly advantages, he will not improbably be called a rascal. Then "Quietism" can never hope much favour in the busy workshop of the West. Though it may seem strange to some minds, self-immolation has by far the greatest chance of winning suffrages; one chief reason being, that the man who sacrifices his own private advantage, has evidently spurned expediency and selfishness. Even those who think his theoretical views erroneous—and possibly mischievous, will applaud his victory over the meaner passions.

Each hour of thought the reader can bestow on moral distinctions, will turn to certain good. At the very least, it must help to form a habit of self-examination. And for this purpose, very simple interrogatories bring out very useful responses. If the reader be a rose grower, let him inquire into his own feelings, when he plucks the fairest flower in his garden, to give fragrance and colour to the sick room of a poor but sensitive little invalid. He will certainly perceive a wide interval between his pleasure in admiring the glowing rose, and his pleasure in adding to the scanty luxuries of the poor sick child. Thus, although a benevolent action be a truly beautiful thing, yet there is a difference between the rose grower's impressions of mere beauty, and of pure benevolence. A difference too between his enjoyment of beauty, and his enjoyment in benevolently resigning to another, the object which charmed him because it was beautiful. Time, also, makes a vast difference between the two emotions. We cannot recal a delicious odour, as truly as we can reproduce a pretty sight before our retrovertive eye. The image of the rose remains, after its sweet fragrance has departed. But much, much longer than either, remains the moral impression graved upon the mind. That little pleasure enjoyed in a brief self-denial, will repeat itself through half a century of years.

Permanence is, indeed, one characteristic which demonstrates the paramount excellence of all moral impressions. It is so difficult to repeat to ourselves the sensation of physical pleasure or physical pain, that many writers on pathologic topics speak of it as a thing impossible. Certainly, its greatest vividness is in dreams; and above all, "aegri somnia"—sick visions—seem to possess the strongest reproductive power. It is curious, however, to observe the manner in which dreams themselves put on a moral meaning. Who does not remember Sir W. Scott's lines in the "Lady of the Lake," on the returning phantoms of early youth,—change, loss, and separation? But those phantoms are pale shadows, compared with what we have all felt in our visionary hours,—the consciousness of our own absolute loneliness,—of our death,—of a hopeless, endless isolation. Even the very thought of our spiritual life [222], as distinguished from mere corporeal life, is terrible to us and hardly to be borne. So overwhelming is the idea of the demand of Justice upon each of us;—the law of human Responsibility.

It is remarkable, too, that the most common-sense practical people sometimes feel these impressions the most acutely. One reason may arise from the circumstance, that the spiritually imaginative temperament of such persons is vigorous,—has few occasions of employment; and throws its unexhausted force into those strong "Michel-Angelesque" realizations.

Whatever may be thought on this point, there is no truth of our whole Manhood more striking, as well as more evident, than the independent vitality of our Moral Consciousness. Let us suppose, for example's sake, that the reader was once unhappy enough to injure a neighbour, a friend, or relation. Let the injury be something which you in your heart know to be truly injurious;—a thing impossible in your better moments,—but still a thing done. Now, let years elapse, and when the thought recurs and the deed is reacted, you feel how wrongful it was. And when you grow old, and there are few left to love you, the feeling will become far more deep. Put oceans, continents, tropics, between yourself and your injured one; the reality is not at all less real. The same stars no longer look down upon you by night,—the sun does not bring back the same seasons at the same time,—but your act is Timeless;—and, though night and day vary, its criminality remains the same. And worst of all,—the injured one may die, whilst no act of reparation may have been performed by you,—no word of love or ruth escaped your lips. The deed is irremediable, and you are the doer of it. Neither Space nor Duration of years can alter the fact. There is a moral mark set upon your conscience; and no human sympathy can heal, nor even alleviate the sorrow. Most likely, you never attempt to explain to others the pain you feel, because were the case another's you would hardly comprehend it yourself. Thousands have gone to the grave, carrying heavy burdens of this kind almost or altogether unsuspected.

Exemption from the laws of Time and Space, is perhaps the most wonderful characteristic of our Moral Consciousness. With this solitary exception, we seem to find ourselves in perpetual subjection to those laws. But in the realm of Morals it is the reverse. The endless theoretical contradictions about the Finite and the Infinite, (to which we have more than once alluded,) bear witness to this fact. Morality at once puts the two together;— what in its sphere of commission was a finite crime, is likewise an infinite immorality. We count up our faults as sins; but, when viewed awhile in the light of conscience, they are most burdensome to us as being, not sins, but Sin. Look at the pre-Christian Eumenides; the last writing of St. John the Evangelist; the confessions of Augustine; and the life of John Bunyan; to which we might add more than one great Oxford life;—and, through them all, the profound sense of Sin underlies every other utterance.

Another salient character of the moral sense, actually existing among mankind, may be outlined as follows. We have already considered the manner in which laws appear to human intelligence, as types, ideas, or relations. Amongst them, we paid particular attention to the relativity between Power and Function. And, when viewing these as polar opposites, with a chain or nexus between them, we saw that the opposition was, in a certain sense, fluent. Function changed into Power more than once, before each complex process of production became entirely accomplished. Power, in accomplishing its errand, continually was lost, and vanished away in Function. But between Right and Wrong, the opposition is fixed, contradictory, and enduring. Any Logic or Rhetoric which attempts to make the antithesis appear fluent, is justly condemned as special pleading, and the art of an oratorical Sophist. The only question asked of the Sophistical speaker, is whether the error he tries to excuse was wilful, or unintentional; whether it was a mistake, or a confusion of distinctly-opposed moral dictates. So Demosthenes says to O'Eschines,

"Among all other men I observe these principles and these distinctions to prevail. Does anyone wilfully do wrong? He is the object of indignation and of punishment. Does anyone commit an error unintentionally? He is pardoned, not punished.... All this is established not only in all our jurisprudence, but by Nature herself in her unwritten laws, and in the very constitution of the human mind" [223].

And we may all feel quite sure that this is the normal decision of Mankind.

Right and Wrong stand out as irreconcileable antagonists, contending for the empire of the world. A man who watches the strife without deep interest, and never mingles in the fray because he thinks its issue immaterial, is no better than a Pessimist.

Compare a Duty with a Function, (in the wide sense we assigned to the latter conception,) and two points will at once be evident. First, how strong the contrast, how wide the interval, between the Law of productive work, and the law of moral activity. Secondly, how inextinguishable the contradiction between Right and Wrong. One man undertakes some mechanical utilitarian function, dependent on the pleasure or life of a superior; to whom he is in no other respect bound, nor in any way accountable. Another is a husband, a father, or a son. The object of his natural affection, is also the being to whom his tender offices of devotion are morally due. For different reasons, the daily lives of both these men have become first irksome,—then, very wearisome,—finally, almost odious to themselves. The man of routine goes to visit his ailing superior, and is permitted to enter the sick room. He undraws a curtain and looks upon the face of a dead man. Between the departed and himself, there existed no natural love, nor any acquired hate, neither duty nor demand. The link was simply official, and it is broken. Next month, there will be a new Superior who knows not Joseph. Another subordinate will occupy the post of routine; and, under the circumstances, to be released from the old toil is a sort of happiness. The tedious function of the past is over; and he carries his powers into a more hopeful employment. Yet Man is always something to Man, if both are genuine; and there arise a thousand regretful memories, and thoughts of kindly interchange of gestures, looks, and words. After a time, the last change of all is thought of as a thing to be deplored, but gone by,—a thing simply irremediable.

But how different, when the man who has been morally bound—say the son—sees a dead face upturned from his father's pillow! Here is another link of service broken;—service of another kind,—a duty. It is gone, the sick bed attendance, the harass, the vexation, endured with a recalcitrant feeling, and sometimes an openly determined opposition. And how much is gone besides! The feeling of resistance vanishes, when there is no longer a Will to be resisted; the harass and vexation appear unwholesome phantoms. To look on the life of a father or a near friend, after death, is like looking on a moonlighted landscape; its harsher features are lost in lengthening shadow; all that we thought rugged and stern, appears subdued and blended with a thousand fondly-remembered softnesses. A mild and silvery radiance flows over the whole familiar scene;—we gaze and sigh,—and sigh and gaze again. To think of its becoming veiled from our eyes, seems like losing a portion of our own existence.

And what more is gone besides? The son's thought, which used to mingle so strangely with his feelings of distaste,—that, some day, he would fill up the measure of that which was consciously lacking in his filial duty and devotion. He has now no power of offering sorrow to obtain the remission of claims unsatisfied, no possibility of saying, "Father, I have sinned"! He would die by inches, if, with each slow degree of mortality he could revoke a short period of the Past.

In other concerns of life all beyond human cure is also beyond human care; but this concern is a matter of Right and Wrong. To say the Wrong is irremediable, is to utter the sharpest cry of Remorse,—the last word of a long Despair.

It is always thus, when the moral rule intervenes. It is so, when an injured friend dies,—the injurer is fast bound by the crime he has committed. It is so, when the Son thinks he has to face things undone which ought to have been done,—the opportunity of doing them now lost for ever. Inability to remedy a wrong makes our sorrow inextinguishable. And we know by experience, that such a sorrow is unlike every other sorrow. It differs in kind from all trains of ordinary feeling, and seems to belong less to our emotional life than to be a dictate of our sovereign reason. And the moral rule is so. In the eye of Practical Reason which (so far as human nature goes), constitutes our supreme guide, a claim of Morality is absolutely rigorous—absolutely supreme—and if unsatisfied, absolutely inexorable.

To suppose anything less, would be to annihilate the whole moral law. For, how can you, or I, or any one, be required to immolate our life, freedom, fortune, or even our ordinary enjoyments, unless the rule be perfectly unyielding; perfectly unchangeable? To be binding now,—it must be binding under all circumstances, and binding always. If a single claim remain unsatisfied the admission is fatal. Broken once, the law is broken everlastingly. Every man might conceive that his own case was, possibly, just one marked for exception. Who, then, would sacrifice at the altar of Right-doing all earthly goods; undergo chains, ignominy, dungeon-solitude, pain, lingering hopelessness, and death? Who, then, would be able to stand by, and see all these inflictions undergone by one he loves best, when compliance with wrong-doing would surely set the sufferer free? It is the certainty of an equal and unrelenting law, which makes all kinds of endurance possible.

If no other reason existed, this one would suffice to prove that, unless human nature is a falsehood, happiness must ultimately coincide with virtue. How distantly removed their final coincidence may be, is a point which can have no influence on the certitude of our knowledge. We speak here, as we speak of parallel lines which cannot meet through infinity;—only we speak the reverse way;—it is for all infinity that virtue must become happiness. If a man will seriously sit down, and try the contrary hypothesis out to himself, he will see that if held true, Morality ceases to be imperial, and Man ceases to be human. The claim of Right is to rule the Universe, entire, and in every part. Before that claim, all knowledge, scientific, phenomenal, inferential, must fail and vanish away. Whatever else be true or untrue, this must be rigorous, unalterable, imperishable truth. Upon this truth, each reasonable being, percipient of it, is required to act in his own individual person. Therefore, in the case of each individual it must hold absolutely true. And thus the moral endowment of Man is not a general sense of Morality; no indeterminate impulse towards excellence floating before him; no mere thought that past generations were made for us, and we for a coming race. What we really know and acknowledge as moral truth, is each Man's strict accountability, individual, isolated, and inalienable. Otherwise, individual rightness cannot be demanded, and individual suffering for conscience-sake must become, in some eyes Utopian,—to most sufferers intolerable. The moral law is therefore supreme, or it would be ineffectual. It is individually specializing, otherwise it could not claim individual obedience. And to be supreme, both in final effect and present empire over each human being, it must obviously be—(as our practical Reason apprehends it)—Universal. To such a sovereignty there is nothing great, nothing small. Time sets no bounds, while Reason beholds in it the ultimate perfection and sum of all that went before it.

Towards that complete coincidence of happiness with virtue, the aspiration of good and the sighs of sorrowful souls, have been breathed continually. In its realization alone, can our noblest capabilities be realized. For, there is nothing in this world commensurate with the capacious longings of the human spirit. Here, too often, it droops like a beautiful plant in a strange unkindly soil; and, when it blooms its brightest, we feel that under other influences it might bloom more brightly still. True humanity is marked by its own specific character, as the fit inhabitant of a far more excellent sphere.

We ask with some eagerness, how may these things be? And the primary answer to this question lies within the circuit of our knowledge. Our own consciousness, the facts of life, and the reason of the thing, all agree in one result. Moral law exists only in, and for, a Will;

and by a Will alone can it be made effectual. In this respect, it resembles the Law of Production, which, apprehended ideally by intelligence, becomes realized by the moving force of Will. Moreover, we have seen that Will is true Causation, and therefore in Will exists the first ground of Movement. We know in fact of no other. Neither is any other Causality conceivable by us, even in hypothesis; and we think this causative power of Will only by knowing its real existence and verifying its workings through their issues.

Yet further. The Moral Law, as a sovereign command, is addressed to our Wills; and unless it were the Expression of a Will, we know it could never be executed. The Law would remain a dead letter,—a thought of Intelligence,—an abstract speculation,—ineffective because impractical. Therefore, when we speak of a Supreme Moral law, we speak of a Supreme Moral Will; an idea we sometimes express by true Being, or true Personality. We speak, that is, of God.

Experience deepens to us every day the meaning of this final word. In the world of our present habitation, we see a confused mass of striving Wills,—the good and just not always in the ascendant,—rightful commands disregarded,—a sovereign rule not visibly asserted. To affirm the possible continuance of these practical contradictions, would be to deny the ultimate Moral Unity of moral purposes. This Divine consummation is, then, the finality towards which all things must in reason be tending. For even as human nature explains all other nature,—as the Moral Law explains all other law,—so God explains Man. Explains his existence, otherwise inexplicable, by the anticipated victory of Right over Wrong,—and the complete satisfaction of his unsatisfied aspirations. By presenting, that is to say, an adequate object,—a Personality infinitely great and infinitely good,—to the eye of Man's reason,—the desire of his heart,—the striving endeavour, and ceaseless energy of Man's whole essential being;—his affections, his will, his spirit.

This elevating thought comes home to each one of us, bringing with it a peace of mind unutterable. We know that the time must come, when thought and memory shall grow faint. Our brain will lose its quick apprehensive motion, and all our bodily powers must sink and languish. Our eyes will refuse to see the faces of those we love; our hands to return their kindly pressure; our nerves to thrill at their voices. But, whosoever has learnt the lesson which God's world, and God's gifts to Man, were meant to teach him, may truthfully say—"My flesh and my heart faileth, but God is the strength of my heart, and my portion for Ever."

Corollary. —One reflection will probably have occurred to every reader of the last few pages. The rigour of the moral law demonstrates to us the necessary existence of a future state of recompense, and the supremacy of a sovereign Will—a divine Judge. Now, does not this very rigour leave man as hopeless, as if he were altogether without God? Can he ever expect to perform the behests of that pure and perfect Will? This difficulty would appear valid, were there nothing in the idea of God thus given us, to furnish rejoinders, such for example, as the following.—How could the Supreme Judge make any difference between those who are His anxious servants, and those who turn away from His infinite purity with hatred or indifference, if all men were alike overwhelmed in one common failure by reason of an inexorable law? How, again, could He satisfy the aspirations of earnest but half-hopeless human souls, without gathering them to His presence and to Himself? The manner in which such a happiness results to men, may be an enigma, so far as Natural Theology is concerned;—but if so, it is an enigma, of which, those who reason on this ground, may foresee that there will certainly be granted some solution. And we are not left quite in the dark as to how that solution may be found;—a truth we may perceive from the ensuing considerations:—

The moral law is presented to Man's practical reason with all its consequences. The divine Idea, when once apprehended, becomes the object of Man's noblest affections. God, Who graved His law of Right and Wrong upon the conscious will of His creature, wrote also a law of love upon His creature's human heart.

Hence we view the Supreme Being, as a God who formed and endowed Man for Himself. It was thus, that Man's nature received its only possible explanation. Hence, also, the sufficient account of a capacity for happiness which this world can never give;—and, along with it, the earnest of its ultimate satisfaction.

But these evidences of the Divine finger, prove also a Divine intention. The supreme ruler of the Universe has, by them, written upon Man's nature a purpose of making His creature happy. And if so, we cannot but conclude that to the Divine attribute of love, which inspired the glad promise, we may look for its certain fulfilment. In this point of view, a miracle worked for such a moral and spiritual purpose as the ennoblement and blessedness of Humanity, ceases in one sense to be a miracle. It becomes not only credible, but probable. And in reality, any event appears less improbable than that incredible and most unlovely issue,—the self-contradictory thought, that God has made Man in vain.

These considerations are drawn from our Moral nature, as just described. There are other considerations at hand to confirm them.

In treating the subject of Production, we saw Intelligence involved in every Idea, and preceding every process. When referred to the Universe, Intelligence was necessarily conceived as vast and immeasurable. In order to discern the other attributes of that universal Intelligence, we examined the characteristics of Design apparent in nature, and saw everywhere a spirit of superhuman tenderness breathed over our beautiful world. Thus, if there be any personal relation between the Author of Nature and our race, it ought to be one of trust on our side, demanded by care and beneficence on His. And this feeling is heightened by the charm of lavish kindness,—the prodigality of a love Divine.

Again, if we turn to one chapter of this Essay farther back, and bring to mind the rise and progress of our primary beliefs, we cannot but ask ourselves the question, how is it that the first religious idea of the Aryan race—the "Heaven-father"—should coincide with the most typical utterances of our loveliest childhood, and our most advanced manhood, now?—Is He really our Father? If so, may we not expect much from His hand? He is a Person, not an Abstract Entity,—a Force,—or a Thing. Our Father will give us, not a stone—but bread;—bread from Heaven—bread from Himself. And we see that He giveth liberally, and upbraideth not.

This is not all. The rigour of the Moral Law is an irreconcileable Antithesis between Right and Wrong,—a gulf which no human subtlety can bridge. But with all this rigour, it leaves unresolved, to a very considerable extent, one set of doubts perpetually recurring to an honest mind. Is this or that particular point a duty;—is it right or wrong;—or is its observance open to debate? There are obvious reasons, arising from the necessities of moral culture and improvement, why such points should, within certain limits, be indeterminate. This whole topic, however, belongs properly to Natural Religion, a separate subject from Natural Theology. Still, for our present purpose, an important consequence of the inexactness is clear.—It gives rise to a reasonable expectation of some more extensive code not unlikely to be vouchsafed us, harmonizing with, and supplementary to, the law of our moral consciousness. And at every age of Man's history, and throughout every country of his habitation, there always did, in fact, prevail an expectant attitude of mind, looking on all sides for the tokens of Divine Revelation. It was felt also by the wisest, that no human foresight could decide beforehand, what aids to higher knowledge and moral virtue might be given along with it. Certainly, every reasonable idea of the great and good God, formed a ground for hope and confident anticipation of the Highest and the Best.

This Essay has reached its close. May it be permitted its writer to drop the tone of an Essayist, and to say that every word of it has come from his heart?

May he likewise ask two favours of the intelligent reader; neither of them he trusts unreasonably onerous?

His first request is that the convergent effect of the separate considerations urged in this Essay, may be fairly taken into account. Indeed, the writer once thought of appending a kind of conspectus or "summing up."—But he would thus have added another full chapter to a book which has grown considerably in his hands. Neither might the summary be altogether welcome to the more candid minds amongst those who doubt, yet honestly debate. Most such readers prefer putting results and consilient reasonings into a connected shape for themselves. The writer may however venture on soliciting some special attention to the breadth of field ranged over;—the wide circumference from which his various arguments and illustrations have converged. This point is one of considerable value. Great credit is given to the accordant testimony of witnesses who have come together from distant parts of the world.

The other favour requested, is that every person who desires to form a deliberate judgment on the grand topics at issue, will carefully weigh in the balance what alternative he can embrace, if he refuses to be a Theist. An alternative, that is, sufficient to account for the human Will and Reason, for such a world as our own, and for so symmetrical and beautiful a Universe.

The system we have advocated on grounds of Reason, asserts that the first Cause of all Things and all Beings known to us, is God. This account alone is sufficingly complete, and coherent. Against it alone, no fatal objection has ever been alleged. And this single fact ought to have a preponderating weight in the balance.

When finally compared together, the motives of our Choice (as presented by Natural Theology), stand thus:—

If explanations of the Universe explain unequally, that account ought to be chosen which is easiest in itself, explains the most, and is the least self-contradictory.

If several explanations appear equal to the deliberative eye, then we must choose the noblest per se; and, as Men, we ought to prefer that which is the most elevating, and most germane to Humanity. In it, will be contained the only true Law of human Progress.

Either motive of our final Choice—still more, both these motives—will bring us to God; and with reason—"For we are also His offspring."

ENDNOTES

[1] *Right and Wrong. A Sermon upon the Question Under what Conditions is a Science of Natural Theology possible?* Preached before the University of Oxford, March 6, 1870.

[2] All citations made in the original draft, or in the foot-notes belonging to it, have been revised and altered to suit later editions of the authorities cited. Thus there are several extracts from books which may appear to be recent publications, but are, in fact, authorized rifaccimenti.

[a] The language of this paragraph is the language of ordinary life. In Coleridge's "Table Talk," for example, the subject of Man's distinguishing prerogative of Immortality is discussed by the great speaker, and his nephew's note of the discussion is headed "Materialism." There appears, indeed, considerable difficulty in finding a precise expression for the form of belief, or unbelief, commonly called Materialism. Most people speak of it as of some clear and well-defined theory until they begin seriously to investigate its rationale. Investigators are then apt to become loud in their complaints of its inexactness. Take by way of instance the following example. Speaking of "the doctrines of Materialism," Lord Brougham remarks: "The vague and indistinct form of the propositions in which they are conveyed affords one strong argument against their truth. It is not easy to annex a definite meaning to the proposition that mind is inseparably connected with a particular arrangement of the particles of matter; it is more difficult to say what they mean who call it a modification of matter; but to consider it as consisting in a combination of matter, as coming into existence the instant that the particles of matter assume a given arrangement, appears to be a wholly unintelligible collocation of words."— (*Discourse of Natural Theology*, p. 102).

Under such circumstances it may seem difficult for many a Materialist to describe himself as the adherent of a distinct or closely reasoned system. The main point we would submit for his earnest consideration is the question whether his hypothesis lands him in certain subtle refinements concerning the nature and connection of Force, Mind, and those generalized facts which have been called the primary properties of Matter,— or whether it leads him onward to the opinions described in the text. Looking at the subject in this light, we might feel inclined to draw a broad distinction between mere scientific Materialism and the Materialistic doctrines of sceptical philosophy.

[b] "I doubt," said Mr. Gladstone at Liverpool on December 21, 1872,—"I doubt whether any such noxious crop has been gathered in such rank abundance from the press of England in any former year of our literary history as in this present year of our redemption,

eighteen hundred and seventy-two." The Premier had before remarked: "I believe that neither Science nor Thought is responsible, any more than Liberty is responsible, for the misdeeds committed in their names."

The passage from which these brief extracts are made is given at greater length in the additional note to this Section (A).

[c] Since writing the above, my attention has been called to Paley's censure of the "disingenuous form" under which Scepticism was placed before the public in his day. He says (Moral Philosophy, B. v. Sect. 9): "Infidelity is served up in every shape that is likely to allure, surprise, or beguile the imagination; in a fable, a tale, a novel, a poem; in interspersed and broken hints, remote and oblique surmises; in books of travels, of philosophy, of natural history; in a word, in any form rather than the right one,—that of a professed and regular disquisition. And because the coarse buffoonery and broad laugh of the old and rude adversaries of the Christian faith would offend the taste, perhaps, rather than the virtue of this cultivated age, a graver irony, a more skilful and delicate banter, is substituted in their place."

[d] "Atheists," says the Pall Mall Gazette of January 18, 1873, "write Atheism because they are Atheists, but Alexandre Dumas writes Atheism, though a good Catholic, who goes to church every Sunday."

[e] Pre-eminent amongst these remonstrants is Mr. Gladstone. In the speech before cited, he says, p. 25: "It is to be hoped that they will cause a shock and a reaction, and will compel many, who may have too lightly valued the inheritance so dearly bought for them, and may have entered upon dangerous paths, to consider, while there is yet time, whither those paths will lead them. In no part of his writings, perhaps, has Strauss been so effective, as where he assails the inconsistency of those who adopt his premises, but decline to follow him to their conclusions. Suffice it to say, these opinions are by no means a merely German brood; there are many writers of kindred sympathies in England, and some of as outspoken courage." (Compare the extracts from this class of writers given along with the Premier's remarks in Note A.)

[f] Die Zustände eines Volkes hängen hauptsächlich von seiner Denkweise ab: diese ist der wichtigste und einflussreichste Zustand. Alle andern können nur nach und in ihr begriffen werden. Sie ist es, die den Menschen zu einem solchen macht; und in ihrer Ausbildung entwickelt sich erst die Menschlichkeit.—(Wilhelm H. J. Bleek, "Ueber den Ursprung der Sprache," p. 12).

[3] Cowper, "The Task," B. III.—It must be confessed that the honest-minded humanitarian may often find in the reception he encounters ample reason and motive enough for taking up Teufelsdroeckh's parable:—"'In vain thou deniest it,' says the Professor; 'thou art my Brother. Thy very hatred, thy very envy, those foolish lies thou tellest of me in thy splenetic humour: what is all this but an inverted sympathy? Were I a steam-engine, wouldst thou take the trouble to tell lies of me? Not thou! I should grind all unheeded, whether badly or well,'"—(*Sartor Resartus*, B. III. c. 7). And when the bigotry of Unbelief is not content with persecuting the honest-minded humanitarian—when he hears some shallow, half-animalized specimen of humanity shouting for a red-handed communism and the blood of the innocent— then he may not irrationally exclaim with the same philosopher:—"Wert thou, my little Brotherkin, suddenly covered up within the largest imaginable glass-bell,—what a thing it were, not for thyself only, but for the world!"

[g] I am indebted to Mr. Gladstone's appendix (p. 40) for the following apposite quotations from Sir George Cornewall Lewis's very scarce work, "On the Influence of Authority in Matters of Opinion." Speaking of "Authority, and its place not as an antagonist of Reason, but as an instrument of Reason for the attainment of Truth," Sir George remarks, in page 35 of his book: "'It is commonly said that the belief is independent of the will,' and that no man can change it 'by merely wishing it to be otherwise.' But 'the operation of a personal interest may cause a man insensibly to adopt prejudices or partial and unexamined opinions.' In page 38 he adds: 'Napoleon affords a striking instance of the corruption of the judgment in consequence of the misdirection of the moral sentiments.'"

All friends, and many casual readers, of S. T. Coleridge will remember that he asserted the same, or perhaps a stronger, conclusion upon metaphysical grounds, and with a force of language not easily surpassed. This—one of Coleridge's bursts of gorgeous eloquence and imagery—will be found in "The Friend," a book which, according to C. Lamb, contains "his best talk." The subject commences on page 260 of Vol. III., Ed. 2, and page 211, seq., Vol. III., Ed. 4. In the latter place it is amplified by a summary of his arguments, pages 213, 214. The position propounded, that true insight cannot exist apart from moral rectitude, receives considerable light from the doctrine of philosophical postulates maintained in the "Biographia Literaria," Vol. I. c. 12, and chiefly borrowed from Schelling, to whom there is an honest reference in the first Edition, I. 250. I mention this circumstance because Coleridge has been held guilty of unjustifiable pillage by writers who have noted his borrowing, but omitted to observe such acknowledgments as he makes, together with the additions and alterations which he introduces.

The corruption of a naturally acute understanding has seldom been more graphically painted than by Judge Talfourd. (See Additional Note, B.)

[4] Compare Lord Macaulay on "Special Pleading in History," Additional Note, C.

[h] These divisions have been sometimes called Physico-Theology and Ethico-Theology; but the latter designation is far too restricted for the line of thought pursued in the latter portion of this Essay.

[i] See Additional Note, D.

[5] Pope, "Essay on Man," Ep. II. Compare Mr. Pattison's notes, pp. 87, 88, and 90. We may remark that the Aphorism "Know thyself" has been often employed to convey a lesson the most distant possible from Pope's,— e.g., "Know thyself; and so shalt thou know God, as far as is permitted to a creature, and in God all things."

[j] See Additional Note, E.

[6] The work referred to, "Der alte und der neue Glaube," appeared in the latter half of 1872.

[7] Compare an illustrative passage, B. III. p. 34. "We have been seeking to determine, whether our point of view, from which the law-governed All, full of life and intelligence, is the summit of thought (die höchste Idee), can still be called a religious point of view, and we have animadverted upon Schopenhauer, who loses no opportunity of flying in the face of this which is our Idea. As I have said, such outbreaks impress our understanding as absurdities; to our feelings, they are blasphemies. It appears to us rash and reckless, on the part of a mere human individual, so boldly to set himself up against the All, out of which he grows, and from which he has the morsel of intelligence that he misuses. We see in this an abnegation of that

feeling of dependence, which we admit to belong to all men. We demand the same piety towards our Universum, as the devout man of the old fashion did for his God."

[8] This declaration we quote in its native German. Its first sentence, together with the sentences immediately preceding, are those passages selected for translation by Mr. Gladstone.

"Historisch genommen, d. h. die ungeheuren Wirkungen dieses Glaubens mit seiner völligen Grundlosigkeit zusammengehalten, lässt sich die Geschichte von der Auferstehung Jesu nur als ein weit historischer Humbug bezeichnen. Es mag demüthigend sein für den menschlichen Stolz, aber es ist so; Jesus könnte all das Wahre und Gute, auch all das Einseitige und Schroffe das ja doch auf die Massen immer den stärksten Eindruck macht, gelehrt und im Leben bethätigt haben; gleichwohl würden seine Lehren wie einzelne Blätter im Winde verweht und zerstreut worden sein, wären diese Blätter nicht von dem Wahnglauben an seine Auferstehung als von einem derben handfesten Einbände zusammengefasst und dadurch erhalten worden." (p. 72.)

[9] As a consequence of the difference in standpoint, the use made by the two men of their several conclusions is marked by very considerable contrast. Comte's Humanity was to be served by a ritual as well as a social set of ordinances. Strauss looks quite another way. Considering the outrage which would be committed upon philosophy and feeling should his Universum find irreverent treatment in the words and writings of men; our emotion, he says, on such occasions becomes thoroughly religious. If then it be asked in express terms whether he and his fellow- thinkers really have a Religion or no, they cannot answer roundly as they will when questioned on Christianity; they must rather say yes or no according to the meaning of the word Religion in the mind of their questioner. (See Strauss, p. 143.)

[10] In the Livraison of the Deux Mondes for November, 1856, M. Cucheval-Clarigny wrote thus: "Personne plus que David Hume n'a éprouvé l'inconstance des jugemens humains. Après avoir été mis au rang des esprits qui ont fait le plus d'honneur à l'humanité, on le compte volontiers aujourd'hui parmi les corrupteurs de la raison et les apôtres du mal." That another kind of interest has been more recently felt in Hume is evidenced by the republication of his works in America and England. While writing this note I learn that a new edition of the seldom-read Treatise on Human Nature will shortly appear, with notes by two well-known members of Balliol College.

[11] Compare with this the subjoined orison for a special gift of moral rectitude penned by Professor Huxley (Lay Sermons, p. 373). "I protest that if some great power would agree to make me always think what is true and do what is right, on condition of being turned into a sort of clock and wound up every morning before I got out of bed, I should instantly close with the offer. The only freedom I care about is the freedom to do right; the freedom to do wrong I am ready to part with on the cheapest terms to any one who will take it of me." It seems wonderful that the talented writer fails to perceive that should his terms be granted the bargain would be dear indeed—it must take place at the expense of his Personality. He would have no choice left, consequently no rightness of choice. With the loss of his volition his manhood would be forfeited; and the Huxley of our praise and blame must needs sink at once and for ever from a Person to a Thing—

"Rolled round in Earth's diurnal course
  With rocks, and stones, and trees."

After all, we may trust that this outpouring of soul after mechanical goodness, is neither more nor less than a fresh rehearsal of the popular fallacy or fable of a learned and intelligent, but somewhat over-hasty, death-watch. The difference between the two myths is not great, and both owe their existence to the prolific fancy of Professor Huxley. About three years ago the teleological beetle speculated in a manner which would have grieved the soul of Aldrich or Whately respecting the purpose of a kitchen clock. The death-watch concluded, like a death-watch, and not like a logician, that the clock's final end was to tick. Man, as Bacon tells us, is the servant and interpreter of nature. Does any one feel sure that a death-watch is the servant and interpreter of kitchen timepieces? Yet his inconsequent thinking served as an implement of Fate to "quail, crush, conclude, and quell" Teleology in general, and the Design argument for Natural Theism in particular. Now, a human Huxley clock always going morally right because it must, is equally conclusive against all freedom and all Conscience. Equally conclusive, we know, because equally true to Nature and to Fact. As conclusive as arguments against received biological tenets drawn from those great natural curiosities the Gorgon, the dragon of St. George, and the fire-breathing Chimaera, who united in her own fair person a lion, a dragon, and a goat. This latter well-known phenomenon may seem nearly as striking as any right-minded clock imaginable, and not much more incongruous.

Many readers may be reminded of Amurath's Ring. But few probably will know, and fewer still recollect, Miss Edgeworth's clever comment upon it in "Rosamond." The book is unfortunately scarce, not having been reprinted along with "Early Lessons," therefore we add the extract ("Rosamond," vol. i., p. 148):—

"Do you remember, brother," said Laura, "your wish when you were reading that story in the 'Adventurer,' last week?"

"Not I. What wish?" said Godfrey. "What story?"

"Don't you remember," said Laura, "when you were reading the story of Amurath and his ring, which always pressed his finger when he was going to do anything wrong?"

"Yes; I wished to have such a ring," said Godfrey.

"Well, a friend is as good as such a ring," said Rosamond; "for a friend is, as somebody observed, a second conscience; I may call Laura my second conscience."

"Mighty fine! but I don't like secondary conscience; a first conscience is, in my opinion, a better thing," said Godfrey.

"You may have that too," said Rosamond.

"Too! but I'd rather have it alone," said Godfrey. "There is something so cowardly in not daring to stand alone."

The lesson seems to be that second-hand goodness falls short of true goodness, and that the impulse to moral action must arise from within—so unmanly is every endeavour at shaking off, either by cowardice or by unreflectiveness, the human burden and birthright of Responsibility. Amurath's ring was a mechanical conscience. Professor Huxley's clock is a mechanism in the outward form of a man. These two imaginations convey the useful lessons that neither Conscience nor Mankind are mere machines. A clock goes because it must go its hourly round; a man chooses which way, when, and whither he will go.

[12] 1 Corinthians ix. 16.

[13] For a useful account of Plato's Dialogue in connection with Plato's philosophy, see "Introduction to the Republic," by Davies and Vaughan, pp. xxi.-xxiv. Cambridge, 1852.

[14] See more particularly Chapter 5, "Production and its Law."

[15] Most literary people are aware that it was borrowed by Paley himself. A reference very accessible to ordinary readers may be made to Knight's *English Cyclopaedia*, Article Nieuwentyt.

"A work," says the biographer, "was published by him at Amsterdam in 1715, in one volume 4to, entitled 'The right use of Contemplating the Works of the Creator': the object of the author is first to convince atheists of the existence of a supreme and benevolent Creator, by contemplating the mechanism of the heavens, the structure of animals, etc.; and, secondly, to remove the doubts of deists concerning revealed religion. It was originally published in Dutch, but has passed through several editions, in German, French, and English. The English editions, translated by Chamberlayne, under the title of the 'Religious Philosopher,' appeared at London in 1718-19 and 1730, in three vols. 8vo. This work, as was first pointed out in the *Athenaeum for 1848*, pp. 803, 907, 930, served as the basis for Paley's 'Natural Theology,' the general argument and many of the illustrations in that remarkable work being directly copied—and without the slightest acknowledgment, though Paley was acquainted with the book—from the 'Religious Philosopher.'" Lord Brougham, who does not appear to have seen Bernard Nieuwentyt's book, believes that Derham supplied the fountain from which Paley drank so freely. Apparently he used both.

To this note it may be added that the want of Natural Philosophy under which the Archdeacon himself laboured, has been recently commented on in the following terms:—

"Paley kicked his foot unconcernedly against the stone he found on the heath; for anything he knew, he says, it might have been there for ever. Geology was then a practically unknown science, or he might have found epochs of history in the stone, and evidence of all manner of special creations for man's benefit. But Paley was no natural philosopher, only a half-learned theologian, who skimmed over all difficulties, and produced a book which has done immense harm in leading Englishmen to anthropomorphic conceptions of God."— Report of an Address by A. J. Ellis, President of the Philological Society, in an American Newspaper (the Index) for August 10th, 1872.

[k] So Hume (Inquiry, Section IV.): "A man, finding a watch or any other machine in a desert island, would conclude that there had once been men in that island." And again (Id. Section V.): "A man who should find in a desert country the remains of pompous buildings, would conclude that the country had in ancient times been cultivated by civilized inhabitants but did nothing of this nature occur to him, he could never form such an inference." The inference is, as Hume says, from effect to cause—a subject which he is here investigating more suo. To the nature of this inference I have found reason for recurring more than once.

[16] A striking peculiarity of this skeleton is thus described by Professor Huxley ("Manual of the Anatomy of Vertebrated Animals," p. 217). "In many Lacertilia (Lacertae, Iguanae, Geckos) the caudal vertebrae have a very singular structure, the middle of each being traversed by a thin, unossified, transverse septum. The vertebra naturally breaks with

great readiness through the plane of the septum, and when such lizards are seized by the tail, that appendage is pretty certain to part at one of these weak points."

[l] "God," says Dogberry, "is a good Man." So others besides Dogberry.

Curiously enough, the charge of Anthropomorphism has been brought by a most eminent naturalist against the greatest authorities on Natural Selection.

M. Edouard Claparède writes as follows in the "Archives des Sciences Physiques et Naturelles" for 1870:—

"Mon but est seulement de montrer que les armes dont M. Wallace se sert victorieusement pour attaquer le duc d'Argyll, se retournent contre lui-même. Sans doute, c'est un pur anthropomorphisme que de supposer chez un Créateur un sentiment du Beau entièrement semblable au nôtre, et une telle hypothèse n'a rien à faire avec la science. Mais cet autre anthropomorphisme par lequel les Darwinistes supposent chez les oiseaux un sens du Beau identique au nôtre, est il plus justifié? Soit M. Darwin, soit M. Wallace, expliquent la formation de la belle voix et du beau plumage chez les oiseaux mâles par sélection sexuelle. Les femelles sont censées donner toujours la préférence aux mâles, qui, au point de vue humain, ont la plus belle voix et les plus brillantes couleurs. Au contraire, chez toutes les espèces à cri désagréable pour l'oreille humaine et à couleur sombre, la nature du cri comme de la couleur a dû sa formation à une autre forme de sélection que la sélection sexuelle. Quel oubli de l'antique dicton: De gustibus et coloribus non est disputandum! Si ce dicton a été reconnu vrai chez toutes les nations civilisées, il acquiert une force bien autrement grande lorsqu'il s'agit de son application à des oiseaux. Serait il absurde de supposer chez certains oiseaux un goût prononcé pour les couleurs sombres, comme ce goût existe chez beaucoup d'hommes? Et alors ne devient-il pas possible, contrairement à MM. Darwin et Wallace, d'expliquer la couleur terne de certaines espèces par sélection sexuelle? N'en peut-il pas être de même pour la voix criarde de tel ou tel volatile? Certes, il est dangereux de baser un édifice sur quelque chose d'aussi subjectif qu'un sentiment, quelque soit du reste la nature de l'être chez lequel on le suppose plus ou moins gratuitement, oiseau ou Créateur!" (pp. 175-6.)

[m] If any one desires to see how early and how persistently this difficulty attached itself to the Design Analogy, I may be permitted to refer him to a thin volume of my own, entitled "Right and Wrong," pp. 17-22 (text and notes), and Appendix, pp. 58-60.

A similar Dualism (coupled with the charge of Anthropomorphism) is frequently urged against Natural Theology at the present day. The alternative proposed has been called Monism. The fixed unyielding realm of Abiology (inorganic nature) is taken as the type of the universe. The sole supposable Divine principle (or Spirit) is identified with its law, which is in turn pronounced identical with philosophical necessity—that is to say, a necessity not imposed by or flowing from the Divine will, but a necessity which annihilates the possibility of all will. The Divine principle thus supposed is simply that law or force which is embodied in the mechanism of the universe. Professor Haeckel of Jena is the author of a book which has been styled in Germany, "The Bible of Darwinism." The following passages will show how he treats the subject under consideration in the text. He writes (*Generelle Morphologie der Organismen*, Book II. cap. vi. sec. 2, "On Creation")
to the following effect:—

"The conception of Creation is either altogether unimaginable, or at least perfectly inconsistent with that pure intuition of Nature founded on an empirical basis. In Abiology a creation is no longer anywhere spoken of at all, and it is in Biology only that people are still closely wrapped up in this error. The conception of creation is perfectly unimaginable, if by it is understood 'an origination of something out of nothing.' This acceptation is quite incompatible with one of the first and chiefest of Nature's laws—one, indeed, universally acknowledged—namely, with the great law, that ALL MATTER IS ETERNAL." (Vol. i. p. 171.)

There is one general reflection which may fairly strike the honest and ingenuous mind respecting the difficulties thus "Now if the conception of such an immaterial force, discoverable exterior to matter, independent of, yet nevertheless acting upon it, is absolutely inadmissible and inconceivable in itself, then so, too, becomes the conception of a creative power from our point of view; and all the more so, since with it are united the most untenable teleological conceptions, and the most palpable Anthropomorphism." ... "In all these teleological conceptions, and similarly in all histories of creation which the poetical phantasy of men has produced, gross Anthropomorphism is so evident, that we may leave the denial of this Creation-idea to the insight of any general reader who thinks for himself, and is not too far involved in traditional prejudices." ... "A creation of organisms is, therefore, partly quite unimaginable, partly in such complete contradiction to all knowledge of nature empirically gained, that we cannot in any case allow ourselves to end by accepting this hypothesis. There remains, consequently, nothing else but to suppose a spontaneous origination of the simplest organisms, from which all more perfect ones developed themselves by gradual metamorphosis—that is to say, a self-forming or self-configuration of matter into organization, which is generally called primordial production or spontaneous generation (generatio aequivoca). (Ibid. 173-4.)

Haeckel commences his section upon Dualism and Monism (Book I. cap. iv. section 6), with the following quotation from August Schleicher (die Darwinische Theorie und die Sprachwissenschaft: Weimar, 1863, p. 8):—

"The tendency of modern thought is undeniably towards Monism. Dualism —whether you are pleased to define it as the contrast of spirit and nature, of contents and form, of appearance and reality—is no longer a firm ground to stand upon, if we wish to survey the field of modern science. To the latter there is no matter without spirit (i.e., without the unavoidable necessity that governs it), nor, on the other hand, is there any spirit without matter. We might say, perhaps, that there is neither matter nor spirit in the usual acceptation of the words, but only a something which is the one and the other at the same time. To charge this view—which is founded on observation—with materialism, is equally unjust as to lay it at the door of spiritualism."

Haeckel concludes this section by avowing an unalterable conviction of the truth of Monism, with which his mind is thoroughly penetrated.

The extracts above given will explain the value of those distinctions respecting Law and Causation, which are drawn in the latter part of this chapter. The wider subject pertains, however, to Chapter 5, where it is discussed at some length.

[17] Many readers may be pleased by a perusal of Lord Brougham's "Dissertation on the Origin of Evil." It gives an account of various hypotheses, and ends with some

interesting remarks. See his "Dissertations on Subjects of Science connected with Natural Theology," vol. ii.

[18] Even Lord Brougham, whom no one will accuse of a too ardent addiction to metaphysical pursuits, chides Paley very severely for this neglect. Dr. Whewell's censure is more grave. Passages from these criticisms are given in Additional Note A, with some explanations which may conduce to a clear insight of what is meant by bad metaphysics, particularly in relation to the subject before us.

[19] Compare the figure employed in Rev. xxi. 1.

[n] There seems little doubt that the popular phrase "Design proves a Designer" has given rise to an extensive distrust of the Design argument in toto. Compare Additional Note B.

[o] Another shape of the objection is stated and examined in Additional Note C.

[20] Essay on the "Spirit of the Inductive Philosophy," Ed. 2, p. 174. The italics and capitals are Professor Powell's.

[p] Were Paley now alive, he might plead the example of Mr. Darwin, whose practice it is to speak of any incidental chasm occasioned by the link sometimes missing from his premises, as "not a long step." "Mr. Darwin's argument," says a reviewer of his "Descent of Man," "is a continuous conjugation of the potential mood. It rings the changes on 'can have been,' 'might have been,' 'would have been,' 'should have been,' until it leaps with a wide bound into 'must have been.'" (*Times*, April 8, 1871.) Any similarity between the reasonings of the Archdeacon and the Naturalist may appear noteworthy. But the coincidence ends here. Paley, though reproved by a Lord Chancellor, had the good fortune to be excused by a Bishop. There is a short account of both censure and defence in the notes to Powell's "Connection of Natural and Divine Truth," pp. 287-9.

[21] P. 177.

[22] Ibid.

[23] Ibid.

[24] Pp. 175-6.

[25] Putting aside workmanship exercised on given material, we may perceive a gliding of thought from the idea of plan, form, or fashion, to adaptation, and so onwards to purpose and intention—that is, conscious adaptation to a designed end.

[26] "Sämmtliche Werke," vol. II., pp. 51, 52.

[27] "Connexion of Natural and Divine Truth," pp. 183-4.

[28] See the work last quoted, pp. 287-9. The Professor substantially agrees with Lord Brougham's censure before referred to, and considers Dr. Turton's defence of Paley an insufficient apology.

[29] "Essays and Reviews," 8vo. p. 125.

[q] The general reader may reasonably feel a difficulty in assigning their proper meaning to terms used in senses so technical. He may possibly be assisted by looking over the field of view thus:—A Force is visible to us as a movement in Nature;—when we try to formulate it intelligently to ourselves, its mental equivalent is Law. If, then, we wish to describe an intelligent prae- conception of Law (such as distinctly involves the Foresight of its operation) we call the Law a Creative Idea, or (less definitely) a Design. Tracing the chain of causation in the reverse or downward direction, the Idea when put in movement appears to our mind's eye as Law; and when we wish to include its actual working upon the realm of Nature we term it a Force.

Both James Mill and his son (a truly affectionate annotator), are careful to point out that the essence of moral causation involves Intention—that is (as Mr. Mill explains), Foresight, or expectation of consequences.—"Analysis of the Human Mind," II., 400, 401.

It should be observed that in many branches of Natural Science the word Law is so employed as to include the conception of Force. Law is in this usage not merely a logical formula expressive of realized facts, but it involves the idea of the coercion or impellent motion which brought those facts into being. "Thus, then," says Dr. Carpenter, "whilst no Law, which is simply a generalisation of phenomena, can be considered as having any coercive action, we may assign that value to Laws which express the universal conditions of the action of a Force, the existence of which we learn from the testimony of our own consciousness." He had before remarked that "it is the substitution of the Dynamical for the mere Phenomenal idea, which gives their highest value to our conceptions of the Order of Nature."— Address to British Association at Brighton, August, 1872. This Order of Nature, as the learned President says in conclusion, is no "sufficient account of its Cause."

[30] See how the matter appears to a Satirist:—"By the great variety of theories here alluded to, every one of which, if thoroughly examined, will be found surprisingly consistent in all its parts; my unlearned readers will perhaps be led to conclude that the creation of a world is not so difficult a task as they at first imagined. I have shown at least a score of ingenious methods in which a world could be constructed; and I have no doubt that had any of the philosophers above quoted the use of a good manageable comet, and the philosophical warehouse, chaos, at his command, he would engage to manufacture a planet as good, or, if you will take his word for it, better than this we inhabit." Such is the dictum of the profound Knickerbocker,—"History of New York," 8vo, p. 16. His variety of theories concludes with that of "the renowned Dr. Darwin," of Lichfield. If the history were brought down to our day, additional variety might be given to this part of it.

[r] It is upon this confusion that Powell charges Pantheistic theories in which physical speculations are mistakenly supposed to have their natural termination. See Additional Note D, where the passage to which more than one reference has already been made, is given in extenso. Compare also our Chapter 6, on Causation. (note: this is reference h Chapter 2 Section D)

[31] Essay as above, p. 165.

[32] The signification attached by the Professor to Law and Cause may be most readily explained by a similitude. Let the physical series of antecedents and consequents be represented by a chain of which we see the present links, but both its beginning and its end are invisible. Physical law is this chain. Cause must not be considered its first link, for Cause differs in kind from the series, is in truth sui generis, and can be illustrated by no physical phenomenon, but by the fact of our own Moral Volition. Cause, therefore, is external to the chain, and originates, not only the first, but every link of it. Each and all—nay, the universal chain in its entirety—may be viewed as owing its existence to one single fiat of an absolute moral Cause. Compare on this subject Chapters 6 and 7. ensuing.

[33] Essay, pp. 155, 173. It should, however, be observed that Sterling's language has been interpreted two opposite ways, and therefore the obscurity may be verbal. Coleridge's

expressions have regard to certain "so-called Demonstrations." His own judgment as to the cumulative proofs of Theism was that "there are so many convincing reasons for it, within and without—a grain of sand sufficing, and a whole universe at hand to echo the decision!—that for every mind not devoid of all reason, and desperately conscience-proof, the Truth which it is the least possible to prove, it is little less than impossible not to believe; only indeed just so much short of impossible, as to leave some room for the will and the moral election, and thereby to keep it a truth of religion, and the possible subject of a commandment."— *Aids to Reflection*, Edition 1843, Vol. I. p. 135. First and rare edition, p. 177.

[34] "There is thus no alternative, but either to abandon the inquiry after an immediate intuition of power, or to seek for it in mind as determining its own modifications; a course open to those who admit an immediate consciousness of self, and to them only. My first and only presentation of power or causality is thus to be found in my consciousness of myself as willing. In every act of volition, I am fully conscious that it is in my power to form the resolution or to abstain; and this constitutes the presentative consciousness of free-will and of power. Like any other simple idea, it cannot be defined; and hence the difficulty of verbally distinguishing causation from mere succession. But every man who has been conscious of an act of will, has been conscious of power therein; and to one who has not been so conscious, no verbal description can supply the deficiency."— *Prolegomena Logica*, p. 151.

[s] It seems singular that this rise of thought has of late years seldom been explicitly put forward as the natural continuation and necessary extension of the argument from Design. "He that planted the ear, shall He not hear? He that formed the eye, shall He not see?... He that teacheth man knowledge, shall not He know?" In other words, if we may argue from the structure of the eye and ear to an Intelligence which comprehends our sense-perceptions, their conditions, and their activities, may we not always argue from the reason of man to an Intelligence comprehending our highest human endowments?

If so, we reflect these attributes back upon our explanation of the natural world. We say, further, that such a Creator would never make a mere machine. Humanity was a necessary complement of all that is set under Man. And thus Francis Bacon's aphorism may be applied in a double sense,—Man not only interprets Nature to himself—but he affords in himself a text for her more complete interpretation. Nature and Human Nature are two correlatives.

[35] Take, as example, the scientific theories on Insanity and its melancholy accompaniments. How many theorizers seem to justify Sir William Ellis's old observation, that few of his medical brethren ever got much notion of Mind?

[36] "Natural Theology attempts to demonstrate the existence of a personal First Cause, supreme Reason, and Will. The relations of mankind towards such a Being are called Natural Religion."— *Right and Wrong*, p. 58.

[37] If any one wishes to convince himself that other meanings proposed are open to serious objections, let him peruse Max Müller's first Lecture on the Science of Religion.

[38] Compare Additional Note E, on the extent and divisions of the *Science of Natural Theology*.

[39] *The Soul*, p. 32, seq.

[40] Any strictures of ours on the language employed by Natural Theologians must be understood as appeals from individual or peculiar usage to world-wide acceptation and old established custom:—

"Quem penes arbitrium est et jus et norma loquendi."

[41] As regards another important word illustrated in this chapter, it may be useful to add that the term Analogy is often employed in a wide or rather vague signification; not only by careless writers, but by philosophers. There is an important passage in Bacon's Plan of the Instauratio (prefixed to the Novum Organon) which Wood translates thus:—"The testimony and information of the senses bears always a relation to man, and not to the universe, and it is altogether a great mistake to assert that our senses are the measure of things.

The Latin original for "bears a relation" is "est ex analogiâ," but Mr. Ellis prefers rendering it by "has reference to," and confirms his decision by comparing two other Latin phrases;—one, "Materia non est cognoscibilis nisi ex analogiâ formae"—the other, "Materia non est scibilis nisi in ordine ad formam;—ut dicit" (adds Thomas Aquinas) "Philosophus in primo Physicorum." Mr. Ellis subjoins "That the meaning of the word Analogy was misconceived by S. Thomas, by Duns Scotus, and by the schoolmen in general, is pointed out by Zabarella, De prim. rerum materiâ, I. 4."

"Philosophus" means Aristotle, who, however, in the passage referred to is faithful to his own correct definition of Analogy, and his instance may readily be stated in four terms, as will appear on reference to the passage (Ed. Bekker 191, a. 8). Argyropylus translates by "similitudine rationis," and St. Hilaire explains "analogia" for the benefit of the general reader by "rapport proportionnel"—(Leçons de Physique I. 8, s. 18).

That Bacon was really thus vague in his use of "ex analogiâ" may be gathered from his substitution of "in ordine ad" as an equivalent in the closely related passage, Nov. Org. II. 20. Such being the case with so great a writer, some little allowance may be made for difference of phrase employed by ordinary reasoners on Natural Theology.

[42] By way of assisting the young student to a clear perception of what is involved in our Science, we illustrate its ground-work at considerable length in an additional note (marked F) on Teleology.

[43] "Die rechte Erkenntniss kann sich erst dann einfinden wenn man weiss wie man erkennt d. h. wenn man seine eigene Natur begriffen hat." Page 5 of "Ueber den Ursprung der Sprache," von W. H. J. Bleek.

[44] *Macaulay's Essays*. Ed. 1852, p. 401.

[45] The division of Sciences into ancillary and "architectonic" is Aristotelian. It seems also founded in the nature of things. That real science tends to ground itself, strives after unification with kindred sciences, and, by so doing, rises into philosophy, is a fact visible in every line and letter of Faraday; and the general reader will find it exemplified throughout many fascinating pages of Dr. Tyndall's Fragments of Science for Unscientific People, particularly in his articles on Vitality, the use of the Imagination, and the life of Faraday, not to mention his own book on the great inductive philosopher.

[46] It is interesting to compare the French-Scotch, and German-Scotch types of intellect. The former flowered in the Stuart men and in David Hume. The latter produced such diversely graven characters as Sir William Hamilton and Mr. Carlyle. Hume's natural acuteness received a subtle refinement from his Jesuit educators at La Flêche. But his

intellectual bent and determination was given by the French parlour-philosophy, which heralded Rousseau and Robespierre. Hume's well-known face is a truthful index to his mind. If compared with Kant's, the lesson is obvious to even an unskilled physiognomist. Self-complacency beams over every feature.

[47] No doubt the actual course of Hume's philosophising was determined by his zeal against everything he deemed superstitious. It was this dominant motive which made him less a calm philosopher than a skilful advocate, and laid him open to the influences of the French Deism of his period. How strong the tendency was we may infer from the following anecdote, which occurs in an account of his declining days by his friend and admirer, Dr. Adam Smith (pp. 47-50):—

Hume had been "reading a few days before, Lucian's Dialogues of the Dead: among all the excuses which are alleged to Charon for not entering readily into his boat, he could not find one that fitted him. He then diverted himself with inventing several jocular excuses, which he supposed he might make to Charon, and with imagining the very surly answers which it might suit the character of Charon to return to them. 'Upon further consideration,' said he, 'I thought I might say to him, Good Charon, I have been correcting my works for a new edition. Allow me a little time that I may see how the Public receives the alterations.' But Charon would answer, 'When you have seen the effect of these, you will be for making other alterations. There will be no end of such excuses; so, honest friend, please step into the boat.' But I might still urge, 'Have a little patience, good Charon; I have been endeavouring to open the eyes of the Public. If I live a few years longer, I may have the satisfaction of seeing the downfall of some of the prevailing systems of superstition.' But Charon would then lose all temper and decency. 'You loitering rogue, that will not happen these many hundred years. Do you fancy I will grant you a lease for so long a term? Get into the boat this instant, you lazy loitering rogue!'"

[48] The "Treatise" was written during his youthful three years' residence in France, chiefly at La Flêche. Hume was twenty-seven years old when he published it. See "Life," pp. 6 and 7, and Burton's *Life of Hume*, Vol. I. pp. 57-124.

[49] This work, the least known of all Hume's writings, but not the least original, is here cited in the not uncommon reprint 2 vols. 8vo, 1817.

[50] It is curious to compare with both Hume and Bacon a brief dictum of S. T. Coleridge. Biog. Lit., last chapter. "Poor unlucky Metaphysics! And what are they? A single sentence expresses the object and thereby the contents of this science. Γνῶθι σεαυτον: et Deum quantum licet et in Deo omnia scibis. Know thyself: and so shalt thou know God, as far as is permitted to a creature, and in God all things. Surely there is a strange—nay, rather a too natural—aversion in many to know themselves." "People," says Guesses at Truth, "can seldom brook contradiction, except within themselves."

[51] *Compare Advancement*. B. II. with *De Augmentis*. B. III. Chap. iii.

[52] *De Augmentis*. B. III. Chap. iv.

[53] Advancement. B. II. (Ed. Basil Montague, Vol. II. p. 134). It is generally an advantage to quote from the enlarged Treatise, the *De Augmentis*, but in some places the Advancement is more simple and more full.

[54] *De Augmentis*. B. III. Chap. iv. init.

[55] *De Augmentis*. B. III. Chap. iv. Ellis and Spedding, iv. 362.

[56] "The cone and vertical point" itself is "the work which God worketh,"—("summariam nempe Naturae legem")—and "it may fairly be doubted whether man's inquiry can attain to it. But these three are the true stages of knowledge." De Augmentis, as before. So too in his Valerius he speaks of this "highest generality of motion or summary law of Nature" as reserved by God "within His own curtain."

[57] The great thinker speaks of it as made up in part "of the common principles and axioms which are promiscuous and indifferent to several Sciences;" in part "of the inquiry touching the operation of the relative and adventitious conditions of Essences, as quantity, similitude, diversity, possibility, and the rest." These he terms "Transcendentals," and they form a highest kind of philosophical arrangements, "with this distinction and provision, that they be handled as they have efficiency in Nature and not logically."

His instances of common principles show how very vaguely this idea of the first division floated before his mind. Some of them are axioms mathematically certain and true in more than one province of philosophy, others are generalized truths obtained by experience or by comparison of objects diverse in appearance, but to his mind identical or very similar. Among these latter occurs his celebrated saying, that "the delight of the quavering upon a stop in music is the same with the playing of light upon the water";— a thought that haunts us by the seaside and on the shore of mountain lakes while listening to some sweet voice or clear-toned instrument.

From his philosophical arrangements Bacon takes away inquiries into the One, the Good, and the Divine, and assigns them to Natural Theology.

[58] Translation of the *De Augmentis* in Ellis and Spedding. Vol. iv. p. 346.

[59] Nov. Org. E. and S., iv. 120.

[60] *De Augmentis*. E. and S., iv. 362.

[61] Kitchin. Nov. Org. p. 134. But Mr. Kitchin believes that could Bacon have witnessed the actual progress of science, it would have led him to recognize the usefulness of Final Causes, in the field of physical inquiry, and by way of illustration proceeds to quote "the famous case of Harvey's discovery of the circulation of the blood from the consideration of the Final Causes of the valves in the veins of the animal body." (Ibid. p. 135.)

[62] Mill's *Analysis of the Human Mind*. Vol. ii. pp. 310, 11.

[63] In a volume of philosophical Romance some unknown Gulliver of the 19th century bestows many pages of pleasant satire on the Utilitarian principle, assumed as a maxim of social life and pushed to its ultimate conclusions. The author travels into the country of Nowhere (Erewhon), and learns by personal experience, first in a prison, and next in the house of a princely swindler Senoj Nosnibor (alias Jones Robinson) those true laws of Sociology which best subserve the great final end—the noble object laid down by Mr. Mill. Ill-health is made criminal. Immorality counts as being out of sorts. The former is an object of penal justice, the latter of condolence joined with alterative discipline. The swindler sends for his family "straightener," and gets well amidst the sympathy of his friends; the consumptive is condemned to imprisonment and hard labour for the rest of his miserable days. And this is reasonable in itself, and justified by the results,—the Erewhonians possess the finest physique in the world, and rob and embezzle only when they happen to feel tempted. Our traveller himself, though full of old-fashioned moral prejudices, becomes convinced by contemplating the great final

cause. "That dislike," he observes, "and even disgust should be felt by the fortunate for the unfortunate, or at any rate for those who have been discovered to have met with any of the more serious and less familiar misfortunes, is not only natural, but desirable for any society, whether of man or brute: what progress either of body or soul had been otherwise possible?"—and again, "I write with great diffidence, but it seems to me that there is no unfairness in punishing people for their misfortunes or rewarding them for their sheer good luck: it is the normal condition of human life that this should be done, and no right-minded person will complain at being subjected to the common treatment. There is no alternative open to us. It is idle to say that men are not responsible for their misfortunes. What is responsibility? Surely to be responsible means to be liable to have to give an answer should it be demanded, and all things which live are responsible for their lives and actions, should society see fit to question them through the mouth of its authorised agent. What is the offence of a lamb that we should rear it, and tend it, and lull it into security, for the express purpose of killing it? Its offence is the misfortune of being something which society wants to eat, and which cannot defend itself. This is ample. Who shall limit the right of society except society itself? And what consideration for the individual is tolerable unless society be the gainer thereby?" *Erewhon*, pp. 85, 86, and 100, 101.

These sentiments considered, the reader will not be surprised to learn that our author, after a preparatory college training in the main doctrines of Self-interest—to wit, Evasion and Inconsistency—ends happily and usefully for himself by the successful abduction of his host's daughter—and by advertising a propaganda of certain European manners and observances unknown in Erewhon, to be carried out by kidnapping its healthy inhabitants and training them properly on our sugar plantations. What genuine disciple of Utilitarianism can conceive a brighter moral triumph than the union of private self-interest with the interested aims of a great sugar- growing people? Matter-of-fact Baconians may argue that Utility substitutes a misplaced and one- sided "why" for the "what" required by Moralists,—but our traveller's answer is plain—he argues on data;—given the premises—his is the inevitable conclusion. The defence of the former will be an interest to plenty of people—philosophic and unphilosophic. Leave the data to them; or if necessary make a further appeal to the religious aims of society. In Erewhon the great feminine Divinity Ydgrun is supreme; she is sovereign amongst ourselves also;—only we twist her name and call the Goddess "Grundy."

[64] *Preface to the Philosophical Works*. pp. 56, 57.

[65] *Works*. Vol. i. p. 167.

[66] *De Augmentis*. iii. 5. init.

[67] Dr. Whewell rises into poetry—yet is not more poetical than the philosopher on whom he thus comments. "If he" (Bacon) "had had occasion to develop his simile, full of latent meaning as his similes so often are, he would probably have said, that to these final causes barrenness was no reproach, seeing they ought to be, not the mothers but the daughters of our natural sciences; and that they were barren, not by imperfection of their nature, but in order that they might be kept pure and undefiled, and so fit ministers in the temple of God."— *Bridgewater Treatise*. B. III. Ch. vii. sub. fin.

[68] It is a pleasure to confirm this paragraph by a definition of Design taken from a writer who must be frequently quoted in these pages, because his philosophy is of unusually wide scope, and embraces the mixed sciences employed by a natural theologian:—"We

direct our thoughts to an action which we are about to perform; we intend to do it: we make it our aim: we place it before us, and act with purpose (propositum): we design it, or mark it out beforehand (designo)."— Whewell's *Elements of Morality*, Book I., Chap. i., p. 7.

[69] *The Soul*, p. 35.

[70] *Right and Wrong*, p. 31.

[71] Dans plusieurs passages de ses écrits, quand il insiste avec le plus de force sur l'impossibilité où est la raison humaine d'atteindre à la certitude, il semble tout près d'accepter la révélation divine comme source de certaines grandes verités que nous ne saurions repousser, quoiqu'il ne nous soit pas possible de les démontrer. Un soir qu'à Paris il soupait chez le baron d'Holbach, on vint à parler de la religion naturelle; Hume déclara que pour sa part il n'avait jamais rencontré d'athée. On sait la réponse de son hôte. "Parbleu, vous avez de la chance; pour la première fois vous en rencontrez dix-sept du même coup." Hume ne demanda point à être compté comme le dix-huitième. Dix ans auparavant, il se trouvait à Londres lorsque lui arriva la nouvelle de la mort de sa mère; son ami Boyle, frère du comte de Glasgow, témoin de la douleur profonde où le jeta cette perte, exprima le regret qu'il ne pût trouver de consolation dans les croyances chrétiennes sur la destinée des justes et sur la vie future. "Ah! mon ami," dit Hume en sanglotant, "je peux bien publier mes spéculations pour occuper les savans et les métaphysiciens; mais ne croyez pas que je sois si loin que vous le supposez de penser comme le reste des hommes." *Deux Mondes*, 1856, Vol. VI., pp. 118, 19. The latter anecdote will be found in Burton at rather greater length. Vol. I. 293, 4.

[72] These Dialogues were posthumously published in obedience to their author's will. Hume had kept the MS. by him for twenty-seven years, and had corrected it from time to time, yet had delayed publication from deference to the judgment of his friends. He directed his literary executor, Adam Smith, to publish the Dialogues within two years of his death; but, in consequence of Smith's distaste for the task, this duty devolved upon Hume's nephew. They were printed in 1779 translated into German in 1781, and commented on by Jacobi in 1787.

Lowndes states that these Dialogues were not republished with the "Essays," but is mistaken in saying so. They appear at the end of Vol. II. in the 8vo. Edition of 1788. As this is not an uncommon or expensive book, I quote its paging. The quantity of matter extends only through 113 8vo. pages, and reference will not be difficult in any other Edition.

It seems true that the Dialogues were withdrawn from later reprints of the Essays. They appear to have been considered particularly objectionable; but there is no doubt that they express Hume's most deliberate and matured convictions, and thus become to fair inquirers particularly valuable. It must, however, be added that Hume valued himself on a conservatism of opinion. Comparing, when forty years old, his recent Essays with his Treatise "planned before I was twenty-one and composed before twenty-five," he says, "The philosophical principles are the same in both; but I was carried away by the heat of youth and invention to publish too precipitately." Burton, I. 337.

[73] There can be no doubt that Cleanthes is meant for the representative man, both from the tenor of the Dialogue itself and from a letter to Sir Gilbert Elliot, of Minto, given by Burton, I. 331-6. The following extracts may be acceptable to the reader:—"You would perceive by the sample I have given you, that I make Cleanthes the hero of the

dialogue: whatever you can think of, to strengthen that side of the argument, will be most acceptable to me. Any propensity you imagine I have to the other side, crept in upon me against my will; and 'tis not long ago that I burned an old manuscript book, wrote before I was twenty, which contained, page after page, the gradual progress of my thoughts on that head. It began with an anxious search after arguments, to confirm the common opinion; doubts stole in, dissipated, returned; were again dissipated, returned again; and it was a perpetual struggle of a restless imagination against inclination, perhaps against reason.... I could wish Cleanthes' argument could be so analyzed, as to be rendered quite formal and regular. The propensity of the mind towards it,—unless that propensity were as strong and universal as that to believe in our senses and experience,—will still, I am afraid, be esteemed a suspicious foundation. 'Tis here I wish for your assistance; we must endeavour to prove that this propensity is somewhat different from our inclination to find our own figures in the clouds, our faces in the moon, our passions and sentiments even in inanimate matter. Such an inclination may, and ought to be controlled, and can never be a legitimate ground of assent.

"The instances I have chosen for Cleanthes are, I hope, tolerably happy, and the confusion in which I represent the sceptic seems natural, but—si quid novisti rectius, etc.... He (Cleanthes) allows, indeed, in part 2nd, that all our inference is founded on the similitude of the works of nature to the usual effects of mind, otherwise they must appear a mere chaos. The only difficulty is, why the other assimilations do not weaken the argument; and indeed it would seem from experience and feeling, that they do not weaken it so much as we might naturally expect."

It seems clear on the whole, that, so far as Physico-Theology went, Hume was not ill qualified for a Natural Theologian. All the more so perhaps, because, while seeing the difficulties which attach themselves to this kind of argument, he pronounced it to hold conclusively at last.

[74] The following quotation is from the Treatise "composed before twenty-five":—"Nor does this reasoning only prove, that morality consists not in any relations, that are the objects of science; but if examined, will prove with equal certainty, that it consists not in any matter of fact, which can be discovered by the understanding. This is the second part of our argument; and if it can be made evident, we may conclude, that morality is not an object of reason. But can there be any difficulty in proving, that vice and virtue are not matters of fact, whose existence we can infer by reason?... So that when you pronounce any action or character to be vicious, you mean nothing, but that from the constitution of your nature you have a feeling or sentiment of blame from the contemplation of it. Vice and virtue, therefore, may be compared to sounds, colours, heat and cold, which, according to modern philosophy, are not qualities in objects, but perceptions in the mind: and this discovery in morals, like that other in physics, is to be regarded as a considerable advancement of the speculative sciences; though, like that too, it has little or no influence on practice." Treatise, Book III., part 1, Vol. II., 170, 1.

This 3rd Book of the Treatise was not printed till Hume was in his 30th year; and he felt some hesitation respecting the latter paragraph. "Is not this," he asks Hutcheson, "laid a little too strong? I desire your opinion of it, though I cannot entirely promise to conform myself to it. I wish from my heart I could avoid concluding, that since morality, according to your opinion, as well as mine, is determined merely by sentiment, it regards only human nature and human life.... If morality were determined by reason, that is the same to all rational beings; but nothing but experience can assure us that the sentiments are the same. What experience have we with regard to superior beings? How can we ascribe to them any sentiments at all? They have implanted those sentiments in us for the conduct of life like our bodily sensations, which they possess not themselves." (Burton, I. 119.) The paragraph was, however, published; and helped by consequence to foster in its author's mind that Utilitarian theory of morals respecting which many late writers have been only Hume's copyists. In this very Treatise he did in fact apply that theory to the most important of Social questions (see same Bk., Pt. II. Sec. 12, more especially p. 299), and was thus led into lax conclusions respecting those bonds between Man and Woman which underlie the other foundations of Society. Hume shares this blame with his disciples; for leading Utilitarians are apt to shew by their own domestic relations that the principle, when applied, results in maxims lower than our present English tone of thought upon this subject.

But let us suppose that Hume had lived to analyze Rousseau's Confessions. Would he not have urged with the force of truth, that to animalize a Man is to destroy his Manhood, to weaken his judgment and impair his Moral sense? Would he not have argued from Rousseau the depraved boy, to Rousseau the shop-man and footman, and pointed out that in such cases Truth, Honesty, and Gratitude become mere names and shadows?—No one could have replied that Hume was wrong in fact and experience, but some might have said that all which lowers the supremacy of the Moral sense lowers the Manhood of Man. As Hume admitted the fact of a Moral sense, he might possibly have felt the cogency of this argument.

[75] No one who reads Hume's account of his own motives on various occasions will think it untrue to say that his judgment was largely influenced by his vanity. Compare for example his well-known letter to Dr. Blair of December 20th, 1765, with another to the same, dated 1st July, 1766;—the first a panegyric on the "celebrated Rousseau," the second a fierce invective against that "blackest and most atrocious villain." Who can help seeing that the motives of the eulogy are derived from a series of self-gratulations;—while the cause of the invective is a sharp wound given to the philosopher's self-love?

[76] In the Inquiry concerning Human Understanding, Section XI., he puts this case: "As the universe shows wisdom and goodness, we infer wisdom and goodness. As it shows a particular degree of these perfections, we infer a particular degree of them, precisely adapted to the effect which we examine. But farther attributes or farther degrees of the same attributes, we can never be authorized to infer or suppose, by any rules of just reasoning." The argument of this section upon which Hume's limitations are based, is put into the mouth of a representative Epicurus; it is acute even to extreme subtlety, but it is also suicidal. The restraints applied to what he explains as the argument from effects to cause, and conversely down again from cause to other effects, cannot be maintained without dealing a death blow at the Inductive Philosophy. How little do we know of the material Universe, yet we apply the principle of gravitation to the Whole, seen and unseen. By its aid we find masses of radiant matter previously unknown, and predict events long before they are phenomenally apparent. The vast power of extending knowledge which the Inductive principle asserts, will occur for our investigation in Chapter 4. Another Epicurean position contained in this same Section

XI. has been quoted in a previous note, together with Hume's own reply to it; see pp. 101, 2 ante.

A criticism of Hume's Tenth and Eleventh sections occupies a long note appended by Lord Brougham to his "Discourse on Natural Theology"—a volume I suppose accessible to almost all students of the science.

[77] The word Creation must here be construed strictly, so as to signify a true Beginning;— the idea that is of a law-governed materies mundi, a substantial force, and movement evoked into primary Existence.

The prospect of final change yet to be, is thus similarly connected by a living philosopher (Helmholtz) with the history of our world's Past:—

"We estimate the duration of human History at 6,000 years; but immeasurable as this time may appear to us, what is it in comparison with the time during which the earth carried successive series of rank plants and mighty animals, and no men; during which in our neighbourhood the amber-tree bloomed, and dropped its costly gum on the earth and in the sea; when in Siberia, Europe, and North America groves of tropical palms flourished; where gigantic lizards, and after them elephants, whose mighty remains we still find buried in the earth, found a home? Different geologists, proceeding from different premises, have sought to estimate the duration of the above- named creative period, and vary from a million to nine million years.——The time during which the earth generated organic beings is again small when compared with the ages during which the world was a ball of fused rocks. For the duration of its cooling from 2,000° to 200° Centigrade the experiments of Bishop upon basalt show that about 350 millions of years would be necessary.——And with regard to the time during which the first nebulous mass condensed into our planetary system, our most daring conjectures must cease. The history of man, therefore, is but a short ripple in the ocean of time.——For a much longer series of years than that during which he has already occupied this world, the existence of the present state of inorganic nature favourable to the duration of man seems to be secured, so that for ourselves and for long generations after us we have nothing to fear. But the same forces of air and water, and of the volcanic interior, which produced former geological revolutions, and buried one series of living forms after another, act still upon the earth's crust. They more probably will bring about the last day of the human race than those distant cosmical alterations of which we have spoken, forcing us perhaps to make way for new and more complete living forms, as the lizards and the mammoth have given place to us and our fellow-creatures which now exist.

"Thus the thread which was spun in darkness by those who sought a perpetual motion has conducted us to a universal law of nature, which radiates light into the distant nights of the beginning and of the end of the history of the universe. To our own race it permits a long but not an endless existence; it threatens it with a day of judgment, the dawn of which is still happily obscured. As each of us singly must endure the thought of his death, the race must endure the same. But above the forms of life gone by, the human race has higher moral problems before it, the bearer of which it is, and in the completion of which it fulfils its destiny." Helmholtz, Popular Lectures on Scientific Subjects, p. 191, seq.

The distinguished German had just before observed, "Even though the force store of our planetary system is so immensely great ... still the inexorable laws of mechanics indicate that this store of force, which can only suffer loss and not gain, must be finally exhausted." On the subject of such vast cosmical changes, the reader may like to peruse the remarks of Littré in his most recent volume—"Les choses, ou, pour mieux dire, nos choses sont d'hier, dût cet hier comporter de prodigieuses durées.

"Cette nouveauté est un témoignage que notre monde, notre univers, auront une fin. Ce qui a commencé doit finir, la raison le dit, et toutes nos connaissances physiques le confirment. Le soleil et les étoiles se refroidissent incessamment, versant dans les espaces une chaleur qui ne leur revient jamais. Quelque chauds qu'ils soient, ils le sont chaque jour un peu moins, le calorique s'y épuisera; ils s'éteindront, comme déjà leurs planètes se sont éteintes. Que deviendront ces masses animées d'un mouvement rapide? Nul ne peut le dire. Mais il suffirait d'un choc entre elles pour y transformer un prodigieux mouvement en une prodigieuse incandescence, et y renouveler un cycle de chaleur et d'expansion.

"Ce serait se perdre en vaines et gratuites hypothèses, que de spéculer sur ce que deviendra notre univers quand il aura pris fin, comme de spéculer sur ce qu'il fut avant qu'il eût pris commencement." Littré, *La Science*, pp. 560, 1.

There are thinkers who believe that these cycles, immeasurable to Man, took their governing laws from a supreme Designer. They will be aided by Helmholtz and Littré in shaping their ideas of His far-reaching wisdom and power. There are also thinkers who find within their own inward Being a consciousness of kinship with the Source of Causation, so infinitely beyond cycles apparently infinite. How great then the value of human Spirits bearing His likeness, and with it a promise of surviving the period when our world's cycles shall vanish away in Space—to be replaced by other hereditary cycles, or to be remembered no more for ever!

[78] This article has been lately reprinted in a volume of "Critiques and Addresses," and Leibniz's censure of Newton will be found on p. 323. It may be convenient for some readers to be informed that the Correspondence between Clarke and Leibniz to which I have referred will be found at the end of Erdmann's Opera Leibnitii (Berlin, 1840), a portable and useful Edition. The sentences quoted by me are on page 747.

[79] J. Müller.

[80] Kant.

[81] *Philosophy of Discovery*, Chap. XXX. 23, pp. 369-70.

[82] It is necessary to observe the Professor's limitations.

[83] They have been noted before. In this place it is necessary to examine the following instances.

[84] *Critiques*, p. 306.

[85] *Lay Sermons*, p. 373.

[86] *Critiques*, p. 281.

[87] Ibid. 349.

[88] Professor Max Müller writes as follows.—"If philosophy has to explain what is, not what ought to be, there will be and can be no rest till we admit, what cannot be denied, that there is in man a (third) faculty, which I call simply the faculty of apprehending the Infinite, not only in religion, but in all things; a power independent of sense and reason, a power in a certain sense contradicted by sense and reason, but yet a very real power, which has held its own from the beginning of the world, neither sense nor reason being able to overcome it, while it alone is able to overcome both reason and sense." Max

Muller's *Lectures on the Science of Religion.*—Lect. I. New Ed. p. 20. The use of the word faculty is defended in a note.

I quote this passage with pleasure, because one main objection brought against the possible existence of such a faculty is taken from the negative form of the word Infinite. The Professor maintains that, as a question of Philology, Infinite signifies an affirmative idea. In his Lectures on Language, second series, p. 576. he writes thus. "There is no Infinite, we are told, for as there is a Finite, the Infinite has its limit in the Finite, it cannot be Infinite. Now all this is mere playing on words without thoughts. Why is infinite a negative idea? Because infinite is derived from finite by means of the negative particle in! But this is a mere accident, it is a fact in the history of language, and no more. The same idea may be expressed by the Perfect, the Eternal, the Self-existing, which are positive terms, or contain at least no negative element. That negative words may express positive ideas was known perfectly to Greek philosophers such as Chrysippus, and they would as little have thought of calling immortal a negative idea as they would have considered blind positive. The true idea of the Infinite is neither a negation nor a modification of any other idea. The Finite, on the contrary, is in reality the limitation or modification of the Infinite, nor is it possible, if we reason in good earnest, to conceive of the Finite in any other sense than as the shadow of the Infinite. Even Language will confess to this, if we cross-examine her properly." He adds a happy quotation from Roger Bacon: "'et dicitur infinitum non per privationem terminorum quantitatis, sed per negationem corruptionis et non esse.' Oxford of the nineteenth century need not be ashamed, as far as metaphysics are concerned, of Oxford of the thirteenth." Coleridge's theory of the Intuitive reason is well known to most readers.

[89] *Metaph.* XII. 7.

[90] *Hamilton's Discussions*, vol. 1. Art. 1.

[91] Very few people have ever sate down and sturdily endeavoured to realize before their mind's eye, the distinct idea of any other mind separate from themselves and independently subsistent. A short trial will shew the difficulty, perhaps impossibility of the proposed realization.

Any one who tries and fails, may be glad to learn that eminent metaphysicians have retreated in despair from the task of justifying, by argument, our belief in any minds other than our own. To common sense, it may seem a natural inquiry whether this metaphysical failure holds morally, in foro conscientiae, as a valid excuse for most men's neglect of other men's rights and interests? If not, it would appear that morality is a more delicate test of certainty, than some sorts of metaphysics.

[t] For the information of some readers, and the entertainment of others, a few of the less popularized theories respecting Self-ness or Personal Identity are thrown into Additional Note A.

[u] Nothing is more common in conversation than for a talker to affirm that such and such a position must be untrue "because it is inconceivable." The assertor ought in return to be asked one or two questions, e.g., "Do you mean inconceivable to yourself or to the generality of Mankind?" If the latter, "Is the contradictory also inconceivable?" Again, "Do you mean by the word inconceivable, unthinkable or unimaginable?" Few people clearly consider this last distinction. Further, "If unthinkable, is it absolutely so, or only very difficult to think?" And it seems likewise important to deliberate whether any

position ought to be pronounced absolutely unthinkable, unless the human mind lies under a stern necessity of thinking and accepting its contradictory.

[92] "Conceivable" and other like expressions are always relative to conceiving minds; and what appears either conceivable or inconceivable to one mind, may be the contrary to another. A painter not only conceives,—but draws a Centaur, and places him feeding on a wide plain or sloping hill side. But, can the Physiologist conceive such a monstrosity? The solution is easy; the painter thinks of his figure, the physiologist of the structure; and this example furnishes a good caution as to the use of similar words.

From words we may pass to ideas. Take any conception involving the condition of Time or Space,—(those two optical tubes of our mind's perceiving eye),—and place it before the understanding; first as a Finite and next as an Infinite. The result is a conflict of arguments, ending in a contradiction of all possibility that either way the conception can be true. Any one moderately acquainted with Kant's best-known work, is aware that, by thus treating the world's existence, he raises overwhelming difficulties against its being either limited or unlimited in extent;—eternal or having a commencement in duration;—(p. 338. Ed. Rosenkranz) yet, the world does exist in fact. Kant goes on to subject other cosmological ideas to the same enigmatical reasoning, with the same consequences.

Some readers of purely modern science, may illustrate this question of the "conceivable "by what has been written on that extraordinary riddle, the "four dimensions of space." They will see opinions pro and con in an article by Professor Sylvester in Nature vol. 1. A note (p. 238) contains one conclusion of the Professor's, interesting as his answer to a question asked by us a few paragraphs back. He says, "If an Aristotle, or Descartes, or Kant assures me that he recognises God in the conscience, I accuse my own blindness if I fail to see with him.... I acknowledge two separate sources of authority,—the collective sense of mankind, and the illumination of privileged intellects." Plato then may have really seen more than Lucretius—Coleridge more than Comte or Littré.

[v] The advantages and defects of the optical structure of our human eyes have been carefully estimated by Helmholtz. He has also discussed the difficulties attending eyesight considered as a sensation and perception. Extracts from his clear yet popular Lectures are given in Additional Note B.

[93] *Proceedings of the Royal Institution.* V. 456.

[94] All theories of light require these immense numbers. Sir J. Herschel says there is no "mode of conceiving the subject which does not call upon us to admit the exertion of mechanical forces which may well be termed infinite." The numeration in the text is a rough and ready shape of statement at once intelligible. But it is interesting to view the subject more exactly.—Light travels in one second 192,000 miles. Each mile contains 63,360 inches, and in each inch are 39,000 waves of red light, calculated at their mean length. Now, multiply these three sets of figures together, and we get a rate of 474,439,680,000,000 red waves per second. The mean length of a violet wave is the 1/57500th part of an inch; and by a like multiplication we find a product of 699,494,400,000,000 of violet light-strokes thrown upon the retina in each second. The phrase "millions of millions" is used in the text, because few people realize the idea of any arithmetical whole beyond a million.

[95] "What we hear" writes Professor Max Müller "when listening to a chorus or a symphony is a commotion of elastic air, of which the wildest sea would give a very inadequate

image. The lowest tone which the ear perceives is due to about 30 vibrations in one second, the highest to about 4,000. Consider then what happens in a Presto when thousands of voices and instruments are simultaneously producing waves of air, each wave crossing the other, not only like the surface waves of the water, but like spherical bodies, and, as it would seem, without any perceptible disturbance; consider that each tone is accompanied by secondary tones, that each instrument has its peculiar timbre, due to secondary vibrations; and, lastly, let us remember that all this cross-fire of waves, all this whirlpool of sound, is moderated by laws which determine what we call harmony, and by certain traditions or habits which determine what we call melody— both these elements being absent in the songs of birds—that all this must be reflected like a microscopic photograph on the two small organs of hearing, and there excite not only perception, but perception followed by a new feeling even more mysterious, which we call either pleasure or pain; and it will be clear that we are surrounded on all sides by miracles transcending all we are accustomed to call miraculous, and yet disclosing to the genius of an Euler or a Newton laws which admit of the most minute mathematical determination." *Science of Language*, Second Series, p. 115.

[96] There is a much more scientific mode of trying this experiment. A description of the instrument (Kaleidophone), and cuts of the figures produced, may be seen in Tyndall on Sound, pp. 132. seq.

[97] There is reason for believing that a large proportion of animal eyes see much as ours do when in a normal state. Colour blindness is frequent in Man and occurs between red and green, yet a bull distinguishes the two like a healthy, human being. He is allured by the sight of a green field, and lashes himself into fury when a red rag is waved before him.

The eyes of insects are very far removed in structure from ours. A butterfly's compound eye contains 17,000 tubes, that of the Mordella beetle 25,000. Their perception of colours appears vivid and distinct. They resemble birds, reptiles, and other creatures in choosing for their lairs and resting-places objects coloured like themselves. It is not difficult to mount one of these compound eyes, so as to look through it by aid of a lens placed in focus. Leeuwenhoeck looked through the eye of a dragon fly (made up of 12,544 tubes), "and viewed the steeple of a church which was 299 feet high, and 750 feet from the place where he stood. He could plainly see the steeple, though not apparently larger than the point of a fine needle. He also viewed a house in the same manner, and could discern the front, distinguish the doors and windows, and perceive whether they were open or shut." See *Insect Miscellanies*, p. 129.

[98] Two points connected with colour admit of being easily experimented on, and deserve from their interest to be made the subjects of repeated observations.

The first has relation to the question of primary colours;—are they alike in man and in all the lower animals?—In birds and reptiles there are anatomical reasons for believing the primaries to be red, yellow, and blue. But are they the same in our race?—may they not more probably be red, green, and violet? In this case yellow is the transition from red to green, blue from green to violet. As colour blindness consists in an insensibility to red, and as the outer circle of the field of vision is feeble in its reds, the number of experiments which might be suggested is evidently considerable. Let a person place two threads respectively red and green near the bridge of the nose, so as to be seen by the inner angle of the pupil only. If dexterously moved, both seem green;—if not, both will in time become black. Where the want of sensitive appreciation of red is great, the same result follows in every part of the field of sight. Thus reverend gentlemen in former times have been induced to wear scarlet hose under the impression that they had put on black silk; and in these railroad days many persons find themselves unable to distinguish between the safety and the danger signal lights. It seems strange indeed that any scientific advisers of railway Boards should have recommended for use the two colours, above all others, most likely to get confounded.

The theory which supposes red, green, and violet to be Man's three primary colours is the hypothesis of our great countryman Dr. Thomas Young, and deserves much more consideration than was for a long time awarded it. If we may judge of his theory by his appreciation of pictures it must have been excellent;—the present writer saw with admiration in 1845 the grand series of Reynolds' portraits which Dr. Young had left behind him.

The second topic of interest is the inquiry into the number and tone of subjective colours. A perfect theory of colour ought, of course, to embrace all possible human sensations of the kind. Now many persons are able to see in dreams a rich amber light far softer and more pure than any tint ever beheld by the Eye. It generally appears to irradiate Space, and silvery figures, most often the celestial orbs, float within it. A still more beautiful production of reflex energy exerted after tranquil rest is the blending of delicate green with a hyacinthine hue quite strange to this world, and indescribably lovely in its tender shadings off. By means of this subjective activity the experiments of Goethe and J. Müller may be varied almost ad libitum. The easiest plan is on first waking to keep the eyelids steadily closed, and watch for the unbidden rise of tints. Persons of strong pictorial and poetic powers can, after some practice, control their appearance and succession; and much diversity may be produced by slightly separating the fringe of eyelashes and looking between the loosely pressed fingers. The remarkable point in these and similar experiments seems to be that we are thus enabled to gaze upon beauties more marvellous than the outward eye ever beheld—yet we see them.

Another and a painful source of knowledge on this subject consists in registering the visual impressions of persons bodily or mentally diseased. The difference between these and the normal impressions of healthy people would seem to arise from reflex action, the disordered sensory or mind reacting upon the optic apparatus; or, as it may be said, the centre of our being is through these aberrations made manifest in its control of the circumference.

Now, it will be obvious to any reflective person how very important all information we can acquire respecting this central empire over the impressions of our sense-nerves may become when we try to estimate the conditions of human knowledge. If it be true that the Mind imposes laws of activity on the nervous system even when receiving impressions from it, then the necessity we are under of thinking in accordance with certain inly imposed laws receives a most striking illustration. And the inference from it carries an a fortiori probability since our thoughts lie nearer to our mental centre than any of our sense-impressions.

[99] Nerves of common feeling are acutely sensitive when divided, and the patient animal under a Majendie or a dentist utters a sharp shriek. The case is different with motor nerves, with those of the sympathetic system, and with (what is more to our purpose) nerves of sensation. It seems clear that mechanical injuries, or even touches, excite

them in the direction of their own special functions. Auditory nerves feel a shock as a sound,—optic nerves receive it as a sudden and brilliant light. We are doubly assured from these effects of the true functions belonging to the several sets of nerves. Disease and injury are great discoverers of what ought to be healthy susceptibilities. In such cases, however, they prove also something more agreeable to think upon.

They prove that suffering is confined within definite limits, and that economy of pain forms part of the universal design, for the sensitive animal as well as the sensitive man. If all our nerves shrank equally with equal tenderness, life would be a history of protracted agony. Yet one might have expected, primâ facie, that a fibre which telegraphs shapes and colours with their blendings, would eloquently tell the story of its own occasional anguish. And our whole nervous framework might have been conceived as an instrument of torture. It has not been so constituted.

Per contra, the nerves of common feeling assert their own vocation.—"A brazen canstick turned" sets the teeth on edge, and troubles the skin with horripilation. Believers in ghosts—and also disbelievers—are aware that some sights

"Make knotted and combined locks to part,
And each particular hair to stand on end."

For extended information on this subject compare Additional Note C.

[100] Aristotle so described it before Mr. Bain and other modern writers, " τὸ γὰρ ὁρατόν ἐστι χρῶμα, " De Anima II. 7. 1. As Kampe carefully observes, "so ist die Farbe (nicht die gefärbten Körper) das Eigenthümliche des Gesichtssinns." See also his note, Erkenntnisstheorie des Aristoteles, p. 88.

[w] Compare Helmholtz on "The Sensation of Sight," *Lectures*, pp. 256, 7, and 259.

"We have already seen enough to answer the question whether it is possible to maintain the natural and innate conviction that the quality of our sensations, and especially our sensations of sight, give us a true impression of corresponding qualities in the outer world. It is clear that they do not. The question was really decided by Johannes Müller's deduction from well ascertained facts of the law of specific nervous energy. Whether the rays of the sun appear to us as colour, or as warmth, does not at all depend upon their own properties, but simply upon whether they excite the fibres of the optic nerve, or those of the skin. Pressure upon the eyeball, a feeble current of electricity passed through it, a narcotic drug carried to the retina by the blood, are capable of exciting the sensation of light just as well as the sunbeams. The most complete difference offered by our several sensations, that namely between those of sight, of hearing, of taste, of smell, and of touch—this deepest of all distinctions, so deep that it is impossible to draw any comparison of likeness, or unlikeness, between the sensations of colour and of musical tones—does not, as we now see, at all depend upon the nature of the external object, but solely upon the central connections of the nerves which are affected.... But not only uneducated persons, who are accustomed to trust blindly to their senses, even the educated, who know that their senses may be deceived, are inclined to demur to so complete a want of any closer correspondence in kind between actual objects and the sensations they produce than the law I have just expounded. For instance, natural philosophers long hesitated to admit the identity of the rays of light and of heat, and exhausted all possible means of escaping a conclusion which seemed to contradict the evidence of their senses.

"Another example is that of Goethe, as I have endeavoured to show elsewhere. He was led to contradict Newton's theory of colours, because he could not persuade himself that white, which appears to our sensation as the purest manifestation of the brightest light, could be composed of darker colours. It was Newton's discovery of the composition of light that was the first germ of the modern doctrine of the true functions of the senses; and in the writings of his contemporary, Locke, were correctly laid down the most important principles on which the right interpretation of sensible qualities depends. But, however clearly we may feel that here lies the difficulty for a large number of people, I have never found the opposite conviction of certainty derived from the senses so distinctly expressed that it is possible to lay hold of the point of error: and the reason seems to me to lie in the fact that beneath the popular notions on the subject lie other and more fundamentally erroneous conceptions."

[101] Is there, asks Idealistic Scepticism, any outside world at all?

We have all of us always believed in the veritable existence of this outside world from our childhood. So have we believed always in our own real and continued personal existence. The unyielding objectivities concerning which our senses inform us—the identical Self which receives their information—are entities no man ordinarily thinks of calling in question.

Let any one sit down and try to imagine himself a human animal let loose upon life without a firm belief in either of these two primary convictions. What could life be to him? to his descendants? to the world of men if similarly unbelieving? Yet what are the conditions or evidences of veracity upon which his and his fellows' present convictions must necessarily repose? Can he and others help believing them true? and why?—This "why" is a safe answer to the most plausible as well as the most refined objection against such primary beliefs as those premised by Natural Theology.

[102] Cheselden's case is reported in the Philosophical Transactions for 1728, and also in his Anatomy. Respecting the point above quoted he is confirmed by Mr. Nunneley, " On the Organs of Vision," 1858.

[103] See Dr. Carpenter's *Principles of Human Physiology*. Ed. 7. p. 713. § 635.

[x] The following quaint apology for our senses at the expense of our understanding may be new to the majority of my readers:—

"We have seen two notorious instances of sensitive deception, which justifie the charge of Petron. Arbiter.

Fallunt nos oculi, vagique sensus
Oppressâ ratione mentiuntur.

And yet to speak properly, and to do our senses right, simply they are not deceived, but only administer an occasion to our forward understandings to deceive themselves: and so though they are some way accessory to our delusion; yet the more principal faculties are the Capital offenders. Thus if the Senses represent the Earth as fixt and immoveable; they give us the truth of their Sentiments: To sense it is so, and it would be deceit to present it otherwise. For (as we have shewn) though it do move in itself; it rests to us, who are carry'd with it.... But if hence our Understandings falsely deduct, that there is the same quality in the external impressor; 'tis, it is criminal, our sense is innocent. When the Ear tingles, we really hear a sound: If we judge it without us, it's the fallacy of our Judgments. The apparitions of our frighted Phancies are real sensibles: But if we translate them without the compass of our Brains, and apprehend them as external objects; it's the unwary rashness of our Understanding deludes us. And if our disaffected Palates resent nought but bitterness from our choicest viands, we truly tast the unpleasing quality, though falsely conceive it in that, which is no more then the occasion of its production. If any find fault with the novelty of the notion; the learned St. Austin stands ready to confute the charge: and they who revere Antiquity, will derive satisfaction from so venerable a suffrage. He tells us, Si quis remum frangi in aquâ opinatur, et, cum aufertur,integrari; non malum habet internuncium, sed malus est Judex. And onward to this purpose, The sense could not otherwise perceive it in the water, neither ought it: For since the Water is one thing, and the Air another; 'tis requisite and necessary, that the sense should be as different as the medium: Wherefore the Eye sees aright; if there be a mistake, 'tis the Judgement's the Deceiver. Elsewhere he saith, that our Eyes misinform us not, but faithfully transmit their resentment to the mind. And against the Scepticks, That it's a piece of injustice to complain of our senses, and to exact from them an account, which is beyond the sphear of their notice: and resolutely determines, Quicquid possunt videre oculi, verum vident. So that what we have said of the senses deceptions, is rigidly to be charg'd only on our careless Understandings, misleading us through the ill management of sensible informations." Glanvill, *Vanity of Dogmatizing*. Chap. x. First Ed. p. 91, seq.

The reader may like to consider how far Glanvill's apology for the senses is removed from the following propositions laid down by a recent writer just quoted who thus defends while he limits the veracity of sense-impressions:—

"What we directly apprehend," writes Professor Helmholtz, "is not the immediate action of the external exciting cause upon the ends of our nerves, but only the changed condition of the nervous fibres which we call the state of excitation or functional activity." And further on:—"The simple rule for all illusions of sight is this: we always believe that we see such objects as would, under conditions of normal vision, produce the retinal image of which we are actually conscious. If these images are such as could not be produced by any normal kind of observation, we judge of them according to their nearest resemblance; and in forming this judgment, we more easily neglect the parts of sensation which are imperfectly than those which are perfectly apprehended. When more than one interpretation is possible, we usually waver involuntarily between them; but it is possible to end this uncertainty by bringing the idea of any of the possible interpretations we choose as vividly as possible before the mind by a conscious effort of the will." Helmholtz on *The Recent Progress of the Theory of Vision*. pp. 230, 31 and p. 307.

[104] Two acute reasoners, who will be alternately acquitted of madness by contending schools of thought, have arrived at conclusions very favourable to the sanity of idealizing men. In his first lecture at the Royal Institution, Professor Masson spoke in the following terms of Hume and Fichte. "There is the system of Nihilism, or, as it may be better called, Non-Substantialism. According to this system, the Phaenomenal Cosmos, whether regarded as consisting of two parallel successions of phaenomena (Mind and Matter), or of only one (Mind or Matter), resolves itself, on analysis, into an absolute Nothingness,—mere appearances with no credible substratum of Reality; a play of phantasms in a void. If there have been no positive or dogmatic Nihilists, yet both Hume for one purpose, and Fichte for another, have propounded Nihilism as the ultimate issue of all reasoning that does not start with some à priori postulate."—Recent

British Philosophy, p. 66. The reader will observe that to raise the question fully, we have spoken of the special form of Idealism to which Mr. Mill gives the first place in his description, (Examination of Hamilton's Philosophy, p. 8.) "According to one of the forms, the sensations which, in common parlance, we are said to receive from objects, are not only all that we can possibly know of the objects, but are all that we have any ground for believing to exist.——Those who hold this opinion are said to doubt or deny the existence of matter. They are sometimes called by the name Idealists, sometimes by that of Sceptics, according to the other opinions which they hold. They include the followers of Berkeley and those of Hume. Among recent thinkers, the acute and accomplished Professor Ferrier, though by a circuitous path, and expressing himself in a very different phraseology, seems to have arrived at essentially the same point of view. These philosophers maintain the Relativity of our knowledge in the most extreme form in which the doctrine can be understood, since they contend, not merely that all we can possibly know of anything is the manner in which it affects the human faculties, but that there is nothing else to be known; that affections of human or of some other minds are all that we can know to exist."

Mr. Mill's own position will be found in his 11th Chapter. After defining Matter to be a "Permanent Possibility of Sensation," (p. 227) and explaining his definition, he writes in a note (p. 232), the following decisive sentences: "My able American critic, Dr. H. B. Smith, contends through several pages that these facts afford no proofs that objects are external to us. I never pretended that they do. I am accounting for our conceiving, or representing to ourselves, the Permanent Possibilities as real objects external to us. I do not believe that the real externality to us of anything, except other minds, is capable of proof."

Mr. O'Hanlon's pamphlet entitled "A Criticism of John Stuart Mill's Pure Idealism; and an attempt to shew that, if logically carried out, it is Pure Nihilism," seems less known than it deserves to be. Mr. Mill noticed and answered it in his 3rd Edition—chiefly among the criticisms commencing p. 244.——Mr. O'Hanlon's early decease has given a painful interest to his promising labours. Some paragraphs from his now scarce pamphlet are placed at the end of Additional Note D, on "Pure Idealism."

[105] On Hamilton. p. 6. Mill is thus echoed from across the broad Atlantic;—"The profoundest question of philosophy turns on the relation of Thought to Being, Mind to Matter, Subject to Object, or (in empiricistic phrase) Organism to Environment. Is the Organism purely the product of the Environment? Then we have Empiricism, Sensationalism, Materialism, whose motto is that of Destutt-Tracy,—" Penser c'est sentir." Is the Environment the product of the Organism? Then we have Transcendentalism, Egoism, Idealism, whose motto is that of Berkeley,—"The esse of objects is percipi." F. E. Abbot, in *The Index (American)*, for July 27, 1872.

[106] Lord Macaulay has some pertinent and characteristic remarks concerning this topic in his literary estimate of Dr. Johnson. "How it chanced that a man who reasoned on his premises so ably, should assume his premises so foolishly, is one of the great mysteries of human nature. The same inconsistency may be observed in the schoolmen of the middle ages. Those writers show so much acuteness and force of mind in arguing on their wretched data, that a modern reader is perpetually at a loss to comprehend how such minds came by such data. Not a flaw in the superstructure of the theory which they are rearing escapes their vigilance. Yet they are blind to the obvious unsoundness of the

foundation. It is the same with some eminent lawyers. Their legal arguments are intellectual prodigies, abounding with the happiest analogies and the most refined distinctions. The principles of their arbitrary science being once admitted, the statute-book and the reports being once assumed as the foundations of reasoning, these men must be allowed to be perfect masters of logic. But if a question arises as to the postulates on which their whole system rests, if they are called upon to vindicate the fundamental maxims of that system which they have passed their lives in studying, these very men often talk the language of savages or of children." (*Essays*, Ed. 1852. p. 175.) As to the schoolmen, any one who wishes to form a fair idea of their acuteness with little trouble to himself, may consult the "Synopsis Distinctionum" of H. L. Castanaeus, a book found in most learned libraries.

[y] See Additional Note E.—The great interest of this subject for our purpose lies in the circumstance that the relation of Theory to Fact is in effect a question most closely akin to the one already mooted concerning the relation of our Sensations to our Perceptions (compare Additional Note B). These two questions are indeed so very similar as to be in the main identical. What we want to learn regarding both relations, is, first, the extent of the relativity to our human nature; in other words how much we have mentally put into our Theories and Sensations before we treat them as Facts and Perceptions. Secondly, what reason we have for believing any of our knowledge comprehended under either or both of these relativities (Perception and Fact) to be true beyond our human sphere; and, above all, whether we are able to assert, on good grounds, that such and such parts of either kind of our knowledge are absolutely and immutably true?—

If, for example, we ask—Is it thus true that there are real objects external to ourselves? "I do not believe," Mr. Mill has told us, "that the real externality to us of anything, except other minds, is capable of proof." And a few lines further, "The view I take of externality, in the sense in which I acknowledge it as real, could not be more accurately expressed than in Professor Fraser's words." These are "For ourselves we can conceive only—(1) An externality to our present and transient experience in our own possible experience past and future, and (2) An externality to our own conscious experience, in the contemporaneous, as well as in the past or future experience of other minds." (On Hamilton. p. 232, note.) This explanation, Mill had just before observed, is an externality in the only sense we need care about; and it means in plain words, that we possess no absolutely true but only some utilitarian knowledge of the real existence of an outside world. We must, however, and do care infinitely more for another kind of answer to quite another kind of question. Is the antithesis between Right and Wrong,—the Moral Imperative "Do this and live, transgress and die,"—absolutely and immutably true? If not, who would calculate profit and loss as they are calculated in the Gospel; who would or could believe in a Righteous that is to say, a Real and True God?

Many minds, appalled by the vastness of these issues, and finding no satisfactory answer to questions of such infinite importance, have fallen back on the position of Dr. Newman in his Grammar of Assent. But the unsatisfactory characteristic attaching to this position, is that there seems to be no limit to such Assents, because there appears no Reasonable canon or maxim to explain, defend, and regulate them. To the far larger number of minds the problem states itself as a dilemma. There are exactly two alternatives open to Man. His choice lies between two contrasted positions—the most antagonistic conceivable, yet both resulting from one common supposed fact. Ignorance

and impotence are the truest characters inscribed upon our Reason. Man must decide either for an unlimited Doubt such as that which Hume delineates, wide as the universal whole of our human Existence; or else yield the kind of Assent to which Dr. Newman invites as being the sole secure refuge for any soul driven by despair into a recoil from utter absence of belief and hope—the want of everything to trust and love. Now, let it be observed that an assent transcending reasonable proof is, in effect, a confession that Reason falls short of establishing those transcendental truths to which the mind has thus assented. And contrariwise, limitless Doubt making all else uncertain, affirms with unmistakeable decisiveness the impotence of human Reason.—"The observation of human blindness and weakness," says Hume, "is the result of all philosophy, and meets us at every turn, in spite of our endeavours to elude or avoid it." Hence, we see that Hume's conclusion is identical with that underlying a position directly antagonistic to his own, and in this respect les extrêmes se touchent.

It follows, then, with equal clearness, that any Dilemma which restricts human choice to the two alternatives above stated, rests upon a denial that Man's Reason can guide Mankind to truth—(and by consequence that he can ever feel after and find his God);—whilst, conversely, this same denial, if posited as a basis of speculation, permits no human choice beyond the two horns of a Dilemma thus made necessarily imperative upon us all.

Neither alternative, however, can be accepted by the Natural Theologian, nor can he possibly receive any such Dilemma as founded in Truth or Reason. On the one hand the Superhuman, and Supernatural lie outside his science which has for its sphere Nature, including Man's Nature; and which steadily endeavours to attain the true interpretation and evidence yielded by both Natures, to a belief extending beyond their present territory and fluent conditions. On the other hand, his science becomes impossible if unlimited Doubt is the sole dreary prospect open to the philosophic inquirer. And with his science all other sciences must perish. Doubt saps the foundations of them all; common-sense facts, scientific theories, and practical every-day beliefs, are all impartially shewn to be baseless. So far as our realities are concerned

"We are such stuff
As dreams are made on; and our little life
Is rounded with a sleep."

Science is therefore an alien from Man's world; the soul an outcast amid her own:—

"As in strange lands a traveller walking slow,
In doubt and great perplexity,
A little before moon-rise hears the low
Moan of an unknown sea;

"And knows not if it be thunder or a sound
Of stones thrown down, or one deep cry
Of great wild beasts; then thinketh, 'I have found
A new land, but I die.'"

"Not for this," says the same reflective poet—

"Not for this
Was common clay ta'en from the common earth,
Moulded by God, and tempered with the tears
Of angels to the perfect shape of man."

Let it be observed in conclusion, that the mode in which common-sense people are accustomed to treat the primary tenets of most sciences, and the validity of their own ordinary beliefs, may be placed in curious contrast with their attitude towards the proofs of Natural Theology. In the former case, acceptance is easy and wholesale; in the latter, every mind seems to bristle with objections. Now there are evidently thousands who must surrender their judgments to the demands of a present and pressing utility, and must take upon trust a multitude of maxims which they can never hope to investigate. The difficulties necessarily involved in each and all of these easy acceptations thus remain unsuspected, and cannot therefore be placed side by side with the difficulties of Theism.

But, next arises a serious question. How far can a similar facility of wholesale acceptance and a similar absence of comparison with deeper truths, be considered a philosophic or even a fair procedure in the case of men and women who think themselves into Atheism?

[z] Neither can it be too often repeated that practical truth involves an enormous amount of speculative difficulty, and is received as the daily basis of human action in the face of doubts, which speculatively considered are absolutely insoluble. There is (as will appear in Chapter 4) reason to extend this remark beyond what is commonly called practical truth far into the realm of speculative knowledge, or to speak more exactly, of all knowledge whatsoever. Suppose, for instance, the continuity of our inward power of receiving sense-impressions, of knowing, and reasoning; (our personal Identity) is a groundless belief;—Suppose too that our sense-impressions are reflections from self-created shadows and not from objective realities;— where can any knowledge be truly subsistent save in that place of exile now generally termed "the Unknowable"? Compare Additional Notes A and B appended to this present Chapter.

[107] *La Philosophie en France.* IX. p. 66.

[108] *First Principles*, p. 108.

[109] *Lay Sermon* delivered on Sunday, Jan. 7, 1866; in the collected vol. pp. 19, 20.

[110] *Essays* I. p. 190.

[111] Ibid. p. 211.

[aa] Mr. Herbert Spencer has been freely criticized by Americans, in part as not being sufficiently thorough—in part as being untrue to his own position. A few quotations will be found in Additional Note F, on "The Unknowable."

[ab] The paragraph, taken in its entireness, is pervaded with the vivid sense of a Moral Law which can neither change nor perish—a Law at once human and Divine. This strong protest is both in thought and expression a complete contrast to the ordinary tone of Mr. Mill's disquisitions, attempered as they generally are between benevolence and expediency. Instead of pondering the Utilities of a race which, comparatively speaking, began to exist yesterday, it appeals with decisive sternness, once and for ever, to the Immutable and the Absolute. It reminds one of a torch-bearing Prometheus pitted against the selfish despot of a new and morally enfeebled Olympus. See Additional Note G.

[112] This sentence contains two propositions; the question of speculative perplexity has been treated in this Chapter—that of reasonable necessity is reserved for our next.

[113] *On Hamilton*, p. 242.

[114] *Mill on Hamilton*, p. 232, note.

[115] Ibid. p. 233, note.

[116] Ibid. p. 227.

[117] *British Association Report*, 1870. lxxvii. lxxxiv.

[118] The remark above made respecting a " living laboratory " will be readily understood by every one who remembers the great mistakes committed, some years ago, in treating the stomach as a mere chemical workshop;—forgetful of its all-important endowment,— vitality. That oversight has been alluded to here because it may yield a lesson to Psychologists; for may not a far higher kind of endowment in like manner be forgotten when men materialize the principles one and all on which is conditioned the transforming power of mental assimilation?

[119] *Lay Sermons*, p. 160.

[120] And of more than one as we shall see hereafter. Its point will be best understood upon a perusal of Additional Notes F and I.

[121] All these quotations will be found between pp. 332 and 360 of the *Treatise*. Ed. 1817.

[122] Compare Mr. Green's *Introduction to Hume's Treatise on Human Nature*, Vol. I., pp. 263, seq., where he discusses the bearing of this subject upon Hume's doctrine of Cause and Effect.

[123] He sums up in the words of Goethe, thus given in the translation of his lectures from which we have quoted—
"Woe! woe!
Thou hast destroyed The beautiful world With powerful fist;
In ruin 'tis hurled,
By the blow of a demigod shattered. The scattered
Fragments into the void we carry, Deploring
The beauty perished beyond restoring."

[124] "All the different sorts of rays which I have mentioned produce one effect in common. They raise the temperature of the objects on which they fall, and accordingly are all felt by our skin as rays of heat." (p. 237.)

[125] The former of these two latter quotations has been cited already in a foot-note on p. 164 ante. It is repeated here for the sake of bringing together Masson's classification of Fichte, first as "Pure Idealist," and secondly as "Nihilist." Mr. O'Hanlon's criticism of Mill reaches exactly the same goal as regards that subtle controversialist. His position is that Mill's Pure Idealism when analysed, turns out to be Pure Nihilism.

[126] Compare Note B preceding.

[127] In the pamphlet referred to p. 165 ante, note. The quotations in our text commence on its 5th page. The subject will be most easily comprehended after a reperusal of the argument of Chap. III. pp. 164-172 inclusive.

[128] On p. 14 the ingenious writer adds a further argument based on Mill's admissions. "If the fire apart from my consciousness be some positive condition or conditions of warmth and light, if the corn be some positive condition or conditions of food, my thesis is made out, and your Pure Idealism falls to the ground. If, on the other hand, 'the fire' be nothing positive apart from my consciousness, then, since it is nothing at all when so apart, you can have no right to speak of 'modifications' taking place in it, whether we are asleep or awake, present or absent."

[129] It is worth observing how truly our Bishop anticipated the vulgar objection against his theory. Towards the end of his Dialogues Hylas (who clings to the olden elemental

nature) speaks thus: "To say, There is no Matter in the World, is still shocking to me. Whereas to say—There is no Matter, if by that Term be meant an unthinking Substance existing without the Mind; but if by Matter is meant some sensible Thing, whose Existence consists in being perceived, then there is Matter:—this Distinction gives it quite another Turn; and Men will come into your Notions with small Difficulty, when they are proposed in that manner." Lord Byron condescended to repeat the "coxcombs' grin"—

"When Bishop Berkeley said there was no matter,
And prov'd it—'twas no matter what he said."

[130] Read for example the following eloquent passages from Berkeley's "Three Dialogues." Philonous, who represents Berkeley himself, says: "To me it is evident, for the Reasons you allow of, that sensible Things cannot exist otherwise than in a Mind or Spirit. Whence I conclude, not that they have no real Existence, but that seeing they depend not on my Thought, and have an Existence distinct from being perceived by me, there must be some other Mind wherein they exist. As sure, therefore, as the sensible World really exists, so sure is there an infinite omnipresent Spirit who contains and supports it. "Hylas. What! This is no more than I and all Christians hold; nay, and all others too who believe there is a God, and that he knows and comprehends all Things.

"Phil. Ay, but here lies the Difference. Men commonly believe that all Things are known or perceived by God, because they believed the Being of a God, whereas I, on the other side, immediately and necessarily conclude the Being of a God, because all sensible Things must be perceived by Him.

"Hylas. But so long as we all believe the same thing, what matter is it how we come by that Belief?

"Phil. But neither do we agree in the same Opinion. For Philosophers, tho' they acknowledge all corporeal Beings to be perceived by God, yet they attribute to them an absolute Subsistence distinct from their being perceived by any Mind whatever, which I do not. Besides, is there no Difference between saying, There is a God, therefore he perceives all Things: and saying, Sensible Things do really exist: and if they really exist, they are necessarily perceived by an infinite Mind: therefore there is an infinite Mind, or God? This furnishes you with a direct and immediate Demonstration, from a most evident Principle, of the Being of a God ....

Hylas. It cannot be denied, there is something highly serviceable to Religion in what you advance. But do you not think it looks very like a Notion entertained by some eminent Moderns, of seeing all things in God?

Phil. I would gladly know that Opinion; pray explain it to me.

Hylas. They conceive that the Soul, being immaterial, is incapable of being united with material Things, so as to perceive them in themselves, but that she perceives them by her Union with the Substance of God, which being spiritual, is therefore purely intelligible, or capable of being the immediate Object of a Spirit's Thought. Besides, the Divine Essence contains in it Perfections correspondent to each created Being; and which are, for that Reason, proper to exhibit or represent them to the Mind.

Phil. I do not understand how our Ideas, which are Things altogether passive and inert, can be the Essence, or any Part (or like any Part) of the Essence or Substance of God, who is an impassive, indivisible, purely active Being. Many more Difficulties and Objections there are, which occur at first View against this Hypothesis, but I shall only add, that it is liable to all the Absurdities of the common Hypotheses in making a created World exist otherwise than in the Mind of a Spirit. Beside all which it has this peculiar to itself; that it makes that material World serve to no Purpose. And if it pass for a good Argument against other Hypotheses in the Sciences, that they suppose Nature or the Divine Wisdom to make something in vain, or do that by tedious round-about Methods, which might have been performed in a much more easy and compendious way, what shall we think of that Hypothesis which supposes the whole World made in vain?

Hylas. But what say you, are not you too of Opinion that we see all Things in God? If I mistake not, what you advance comes near it.

Phil. I entirely agree with what the Holy Scripture saith, That in God we live, and move, and have our Being. But that we see Things in his Essence after the manner above set forth, I am far from believing. Take here in brief my Meaning. It is evident that the Things I perceive are my own Ideas, and that no Idea can exist, unless it be in a Mind. Nor is it less plain that these Ideas or Things by me perceived, either themselves or their Archetypes exist independently of my Mind, since I know myself not to be their Author, it being out of my Power to determine at Pleasure what particular Ideas I shall be affected with upon opening my Eyes or Ears. They must therefore exist in some other Mind, whose Will it is they should be exhibited to me. The Things, I say, immediately perceived, are Ideas or Sensations, call them which you will. But how can any Idea or Sensation exist in, or be produced by, anything but a Mind or Spirit? This, indeed, is inconceivable: and to assert that which is inconceivable, is to talk Nonsense: Is it not?.

Hylas. Without doubt.

Phil. But on the other hand, it is very conceivable that they should exist in, and be produced by, a Spirit; since this is no more than I daily experience in myself, inasmuch as I perceive numberless Ideas; and by an Act of my Will can form a great Variety of them, and raise them up in my Imagination: Tho' it must be confessed, these Creatures of the Fancy are not altogether so distinct, so strong, vivid, and permanent, as those perceived by my Senses, which latter are called Real Things. From all which I conclude, there is a Mind which affects me every Moment with all the sensible Impressions I perceive. And from the Variety, Order, and Manner of these, I conclude the Author of them to be wise, powerful, and good, beyond comprehension. Mark it well, I do not say, I see Things by perceiving that which represents them in the intelligible Substance of God. This I do not understand; but I say, The Things by me perceived are known by the Understanding, and produced by the Will, of an infinite Spirit. And is not all this most plain and evident? Is there any more in it, than what a little Observation of our own Minds, and that which passes in them not only enables us to conceive, but also obliges us to acknowledge?"

Numberless charming quotations might be added from the "Principles" as well as the Dialogues, but those already given may suffice, and they have been chosen now because not very commonly quoted.

[131] *Hegel Encyklopädie T.* i. S. 95. (Werke VI. 189.) The quotation above is from Mr. Wallace's translation p. 153. Compare his Index.

[132] In the just published Edition of Hume's Treatise on Human Nature, I. p. 140. We must all regret the loss of Dean Mansel's ultimate thoughts on "The real error of Berkeley's Idealism."

Letters &c. p. 391. But more than a dozen years earlier, he wrote, (*Prolegomena Logica*, Chap. V.) "The fault of Berkeley did not consist in doubting the existence of matter, but in asserting its non-existence." How far Mansel himself went in the direction of this same doubt may be judged from the following passage, which occurs in the Prolegomena one page before. "Beyond the range of conscious beings, we can have only a negative idea of substance. The name is applied in relation to certain collections of sensible phenomena, natural or artificial, connected with each other in various ways; by locomotion, by vegetation, by contributing to a common end, by certain positions in space. But here we have no positive notion of substance distinct from phenomena. I do not attribute to the billiard ball a consciousness of its own figure, colour, and motion; but, in denying consciousness, I deny the only form in which unity and substance have been presented to me. I have therefore no data for thinking one way or the other on the question. Some kind of unity between the several phenomena may exist, or it may not; but if it does exist, it exists in a manner of which I can form no conception; and if it does not exist, my faculties do not enable me to detect its absence." In other words (as Mr. O'Hanlon might have phrased it) "My friend Smith is I know a person,—therefore a substance. But Smith's hat and coat, being unconscious, lack the only forms in which unity and substance have been presented to me. Smith's coat is blue, its fabric woollen; his hat black, and of silken texture;—there may or may not be unities in which these phenomena of colour and structural appearance cohere; my faculties do not, however, enable me to decide whether hat and coat are or are not positively substantial unifications.

It would appear from all this, that hats and coats and other familiar so-called substances, are as little essentially known to us as that vast territory of supernatural Being which has been named the "Unknowable."

[133] From Mr. Wallace's translation of Hegel's Logik, pp. 65, 8, and 9. As the translator preserves the numbering of the Sections, reference is easy to the original German. Hegel adds a remark well worthy of attention:—"The scepticism of Hume, by whom this observation was chiefly made, should be clearly marked off from Greek scepticism. Hume founds his remarks on the truth of the empirical element, on feeling and sensation, and proceeds to attack universal truths and laws, because they do not derive their authority from sense-perception. So far was ancient scepticism from making feeling and sensation a canon of truth, that it turned against the deliverances of sense first of all."—Ibid. p. 69.

[134] Pp. 234-341. The preface to this volume is dated February 1874.

[135] Martineau's conception discussed by Spencer is hampered by a theory of Matter difficult per se.

[136] See back pp. 76-8 and 107 (end of note) and connect with these passages the oft-repeated Wordsworthian maxim:— "We murder to dissect."

[137] See our Chapter 6. On Causation.

[138] The paragraph cited in the text of Chapter 3 concludes with these words:—"I will call no being good, who is not what I mean when I apply that epithet to my fellow-

creatures; and if such a being can sentence me to hell for not so calling him, to hell I will go."

Now, no man can sit down and calculate himself into Mr. Mill's conviction thus enounced; neither could any cool process of argument have ever kindled such a flame. A sternness of purpose like his must be either the skeleton-armour covering the thoughtless boy in Tennyson's Gareth and Lynette, or it is the reflection of a light intuitively flashed through the soul—the echo of a chord struck upon the writer's very heart-strings. Such and so deep, beyond doubt, was the ingenuous feeling of Mr. Mill.

[139] *La Science au point de Vue Philosophique*, pp. 539-542.

[140] *Psychological Inquiries*, second part, pp. 195-197.

[141] Address (Presidential) to British Association at Liverpool, 1870, p. 15.

[142] Loc. cit. pp. 199-200.

[143] *Quarterly Journal of Microscopical Science*, January, 1873, p. 74.

[144] Loc. cit. p. 64.

[145] Loc. cit. pp. 69-70.

[146] Loc. cit. pp. 16-17.

[147] This quotation is from his Matter and Force, Chapter 19. Büchner is never tired of emphasizing the Materialism of thought. In an address prefixed to his tenth Edition, speaking of the hypothesis of Mind acting on Brain he calls it "the tragi-comic pianoforte theory," and regrets that there should be so many "human pianofortes out of tune in the world." Büchner's own Materialism is outspoken, as may be judged from the following propositions:—

1. Spirit without Body is unimaginable.

2. The Soul brings with it "no innate intuitions"; and

3. It is not an ens per se, but a product of external influences.

4. There is no individual immortality nor personal continuance after death.

5. The Soul's knowledge relates only to earthly things.

6. It becomes a person by being opposed to earthly individualities.

7. (Adopted from C. Vogt) "The soul ... is a product of the development of the brain; just as muscular activity is a product of muscular development, and secretion a product of glandular development. So soon as the substances composing the brain are aggregated in a similar form, will they exhibit the same functions.... Mental activity changes with the periods of life, and ceases altogether at death."

Büchner's writings are sufficiently known in this country. In America they are food for the million. Proposition No. 6 is particularly noticeable because it re-echoes the fallacy of Locke (see page 182-3 ante) on personal identity. By opposition to earthly individualities we do not "become" persons, but the sense of antagonism between ourselves and other externalities (both men and things), sharpens every day our belief in our own personality, and furnishes its daily verification. The grossness of this writer's Materialism does not hinder him from using the word "soul" on almost every page; and in one of his more recent publications he is candid enough to acknowledge that this old-fashioned entity is not yet quite improved off the face of the Earth. He says:—"Just the properties of the human mind and the impossibility of explaining them, were from the most ancient times one of the main supports of spiritualism and theological systems. True, their explanation is still wanting." Büchner, of course, looks for the speedy elimination of "Soul" proper, on exactly the same grounds which underlie his own whole system. Mental activity and Brain go together (he argues), as Force and Matter go together. It may be answered, that every practical reasoner knows the danger of arguing from concomitancies, however well-established, to Causality; and the risk is evidently much increased when a like argument is used to Identity. Besides, if Mental activity is resolvable into Brain, why should not Matter be likewise resolved into Force? Thus the whole Universe, inanimate and animated, material and psychical, becomes Force. The chain would run in this manner: Mind = Brain = Matter = Force. But how are we to know that Force must be all of one kind and description? Or, again, why may not the concomitancies be rather resolved some other way;— e.g., Matter (including Brain) = Force = Mind? Thus Materialism might slide into Idealism, Pantheism, or even Theism; since in some shape or other Mind would form and sustain the Universe. Our last citation of Büchner is taken from a New York Edition of his Materialism, p. 19.

[148] In other words, that kind of law which pervades the lowest sphere of Nature is conceived as dominant over the highest also. The whole Universe is submitted to its iron rule. There is of Man's Mind as well as of the flagstone with which he paves his streets, one account, one law, one science, one philosophy; nay, strangely enough, as we shall see further on, one religion! The law of stocks and stones is supreme, it rules alike Man's present and his future, and ought to be the sole object of his veneration.

Positivism, as is well known, makes many sciences and classifies them by an ascending scale of Laws. "La Philosophie Positive," writes Littré (Paroles, p. 10) ... "apercevant que, suivant la vraie conception, où la matière n'est pas séparable de ses propriétés, le mot de matérialisme n'avait plus d'emploi philosophique qu'en histoire, elle l'a renouvelé, et s'en est servie pour caractériser l'intrusion de la méthode de toute science inférieure dans la science supérieure."

If Littré had said, "the intrusion of the lowest into the highest," he would have rightly characterized the systems we are describing.

Von Feuchtersleben puts the practical state of the question thus:—"All we can say is, that an intellectual world reveals itself to us, by the law of the true, the good, and the beautiful, and that a physical world manifests itself by those laws which act in space and time. What lies beyond these laws, as it were the substance of both worlds, we know not; we only call that of the physical world, matter or body in the abstract, that of the super-physical, we call spirit (Geist), and must never forget that hereby we have only pronounced an abstraction.

"But now we ask further, wherein does this higher law manifest itself to us, as the physical law does in the material world? Nowhere but in man, and in him only through the medium of his cultivated and refined reason. What we feel, what we remember, nay, the very inmost sensations of our individual existence, may be referred to the world which surrounds us. Thought alone, exalted to the highest degree shows us another world. We are ourselves therefore not spirit, but we watch, as it were, what we call by that name, and which manifests itself to us only by its laws. (Est Deus in nobis.) Man, therefore, should be the link which connects the two worlds; and this is the problem, this is the enigma, which can never be solved." He adds in a note: "Materialism, that is, the view which will not allow the separation of the intellectual principle from the corporeal, but looks upon the former as a higher power of the latter, not only explains nothing, but makes the enigma still more obscure. Medical Psychology, Ed. Sydenham, pp. 15-16.

[149] Compare footnote (c) pp. 56-7 ante. This whole theory is dreamlike,—a sort of romance or revel of a half-metaphysical, half-materializing imagination. The following rather long extract from Haeckel's book will shew the hypothesis on its most poetical side. But alas for its prose, and its plain practical application! "It is indeed," he writes, "not difficult to arrive through an unprejudiced consideration of facts, at a clear conviction that Theism, which has its origin in Mythology, and which, under the name of "Pure Monotheism," rules the civilized peoples of modern day, and plays even now so conspicuous a part in organic Morphology as the Myth of Creation, is in fact not Monotheism but Amphitheism. This predominant religion was Monotheism only so long as all Natural Phenomena were, without any exception, taken to be the direct result of the personal divine government of the world,—only so long as all inorganic or organic Phenomena—from the blowing of the wind and the rolling of the thunder, to the light of the sun and the course of the stars; from the flowery fragrance of plants and the wing of the bird, to the Mind-formation of Man and the development-history of peoples;—were direct actions of a monarchical, personal Creator. But when modern Natural Science demonstrated that the whole realm of inorganic Nature was governed by fixed, unvarying laws of Nature; when Physics and Chemistry reduced Abiology to mathematical formulae, then the half of his realm was wrested from the personal Creator, and there remained to him organic Nature alone, and even the half of this was next set free by recent Physiology, so that organic Morphology alone remained subject to the personal, arbitrary government of the mediatised ruler of the world. Thus, out of the earlier Monotheism grew up that full-blown Amphitheism which at present rules the modern Cosmology of civilized peoples; and which appears in Science as the thoroughly perverted Dualism against which we have contended most determinedly in our General Morphology. For, what else is this Dualism but the battle between two Gods of fundamentally distinct natures? On the one hand, we see in the realm of Abiology, dominated by Mechanism, the exclusive sovereignty of unvarying and necessary Nature-laws, of the ἀναγκη, which at all times and in all places constantly remains one and the same.

"On the other hand, in the realm of Biology (which is still governed by Teleology), and especially in the realm of organic Morphology, we see the ridiculous arbitrary government of a personal and thoroughly humanlike Creator, who vainly wearies himself with endeavouring to create a 'perfect' Organism, and constantly rejects the earlier creations of a 'former age,' in that he is continually setting up new and improved editions in their places. We have already shewn, in our sixth chapter, why we must entirely reject this pitiful idea of a personal Creator (Vol. I. p. 173). It is in fact a degradation of the pure God-Idea. Most men picture to themselves this 'beloved God' as being thoroughly humanlike: he is in their eyes an architect, who is engaged in carrying on the construction of the world according to some previously rejected plan; but who never gets done with it, because during the process of completion, he is always hitting on new and better ideas; he is a Stage-manager, who directs the earth like a great puppet-play, and generally knows how to handle with tolerable skill the numerous threads by which he manages the hearts of men: he is a half-deprived king who only rules over the inorganic realm conditionally, and according to firmly fixed laws; rules on the other hand over the organic realm absolutely as patriarchal land-father, who in this domain allows himself to be led into a daily alteration of his world-plan by the wishes and prayers of his own children, among whom the most perfect Vertebrates are those principally favoured.

"Let us turn away from this unworthy Anthropomorphism of modern Dogmatics, which degrade God himself into an aerial Vertebrate, and let us look on the contrary at the infinitely higher God-Idea to which Monism conducts us; in that it demonstrates the Unity of God in the whole of Nature, and abolishes the antithesis of an organic and inorganic God which sows the germ of a death- agony in the heart of that predominating Amphitheism. Our Cosmology knows only One Sole God, and this Almighty God rules the whole of Nature without exception. We contemplate his operation in all phenomena of every description. To it the whole inorganic material world is subject, and so too the whole world of organization. If each body in vacuo falls fifteen feet in the first second; if three atoms of Oxygen to one of Sulphur always produce Sulphuric Acid; if the angle which one columnar surface of rock crystal makes with the neighbouring one is always 120°; then, these phenomena are the immediate operations of God, equally with the blossoms of plants, the movements of animals, the thoughts of Mankind. We all exist by 'God's grace'; the stone as well as the water, the Radiolarian as well as the pine tree, the gorilla as much as the Emperor of China. "This Cosmology which contemplates God's spirit and power in all natural phenomena is alone worthy of His all-comprehensive greatness; only when we refer all forces and all phenomena of movement, all forms and properties of matter, to God, as the Author of all things, do we attain to that human intuition of God, and veneration of God, which really befits his immeasurable greatness. For 'in Him we live and move and have our being.' Thus the philosophy of Nature becomes in fact Theology. The worship of Nature becomes that true worship of God of which Göethe says:—' Certainly there is no more beautiful veneration of God, than that which arises from communion with Nature in our own breasts.'

"God is Almighty; he is the sole Author, the prime Cause of all things; that is, in other words, God is the Universal Causal Law. God is absolutely perfect; he can never act otherwise than perfectly rightly, therefore he can never act arbitrarily or freely; that is to say, God is Necessity. God is the sum of all forces; so also, therefore, of all Matter. Every conception of God, which separates him from Matter, opposes to him a sum of forces which are not of divine Nature; every such conception leads to Amphitheism, consequently to Polytheism.

"Since Monism demonstrates the Unity of the whole of Nature, it proves, likewise, that only One God exists, and that this God manifests himself in the collective phenomena of Nature. Since Monism grounds the collective phenomena of organic and inorganic Nature on the Universal Causal Law, and displays them as the effects of 'active causes,' it shews at the same time, that God is the necessary Cause of all things and is the Law itself. Since Monism acknowledges no other beside the divine Forces in Nature, since it recognizes all laws of Nature as divine, it raises itself to the greatest and most elevated conception of which man, as the most perfect of all animals, is capable, to the conception of the Unity of God and Nature.

'Was wär' ein Gott, der nur von aussen stiesse,
Im Kreis das All am Finger laufen liesse!

Ihm ziemt's, die Welt im Innern zu bewegen,
Natur in Sich, Sich in Natur zu hegen,
So dass, was in Ihm lebt und webt und ist,
Nie Seine Kraft, nie Seinen Geist vermisst.'"
Haeckel's *Generelle Morphologie der Organismen*. Vol. II. Book viii. Chap. 30.
No one who reads the latter part of this quotation will doubt that Haeckel is a refined, or, in other words, a metaphysical Materialist. That he has produced an effect in materializing circles is evident; witness the following passages from Büchner "the crass." "To any one who does not stubbornly and obstinately cling to old prejudices, this new Cosmology which has superseded the dualism of former systems of philosophy and thought, must appear as clear, simple, free of dualism, easily intelligible and perfectly satisfactory. On account of this very antagonism to the dualistic character of the speculative philosophy of the past, I should like best to designate the philosophy of Materialism as monistic philosophy, or philosophy of unity; and the cosmology founded upon it as monism, in accordance with the suggestion of Professor Haeckel.... Since the indestructibility of matter, as previously described, has found its necessary complement in the indestructibility of force; and since the separation of force and matter has been recognized as a mere abstraction and existing only in our thoughts: it is really impossible to speak any longer of Materialism as a system which derives everything from matter only. Otherwise we might just as well speak of Dynamism, that is of a system that derives everything from force (dynamis). But in reality both are identical and inseparable; and therefore a philosophy built upon those ideas cannot be better designated than as monistic, or a philosophy of unity." (Materialism, ut supra p.24.) This last phrase is more metaphysical than Büchner's wont; but S. T. Coleridge, if alive, would tell him that what the world really wants, is a "Philosophy of Multeity in Unity." To annihilate the Manifold is to destroy our sole knowledge of the One.

[150] It was previously intimated that the idealizing philosopher often escapes ethical censure more easily than he deserves. Idealism may, or may not, be a bar to irreligious materialism. For example:—"The materialism of Strauss was not inconsistent with an idealism of the Hegelian type; for, as he showed in his last work, the question between logically consistent idealists and materialists who carry out their principles is, at its roots, one of names and terms rather than of antagonistic principles." Pall Mall Gazette for Feb. 11, 1874. The Idealism referred to, is that which identifies pure Being with Impersonal Thought. Now Berkeley's idealism culminated with the Divine Personality, through whose omnipresence and spiritual subsistence those properties or modes of existence, called material, are realized to us, who, together with all the world, exist in and by Him. Yet, as far as Berkeley's argument rests upon the common ground of idealistic reasoning, it is approachable by the Atheist or the Sceptic. Of Hobbes a reviewer has lately remarked: "He clearly demonstrated that the secondary qualities of body are purely subjective, and his language is almost strong enough to lead us to believe that he would have gone a long way with Berkeley. For he claims to have proved that 'as in vision, so also in conceptions that arise from the other senses, the subject of their inherence is not the object but the sentient.'" *Westminster Review*, April, 1874, p. 387.

The truth from which so many theories, physical and metaphysical, branch out, is thus clearly stated by Professor Huxley. "All the phenomena of nature are, in their ultimate analysis, known to us only as facts of consciousness." "On Descartes," *Lay Sermons*, p. 374. This statement is an incontrovertible proposition; and may help in persuading us to believe our own souls. At all events, we plainly see that the sum total of our human knowledge is potentially contained in their evidence.

[151] A mongrel Word-book would be a valuable addition to popular science. How many metaphysicians proper, or how many skilled students of Natural Science, can explain that novel compound "Psychoplasm"? The Westminster Review is not lost in admiration for either this new coinage, or another specimen from the same mint,— "Metempirics." (See No. for July, 1874.) The Fortnightly is more congratulatory.

[152] Ravaisson, the great philosophical critic of France, considers Biology among the sciences directly antagonistic to Materialism. He classifies the tendencies of scientific studies thus. There are, he says, "Deux directions opposées auxquelles nous inclinent les deux ordres differents de connaissances:—la direction qui aboutit au Materialisme, et c'est celle dans laquelle nous engagent les mathématiques et la physique, et la direction qui mène au spiritualisme, et c'est celle où acheminent la biologie et surtout les sciences morales et esthétiques." (*La Philosophie en France*, p. 98.) His description of a certain degree of progress in the mind of Comte illustrates this same idea:—"Il comprit, en présence de la vie, que ce n'était pas assez, comme il avait pu le croire dans la sphère des choses mécaniques et physiques, de considérer des phénomènes à la suite ou à côté les uns des autres, mais que, de plus, que surtout il fallait prendre en considération l'ordre et l'ensemble.

"En présence des êtres organisés, on s'aperçoit, disait-il, que le détail des phénomènes, quelque explication plus ou moins suffisante qu'on en donne, n'est ni le tout ni même le principal; que le principal, et l'on pourrait presque dire le tout, c'est l'ensemble dans l'espace, le progrès dans le temps, et qu'expliquer un être vivant, ce serait montrer la raison de cet ensemble et de ce progrès, qui est la vie même....

"Dans les sciences des choses inorganiques, disait-il encore, on procède par déduction des détails au tout; dans les sciences des êtres organisés, c'est de l'ensemble que se tire par déduction, la vraie connaissance des parties.

"De plus, d'accord maintenant avec Platon, Aristote, Leibniz, il déclarait que l'ensemble étant le résultat et l'expression d'une certaine unité, à laquelle tout concourt et se co-ordonne et qui est le but où tout marche, c'est dans cette unité, c'est dans le but, c'est dans la fin ou cause finale qu'est le secret de l'organisme.

"Le 16 Juillet 1843, écrivant à M. Stuart Mill, il exprimait l'opinion que, si ce savant ne le suivait pas dans les voies plus larges où dorénavant il allait marchait, c'est que, très-versé dans les études mathématiques et physiques, il n'était pas assez familier avec les phénomènes de la vie. Plus avancé dans la science biologique, M. Mill aurait mieux compris comment il faut, outre le détail des faits, quelque chose qui les domine, qui les combine et les co-ordonne." (Ibid. p. 75, seq.)

[153] These pages are inappropriate to that wide and momentous controversy:—Has each Science a Method of its own?—and by consequence its own terminology? That such a question remains to be debated, is a clear proof that most of our philosophizing is yet tentative; and has not passed over the critical "first stage."

[ac] "In vain," says Hume's Cleanthes, "In vain would the sceptic make a distinction between science and common life, or between one science and another. The arguments, employed in all, if just, are of a similar nature, and contain the same force and evidence.

Or if there be any difference among them, the advantage lies entirely on the side of theology and natural religion."— Dialogues, etc., Part I. sub. fin.

And our ultimate appeal—as for example concerning the subject next discussed in this chapter—is, he observes, to an instinctive operation of the mind which obliges us to accept and act upon what we cannot explain. Writing in his own person, Mr. Hume observes, "As nature has taught us the use of our limbs, without giving us the knowledge of the muscles and nerves by which they are actuated, so has she implanted in us an instinct, which carries forward the thought in a correspondent course to that which she has established among external objects; though we are ignorant of those powers and forces on which this regular course and succession of objects totally depends."— Inquiry concerning the Human Understanding. Section V., end. Compare footnote [d]. to this chapter, p. 269 post.

[ad] The word Belief has been used in a variety of senses by modern writers of differing views from Jacobi to Sir. W. Hamilton, from Dr. Newman to Mr. Herbert Spencer.

"This word," Mr. Spencer says, "is habitually applied to dicta of consciousness for which no proof can be assigned: both those which are unprovable because they underlie all proof, and those which are unprovable because of the absence of evidence." And again; "we commonly say we 'believe' a thing for which we can assign some preponderating evidence, or concerning which we have received some indefinable impression.... And it is the peculiarity of these beliefs, as contrasted with cognitions, that their connexions with antecedent states of consciousness may be easily severed, instead of being difficult to sever. But unhappily, the word 'belief' is also applied to each of those temporarily or permanently indissoluble connexions in consciousness, for the acceptance of which the only warrant is that it cannot be got rid of.... Thus the two opposite poles of knowledge go under the same name; and by the reverse connotations of this name, as used for the most coherent and least coherent relations of thought, profound misconceptions have been generated."

Mr. Spencer made these remarks at separate intervals of time, and has repeated them in 1874 (Essays, III. 259-60). It would therefore appear that he thinks little has recently been done to discriminate the significations of so ambiguous a term.

This chapter endeavours to investigate a small number of the genus "Beliefs" to which the differentia "Of Reason" has been added by way of distinction. It also attempts to offer a contribution towards the useful work of explaining their specific validity, and if its argument be correct, they constitute a very important definable species of the Genus, carrying with them a persuasion pre-eminently their own.

On his page 260, last referred to, Mr. Spencer remarks,—"that the belief which the moral and religious feelings are said to yield of a personal God, is not one of the beliefs which are unprovable because they underlie all proof"—and adds that works on Natural Theology treat that Belief as inferential.

The view taken of this moral and religious belief in the present Essay, is that it is in its own nature both primary and inferential. The former of these aspects is the one now under discussion.

[154] Compare Fowler's Inductive Logic, p. 29. [Since the reference was made, Mr. Fowler has become Professor of Logic in the University of Oxford.]

[155] Mr. Fowler, in the little volume just referred to, describes another "Theory of the Origin of Universal Beliefs," as follows:—"It would admit that all beliefs alike are ultimately

derived from experience, and still it would freely adopt the language that there are some beliefs which are 'native to the human mind.' The word 'experience' as ordinarily employed by psychologists, includes not only the experience of the individual, but the recorded experience of mankind. On the theory, however, of which we are now speaking, it has a still more extended meaning; it includes experience, or to speak more strictly, a peculiar facility for forming certain experiences, transmitted by hereditary descent from generation to generation. While some ideas occur only to particular individuals, at particular times, there are others which, from the frequency and constancy with which they are obtruded upon men's minds at all times and under all circumstances, become, after an accumulated experience of many generations, connatural, as it were, to the human mind. We assume them, often unconsciously, in our special perceptions, and when the propositions, which embody them, are propounded to us, we find it impossible, on reflection, to doubt their truth. It is by personal experience of external objects and their relations that each man recognises them, but the tendency to recognise them is transmitted, like the physical or mental peculiarities of race, from preceding generations, and is anterior to any special experience whatever on the part of the individual. This theory, to which much of modern speculation appears to be converging, is advocated with great ability in the works of Mr. Herbert Spencer." *Inductive Logic*, p. 31.

This account of our Belief in the Inductive Principle agrees, in effect, with the opinion of those who hold that our acceptance of its truth resembles our acceptance of Mathematical Truths in two very important respects: (1) Its Certitude. To use Dr. Whewell's words; "We are as certain of it as of the truths of arithmetic and geometry. We cannot doubt that it must apply to all events past and future, in every part of the universe, just as truly as to those occurrences which we have ourselves observed. What causes produce what effects;—what is the cause of any particular event;—what will be the effect of any peculiar process;—these are points on which experience may enlighten us. Observation and experience may be requisite, to enable us to judge respecting such matters. But that every event has some cause, Experience cannot prove any more than she can disprove. She can add nothing to the evidence of the truth, however often she may exemplify it. This doctrine, then, cannot have been acquired by her teaching," Whewell's *Hist. of Scientific Ideas*, B. III. Cap. ii.

(2) In the fact of its being intuitive; that is, as Mr. Fowler says, "connatural," or "native to the human mind."

Whether we can trace the process through which it became one of the mental possessions characteristic of Mankind is a further question, and a very curious one. The subjects of improvement by education, and of the transmission of improvements thus acquired among men and the lower animals, belong in part to our next Chapter;—they are, of course, deeply interesting to every philanthropist, every promoter of true progress and wholesome civilization.

[156] Galen remarks upon the immediate activity of animal instinct prior to example or habituation. Most Naturalists know his experiment of hatching three different sorts of eggs together. He was much struck to see the young aquatic bird, reptile, and eaglet, betake themselves at once, each to his vocation. Some persons referred these instincts to the influence of organs fitted for definite uses, yet, observes Galen, the young calf will butt before he has got horns. A good deal might be added to Galen's rejoinder. Animals

seem often to work without fitness of organization,—or one might almost say in defiance of their organs. "There is nothing," says Sir C. Bell, "in the configuration of the black bear, particularly adapted for his catching fish; yet he will sit, on his hinder extremities, by the side of a stream, morning or evening, on the watch, like a practised fisher, and so perfectly motionless as to deceive the eye of the Indian, who mistakes him for the burnt trunk of a tree; when he sees his opportunity favourable, he will thrust out his fore-paw, and seize a fish with incredible celerity. The exterior organ is not, in this instance, the cause of the habit or of the propensity; and if we thus see the instinct bestowed without the appropriate organ, may we not the more readily believe, in other examples, when the two are conjoined, that the habit exists with the instrument, although not through it?" (Bridgewater Treatise, Chap. x. p. 250.)—In Captain Cook's third voyage there is another anecdote of bears equally curious. "The wild deer (barein) are far too swift for those lumbering sportsmen; so the bear perceives them at a distance by the scent; and, as they herd in low grounds, when he approaches them, he gets upon the adjoining eminence, from whence he rolls down pieces of rock; nor does he quit his ambush, and pursue, until he finds that some have been maimed." (Vol. 3, p. 306.)

In such cases as these, there is a manifest want of correspondence between animal organisms and animal instincts, which many naturalists consider essentially interdependent. Yet on their mutual action and reaction some have founded a theory of evolution.

[157] "We have in the Veda the invocation Dyaūs pítar, the Greek Ζεῦ πατερ, the Latin Jupiter; and that means in all the three languages what it meant before these three languages were torn asunder—it means Heaven-Father. These two words are not mere words; they are to my mind the oldest poem, the oldest prayer of mankind, or at least of that pure branch of it to which we belong—and I am as firmly convinced that this prayer was uttered, that this name was given to the unknown God before Sanskrit was Sanskrit, and Greek was Greek, as when I see the Lord's Prayer in the languages of Polynesia and Melanesia, I feel certain that it was first uttered in the language of Jerusalem." Professor Max Müller's *Science of Religion*. New Ed. p. 172.

[158] This then would seem to be an instance of wide spread "moral regression."

[ae] Our deep-rooted tendency to trust human testimony may yield a very curious example of the difficulties presented by the whole class of pre-rational beliefs. Mr. J. Mill in accordance with his system of foregone Associations "resolves" this case as follows (Analysis I. p. 385-6): "Belief in testimony is but a case of the anticipation of the future from the past; and belief in the uniformity of the laws of nature is but another name for the same thing.... The testimony uniformly calls up the idea of the reality of the event, so closely, that I cannot disjoin them. But the idea, irresistibly forced upon me, of a real event, is Belief."

On this explanation Mr. Bain remarks, "The belief in Testimony is derived from the primary credulity of the mind, in certain instances left intact under the wear and tear of adverse experience. Hardly any fact of the human mind is better attested than the primitive disposition to receive all testimony with unflinching credence. It never occurs to the child to question any statement made to it, until some positive force on the side of scepticism has been developed. Gradually we find that certain testimonies are inconsistent with fact; we have, therefore, to go through a long education in discriminating the good testimonies from the bad. To the one class, we adhere with the primitive force of conviction that in the other class has been shaken and worn away by the shocks of repeated contradictions."

It seems quite possible that our "primary credulity" may be one example of a wider spread feeling of reliance engendered in part by affection and dependence. Its force varies considerably in various minds. Women whose lives have been happy and free from disappointment retain much of this primary intuitive belief to the end of their days. Among men, the trust in Testimony becomes controlled by their power of balancing probabilities; a faculty in which the very credulous and also the very sceptical are often observed to be deficient. The disappointed of both sexes proverbially incline to Scepticism.

[159] *Metaph*. I. 44.

[160] Acts xvii. 27, 28. Romans i. 32; ii. 14 seq.

[161] Most persons have read with delight the observations on Insect Architecture from Huber downwards. Birds are generally well watched and well reported. Many Naturalists have written on these subjects, from a hope of creating in the minds of men some softer interest for their humble companions. Mr. Jesse naïvely prefaces a collection of anecdotes, by saying that, of all the nations in Europe, our own countrymen are perhaps the least inclined to treat the brute creation with tenderness.

Wilson long ago observed that the nest building of birds was not always the same in the same species. The older birds built the better nests.

M. Pouchet of Rouen proved that when the new streets of that city were erected, the window- swallows altered their nests and substantially improved them. A short account of his observations will be found in Wallace's Contributions, 228 A. Mr. Wallace adds several instances of bad nest building, especially by pigeons, rooks, and window-swallows, a circumstance also noticed by White of Selborne.

Amongst the most remarkable bird-families with special ideas of construction, are the mound-builders, and bower birds of Australia, described by Mr. Gould. The former hatch their eggs in hillocks contrived to retain during the night, amid their warm vegetable linings, the solar heat of each successive day. The nests of one family are about a yard high and three wide. In another family, mounds of five yards in height and twelve in girth seem not uncommon; and the circumference of one mound in particular measured full fifty yards. These larger mounds are the work of many birds, through many years, and their firm sides are covered by ancient forest growth.

The bower birds construct over-arching alleys of curved branches, decorated with pretty grasses, gay feathers, shells and bones, particularly near the entrances. These bowers seem to be used as meeting and recreation places for both sexes. They vary to some extent amongst the different species of this singular tribe.

There can be no doubt of the power of adaptation among animals;—and those who study them most are least surprised at its extent. Horses will learn to go up and down stairs, cats to undo door latches; and one pony mentioned by Jesse used to unfasten the stable door, open and rob the corn chest. Still more curious, is the American bird called neuntödter, which catches grasshoppers and spears them upon twigs, not for the shamble-purposes of the butcher bird, but simply as baits to catch and eat the smaller birds attracted by the spoil.

Schleiden (Plant 232), tells a most singular story of a Kangaroo who tried to drown his pursuer, and shewed considerable craft in the way he set about the drowning. After knocking the hunter backwards into a pond, the "old man" (Australian for Kangaroo) kept pushing the poor fellow's head under water every time he raised it up. If Kangaroo had never drowned a human being before, he must have proceeded by analogy, and argued, as some Naturalists do, from the brute to the man. A dog, mentioned by Jesse, endeavoured to save his drowning master's life by the reverse process to Kangaroo's, and would not let the beloved head disappear under water for many a wintry hour after life had been extinguished. (*Country Life*, p. 119.)

A person reflecting on these and similar facts, does not feel much surprised at Aristotle's appreciation of animal intelligence, (e.g., *Historiae* viii. 1, 2,) "[Greek: hôs gar en anthrôpô technê kai sophia kai synesis, houtôs eniois tôn zôôn esti tis hetera toiautê physikê dynamis.]" The animal power of adaptation, travelling beyond the routine of instinctive action, probably struck the philosopher very strongly.

[162] These barricades are curiously galleried and casemated, like the defences of a fortress. The best account of them is given by the accurate and interesting Huber.

[163] In Aristotle's Introduction to Physical Science, he remarks that Sense grasps at Wholes, so that in a certain way, the general may seem to take precedence with us of the particular. Language is a proof of this—Children's talk is apt to run in concretes;—every man or woman is a father or mother to them. See Phys. Ausc. I. 1, with Pacius' note. The old commentator unties a knot which some moderns appear to have tied fast again.

>Addition. Aristotle's illustration, it is alleged (e.g., by Dr. Whewell), goes in the wrong direction; fathers and mothers are less comprehensive terms than men and women; the truth seems to be that children fail to perceive the differences between parents and other human beings;—therefore they call men and women, parents. Pacius says:—"Nunc igitur totum esse nobis notius, probat à signo, id est, argumento sumto ab infantibus, qui initiò non distinguunt patrem ab aliis viris, nec matrem ab aliis mulieribus: postea verò distinguunt: nempe, quia ab initio habuerunt cognitionem magis confusam, neque cognoverunt proprietates parentis, sed tantum eum noverunt sub ratione universali, quatenus est homo, ideoque non potuerunt eum ab aliis hominibus sejungere. Postea verò progredientes ad cognitionem magis particularem, possunt patrem ab aliis discernere." Ed. 1608, p. 346.

[af] It is quite conceivable that the presence of Reason may from its first dawn, give rise to a very wide difference between the highest animal instincts, and the lowest instinctive impulses of Man. The discussion would be far too extensive for these pages; but it is obvious that such a difference might clearly account for much that is obscure in the twilight territory of Mind.

Hume, however, appears to have thought otherwise, as may be perceived in the Conclusion of his Reason of Animals. From his mention of "experimental reasoning" and the instances adduced, he would seem to attribute our Inductive process to a simple instinct. He writes thus:—"Though animals learn many parts of their knowledge from observation, there are also many parts of it which they derive from the original hand of Nature, which much exceed the share of capacity they possess on ordinary occasions, and in which they improve little or nothing, by the longest practice and experience. These we denominate Instincts, and are so apt to admire as something very extraordinary and inexplicable by all the disquisitions of human understanding. But our wonder will perhaps cease or diminish when we consider that the experimental reasoning itself, which we possess in common with beasts, and on which the whole conduct of life depends, is nothing but a species of instinct or mechanical power, that acts in us unknown to ourselves, and in its chief operations is not directed by any such relations or comparison of ideas as are the proper objects of our intellectual faculties. Though the instinct be different, yet still it is an instinct, which teaches a man to avoid the fire, as much as that which teaches a bird, with such exactness, the art of incubation, and the whole economy and order of its nursery." Compare foot-note (a) to this chapter, p. 255 ante.

[ag] "Wisdom is Alchemy. Else it could not be Wisdom. This is its unfailing characteristic, that it 'finds good in everything,' that it renders all things more precious. In this respect also does it renew the spirit of childhood within us: while foolishness hardens our hearts and narrows our thoughts, it makes us feel a childlike curiosity and a childlike interest about all things. When our view is confined to ourselves, nothing is of value, except what ministers in one way or other to our own personal gratification: but in proportion as it widens, our sympathies increase and multiply: and when we have learnt to look on all things as God's works, then, as His works, they are all endeared to us.

"Hence nothing can be further from true wisdom, than the mask of it assumed by men of the world, who affect a cold indifference about whatever does not belong to their own immediate circle of interests or pleasures." *Guesses at Truth*, 2nd Ed. 2nd Series, p. 200.

[164] "Try to conceive a man without the ideas of God, eternity, freedom, will, absolute truth, of the good, the true, the beautiful, the infinite. An animal endowed with a memory of appearances and of facts might remain. But the man will have vanished, and you have instead a creature, more subtle than any beast of the field, but likewise cursed above every beast of the field; upon the belly must it go, and dust must it eat all the days of its life. But I recal myself from a train of thoughts little likely to find favour in this age of sense and selfishness." Coleridge, *Church and State*. Note p. 50, Ed. 1839.

[165] Some people we may remark are unable to see any difference between sentiments and sentimentalities.

[166] It was by a reverse procedure that Kant shewed his greatness. He kept the two fields of thought apart, and applied to each a criticism unsparing, but appropriate. Nothing could be more decisive than the result, though darkened in some degree by the critic's peculiar technicalities. Moral truth was placed upon the most sublime of elevations. Speculative reason could never rise beyond the limits of conditioned truth; any attempt to extend its sphere issued in antinomy or blank negation. It left the human mind apparently oscillating between Idealism and limited Insight. But to this must be added a most important point too commonly forgotten. Though Speculative reason does not demonstrably prove, it renders conceivable by us those highest of all Ideas which our Practical reason shews to be necessarily and unquestionably certain for every one of us. Moral Truth thus opens to Man's eye a clear vista into the Timeless and the Absolute, to an immortal life beyond the grave, and to God the Sovereign both of Nature and of Man. It tells us the secret of true Causation, and with it of all that is most worth living for, the intrinsically greatest and Best of Humanity. And it binds every human being, as by golden links, to that ever present Divine throne, the shrine and oracle set up within his own breast. We ought always to remember that upon those grand truths which if

practically certain cannot be ultimately false, Kant staked his all. They were the crown alike of his labours and his life.

Addition. —By these remarks the present writer does not intend subscribing to all the Kantian conclusions respecting pure Speculative Reason, much less to those that have been asserted by many of Kant's disciples. Difference of opinion on such conclusions cannot, however, effect an honest appreciation of the clear and elevated principles maintained by Kant on the subject of independent Morality, as contradistinguished from the scheme which used to be termed Selfish, but is now commonly called Utilitarian.— See pp. 93-6 ante.

[ah] "Thousands of years it may be before Homer and the Veda ... Dyaus did not mean the blue sky, nor was it simply the sky personified; it was meant for something else.... We shall have to learn the same lesson again and again in the Science of Religion, viz. that the place whereon we stand is holy ground. Thousands of years have passed since the Aryan nations separated to travel to the North and the South, the West and the East: they have each formed their languages, they have each founded empires and philosophies, they have each built temples and razed them to the ground; they have all grown older, and it may be wiser and better; but when they search for a name for what is most exalted and yet most dear to every one of us, when they wish to express both awe and love, the infinite and the finite, they can but do what their old fathers did when gazing up to the eternal sky, and feeling the presence of a Being as far as far and as near as near can be: they can but combine the self-same words, and utter once more the primeval Aryan prayer, Heaven-Father, in that form which will endure for ever, 'Our Father which art in Heaven.'"—Max Müller, *Lectures on the Science of Religion*, pp. 171-2, 3.

[167] Compare the Indian phrase "the magical illusions of reality, the so-called Mâyâ of creation." Max Müller's Sanskrit Literature, p. 19. Also Ritter's Gesch. der Philosophie, I. 101 seq., and the account in both of the philosophy of Quietism. The attractive side of it is given by Max Müller, pp. 18, 19, and 29. The National results are elegantly painted, pp. 30, 31. He concludes: "It might therefore be justly said that India has no place in the political history of the world.... India has moved in such a small and degraded circle of political existence that it remained almost invisible to the eyes of other nations."

Few feelings are more deeply rooted, as in our individual, so in our collective human nature, than this same conclusion. Quietism culminates when Action appears useless because of a conceived Necessity or Unreality of Nature:—"Life is but a Dream—Let all sit still and fold their hands to slumber."

[168] Speculatively considered, what can the weapon commonly called argument do against Idealism? Both sides allow that man can neither cause nor annihilate sensible impressions. But they are supposably ideal phrases of susceptibility, which may be explained in more ways than one. On the inability of most men—(particularly Scotchmen,) to comprehend Berkeley's position, see Fraser's Ed., IV. 366, 7, 8, note. It gave rise to notably absurd rejoinders: "With the witty Voltaire ten thousand cannon balls, and ten thousand dead men, were ten thousand ideas, according to Berkeley. There is as much subtlety of thought, and more humour, in the Irish story of Berkeley's visit to Swift on a rainy day, when, by the Dean's orders, he was left to stand before the

unopened door, because, if his philosophy was true, he could as easily enter with the door shut as open."

[169] "We cannot possibly identify the perception of expanded colour, which is all that originally constitutes seeing, with the perception of felt resistance, which is all that originally constitutes touching. Coloured extension is antithetical to felt extension. In fact, we do not see, we never saw, and we never can see the orange of mere touch; we do not touch, we never touched, and we never can touch the orange of mere sight." Ibid. p. 394.

[170] "From floating elements in chaos hurl'd,
Self-form'd of atoms, sprang the infant world:
No great First Cause inspired the happy plot,
But all was matter—and no matter what.
Atoms, attracted by some law occult,
Settling in spheres, the globe was the result:
Pure child of Chance, which still directs the ball,
As rotatory atoms rise or fall.
In ether launch'd, the peopled bubble floats,
A mass of particles, and confluent motes,
"So nicely poised, that if one atom flings
Its weight away, aloft the planet springs,
And wings its course through realms of boundless space,
Outstripping comets in eccentric race.
Add but one atom more, it sinks outright
Down to the realms of Tartarus and night."
"Rejected Addresses," pp. 115, 116.

[171] "What are the core and essence of this hypothesis? Strip it naked and you stand face to face with the notion that not alone the more ignoble forms of animalcular or animal life, not alone the nobler forms of the horse and lion, not alone the exquisite and wonderful mechanism of the human body, but that the human mind itself—emotion, intellect, will, and all their phenomena—were once latent in a fiery cloud. Surely the mere statement of such a notion is more than a refutation." Tyndall, Fragments of Science, p. 163.

[172] Mr. Mill speaks thus of the Design argument. "It is the best; and besides, it is by far the most persuasive. It would be difficult to find a stronger argument in favour of Theism, than that the eye must have been made by one who sees, and the ear by one who hears." *Mill On Hamilton*, p. 551.

[173] So in Thomson's Hymn:—
"Thy beauty walks, Thy tenderness and love.
Wide flush the fields; the softening air is balm;
Echo the mountains round; the forest smiles;
And every sense, and every heart, is joy."

[ai] "The idea of God, beyond all question or comparison, is the one great seminal principle; inasmuch as it combines and comprehends all the faculties of our nature, converging in it as their common centre; brings the reason to sanction the aspirations of the imagination; impregnates law with the vitality and attractiveness of the affections; and establishes the natural legitimate subordination of the body to the will, and of both to

the vis logica or reason, by involving the necessary and entire dependence of the created on the creator." *Guesses at Truth*. 1st Ed., pp. 122, 3.

[aj] Perhaps every cynic delighting in those records should be asked to define what he means by Savagery. Of savages there are evidently many sorts, e. g.:—

(1) The children of our race;—a condition not beautiful, yet not without hope.

(2) Semi-civilized tribes, generally addicted to "fire-water" and other vices of civilization, without possession of its better things.

(3) Barbarian princedoms, grown decrepit by reason of wars, caste domination, or a sensual and effete culture.

(4) There are also a few wholly uncultured folk, who are more of gentlemen and ladies than our highly civilized peoples;—more truthful, honourable, and courteous;—while,

(5) Not a few are savages indeed!

These strictures serve as a reminder to add that by Theism is here intended the belief in a Supreme Being, the Father of Spirits, to Whom we shall give solemn account. But it is not meant to include some civilized superstitions, by means of which many men degrade and torment their fellows. Of such men we say, They too are savages indeed!

[174] *Reid's Works*, p. 751.

[175] *Reid's Works*, p. 743.

[176] *Metaph.* II. p. 530.

[177] *The Friend*, vol iii. p. 214. Ed. 1844.

[ak] The portrait of a lonely thinker searching out God has been painted in lively colours, as follows:—"O my friend, you would do me most grievous wrong, if you thought my heart empty of those feelings which make man the standing miracle of Nature. If your child fell into the river, would you stop to tell or think how you loved it, how dear and winsome and precious it was to you, how blank your home and bruised your heart would be without it? Or would you plunge into the stream in utter recklessness of your life, bear it swiftly out of the devouring flood, and then in silence strain the rescued little one to your bosom? Characters differ. It is mine to act, as well as to feel. What, do you imagine, prompts a thinker to give his days and nights to the rescue of man's faith in God, his heart-trust and moral inspiration and spiritual joy, when all these are put in jeopardy by the increase of a knowledge that is but half comprehended, even by those who in their own special lines are nobly increasing it? What lies back of the intense activity of his brain, as he toils over problems that wring the beads from his brow, gives up to the lonely pursuit of truth the hours that might be fertile of the prizes clutched after by the crowd, and turns his back on prizes that even he holds dear? What but a mighty hunger for God can explain this weary, unending search for Him? What else can explain the unthanked effort to make plain a path to Him that no man wants to travel?" *American Index*, Jan. 15, 1874.

[178] Butler's *Sermons*, p. 184 seq.

[179] *The Soul, her Sorrows and her Aspirations*, pp. 103, 104.

[180] Nov. Org. II. 4, last paragraph. "For a true and perfect rule of operation then the direction will be that it be certain, free, and disposing or leading to action. And this is the same thing with the discovery of the true Form. For the Form of a nature is such, that given the Form the nature infallibly follows. Therefore it is always present when the nature is present, and universally implies it, and is constantly inherent in it. Again, the Form is such, that if it be taken away the nature infallibly vanishes. Therefore it is

always absent when the nature is absent, and implies its absence, and inheres in nothing else."

[181] Sentence following immediately in N. O. II. 4. "Lastly, the true Form is such that it deduces the given nature from some source of being which is inherent in more natures, and which is better known in the natural order of things than the Form itself. For a true and perfect axiom of knowledge then the direction and precept will be, that another nature be discovered which is convertible with the given nature, and yet is a limitation of a more general nature, as of a true and real genus. Now these two directions, the one active the other contemplative, are one and the same thing; and what in operation is most useful, that in knowledge is most true." *Ellis and Spedding*, Vol. IV. pp. 121, 2.

[182] Savery was celebrated by Dr. Darwin as the man, who,—

"Bade with cold streams the quick expansion stop

And sank the immense of vapour to a drop."

Savery's patent (the first granted for a steam engine), is dated 1698. Papin suggested in 1695 a partial vacuum under a piston for raising water, so as to make the pressure of the air the moving power. Most people are aware of the effect upon invention produced by the great mining interest,—the necessity of pumping out underground adits, water logged, and therefore inaccessible.

[183] At the end of his *Lectures on the Steam Engine*.

Hulls' was the first attempt to convert the reciprocating movement of the piston-rod into rotation; and it does not rival the crank in simplicity. But there is a contrivance for equalizing the first irregular motion by weights, which possesses real beauty, and has the further advantage of readily increasing or diminishing the velocity of the wheels. The wheels themselves are fixed at some little distance astern of his boat which he intends to be used for towing ships. They are thus (as Professor Rigaud observes) nearer "to what may be considered as the centre of the compound body, which they were the means of propelling."

Such was the earliest patent; but proposals for the same object had been made still earlier. Papin submitted one to the Royal Society in 1708, comprehending a "boat to be rowed with oars moved with heat," and engines capable of throwing bullets and raising water. Sir Isaac Newton reported on the invention and recommended experiments, but the Society could not or would not grant a sum not exceeding £15 for the purpose. Again, the Acta Eruditorum for 1690, preserves a previous proposal made by Papin, accounts of which will be found in Farey's Treatise on the Steam Engine, and Professor Rigaud's Early Proposals for Steam Navigation. In the latter publication (a paper read to the Ashmolean Society) is also contained (pp. 11-14) a summary of the most wonderful among all records relating to this subject;—the trial of Blasco de Garay's steam-boat at Barcelona under Charles V. "The experiment was made the 17th June 1543 on board a vessel called the Trinidad, of 200 barrels burden, which had lately arrived with wheat from Colibre. The vessel was seen at a given moment to move forward and turn about at pleasure, without sail, or oar, or human agency, and without any visible mechanism except a huge boiler of hot water, and a complicated combination of wheels and paddles." The entire or partial credibility of this record has been often argued pro and con. Professor Rigaud thinks it "not impossible that even a magnificent invention, like this, may have sunk into oblivion." Perhaps not, considering that the Spain of Cervantes is the Spain of Southey, and Mr. Borrow. A clock may stand still, but a nation which does so is retrograde.

[184] The Chinese seeing our steam-ships at Chusan (in the war of 1841, 2), made paddlewheel vessels driven by men inside their hulls. Ignorant of steam-power, they achieved an engine without its principle. So too Prince Rupert gave a rotary motion to oars by horse-power, producing a greater velocity than sixteen watermen could impart to the Royal barge.

[185] See second note on this chapter.

[186] Darwin's Descent of Man, I. p. 179. Mr. Darwin adds in a note that "Sir C. Lyell had already (*Principles of Geology*, 1868. II. 489) called attention, in a striking passage, to the evil influence of the Holy Inquisition, in having lowered, through selection, the general standard of intelligence in Europe."

[al] The term "relativity" is employed here on account of its breadth and comprehensiveness, and because it does not imply the adoption of some special hypothesis as to the essence of things or formative principles themselves;—such theorizing being no necessary condition of the present line of thought.

Let it be observed, however, that any law of the natural world by virtue of which, the apprehended relativity becomes operative, must be conceived as in its own nature genetic or causative, in order to explain Production. What is here meant may easily be understood by a few common-sense reflections.

The word "Law" is one of the most ambiguous expressions possible. Perhaps its most familiar use is in statistical science, where it usually means the result gained from averages. For example, birth-rates, death-rates, and rates of exchange are spoken of as laws of increase, of mortality, and of the money market. Sometimes nothing but the generalized fact is signified; sometimes it is intended to imply that these formulae govern, or ought to govern social questions, or problems of political economy.

In like manner, when a law is the verbal embodiment of any principle, it may be considered as a perfectly abstract proposition; or else as a governing rule or maxim, under which definite and actual cases can be brought. The principles of arithmetic or geometry are laws to which every practical question involving number or measurement must be submitted. The laws of thought govern our reasonings, or at least they ought to do so.

Another way of looking at Law is to consider it in its commonest origin— i.e., as the expression of a law-maker's will. But when a writer on Natural Theology speaks of the laws of the physical world, and then adds that "law implies a lawgiver," he either supposes himself to have demonstrated the applicability of this maxim in relation to his own science;—or if not he is simply assuming the whole question at issue. [Compare Additional Note B, to Chapter 2. p. 98, seq.]

The remaining most usual employment of the word, is to designate a Force, some actual moving power tending to realize itself in some way, working out a function either for good or evil, developing the secret of its own existence by the effects which it produces. Take an example from real life. A medical man coming to a certain rural district, observed its high death-rate, traced it to the very great prevalence of small-pox in the place, and formulated a law embodying the results of several years averages which appeared sufficiently surprising. A further acquaintance with the habits of the neighbourhood disclosed the fact that inoculation was continually practised, and as continually kept secret on account of the penalties attached to it. The inquirer took advantage of the opportunity afforded by a custom he could not control to investigate its consequences. A few years later, he arrived at exact conclusions determining the law of activity exerted by the virus, under certain conditions. In other words, he found the genetic law of its operation.

Now, if the death-rate,—a piece of statistical law,—be contrasted with this last named law of virus-growth, the difference between these two formulae is at once obvious. Without any scientific discussion or refining, we grasp a broad common-sense distinction, which is all that seems needed here. For our purpose, it would be useless to inquire whether the law of virus-growth may be resolved into laws higher and far more recondite still. An inventor seizing the useful law he wants, will not stop to ask any such questions; he will apply his power and realize the function he has in view at the moment.

Another common-sense instance is to think of the properties of any familiar substance; the acridity of an alkali, for instance; its power of effervescing with acids, and neutralizing them; its behaviour as a reagent in a variety of ways, long to enumerate, but practically useful. When we have described all these properties, have we defined the whole substance? In other words, is the alkali anything more than a bundle of properties momentarily known to us? Undoubtedly there is one point more to be noticed; its principle of permanence, until brought under new conditions which dissolve its unity, and destroy the inter-coherence of its properties. Now whatever maintains this unity is the law of its substance. There are laws of nature under which both it and countless other substances are formed, continue, and are dissolved, making way for unending series of fresh combinations. And this mode of apprehending the unities we call substances, raises the self- same idea of genetic law which has been under consideration. If we are asked whether we can explain such laws further, we usually reply by saying "these are the forces of the natural world." Their correlations and modifications rule the kingdom of nature, and the great globe itself;—nay, they wield the empire of the Universe!

Such laws, such forces, have engrossed the attention of physical philosophers from the rude beginnings of inquiry. They have led to speculations of all kinds;—the best known of which is the distinction between Form and Matter in existing objects;—a distinction in common use amongst persons who but dimly guess at the past issues which it raises. Nothing, however, can be said on such a topic here, except by way of reference to the philosophic system of Francis Bacon. [Compare p. 92 ante, and the Synopsis prefixed to this chapter.]

[am] One of the most curious morceaux in the history of Science, is the fact that the nature of Heat has been several times thus determined, viz., by Bacon, Locke, and Count Rumford. See Tyndall on Heat as a Mode of Motion, Section II., and Appendix.

Bacon determines the nature of Heat by way of exemplifying "The Investigation of Forms." It is his sole instance, and is most instructive. (Nov. Org. II., 11 seq., in E. and S. Vol. IV., pp. 127-155.) "For example," he begins, "let the investigation be into the Form of Heat." It need scarcely be observed that the twofold relation of his "Forms" to Metaphysic and to Physic is one of the least explained parts of Bacon's vast system. How little his theory of Induction is commonly understood may be perceived by any skilled reader of Macaulay's well known Essay—a composition (to borrow a great schoolmaster's words) "displaying an almost inconceivable amount of nescience."

[187] It is worth observation how often the abstract entity—(the principle of the whole realization)—is forgotten even by scientific persons. Forgotten, we say, since surely forgetfulness is the true origin of many futile attempts at explaining away essential principles. The following very curious case in point is narrated by S. T. Coleridge:— "There is still preserved in the Royal Observatory at Richmond the model of a bridge, constructed by the late justly celebrated Mr. Atwood (at that time, however, in the decline of life), in the confidence that he had explained the wonderful properties of the arch as resulting from the compound action of simple wedges, or of the rectilinear solids of which the material arch was composed; and of which supposed discovery his model was to exhibit ocular proof. Accordingly, he took a sufficient number of wedges of brass highly polished. Arranging these at first on a skeleton arch of wood, he then removed this scaffolding or support; and the bridge not only stood firm, without any cement between the squares, but he could take away any given portion of them, as a third or a half, and appending a correspondent weight, at either side, the remaining part stood as before. Our venerable sovereign, who is known to have had a particular interest and pleasure in all works and discoveries of mechanic science or ingenuity, looked at it for awhile stedfastly, and, as his manner was, with quick and broken expressions of praise and courteous approbation, in the form of answers to his own questions. At length turning to the constructor, he said, 'But Mr. Atwood, you have presumed the figure. You have put the arch first in this wooden skeleton. Can you build a bridge of the same wedges in any other figure? A straight bridge, or with two lines touching at the apex? If not, is it not evident that the bits of brass derive their continuance in the present position from the property of the arch, and not the arch from the property of the wedge?' The objection was fatal, the justice of the remark not to be resisted."— (*The Friend.* Vol. III., pp. 176, 7.)

Addition. Of "those abstract entities absolute in truth," Bacon writes (Nov. Org. II. 9), "Let the investigation of Forms, which are (in the eye of reason at least, and in their essential law) eternal and immutable, constitute Metaphysics:" and again (Ibid. 15), "To God, truly, the Giver and Architect of Forms, and it may be to the angels and higher intelligences, it belongs to have an affirmative knowledge of forms immediately, and from the first contemplation. But this assuredly is more than man can do, to whom it is granted only to proceed at first by negatives, and at last to end in affirmatives, after exclusion has been exhausted." And of their utility, as applied truths, he says (Ibid. 2), "Though in nature nothing really exists beside individual bodies, performing pure individual acts according to a fixed law, yet in philosophy this very law, and the investigation, discovery, and explanation of it, is the foundation as well of knowledge as of operation. And it is this law, with its clauses, that I mean when I speak of Forms; a name which I the rather adopt because it has grown into use and become familiar."

And these passages are in perfect harmony with Bacon's precept "that Physic should handle that which supposeth in Nature only a being and moving (and natural necessity), and Metaphysic should handle that which supposeth further in nature a reason, understanding, and platform (ideam)." (*Advancement.* II. E. and S. p. 353.) The reader will also perceive how natural it was for Bacon to place mathematical science "as a branch of metaphysic; for the subject of it being Quantity; not Quantity indefinite, which is but a relative and belongeth to philosophia prima (as hath been said,) but Quantity determined or proportionable; it appeareth to be one of the Essential Forms of things; as that that is causative in nature of a number of effects; ... and it is true also that of all other forms (as we understand forms) it is the most abstracted and separable from matter, and therefore most proper to metaphysic; which hath likewise been the cause why it hath been better laboured and enquired than any of the other forms, which are more immersed into matter. For it being the nature of the mind of man (to the extreme prejudice of knowledge) to delight in the spacious liberty of generalities, as in a champion region, and not in the inclosures of particularity; the mathematics of all other knowledge were the goodliest fields to satisfy that appetite." (Ibid. p. 359.) Compare this Essay, p. 91 ante, together with foot-note.

[an] "Observe," writes the late Sir B. Brodie, "observe the effect which the general diffusion of knowledge produces on society at large; how it draws the different classes of it into more free communication with each other; how its tendency is to make the laws more impartial, bring even the most despotic governments under the influence of public opinion, and show them that they have no real security except in the good will of the people. Knowledge goes hand-in-hand with civilization. It is necessary to the giving full effect to the precepts of the Christian faith. It was from the want of it that Galileo was tortured by the Inquisition, that Servetus was burned by Calvin, that the Huguenots were persecuted and slaughtered by Louis XIV., and that in numerous other instances one sect of Christians has conceived it to be their duty to exterminate another. It is a misapplication of the term civilization to apply it to any form of society in which ignorance is the rule and knowledge the exception. If a Being of superior intelligence were to look down from some higher sphere on our doings here on the earth, is it to be supposed that he would regard the Duke of Buckingham, dancing at the French Court, and scattering the pearls with which his dress was ornamented, on the floor, as being really superior to an Australian savage; or that he would see in the foreign Prince, who at a later period exhibited himself at another Court with his boots glittering with diamonds, any better emblem of civilization than in the negro chief, who gratifies his vanity by strutting about in the cast-off uniform of a general officer?" *Psychological Inquiries*. Part II., pp. 14, 15.

[188] "A few phrases of Aristotle," says Dr. Brown, (Works I. p. 341,) "are perhaps even at this moment exercising no small sway on the very minds which smile at them with scorn." Mr. Carlyle asks, "Do not Books still accomplish miracles, as Runes were fabled to do?... Consider whether any Rune, in the wildest imagination of Mythologist, ever did such wonders as, on the actual firm Earth, some Books have done." *Heroes*, p. 252.

[189] No writer has ever dwelt more on this truth than Coleridge, and no writer ever had a stronger reason for dwelling upon it. Perhaps the ordinary public has seldom been more unjust than in its estimate of Coleridge's addiction to opium. The occasion of his first use of it was a venial error, his servitude was heavy, and the account of his sufferings and struggles most deeply affecting. Then, his final victory (respecting which so little is generally said) was a very noble moral achievement.

[ao] Men have aimed at accomplishing their purpose partly by training animals, and partly by breeding through select specimens of each race. The two principles thus relied on are habit and heredity. Respecting the latter of these a note of considerable length had been

intended in this place. But the reader interested in the general question can learn sufficient details in Dr. Carpenter's Mental Physiology together with the authorities therein referred to by him.

The following instances adduced by Mr. Wallace to show how improvement through heredity is visibly limited are very remarkable. "In the matter of speed, a limit of a definite kind as regards land animals does exist in nature. All the swiftest animals— deer, antelopes, hares, foxes, lions, leopards, horses, zebras, and many others—have reached very nearly the same degree of speed. Although the swiftest of each must have been for ages preserved, and the slowest must have perished, we have no reason to believe there is any advance of speed. The possible limit under existing conditions, and perhaps under possible terrestrial conditions, has been long ago reached." He immediately proceeds to place in contrast with these, some examples where progress is not thus barred. "In cases, however, where this limit had not been so nearly reached as in the horse, we have been enabled to make a more marked advance and to produce a greater difference of form. The wild dog is an animal that hunts much in company, and trusts more to endurance than to speed. Man has produced the greyhound, which differs much more from the wolf or the dingo than the racer does from the wild Arabian. Domestic dogs, again, have varied more in size and in form than the whole family of Canidae in a state of Nature. No wild dog, fox, or wolf, is either so small as some of the smallest terriers and spaniels, or so large as the largest varieties of hound or Newfoundland dog. And, certainly, no two wild animals of the family differ so widely in form and proportions as the Chinese pug and the Italian greyhound, or the bulldog and the common greyhound. The known range of variation is, therefore, more than enough for the derivation of all the forms of Dogs, Wolves, and Foxes from a common ancestor." Wallace. *Natural Selection*, pp. 292, 3.

Dr. Prichard's accounts of similar variations in his *Natural History of Man* and other ethnological works are particularly interesting.

Habit is a topic more germane to the subject of self-training, and is therefore examined at some length in our text.

It seems natural that the empire of both Habit and Heredity should be strongest over the purely automatous, and the instinctive or semi-instinctive actions of mankind. Witness the effect of Caste institutions, Guilds, and family vocations. Regular occupation struck a certain visitor to this world as producing a like result:—

"Nimbly," quoth he, "do the fingers move
If a man be but used to his trade."

[ap] "They that deny a God destroy man's nobility; for certainly man is of kin to the beast by his body; and, if he be not of kin to God by his spirit, he is a base and ignoble creature. It destroys likewise magnanimity, and the raising of human nature; for take an example of a dog, and mark what a generosity and courage he will put on when he finds himself maintained by a man, who to him is instead of a God, or 'melior natura'; which courage is manifestly such as that creature, without that confidence of a better nature than his own, could never attain. So man, when he resteth and assureth himself upon divine protection and favour, gathereth a force and faith, which human nature in itself could not obtain'; therefore, as atheism is in all respects hateful, so in this, that it depriveth human nature of the means to exalt itself above human frailty." Bacon. *Essay on Atheism*, p. 56.

"What joy to watch in lower creature
Such dawning of a moral nature,
And how (the rule all things obey)
They look to a higher mind to be their law and stay!" /div
Remains of A. H. Hallam, privately printed.

[aq] The difference between brute and Man appeared so vast to Bacon that, following Telesius in this as in some other respects, he adopted as a doctrine the duality of the human soul. He maintains it at length in the De Augmentis iv. 3, a chapter which begins thus:—"Let us now proceed to the doctrine which concerns the Human Soul, from the treasures whereof all other doctrines are derived. The parts thereof are two; the one treats of the rational soul, which is divine; the other of the irrational, which is common with brutes.... Now this soul (as it exists in man) is only the instrument of the rational soul, and has its origin like that of the brutes in the dust of the earth.... For there are many and great excellencies of the human soul above the souls of brutes, manifest even to those who philosophise according to the sense. Now wherever the mark of so many and great excellencies is found, there also a specific difference ought to be constituted; and therefore I do not much like the confused and promiscuous manner in which philosophers have handled the functions of the soul; as if the human soul differed from the spirit of brutes in degree rather than in kind; as the sun differs from the stars, or gold from metals."

[190] We have it on Coleridge's authority that "Lord Erskine, speaking of animals, hesitating to call them brutes, hit upon that happy phrase—'the mute creation.'" Would this were true! exclaims some invalid, nervously agonized by cats and dogs, cocks and hens, and listening with horror to their various cries and noises. But strictly speaking Lord Erskine was right,—for the animal world is mute as far as real language is concerned. Compare Max Müller on the "Bow-wow Theory." *Lectures on Language*, Series I. Lecture ix.

[191] The Poet's thought, not more imaginative than true, should be kept in mind when estimating the difference between gregariousness and society. If the latter be held a development of the former, it must have been transformed in the progress of its descent. Where affinities are really traceable between the human and the unreasoning world, they may perhaps be referred with greater probability to a common ancestry than to a lineal pedigree. And the more remote the alleged origin, the less unlikely it may appear.

[192] "Sir Humphrey Davy, when a boy, was placed under a schoolmaster who neglected his duties, and adverting to this subject in a letter addressed to his mother after he was settled in London, he says, 'I consider it as fortunate that I was left much to myself as a child, and put on no particular plan of study, and that I enjoyed much idleness at Mr. Coryton's school. I, perhaps, owe to these circumstances the little talents I have, and their peculiar application. What I am I made myself. I say this without vanity, and in pure simplicity of heart.'" *Brodie's Psychological Inquiries*, I. 29.

"The regular course of studies, the years of academical and professional education, have not yielded me better facts than some idle books under the bench at the Latin School. What we do not call education is more precious than that which we call so. We form no guess, at the time of receiving a thought, of its comparative value. And education often wastes its efforts in attempts to thwart and balk this natural magnetism, which is sure to select what belongs to it." Emerson. *Spiritual Laws.*

[ar] "We can command Nature only by obeying her; nor can Art avail anything except as Nature's handmaiden. We can affect the conditions under which Nature works; but things artificial as well as things natural are in reality produced Not by Art but Nature. Our power is merely based upon our knowledge of the procedure which Nature follows. She is never really thwarted or controlled by our operations, though she may be induced to depart from her usual course, and under new and artificial conditions to produce new phenomena and new substances.

"Natural philosophy, considered from this point of view, is therefore only an answer to the question, How does Nature work in the production of phenomena?" R. L. Ellis. Preface to Bacon's *Philosophical Works*, Vol. I. p. 59.

[as] "The philosopher, not less than the poet, postpones the apparent order and relations of things to the empire of thought. 'The problem of philosophy,' according to Plato, 'is, for all that exists conditionally, to find a ground unconditioned and absolute.' It proceeds on the faith that a law determines all phenomena, which being known, the phenomena can be predicted. That law, when in the mind, is an idea. Its beauty is infinite. The true philosopher and the true poet are one, and a beauty, which is truth, and a truth, which is beauty, is the aim of both. Is not the charm of one of Plato's or Aristotle's definitions, strictly like that of the Antigone of Sophocles? It is, in both cases, that a spiritual life has been imparted to nature; that the solid seeming block of matter has been pervaded and dissolved by a thought; that this feeble human being has penetrated the vast masses of nature with an informing soul, and recognized itself in their harmony, that is, seized their law. In physics, when this is attained, the memory disburthens itself of its cumbrous catalogues of particulars, and carries centuries of observation in a single formula." Emerson. *Idealism*.

"He who studies the concrete and neglects the abstract cannot be called an interpreter of nature. Such was Bacon's judgment." Robert Leslie Ellis, in Bacon's *Works*, Vol. I. p. 26.

"If a man's knowledge be confined to the efficient and material causes (which are unstable causes, and merely vehicles, or causes which convey the form in certain cases) he may arrive at new discoveries in reference to substances in some degree similar to one another, and selected beforehand; but he does not touch the deeper boundaries of things. But whosoever is acquainted with Forms, embraces the unity of nature in substances the most unlike; and is able therefore to detect and bring to light things never yet done, and such as neither the vicissitudes of nature, nor industry in experimenting, nor accident itself, would ever have brought into act, and which would never have occurred to the thought of man. From the discovery of Forms therefore results truth in speculation and freedom in operation."—Bacon. Novum Organon, *Book II. Aph. III.*

[at] The problem awaiting the philosophic physicist runs as follows:—

It remains to be seen how closely and with what degree of distinctness, science can approximate these impalpable forces governing the natural world, to the forces we are accustomed to call immaterial, because they become known to us by the activities of Thought and Will.

This problem—the incorporeity of Matter, or a near approach to it—has been a favourite subject of speculation in all ages. The curious reader may track it from the pre-and post-Christian Greeks through Arabian and Jewish philosophies to the

Schoolmen (who borrowed from Jews unknowingly) and so transmitted it down like an heirloom to our own later controversialists. The subject has been treated on Metaphysical grounds, for Religious interests, or as a weapon keen edged in demolishing antagonistic cosmologies. But it has not often been entertained for purely scientific reasons, and as one of those so-called "useless questions" which always turn out most prolific seminal principles, fertile in explaining nature and throwing out branches in numerous unforeseen directions.

It was thus however and with no side views that the illustrious Faraday looked at this subject. With what effect may be best learned by putting together two separate accounts of his reasoning.

In 1844, Dr. Bence Jones informs us Faraday (then in his 53rd year) indulged in "A speculation respecting that view of the nature of matter which considers its ultimate atoms as centres of force, and not as so many little bodies surrounded by forces .... The particle, indeed, is supposed to exist only by these forces, and where they are it is."

This speculation did in fact give a tone to that memorable season—now thirty years ago.

Dr. Tyndall says:—"On Friday, January 19, 1844, he opened the weekly evening meetings of the Royal Institution by a discourse entitled 'A speculation touching Electric Conduction and the nature of Matter.' In this discourse he not only attempts the overthrow of Dalton's Theory of Atoms, but also the subversion of all ordinary scientific ideas regarding the nature and relations of Matter and Force. He objected to the use of the term atom:—'I have not yet found a mind,' he says, 'that did habitually separate it from its accompanying temptations; and there can be no doubt that the words definite proportions, equivalent, primes, etc., which did and do fully express all the facts of what is usually called the atomic theory in chemistry, were dismissed because they were not expressive enough, and did not say all that was in the mind of him who used the word atom in their stead,'" (*Faraday as a Discoverer*, pp. 119-20.)

And again:—"With his usual courage and sincerity he pushes his view to its utmost consequences. 'This view of the constitution of matter,' he continues, 'would seem to involve necessarily the conclusion that matter fills all space, or at least all space to which gravitation extends; for gravitation is a property of matter dependent on a certain force, and it is this force which constitutes the matter. In that view matter is not merely mutually penetrable; but each atom extends, so to say, throughout the whole of the solar system, yet always retaining its own centre of force.'" Faraday "compares the interpenetration of two atoms to the coalescence of two distinct waves, which though for a moment blended to a single mass, preserve their individuality, and afterwards separate." (Ibid. pp. 123-4 and note.)

The subject did not easily lose its hold on the philosopher's mind. "At the Institution," writes Dr. Bence Jones, "he gave eight lectures after Easter on the phenomena and philosophy of heat. He ended this course thus:—'We know nothing about matter but its forces—nothing in the creation but the effect of these forces; further our sensations and perceptions are not fitted to carry us; all the rest, which we may conceive we know, is only imagination.' He gave two Friday discourses: the first on the nature of matter, the other on recent improvements in the silvering of mirrors.

"His notes of the first lecture begin thus:—'Speculations dangerous temptations; generally avoid them; but a time to speculate as well as to refrain, all depends upon the temper of the mind. I was led to consider the nature of space in relation to electric conduction, and so of matter, i.e., whether continuous or consisting of particles with intervening space, according to its supposed constitution. Consider this point, remarking the assumptions everywhere.

"'Chemical considerations abundant, but almost all assumption. Easy to speak of atomic proportions, multiple proportions, isomeric and isomorphic phenomena and compound bases; and to account for effects we have only to hang on to assumed atoms the properties or arrangement of properties assumed to be sufficient for the purpose. But the fundamental and main facts are expressed by the term definite proportion,—the rest, including the atomic notion, is assumption. "'The view that physical chemistry necessarily takes of atoms is now very large and complicated; first many elementary atoms—next compound and complicated atoms. System within system, like the starry heavens, may be right —but may be all wrong. Thus see how little of general theory of matter is known as fact, and how much is assumption.

"'Final brooding impression, that particles are only centres of force; that the force or forces constitute the matter; that therefore there is no space between the particles distinct from the particles of matter; that they touch each other just as much in gases as in liquids or solids; and that they are materially penetrable, probably even to their very centres. That, for instance, water is not two particles of oxygen side by side, but two spheres of power mutually penetrated, and the centres even coinciding.'" Bence Jones— *Life of Faraday*, Vol. II., pp. 177-78.

These views (best known as Boscovich's theory), though not generally held in scientific circles, are favoured by Bacon's most able commentator, Robert Leslie Ellis, and are pronounced by Professor Huxley a "tenable hypothesis." Mr. Spencer poises the balance as follows:—"Though the combining weights of the respective elements are termed by chemists their 'equivalents,' for the purpose of avoiding a questionable assumption, we are unable to think of the combination of such definite weights, without supposing it to take place between definite numbers of definite particles. And thus it would appear that the Newtonian view is at any rate preferable to that of Boscovich. A disciple of Boscovich, however, may reply that his master's theory is involved in that of Newton; and cannot indeed be escaped. 'What,' he may ask, 'is it that holds together the parts of these ultimate atoms?' 'A cohesive force,' his opponent must answer. 'And what,' he may continue, 'is it that holds together the parts of any fragments, into which, by sufficient force, an ultimate atom might be broken?' Again the answer must be—a cohesive force. 'And what,' he may still ask, 'if the ultimate atom were, as we can imagine it to be, reduced to parts as small in proportion to it, as it is in proportion to a tangible mass of matter—what must give each part the ability to sustain itself, and to occupy space?' Still there is no answer but—a cohesive force. Carry the process in thought as far as we may, until the extension of the parts is less than can be imagined, we still cannot escape the admission of forces by which the extension is upheld; and we can find no limit until we arrive at the conception of centres of force without any extension." *First Principles*, p. 54.

It is evident that Faraday was able to think in a manner which has been often declared impossible. Mr. Spencer's statement of the counter case is alone sufficient to prove that the inquiry is sure to be recurrent. We may add with Dr. Tyndall that facts alone cannot satisfy the mind, and that when a law is established, the question "why" is inevitable. Compare foot-note p. 324 post.

[193] A familiar instance of one among these abstract entities may convey to some readers a clearer idea of their nature than many careful explanations. Three balks of timber are lying in our road,—one, a very large and heavy monster, directly across it. Desirous of driving by, and being without adequate help to remove an obstacle beyond our strength, we call to mind the following definition. "The lever is an inflexible bar, capable of free motion about a fixed axis, called the fulcrum." (Newth. *Natural Philosophy*, p. 33.) Acting upon this idea, we place one balk we can manage to move, upon a second which happens to lie conveniently, and so roll away the third heavy monster. This done, we replace No. 1 peaceably beside No. 2, and wend on our way rejoicing. Now the lever, as defined by Newth, existed ideally in our mind, and we realised and used it. Our lever and fulcrum are still lying on the road, though they are lever and fulcrum no longer. The leverage was an applied mental Form, but we no longer want the Form to be operative,—and along with it the Force has disappeared.

[au] Our knowledge of Matter and of Motion;—our knowledge of their continuance while our forms and other forms are undergoing change;—all we most certainly know of the material world, resolves itself into our knowledge of Force. Thus far Mr. Herbert Spencer is with us, as may be seen from the following paragraphs from his First Principles. "By the indestructibility of Matter, we really mean the indestructibility of the force with which Matter affects us. As we become conscious of Matter only through that resistance which it opposes to our muscular energy, so do we become conscious of the permanence of Matter only through the permanence of this resistance; as either immediately or mediately proved to us. And this truth is made manifest not only by analysis of the à posteriori cognition, but equally so by analysis of the à priori one. For that which we cannot conceive to be diminished by the continued compression of Matter, is not its occupancy of space, but its ability to resist." (p. 179.) "It remains to be pointed out that the continuity of Motion, as well as the indestructibility of Matter, is really known to us in terms of force. That a certain manifestation of force remains for ever undiminished, is the ultimate content of the thought; whether reached à posteriori or à priori." (p. 182.) And again (pp. 191-2). "What, in these two foregoing chapters, was proved true of Matter and Motion, is, à fortiori, true of the Force out of which our conceptions of Matter and Motion are built. Indeed, as we saw, that which is indestructible in matter and motion, is the force they present. And, as we here see, the truth that Force is indestructible, is the obverse of the truth that the Unknown Cause of the changes going on in consciousness is indestructible. So that the persistence of consciousness, constitutes at once our immediate experience of the persistence of Force, and imposes on us the necessity we are under of asserting its persistence.... Consciousness without this or that particular form is possible; but consciousness without contents is impossible."

We are also quite at one with Mr. Herbert Spencer as regards an assertion made in his *Principles of Psychology* (I. 161,) and repeated, to shew how anti-materialistic he is, in his last book. (*Essays*, III., p. 250.) "Of the two it seems easier to translate so-called Matter into so-called Spirit, than to translate so-called Spirit into so-called Matter, which latter is, indeed, wholly impossible." But though it is true, as he adds, that "no translation can carry us beyond our symbols," it is no less true that we are impelled to inquire into that which underlies them. Mr. Spencer says further (*Psychology I.* 162,) "The conditioned form under which Being is presented in the Subject, cannot, any more than the conditioned form under which Being is presented in the Object, be the Unconditioned Being common to the two." In this negation we are less at one with him, for, as we firmly believe, in that conditioned sphere we call our own subjective nature there is a Reality presented to our consciousness by every act of Volition which brings us far nearer than any objective or outside form of existence can bring us to that Unconditioned Being which is common to the two, and infinitely superior to them both.

[194] *Spirit of Inductive Philosophy*, p. 165.

[195] Ibid. pp. 169-170. "In the confined and literal notions, often ignorantly entertained, of the sciences of observation, our conclusions might be supposed restricted to the field of mere sensible experience; and in this sense we should fall short of any worthy apprehension of the Supreme Intelligence. But the truly inductive philosopher extends his contemplation to intellectual conceptions of a higher class, pointing to order and uniformity as constant and universal as the extent of nature itself in space and in time; and in the same proportion he recognises harmony and arrangement invested with the attributes of universality and eternity, and thus derives his loftier ideas of the Divine perfections."

[196] See Ravaisson (La Philosophie en France, p. 82,) for an account of Comte's position in this particular. He characterizes it thus: "Du positivisme physique superficiel il est arrivé au positivisme moral."

[av] Or else as some may prefer to state it, Mind is the intelligible law. In other words, Law is the manifestation and energizing of the Mind in Nature, and we recognize mind in the energy of Law.

Canon Mozley spoke as follows in 1872. "There is a great deal said now about Mind in Nature, and scientific men talk enthusiastically about Mind; the old notion of chance is obsolete, and in spite of the strength of a materialist school, there is a tendency to a consensus of scientific men that there is Mind in the universe. Would any one in any public meeting of scientific men dare to stand up and deny that there was Mind in Nature? It would be thought monstrous. It would be set down as the revival of an old stupidity. It is the only form in which they find they can speak of nature which at all ennobles it or which satisfies their own idea of the sublimity of nature." The Principle of Causation considered in opposition to Atheistic Theories, p. 41.

The learned writer goes on to connect this admitted idea of Mind with the collateral idea of Design. And this is a most natural sequence of thought. But, for reasons already mentioned, the main argument of this chapter pursues another track. Mind in Nature being directly intuited, (to use an expressive Kantian phrase) we supplement the evidence thus given by a cross-examination of facts for the purpose of eliciting an account of what manner of Intelligence this Mind in Nature must be.

[aw] "It is true," says Canon Mozley, "that matter has lately been set before us as claiming more vicinity to mind than it has been usual to assign it; and a scientific man, of the highest genius, has regretted that 'mind and matter have ever been presented to us in the rudest contrast—the one as all noble, the other as all vile.' ... Hobbes, in the 17th century, anticipated this claim, and laid down 'that all matter as matter is endued not only with figure and a capacity of motion, but also with an actual sense and perception,

and wants only the organs and memory of animals to express its sensations,'" On Causation, as before, p. 38.

The doctrine of an inferior and irrational, or as some phrase it "a blind intelligence" is the topic next discussed with some fulness in our text.

This "blind intelligence" makes Nature, so to speak, "the instinct of the Universe." Thence it is "no long step" to a belief that the world is a living creature, neither are there wanting modern accounts of the principle of Vitality, and its powers of assimilation,—equally applicable to the accretive growth of a crystal.

The renovators of philosophy were (as Mr. Leslie Ellis remarks) strongly inclined to this belief, its typical teacher being Campanella. Leibniz points out with his usual energy its affinity with the Scholastic doctrine of "substantial forms"—(a very different theory from Bacon's) "formas quasdam substantiales ejusmodi sibi imaginatus videtur, quae per se sint causa motus in corporibus, quemadmodum Scholastici capiunt;" and proceeds to say, "ita reditur ad tot deunculos, quot formas substantiales, et Gentilem prope polytheismum.... Quum tamen revera in natura nulla sit sapientia, nullus appetitus, ordo vero pulcher ex eo oriatur, quia est horologium Dei." *Leibnitii Opera Philosophica*, Ed. Erdmann, pp. 52-3.

[197] "Easiest" is here and elsewhere used to mean that which accounts in the most natural and perfect manner alike for a single fact and for the complex whole of facts presented to us. Such an "easiest account" is the law of Gravitation—it is at once the simplest and the most complete.

[198] *Fragments of Science*, p. 88.

[199] Struck it so truly that (to borrow Mr. Huxley's expression) a sufficient Intelligence might have predicted the Universe. But what an infinitude of knowledge would this "sufficiency" seem to presuppose!

[ax] Taking an optical structure of the Eye as a test example, the chances of its Evolution per accidens have been calculated by an eminent mathematician. His results may be seen in the Additional Note appended to this Chapter. They are extracted from the Hulsean Lectures for 1867.

[ay] For example:—No one holds the doctrine of Natural Selection more firmly than Mr. Wallace;—he is, in fact, known to have anticipated the Darwinian theory of Evolution. But he also holds that Natural Selection cannot account for certain of the physical peculiarities of Man; much less for his consciousness, his language, his moral sense, or his Volition.

Mr. Wallace maintains likewise that

(1) Atoms are centres of Force.

(2) Force is known to us as Will.

(3) The Will that governs the world is the Will of higher intelligences or of one supreme Intelligence.

He quotes, as representing his own thought, the following lines from an American poetess:—

"God of the Granite and the Rose!
Soul of the Sparrow and the Bee!
The mighty tide of Being flows
Through countless channels,
Lord, from thee. It leaps to life in grass and flowers,

Through every grade of being runs,
While from Creation's radiant towers
Its glory flames in Stars and Suns."

To the above-mentioned points Mr. Wallace adds a spiritualistic belief in many sublime intelligences intermediate between the Deity and the Universe. Compare *Natural Selection*, Ed. 2. *Essay X.* with Notes.

[az] That the perception of fitness, even when of the most exalted kind, does not to some thinkers carry with it a perception of Design, is plainly manifest from the ensuing paragraph:—

"The absurdity of the à posteriori argument for a God consists in the assumption that what we call order, harmony, and adaptation are evidence of design, when it is evident that, whether there be a God or not, order, harmony, and adaptation must have existed from eternity, and are not therefore necessary proof of a designing cause." (*American Index*, Jan. 11, 1873.)

It is to be hoped that the writer of this rather strong statement had insight enough to perceive that these eternal harmonizers of the whole Universe do, in fact, constitute a self-existent Mind.

[ba] With perfect fairness, Professor Huxley admits the force of this distinction. In a paragraph quoted p. 133, he wrote thus:—"It is necessary to remember that there is a wider Teleology, which is not touched by the doctrine of Evolution, but is actually based upon the fundamental proposition of Evolution. That proposition is, that the whole world, living and not living, is the result of the mutual interaction, according to definite laws, of the forces possessed by the molecules of which the primitive nebulosity of the universe was composed. If this be true, it is no less certain that the existing world lay, potentially, in the cosmic vapour; and that a sufficient intelligence could, from a knowledge of the properties of the molecules of that vapour, have predicted, say the state of the Fauna of Britain in 1869, with as much certainty as one can say what will happen to the vapour of the breath in a cold winter's day."

It is curious to compare Mr. Huxley's dictum on the Eye (cited p. 133) with a passage before part- quoted from Mr. Newman. "In saying that lungs were intended to breathe, and eyes to see, we imply an argument from Fitness to Design, which carries conviction to the overwhelming majority of cultivated as well as uncultivated minds. Yet, in calling it an argument, we may seem to appeal to the logical faculty; and this would be an error. No syllogism is pretended, that proves a lung to have been made to breathe; but we see it by what some call Common-Sense, and some Intuition. If such a fact stood alone in the universe, and no other existences spoke of Design, it would probably remain a mere enigma to us; but when the whole human world is pervaded by similar instances, not to see a Universal Mind in nature appears almost a brutal insensibility; and if any one intelligently professes Atheism, the more acute he is, the more distinctly we perceive that he is deficient in the Religious Faculty. Just as, if he had no sense of Beauty in anything, we should not imagine that we could impart it by argument, so neither here.... No stress whatever needs here to be laid upon minute anatomy, as, for instance, of the eye: it signifies not, whether we do or do not understand its optical structure as a matter of science. If it had no optical structure at all, if it differed in no respect (that we could discover) from a piece of marble, except that it sees, this would not impair the reasons for believing that it is meant to see." *The Soul*, pp. 32-3.

This extract from Mr. Newman raises the question—Is an eminent Biologist any better judge on the subject of Design, than any other eminent thinker? Clearly he is a judge of Fitness, but that fact is admitted on all sides;—the eyes of animals are practically fit for seeing with, and, what is more, they are fitted to the special fields of vision useful to their several owners. The first question is, Does the fact of seeing or the fitness to see raise a moral certainty or very strong probability of Design? And should a Biologist rejoin that there exists another account of organic facts and fitnesses probable and adequate; next comes the further inquiry, which is the most probable, the most adequate, in a word the easiest? In this connection it must likewise be asked with some urgency, what non -Biological reasons there are for preferring Design? Whether for instance any good reasons may be found for believing that there is somewhere subsisting in and over the Natural world an Intelligence of such order as to be capable of arranging fitness with a view to the harmony and general co-operation of natural Forces?

The attempt has been made to shew cause on this side in the present Chapter. Of course, the case for Design must be rendered unanswerable if a certitude of Reason, either speculative or practical, or a very strong conclusion of moral argument, or a probability outweighing all other probabilities, shall in any way be shewn for accepting the still nobler belief in a self-existent Will and Personality. Now this latter idea is the subject of our two closing Chapters, and is contemplated on grounds with which the Biologist or Physicist, quâ Biologist or Physicist has no very special concern.

It seems plain, however, that when a great Biologist is pre-eminently a philosophic thinker (as an author like Mr. Huxley must be acknowledged by competent judges)—then he possesses a strong vantage ground, and vast opportunities either for good or for evil. And these last six words remind us to add with Mr. Newman that after all subjective conditions must not be forgotten.

Would not a man without sense of the Beautiful be "colour-blind" to many among the harmonies of Nature? And is there not something in the "Religious insight" Mr. Newman speaks of which seems nothing less than a gift of vision and faculty divine? Man thus endowed may be in the highest sense Nature's interpreter, when he sees in her moving mirror the reflected lineaments of his own and Nature's God. To such a mind no idea can be more sublimely magnificent than the philosophic Teleology which Mr. Huxley bases on Evolution; it seems to compress into one the Past, the Present, and the Future; and to follow with winged thought that glance of an omniscient Creator which tongues of men and angels must for ever fail to describe.

We ought to add that the principle of Evolution has been defined in more than one way. Some definitions would exclude the wide Teleologic view. What is here meant might (to borrow Mr. Spencer's remark) be more justly characterized as "Involution."

[200] Comparing the life of Humanity with the life of an individual, and arguing for an all-pervading optimism as the general Law in both, Littré observes, "Pas plus dans un cas que dans l'autre, ne sont elimineés les maladies, les perturbations, les dérangements, en un mot, tous les accidents qui interviennent dans le fonctionnement de chaque loi, et qui sont d'autant plus fréquents et plus graves que la loi dont il s'agit gouverne des rapports plus compliqués et plus élevés." *Paroles de Philosophie Positive*, p. 26. The italics are our own.

[201] It is a curious problem to put testimony in the scale against alleged necessities, regarding the course of Nature. A certain Eastern prince had never seen ice—and obstinately rejected the idea of its possible existence. Was he wise or unwise in his disbelief? Wise, if we make the rule of actual experience our canon;—unwise if we admit the rule of modification by unseen possibilities; and still more, if we allow that a small amount of affirmative testimony ought in reason to outweigh a large amount of negative presupposition, or difficulty. A curious instance of this last rule is the natural history of the duck-billed platypus (the ornithorynchus), rightly called "paradoxus." The contradictory appearance of its organs created a world of scepticism, when its history was first reported to Naturalists. It was a question of improbability versus testimony;— and, to use the established phrase, "every school boy" now knows that Testimony was right. Compare Note (c) p. 264, ante.

[bb] How Bacon can have been pictured by his admirers as neither ideal, nor metaphysical, seems to be one of those unintelligible mysteries of idolatry which idol-worshippers cannot themselves explain. How impossible it is on such a supposition to reconcile Bacon with himself will appear evident to any informed reader of Mr. Ellis's *Preface to the Philosophical Works.*

Bacon's tribute to Plato was just, as well as discriminating, and to our purpose is most appropriate. He says (De Augmentis, III. 4) "For Metaphysic, I have already assigned to it the inquiry of Formal and Final Causes; which assignation, as far as it relates to Forms, may seem nugatory; because of a received and inveterate opinion that the Essential Forms or true differences of things cannot by any human diligence be found out; an opinion which in the meantime implies and admits that the invention of Forms is of all parts of knowledge the worthiest to be sought, if it be possible to be found. And as for the possibility of finding it, they are ill discoverers who think there is no land where they can see nothing but sea. But it is manifest that Plato, a man of sublime wit (and one that surveyed all things as from a lofty cliff), did in his doctrine concerning Ideas descry that Forms were the true object of knowledge; howsoever he lost the fruit of this most true opinion by considering and trying to apprehend Forms as absolutely abstracted from matter." This last path we have endeavoured to avoid; and have ourselves elected to follow the Baconian precept, and to treat the Law or Form of Production not logically, but as seen in operation, and existent in rerum naturâ; not in ordine ad hominem but in ordine ad Universum.

What Bacon himself expected from the investigation, he states plainly enough in continuation. "If we fix our eyes diligently seriously and sincerely upon action and use, it will not be difficult to discern and understand what those Forms are the knowledge whereof may wonderfully enrich and benefit the condition of men.... This part of Metaphysic I find deficient; whereat I marvel not, because I hold it not possible that the Forms of things can be invented by that course of invention hitherto used; the root of the evil, as of all others, being this: that men have used to sever and withdraw their thoughts too soon and too far from experience and particulars, and have given themselves wholly up to their own meditation and arguments.

"But the use of this part of Metaphysic, which I reckon amongst the deficient, is of the rest the most excellent in two respects; the one, because it is the duty and virtue of all knowledge to abridge the circuits and long ways of experience (as much as truth will permit), and to remedy the ancient complaint that 'life is short and art is long.' ... For

God is holy in the multitude of his works, holy in the order or connexion of them, and holy in the union of them. And therefore the speculation was excellent in Parmenides and Plato (although in them it was but a bare speculation), 'that all things by a certain scale ascend to unity.'" (Ibid. Ellis and Spedding, IV. 360-362.)

[bc] The Hulsean Lecturer before alluded to states this point with most distinct emphasis. Speaking of the Eye as an optical instrument, he says, "Here are four conditions of things each utterly independent of the others, viz. the nerve, then its non-reflecting coating, then a transparent medium investing it, then a most remarkable ether surrounding the whole, the concurrence of all four being essential to the production of vision, nevertheless we are to believe that all these adjustments and adaptations are accidentally made, retained and handed down by inheritance. If there be not evidence here of the selecting, arranging, controlling power of mind, will, forethought, contrivance, then I feel that I have no evidence for the existence of the individuality of my own being." *Analogies*, etc., p. 124.

[202] There is perhaps no familiar tribe in which the wonders of this mechanical arrangement, can be more easily studied than in the venerable family of owls.

[203] The stalk-eyed Crustacea are known to most readers through the fascinating volume of Mr. Bell.

[204] De Anima, III. 1, 4. Hist. Animal., I. 9, IV. 8. The structural eye is reduced to an ocellus.

[205] M. Le Court: see Geoffrey St. Hilaire, *Cours d'Histoire Naturelle*, des Mammifères.

[206] One is glad of this result for Shakespeare's sake, as well as Aristotle's; though a Warwickshire man might have been expected to know the exact truth so far as his county is concerned; which Shakespeare did not:—

"The blind mole casts

Copp'd hills towards heaven." (Pericles, I. 1.)

"Pray you tread softly that the blind mole may not

Hear a footfall." (*Tempest*, IV. 1.)

[207] The Proteus Anguinus has been rendered illustrious by Sir H. Davy's Consolations in Travel. Since his time, living specimens have been kept in England.

[208] The English reader will be charmed with the account of him in Bell's British Quadrupeds.

[209] "In the organ of hearing in man we have first of all the external orifice of the ear, which is closed at the bottom by the circular tympanic membrane. Behind that membrane is the cavity called the drum of the ear, this cavity being separated from the space between it and the brain by a bony partition, in which there are two orifices, the one round and the other oval. These orifices are also closed by fine membranes. Across the cavity of the drum stretches a series of four little bones: the first, called the hammer, is attached to the tympanic membrane; the second, called the anvil, is connected by a joint with the hammer; a third little round bone connects the anvil with the stirrup bone, which has its oval base planted against the membrane of the oval orifice above referred to. The base of the stirrup bone abuts against this membrane, almost covering it, and leaving but a narrow rim of the membrane surrounding the bone. Behind the bony partition, and between it and the brain, we have the extraordinary organ called the labyrinth, which is filled with water, and over the lining membrane of which, the terminal fibres of the auditory nerve are distributed. When the tympanic membrane receives a shock, that

shock is transmitted through the series of bones above referred to, and is concentrated on the membrane against which the base of the stirrup bone is planted. That membrane transfers the shock to the water of the labyrinth, which, in its turn, transfers it to the nerves.

"The transmission, however, is not direct. At a certain place within the labyrinth exceedingly fine elastic bristles, terminating in sharp points, grow up between the terminal nerve fibres. These bristles, discovered by Max Schultze, are eminently calculated to sympathise with those vibrations of the water which correspond to their proper periods. Thrown thus into vibration, the bristles stir the nerve fibres which lie between their roots, and excite audition. At another place in the labyrinth we have little crystalline particles called otolithes —the Hörsteine of the Germans—embedded among the nervous filaments, and which, when they vibrate, exert an intermittent pressure upon the adjacent nerve fibres, thus exciting audition. The otolithes probably subserve a different purpose from that fulfilled by the bristles of Schultze. They are fitted, by their weight, to accept and prolong the vibrations of evanescent sounds, which might otherwise escape attention. The bristles of Schultze, on the contrary, because of their extreme lightness, would instantly yield up an evanescent motion, while they are eminently fitted for the transmission of continuous vibrations. Finally, there is in the labyrinth a wonderful organ, discovered by the Marchese Corti, which is to all appearance a musical instrument, with its chords so stretched as to accept vibrations of different periods, and transmit them to the nerve filaments which traverse the organ. Within the ears of men, and without their knowledge or contrivance, this lute of 3,000 strings has existed for ages, accepting the music of the outer world, and rendering it fit for reception by the brain. Each musical tremor which falls upon this organ selects from its tensioned fibres the one appropriate to its own pitch, and throws that fibre into unisonant vibration. And thus, no matter how complicated the motion of the external air may be, those microscopic strings can analyse it and reveal the constituents of which it is composed." Tyndall. On Sound, pp. 323-4 and 5. We may add that the "fine elastic bristles," mentioned by Dr. Tyndall, are known to be prolongations of the free ends of the epithelial cells. The other ends of these cells—(i.e., the deep or attached ends) are delicately ramified, and are said to be in connection with slender nerve-fibrils.

[210] E.g., Coleridge. "I have at this moment before me, in the flowery meadow, on which my eye is now reposing, one of its most soothing chapters, in which there is no lamenting word, no one character of guilt or anguish. For never can I look and meditate on the vegetable creation without a feeling similar to that with which we gaze at a beautiful infant that has fed itself asleep at its mother's bosom, and smiles in its strange dream of obscure yet happy sensations. The same tender and genial pleasure takes possession of me, and this pleasure is checked and drawn inward by the like aching melancholy, by the same whispered remonstrance, and made restless by a similar impulse of aspiration. It seems as if the soul said to herself: From this state hast thou fallen! Such shouldst thou still become, thyself all permeable to a holier power! thyself at once hidden and glorified by its own transparency, as the accidental and dividuous in this quiet and harmonious object is subjected to the life and light of nature; to that life and light of nature, I say, which shines in every plant and flower, even as the transmitted power, love and wisdom of God over all fills, and shines through, nature! But what the plant is, by an act not its own and unconsciously— that must thou make

thyself to become —must by prayer and by a watchful and unresisting spirit, join at least with the preventive and assisting grace to make thyself, in that light of conscience which inflameth not, and with that knowledge which puffeth not up!" *Statesman's Manual*. Appendix B. pp. 267, 8. Ed. 1839.

[211] Tyndall's *Earlier Thoughts*; in his *Essays*, p. 72. Dr. Tyndall is never weary of repeating this useful truth, and we may honour him for so doing. The following references are to his last very popular work, and in each place the same thought will be found differently expressed according to the difference of subject-matter. *Fragments of Science*, pp. 93, 105, 121, 163, 442.

[212] George Stephenson used to watch the speed of his locomotive, and pleasantly remark that he was utilizing the solar heat of the great coal-period. The words were his own. The idea was Herschel's.

[213] "Time is no agent, as some people appear to think it, that it should accomplish anything of itself. Looking at a heap of stones for a thousand years, will do no more toward making a house of them, than looking at it for one moment. The cause is obvious. Time, when applied to works of any kind, being only a succession of relevant acts, each furthering the work to be accomplished, it is clear that even an infinite succession of irrelevant, and consequently useless acts, would no more achieve or forward the completion of it, than an infinite number of jumps in the same place would advance one toward a journey's end; for there is a motion without progress, in time as well as space; where that has often remained stationary which appeared to us, in leaving it behind, to have receded."— *Guesses at Truth*. First Ed., pp. 61-2.

[214] *Fragments of Science*, p. 442. The passage has been referred to before—and its pith alone is given here— i.e., the central sentence.

[215] *Astronomy*, Chapter 8. init., note p. 264. Ed. 1850.

[216] Page 178, seq.

[bd] Compare our summary of Powell's argument on this point, pp. 173-4 ante. "We see the necessity of a Moral cause as distinguished from a physical antecedent, when we survey Nature. But Nature does not contain the idea in an explicit shape. She only necessitates its acceptance."

[217] Having before quoted at some length from this distinguished Professor, it seems needless to add anything here, except that the same sentiments will be found reasserted in his later works.—See *Spirit of Inductive Philosophy*, pp. 152-3, and 175-9; and compare Chapter 2. ante, Additional notes D and E, pp. 103-107, where these passages are in part quoted and commented on.

[218] Of course, if any man pronounces anything absolutely unknowable, he says virtually, "my knowledge equals the sum total of all knowledge."

[219] Every one who writes this word, must feel tempted to ask why such a condition attaches to any truth. This Essay avoids metaphysical inquiries; we must, therefore, rest content with having plainly shewn that it does attach to the most certain and necessary of all truths.

[be] The reader may be pleased to recall Professor Huxley's two necessary beliefs— necessary, that is, for making the world we live in less miserable and less ignorant. First, that the Order of Nature is practically ascertainable. Secondly, that our Volition counts for something as a condition in the course of Events. (*Lay Sermons*, p. 159,— already quoted pp. 247 and 8 ante.)

Evidently, to count for anything, Volition must produce effects; that is, cause certain changes in the natural order of things. This principle, therefore, is clearly asserted by the Professor,—and its consequences follow by logical necessity, as here deduced.

Mr. Huxley's idea of the Order of Nature is also coincident with the view of it taken in this Chapter.

The present writer is glad to mark these undesigned coincidences of thought. "Lay Sermons" had not reached him when this Essay was sent to the Oxford Registrar. Neither had he seen the Professor's Article in the *Fortnightly Review*.

Addition. —The doctrine in most complete antagonism with Mr. Huxley's position is described as follows by Dr. Carpenter:—

"The most thorough-going expression of this doctrine will be found in the 'Letters of the Laws of Man's Nature and Development,' by Henry G. Atkinson and Harriet Martineau. A few extracts will suffice to show the character of this system of Philosophy. 'Instinct, passion, thought, etc., are effects of organized substances.' 'All causes are material causes.' 'In material conditions I find the origin of all religions, all philosophies, all opinions, all virtues, all "spiritual conditions and influences," in the same manner that I find the origin of all diseases and of all insanities in material conditions and causes.' 'I am what I am; a creature of necessity; I claim neither merit nor demerit.'

'I feel that I am as completely the result of my nature, and impelled to do what I do, as the needle to point to the north, or the puppet to move according as the string is pulled.' 'I cannot alter my will, or be other than what I am, and cannot deserve either reward or punishment.'" Carpenter. *Mental Physiology*, p. 4.

[220] Horace would have felt himself bewildered by some modern Philosophies. He says:—

"Unde nil majus generatur ipso

Nec viget quidquam simile aut secundum."

[221] Every reader of Ben Jonson must recal the Alchemical process of "Exaltation":—

"Son, be not hasty, I exalt our med'cine,

By hanging him in balneo vaporoso,

And giving him solution; then congeal him;

And then dissolve him; then again congeal him."

The Alchemist, Act II. Scene i.

But who would wish the congelation of our Moral sense? If indeed it could possibly survive the rest of the process.

Reading these lines, can any one wonder at the celebrated chemical analysis of bygone days, which ended in discovering an undetermined residuum of dirt?

[222] Compare Job iv. 13, seq.

[223] De Corona. Sect. 274. The translation in the text is Lord Brougham's, and his note on this passage is worth perusal. Trans. p. 185.

INDEX